Affective Information Processing

Jianhua Tao · Tieniu Tan

Editors

Affective Information Processing

🐎 Springer

Dr. Jianhua Tao, PhD
Professor Tieniu Tan, BSc, MSc, PhD
Institute of Automation, Chinese Academy of Sciences
95 Zhongguancun East Road
Haidian, Beijing, 100080, P.R. China

ISBN: 978-1-84800-305-7   e-ISBN: 978-1-84800-306-4
DOI: 10.1007/978-1-84800-306-4

British Library Cataloguing in Publication Data
A catalogue record for this book is available from the British Library

Library of Congress Control Number: 2008937467

Printed on acid-free paper

Springer Science+Business Media
springer.com

Preface

Affective information processing involves studies that attempt to give computers the humanlike capabilities of observation, interpretation, and generation of affect features. It is an important topic in human–computer interaction (HCI), because it helps improve the quality and effectiveness of human to computer communications. Words such as "affect," "affective," and "affection" are usually linked to humans and have rarely been used for lifeless machines. Affective information processing is quite new in HCI which considers affect features and investigates ways of capturing and processing these by computers. The computation of affective multimodal information is also known as "affective computing" and has become a very hot research topic.

In 2005, we organized the first international conference on affective computing and intelligent interaction (ACII2005) in Beijing. There were 134 papers accepted for the conference in total, and about 140 people from 32 countries attended the conference. The conference proceedings were published as a volume in Springer LNCS. In 2007, the second ACII was held in Lisbon with an attendance of around 150. ACII is now an event of the HUMAINE Association. From that time on, ACII has become a central event for researchers studying and developing the role of emotion and other affective phenomena as these relate to human–computer and human–robot interaction, graphics, artificial intelligence, robotics, vision, speech, synthetic characters, games, educational software, and so on.

The international enthusiasm at ACII encouraged us to edit a book on affective information processing by soliciting original theoretical and practical work offering new and broad views of the latest research in this new and exciting area. Most of the authors were selected and invited from among the attendees of ACII2005, and some chapters were written by other leading researchers outside ACII2005. This ensures that the book has a balanced coverage of the important topics.

The book summarizes some key technologies that are organized into four parts: "Cognitive Emotion Model," "Affect in Speech," "Affect in Face," and "Affect in Multimodal Information," with 17 chapters. Unlike other books which often focus on psychological problems or cognitive models for emotions, this book gives more content on how to process affective information for the next generation of

HCI technologies. Thus the multimodalities of affective information in the form of language, speech, and face are emphasized in this book.

We have no intention of addressing all problems in affective information processing within this book, but try to give a wide description and some detailed knowledge in this area. We hope that the book can be taken as a useful reference book and will help promote more and deeper studies in this exciting area.

As a final word, we would like to thank all the authors for their quality contributions. Our thanks also go to Wayne Wheeler and Catherine Brett from Springer for their invaluable help and guidance throughout the project. This book is supported in part by the National Natural Science Foundation of China under Grant (60575032)

Beijing, China   *Jianhua Tao*
May 10, 2008   *Tieniu Tan*

Contents

Part III Affect in Face

Part IV Affect in Multimodal Interaction

Contributors

Aijun Li Institute of Linguistic, Chinese Academy of Social Science, Beijing, liaj@cass.org.cn

Ana Paiva IST – Technical University of Lisbon and INESC-ID, Avenida Prof. Cavaco Silva – Taguspark, 2780-990 Porto Salvo, Portugal, ana.paiva@inesc-id.pt

Ana Paiva INESC-ID, TagusPark, Av. Prof. Dr. Cavaco Silva, 2780-990 Porto Salvo, Portugal, ana.paiva@inesc-id.pt

Andrew Ortony Northwestern University, 2120 North Campus Drive, Annenberg Hall, Evanston IL 60208-2610, USA ortony@northwestern.edu

Anna Esposito Dipartimento di Psicologia, Seconda Università di Napoli Via Vivaldi 43, 81100 Caserta, Italy IIASS, Via Pellegrino 19, 84019, Vietri sul Mare, SA, Italy, iiass.annaesp@tin.it,anna.esposito@unina2.it

Celso M. de Melo USC, University of Southern California, demelo@usc.edu

Christian Peter Fraunhofer Institute for Computer Graphics Rostock, Joachim Jungius Str. 11, 18059 Rostock, Germany

Chung-Hsien Wu Department of Computer Science and Information Engineering, National Cheng Kung University, Tainan, chwu@csie.ncku.edu.tw

Eric Ebert arivis Multiple Image Tools GmbH, Schwaansche Straße 1, 18055 Rostock, Germany

Fiorella de Rosis Department of Informatics, Via Orabona 4, 70124 Bari, Italy

Helmut Beikirch University of Rostock, Faculty of Computer Science and Electrical Engineering, Albert-Einstein-Str. 2, 18059 Rostock, Germany

Helmut Prendinger Digital Contents and Media Sciences Research Division, National Institute of Informatics, 2-1-2 Hitotsubashi, Chiyoda-ku, 101-8430 Tokyo, Japan, helmut@nii.ac.jp

Jean-Claude Martin LIMSI-CNRS, France

Laurence Devillers LIMSI-CNRS, France

Jianhua Tao National Laboratory of Pattern Recognition, Institute of Automation, Chinese Academy of Sciences, Beijing, jhtao@nlpr.ia.ac.cn

Joao Dias NESC-ID, TagusPark, Av. Prof. Dr. Cavaco Silva, 2780-990 Porto Salvo, Portugal, joao.assis@tagus.ist.utl.pt

Jui-Feng Yeh National Chia-Yi University, Chia Yi

Kristiina Jokinen University of Helsinki and Tampere, Finland, Kristiina.Jokinen@helsinki.fi

Le Xin National Laboratory of Pattern Recognition, Institute of Automation, Chinese Academy of Sciences, Beijing

Lynne.Hall School of Computing and Technology, University of Sunderland, Sunderland, SR6 0DD, UK, lynne.hall@sunderland.ac.uk

Mostafa Al Masum Shaikh Department of Information and Communication Engineering, University of Tokyo, 7-3-1 Hongo, Bunkyo-ku, 113-8656 Tokyo, Japan, mostafa@mi.ci.i.u-tokyo.ac.jp

Mitsuru Ishizuka Department of Information and Communication Engineering, University of Tokyo, 7-3-1 Hongo, Bunkyo-ku, 113-8656 Tokyo, Japan, ishizuka@i.u-tokyo.ac.jp

Maja Pantic Imperial College London University of Twente, Netherlands, m.pantic@imperial.ac.uk

Marc Schröder DFKI GmbH, Saarbrücken, Germany, schroed@dfki.de

Nicole Novielli Department of Informatics, Via Orabona 4, 70124 Bari, Italy

Panrong Yin National Laboratory of Pattern Recognition, Institute of Automation, Chinese Academy of Sciences, Beijing

Pascal Thibault Department of Psychology, McGill University, Montreal, Canada, pascal.thibault@videotron.ca

Qiang Ji Department of Electrical, Computer and Systems Engineering, Rensselaer Polytechnic Institute, Troy, NY, qji@ecse.rpi.edu

Ruth Aylett Mathematics and Computer Science, Heriot-Watt University, Edinburgh, EH14 4AS, UK, ruth@macs.hw.ac.uk

Sarah Woods Psychology Department, University of Hertfordshire, Hatfield, Herts, AL10 9AB, UK s.n.woods@herts.ac.uk

Tieniu Tan National Laboratory of Pattern Recognition, Institute of Automation, Chinese Academy of Sciences, Beijing

Thomas S. Huang University of Illinois at Urbana-Champaign Imperial College London, huang@ifp.uiuc.edu

Ursula Hess Department of Psychology, University of Quebec at Montreal, PO Box 8888, station A, Montreal Qc. H3C3P8, Hess.Ursula@uqam.ca

Valeria Carofiglio Department of Informatics, Via Orabona 4, 70124 Bari, Italy

Wenhui Liao The Thomson Corporation, Eagan, MN, wenhui.liao@thomson

Yan Tong General Electric Global Research Center, Schenectady, NY, tongyan@ge.com

Ze-Jing Chuang Department of Computer Science and Information Engineering, National Cheng Kung University, Tainan

Zhihong Zeng University of Illinois at Urbana-Champaign Imperial College London, zhzeng@ifp.uiuc.edu

Chapter 1
Introduction

Jianhua Tao and Tieniu Tan

Before we use the concept of "affect" in human–computer interaction (HCI), research on emotions has been done for a long time, a history of which has been detailed in the book *Handbook of Emotions* (Lewis & Haviland-Jones, 2000). Emotion is a positive or negative mental state that combines physiological input with cognitive appraisal (Oatley, 1987; Ortony et al., 1990; Thagard, 2005). Although not traditionally considered an aspect of cognitive science, it has recently been attributed to be effective on rational decision making. Predominant theories about emotion explain it as either making judgments, or having bodily reactions, or the combination of the two. Judgments are made (such as satisfaction from the outcome of hard work) and/or bodily reactions (such as sweating from fear of a task, or nervousness) take place based on a person's interactions or disposition.

Emotional communication is important to understanding social emotional influences in the workplace. Nowadays, more and more researchers are interested in how to integrate emotions into HCI, which has become known as "affective computing" (Picard, 1997). Affective computing builds an "affect model" based on a variety of information, which results in a personalized computing system with the capability of perception and interpretation of human feelings as well as generating intelligent, sensitive, and friendly responses.

Most of the existing affect models are based on discrete emotion states, which do not have significant correspondence to the real environment. In 1998, Goleman published a book called *Working with Emotional Intelligence* (Goleman, 1998). In his work, he widened the definition of emotional intelligence, saying that it consists of 25 "skills, abilities and competencies." There are many arguments about how best to define emotions. Some individuals think it is not possible to model affect, and thus, facilitate affective understanding. This question has been discussed by Picard (1997).

J.H. Tao (✉) and T.N. Tan
National Laboratory of Pattern Recognition, Institute of Automation,
Chinese Academy of Sciences, Beijing
e-mail: jhtao@nlpr.ia.ac.cn

J.H. Tao, T.N. Tan (eds.), *Affective Information Processing,*
© Springer Science+Business Media LLC 2009

1

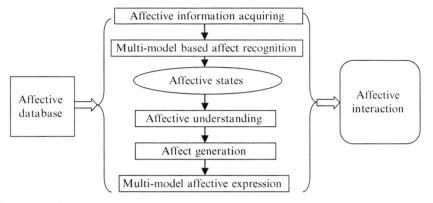

Fig. 1.1 Multimodal affective interaction system.

With any complex modelling problem, there are ways to handle complexity and contribute to progress in understanding. If we want to model affect at the neuropeptide signalling level, then we are limited indeed, because we know only a small part about how such molecules communicate among the organs in our body and realtime sensing of local molecular activity is not easily accomplished. (Picard, 2003)

On the basis of perception, analysis, and modelling of affective features, the interrelation among research contents can be illustrated as shown in Figure 1.1. The framework involves several modules on information acquiring, recognition, understanding, generation, and expression. Both verbal and nonverbal means of communication are used to transmit values from one individual to another. Affective states are used in order to transfer status for the interaction. Some use agents to describe them whereas others use a markup language to represent them, such as eXtended Markup Language (XML) based emotion language, among others.

Although affective information processing for HCI is a relatively new concept, there are already some related projects, such as HUMAINE,[1] affective computing,[2] Oz,[3] BlueEyes,[4] affect sensitive human–robot collaboration,[5] verbal and nonverbal face-to-face communication,[6] and so on.

In this book, the remaining 16 chapters are divided into four parts, "Cognitive Emotion Model," "Affect in Speech," "Affect in Face," and "Affect in Multimodal Information."

---

[1] http://emotion-research.net/.

[2] http://affect.media.mit.edu/.

[3] http://www.cs.cmu.edu/afs/cs.cmu.edu/project/oz/web/oz.html.

[4] http://www.almaden.ibm.com/cs/BlueEyes/index.html.

[5] http://robotics.vuse.vanderbilt.edu/affect.htm.

[6] http://www.cost2102.eu/joomla/.

1.1 Cognitive Emotion Model

The cognitive model of the emotion may contain the functions by absorbing and remembering the information, modelling the user's current mood and affect states. Furthermore, it will build a more complete model of the user's behavior by eventually modelling the user's context and affect states (Picard, 2003).

With the cognitive emotion model, the ultimate purpose of affective computing is to assist the computer to react accurately after it understands the user's meaning, and to be accustomed to the changes of the user's affect.

Affects are closely related to cognition, and associated with personalities, environment, and cultural background. Psychologists have been exploring this issue for a long time. In recent years, there has been an attempt to verify the relations between affects and cognition through various experiments; for instance, the emotion group of Geneva University[7] designed a set of computer games dealing with questions and answers. Experiment participants experienced emotional changes when playing the games, and their facial expressions and sounds emitted during the game were collected as samples to be analysed. These kinds of games trigger emotions that can be used to help researchers study and explore the interaction of emotion triggering and cognition levels.

Although there is much work to be done on the cognition of affects or emotions, the OCC (Ortony, Clore, & Collins, 1998) model might be one of the most successful. It classifies people's emotions as a result of events, objects, and other agents under three categories. People are happy or unhappy with an event, like or dislike an object, or approve or disapprove an agent. In Chapter 2, Ortony (one of the authors of the OCC model) tries to extend the work by using the term "affect" to refer to any aspect of mental life that has to do with value and the assessment of the environment.

Chapter 3 describes some psychological theories that are at the foundation of research on cognitive models of emotions, and then reviews the most significant projects in this domain in recent years.

Chapter 4 proposes to relate cognitive variables of the emotion model to linguistic components in text, and provide tailored rules for textural emotion recognition, which are inspired by the rules of the OCC emotion model. The resulting linguistics-based rule set for the OCC emotion types and cognitive states allows us to determine a broad class of emotions conveyed by text.

Chapter 5 introduces a virtual drama system (FearNot!) for use in education against bullying. An emotion cognitive model is introduced for the system to make decisions. It describes the emotionally driven architecture used for characters as well as the management of the overall story.

---

[7] http://www.unige.ch/fapse/emotion/.

1.2 Affect in Speech

For affective (expressive) speech processing, it is widely known that affective (expressive) speech differs with respect to the acoustic features (Scherer, 1986; Cahn, 1990; Schröder, 2001). Some prosody features, such as pitch variables (F0 level, range, contour, and jitter), and speaking rate have been analyzed by researchers (Cahn, 1990; Schröder, 2001). Parameters describing laryngal processes on voice quality have also been taken into account (Gobl and Chasaide, 2003). Some experiments (Tato, Santos, Kompe, & Pardo, 2002) also showed that "quality features" are important in addition to "prosody features". These acoustic features are widely used in the research of expressive speech. In Chapters 6 through 8, the book introduces the work on "emotion perception and recognition from speech" and "expressive speech synthesis".

Chapter 6 summarizes several recognition methods for emotion recognition from speech, including support vector machines (SVMs), K-nearest neighbors (KNN), neural networks, and so on. To give a more practical description of the emotion recognition procedure, a new approach to emotion recognition is provided as a case study. In this case study, a feature compensation approach is proposed to characterize the feature space with better discriminability among emotional states, with the assumption of linear mapping between feature spaces in different emotional states.

In Chapter 7, the book traces the development of expressive speech synthesis since its beginnings to current challenges in the area, and addresses the issue of how to combine a high degree of naturalness with a suitable level of control over the expression. Based on the current state of affairs, the chapter also ventures some speculation about future developments.

Chapter 8 introduces a specific technology on a prosody conversion method for expressive speech generation by using a Gaussian Mixture Model (GMM) and a Classification and Regression Tree (CART) model. Unlike the rule-based or linear modification methods, these statistic models are able to get the subtle prosody variations between neutral and expressive speech. A sample case for Mandarin emotional speech generation is presented.

1.3 Affect in Face

Facial expressions and movements such as a smile or a nod are used either to fulfill a semantic function, or to communicate emotions or conversational cues. Similar to speech processing, the research of facial expression consists of work on coding, recognition, and generation, and have been carried out for a very long time.

How emotions are expressed is subject to cultural precepts and proscriptions. Those who disregard these conventions are either misunderstood or marginalized. In this sense, there is little difference between European and Asian societies. Nevertheless, differences between cultures become obvious when one considers concrete rules of emotional expression. To examine these similarities and differences among individuals, Chapter 9 presents some findings about the importance of faces in the context of emotion communication, and explains why the same expression may not mean the same when shown on different faces or seen by different people. Finally, the chapter points out that faces convey information relevant to the interpretation of emotion expressions and they have a meaning of their own which interacts with the facial expression shown.

For facial coding technologies, Chapter 10 introduces a system that could automatically analyse facial actions in real-time. Considering the previous facial Action Unit (AU) recognition approaches which ignore the semantic relationships among AUs and the dynamics of AUs, the chapter introduces a new AU recognition system to systematically account for the relationships among AUs and their temporal evolutions based on a dynamic Bayesian network (DBN).

Furthermore, Chapter 11 presents two methods (the unit selection method and the fused HMM inversion method) for the speech-driven facial animation system. It systematically addresses audiovisual data acquisition, expressive trajectory analysis, and audiovisual mapping. Based on this framework, the chapter also introduces a method to map neutral facial deformation to expressive facial deformation with a Gaussian Mixture Model (GMM).

1.4 Affect in Multimodal Information

Direct human-to-human interaction is, by definition, multimodal interaction in which participants encounter a steady stream of facial expressions, gestures, body postures, head movements, words, grammatical constructions, prosodic controlling, and so on. Multimodal systems are thought by most researchers and users to improve the results of affect recognition and to generate more vivid expressions in human–computer interaction (HCI; Cowie, 2001). They are able to meet the stringent performance requirements imposed by various applications.

But till now, the lack of a coordination mechanism of affective parameters under multimodal conditions limits affective understanding and affect prompts. The fusing of different channels involves not just their combination, but also finding the mutual relations among them. Chapter 12 introduces the emotional states in the face-to-face communication system that involve both the verbal and the nonverbal modalities of communication. It points out that the same information is transferred through several channels. And the chapter answers questions on how much information about the speaker's emotional state is transmitted by each channel and which channel plays the major role in transferring such information, and suggests that each channel performs a robust encoding of the emotional features that is very helpful in recovering the perception of the emotional state when one of the channels is degraded by noise.

Furthermore, Chapter 13 looks at verbal and nonverbal feedback for the purposes of designing and developing dialogue systems. Chapter 14 provides an overview of the research on automatic human emotion recognition based on information from multiple modalities (audio, visual, and physiological responses).

The design of future interactive affective interactive systems requires the representation of spontaneous emotions and their associated multimodal signs. In order to model the sophisticated relations between spontaneous emotions and their expressions in different modalities, Chapter 15 defines an exploratory approach in which a TV corpus of interviews was collected and annotated. The collected data displayed emotions that are more complex than the basic emotions. Superpositions, masking, and conflicts between positive and negative emotions are also observed.

Chapter 16 summarizes the physiological process's affective applications. After this, the chapter presents the requirements of affective applications for physiological sensors. A design concept meeting the requirements is drawn and exemplary implementations including evaluation results are also described.

Although most researchers tend to focus on gesture, face, and voice for the expression of emotions, in order to go beyond the limitation on the body, Chapter 17 describes an evolutionary model for the expression of emotions in virtual humans using light, shadows, filters, and composition. In this chapter, lighting expression relies on a local pixel-based model supporting light and shadow parameters regularly manipulated in the visual arts. Screen expression uses filters and composition to manipulate the virtual human's pixels themselves in a way akin to painting. Emotions are synthesized using the OCC model. Finally, to learn mappings between affective states and lighting and screen expression, an evolutionary model that relies on genetic algorithms is proposed.

1.5 Summary

Although the research on affective interaction is relatively new, it has attracted extensive attention from researchers around the world. With the integration of affective multimodal features, the computer is now able to recognize human affect states, better understand human meaning, and make better humanlike responses in human–machine interaction systems. Various problems are not well solved, however, there is considerable scope for applications: for instance, adding the function of automatic emotion perception in household appliances to provide better services to people, making use of the affect analysis in information retrieval systems to improve the accuracy and efficiency of information retrieval, adding affect factors in remote education systems, processing human emotions in virtual reality applications to enhance the virtual scenario, and so on. In addition, affective interaction may also be applied in games, robots, and intelligent toys to create objects with more personality. The technology will give us a remarkable change in our research of human–computer interactions.

For this book, we solicited original theoretical and practical work offering new and broad views of the latest research in affective information processing. We organized many chapters spanning a variety of topics ranging from a cognitive model of emotion and affect model for speech and language, to affective multimodal information processing. We hope the book will be a useful reference book for research.

References

Aggarwal, J. K., & Cai, Q. (1999). Human motion analysis: A review, *Computer Vision and Image Understanding, 73*(3), 428–440.

Antonio, R., & Damasio, H. (1992). Brain and language, *Scientific American*, September, 89–95.

Blaney, P. H. (1986). Affect and memory: A review. *Psychological Bulletin*, 99(2), 229–246.

Bregler, C., Covell, M., & Slaney, M. (1997). Video rewrite: Driving visual speech with audio. *ACM SIGGRAPH'97*, 353–360.

Cahn, J. E. (1990). The generation of affect in synthesized speech. *Journal of the American Voice I/O Society, 8*, 1–19.

Campbell, N. (2004). Perception of affect in speech – Towards an automatic processing of paralinguistic information in spoken conversation. In *ICSLP2004*, Jeju (pp. 881–884).

Cowie, R. (2001). Emotion recognition in human–computer interaction. *IEEE Signal Processing Magazine, 18*(1), 32–80.

Damasio, A. R. (1994). *Error: Emotion, reason, and the human brain*. New York: Gosset/Putnam Press.

Eide, E., Aaron, A., & Bakis, R., et al. (2002). A corpus-based approach to < ahem/ > expressive speech synthesis. In *IEEE Speech Synthesis Workshop*, Santa Monica (pp. 79–84).

Ekman, P. (1999). *Basic emotions. Handbook of cognition and emotion*. New York: John Wiley.

Ekman, P., & Friesen, W. V. (1997). *Manual for the facial action coding system*. Palo Alto, CA: Consulting Psychologists Press.

Etcoff, N. L., & Magee J. J. (1992). Categorical perception of facial expressions. *Cognition, 44*, 227–240.

Gavrila, D. M. (1999). The visual analysis of human movement: A survey. *Computer Vision and Image Understanding, 73* (1) January. 82–98.

Gobl, C., & Chasaide, A. N. (2003). The role of voice quality in communicating emotion, mood and attitude. *Speech Communication*, 40, 189–212.

Goleman, D. (1998). *Working with emotional intelligence*, New York: Bantam Books.

Gutierrez-Osuna, R., Kakumanu, P.K., Esposito, A., Garcia, O.N., Bojorquez, A., Castillo, J.L., & Rudomin, I. (2005). Speech-driven facial animation with realistic dynamics. *IEEE Transactions on Multimedia, 7*(1), 33–42.

Hong, P. Y., Wen, Z., & Huang, T. S. (2002). Real-time speech-driven face animation with expressions using neural networks. *IEEE Transactions on Neural Networks, 13*(4), 916–927.

James, W. (1884). What is emotion? *Mind, 9*, 188–205.

Lewis, M., & Haviland-Jones, J. M. (2000). *Handbook of emotions*. New York: Guilford Press.

Massaro, D. W., Beskow, J., Cohen, M. M., Fry, C. L., & Rodriguez, T. (1999). Picture my voice: Audio to visual speech synthesis using artificial neural networks. In *AVSP'99*, Santa Cruz, CA (pp. 133–138).

Moriyama, T., & Ozawa, S. (1999). Emotion recognition and synthesis system on speech. In *IEEE International Conference on Multimedia Computing and Systems*, Florence, Italy, Vol. 1, 840–844.

Mozziconacci, S. J. L., & Hermes, D. J. (2000). Expression of emotion and attitude through temporal speech variations. In *6th International Conference on Spoken Language Processing*, ICSLP2000, Beijing.

Oatley, K. (1987). Cognitive science and the understanding of emotions. *Cognition and Emotion*, *3*(1), 209–216.

Ortony, A., Clore, G. L., & Collins A. (1990). The cognitive structure of emotions, Cambridge, UK: Cambridge University Press.

Osgood, C. E., Suci, G. J., & Tannenbaum, P. H. (1957). The measurements of meaning, Champaign, IL: University of Illinois Press.

Pavlovic, V. I., Sharma, R., & Huang T. S. (1997). Visual interpretation of hand gestures for human–computer interaction: A review. *IEEE Transactions on Pattern Analysis and Machine Intelligence*, *19*(7), 677–695.

Petrushin, V. A. (2000). Emotion recognition in speech signal: Experimental study, development and application. In *6th International Conference on Spoken Language Processing, ICSLP2000*, Beijing (pp. 222–225).

Picard, R. W. (1997). *Affective computing*. Cambridge, MA: MIT Press.

Picard, R. W. (2003). Affective computing: Challenges. *International Journal of Human–Computer Studies*, *59*(1–2), 55–64.

Rapaport, D. (1961). Emotions and memory. New York: Science Editions.

Scherer, K. R. (1986). Vocal affect expression: A review and a model for future research. *Psychological Bulletin*, *99*, 143–165.

Schlossberg, H. (1954). Three dimensions of emotion. *Psychological review*, *61*, 81–88.

Schröder, M. (2001). Emotional speech synthesis: A review. In *Eurospeech 2001*, Aalborg, Denmark (pp. 561–564).

Tao, J., & Tan, T. (2005). Affective computing: A review. In *ACII 2005*, 981–995.

Tato, R., Santos, R., Kompe, R., & Pardo, J. M. (2002). Emotional space improves emotion recognition. In *ICSLP2002*, Denver (pp. 2029–2032).

Thagard, P. (2005). *MIND: Introduction to cognitive science*, Cambridge, MA: MIT Press.

Verma, A., Subramaniam, L. V., & Rajput N., et al. (2004). Animating expressive faces across languages. *IEEE Transactions on Multimedia*, *6*(6), 791– 800.

Yamamoto, E., Nakamura, S., and Shikano K. (1998). Lip movement synthesis from speech based on hidden Markov models. *Speech Communication*, *26*, 105–115.

Part I
Cognitive Emotion Models

Chapter 2
Affect and Emotions in Intelligent Agents: Why and How?

Andrew Ortony

Abstract Starting with a strong distinction between affect and emotion, a characterization of an organism's effective functioning is presented in terms of the fit between an organism's functioning and the demands and opportunities that are presented by the environment in which it finds itself. It is proposed that effective functioning requires the interplay of four elements—affect, cognition, motivation, and behavior—and that the level of information processing (reactive, routine, or reflective) determines the manner in which the affect is differentiated. Two particular claims about emotion are then explored, namely, that typical full-blown emotions usually have all four elements present, and that emotions arise from the cognitive elaboration of undifferentiated affect. On this view, positive feelings about something deemed to be good, and negative feelings about something deemed to be bad are the bedrock of emotion, which, with the incorporation of cognition, break apart into conditions that look increasingly like emotions. Evidence of the value and utility of affect in humans is discussed, with three classic studies being summarized to demonstrate the consequences of positive and negative affect for attention and for judgment, as well as the effect of positive affect on altruistic behavior. Finally, problems associated with modeling the behavioral manifestations of emotions are discussed, with special attention to the potential ambiguity of facial expressions and emotion-relevant actions.

2.1 Preliminaries

In this chapter, the term "affect" is used to refer to any aspect of mental life that has to do with value, that is, with the assessment of the environment—either spontaneous and automatic, or deliberate and conscious—as good or bad, beneficial or harmful, hospitable or inhospitable, and so on. Examples of aspects of mental life

A. Ortony
Northwestern University, 2120 North Campus Drive, Annenberg Hall,
Evanston IL 60208-2610, USA
e-mail: ortony@northwestern.edu

J.H. Tao, T.N. Tan (eds.), *Affective Information Processing*, that are affective in this way include moods and preferences, as well, of course, as emotions. "Affect," therefore, is a superordinate term, more general than "emotion." It always has one of two possible values, and it is helpful to think of it as lying along a continuum from undifferentiated to differentiated, with vague positive and negative feelings being the most obvious examples of undifferentiated affect, and specific discrete emotions as the best examples of differentiated affect. In fact, one way in which to characterize the difference between affect and emotion is to view emotions as cognitively elaborated undifferentiated affect (Ortony, Norman, and Revelle, 2005) with the differentiation that corresponds to the difference between one emotion and another depending on the way in which the underlying undifferentiated affect is cognitively elaborated. Given this view, emotions (as opposed to undifferentiated affect) always involve cognition (Clore and Ortony, 2000), even though these cognitions are not necessarily conscious.

A second preliminary issue is the clarification of what is meant by "intelligent agent" in the present context. Here it is meant to be very general and to include not only computational artifacts such as autonomous humanoid robots, artificial and lifelike characters, ECAs, and so on, but also, yes, humans. It is important to understand that the issue is not whether all such agents can have genuine affect. Indeed, in my opinion this is not possible for computational artifacts, not only because they lack a somatic component, but also because they lack what in humans we consider to be phenomenological experience, and such experience is taken to be a prerequisite for "having" emotions (but see Sloman and Croucher (1981)). Some might argue that this is not a problem in principle, and therefore, not a deal breaker. My own view is that such arguments are best left to philosophers. What I do think is that by trying to incorporate into computational artifacts those components of affect and emotions that can be modeled we stand to gain many benefits. One obvious benefit is that it will enable us to build more lifelike, believable, and helpful agents.

Whereas I suspect that there are many applications where the agents we build do not need such features, there are many applications for which lifelike, believable agents are likely to be important (e.g., social robots, therapy, training simulations). And at the very least, we need to take care to avoid conflicts between the information that such agents are receiving or transmitting (or the actions in which they engage) and any display (or lack thereof) of affect that they might exhibit.

Finally, another benefit of implementing models of emotion is that we can explore, and thus to some extent test (some aspects of) the implications of the theories those implementations embody. We can see whether the models behave as they are supposed to behave.

2.2 Affect and Emotions in Intelligent Agents: Why?

2.2.1 The Function of Affect and Emotion

If we plan to introduce at least some aspects of affect and emotion into computational artifacts, it's worth spending a few moments addressing the question of what their value might be. One way to approach this is to consider the utility of affect for biological (especially, human) agents. It used to be thought that emotions were disruptive, frequently interfering with efficient rational functioning. And indeed, under extreme conditions, this is a reasonable perspective to take. When emotions are not well regulated by an individual, either in the moment, as in crimes of passion, or chronically, as in emotional disorders such as phobias and depression, it is hard to argue that they have beneficial effects. However, under normal conditions, when under control, affect and emotion, by modulating attention, action, and information processing and judgment, contribute in important ways to effective functioning.

Ortony, Norman, and Revelle, (2005) characterized effective functioning in terms of the quality of fit between an organism's functioning and the demands and opportunities that are presented by the environment in which it finds itself. We elaborated this idea by exploring the interplay between what an organism does and how it does it. With respect to what (i.e., the kinds of things) the organism does, we specified four modes: affect, motivation, cognition, and action. With respect to the ways in which an organism does those things, we specified three levels: reactive (fast, often, pattern-matching mechanisms), routine (learned automatic procedures), and reflective (controlled conscious activity).

Of particular relevance here are the four proposed modes of affect, motivation, cognition, and action, roughly: feeling, wanting, thinking, and acting. The claim is that effective functioning requires that all four of these modes (together, in fact, with perception) interact in concert, but with each operating in a somewhat different manner depending on the level (reactive, routine, or reflective) at which it is operating. In particular, we proposed that affect manifests itself as progressively more differentiated; at the reactive level, it tends to be quite diffuse and undifferentiated, whereas at the highest, reflective, level it is maximally differentiated and shows up as discrete full-blown emotions. But regardless of how affect is manifested, there is considerable evidence, some of which is discussed below, that affect is important for effective functioning, not least because of its role in modulating attention, action, and information processing and judgment.

Affect and Attention

In a seminal paper some 40 years ago, Herbert Simon made the point that affect influences attention (Simon, 1967). We now know much more about the nature of this influence. We now know that negative affect tends to narrow attention to relatively local information—to the here and now, to what's in the immediate vicinity—whereas positive affect allows attention to be drawn to more global "out there" information.

It is easy to see the adaptive value of these attentional correlates of affect. Assuming that negative affect arises because the environment is presenting the organism with some kind of problem, vigilance to local conditions is likely to be beneficial with respect to, for example, threat detection and avoidance. Meanwhile, if we regard positive affect as a kind of "all's well" signal, then the organism is more likely

Fig. 2.1 Sample stimulus used in Gasper and Clore (2002).

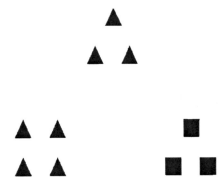

to be able to safely engage in more wide-ranging exploratory behaviors. There are many studies demonstrating the phenomenon of attentional narrowing with negative affect and attentional broadening with positive affect. I briefly review just one.

Consider a stimulus display such as the one shown in Figure 2.1 The way to view this particular stimulus is as, on top, a large (global) triangle composed of small (local) triangles, below which, on the left, is a large square also composed of small triangles, and on the right, a large triangle composed of small squares. Using stimuli like this, Gasper and Clore (2002), after inducing either positive or negative affect in participants by having them re-live highly emotional autobiographical experiences, asked participants to select whichever of the two lower figures they judged to be more similar to the upper figure. Results showed a marked preference (about 2:1) for people in negative affective states to select the square (on the left), whose similarity to the target triangle depends on the fact the both are comprised of small triangles, whereas people in positive affective states preferred (again, close to 2:1) the triangle (on the right), whose similarity to the target triangle depends on the fact both are (globally speaking) triangles, even though they are locally different in that one is comprised of small triangles and the other of small squares. This is exactly what one would expect if negative affect tends to focus attention on local features and details and positive affect tends to encourage attention to be focused on the bigger picture.

Affect and Action

How does affect influence what people do? It turns out that a little bit of positive affect can have powerful effects on what people do. In a classic experiment, Isen and Levin (1972) observed the helping behaviors of people in a shopping mall after they had used a public telephone to make a call. When the phone was not in use, the experimenters sometimes placed a dime in the return slot of the phone. They then compared the helping behaviors of individuals who unexpectedly found a dime with those not blessed with such good fortune. As each person left the call box, a confederate "happened" to drop a stack of papers close to and in plain view of the caller.

The results were truly astonishing. Of callers who had found a dime, almost 90 percent stopped to help pick up the papers. Of those who found nothing (which is what usually happens when one uses a public call box), only 4 percent stopped to help—a huge effect resulting from an apparently tiny, 10 cent, manipulation of affect.

Affect and Judgment

Everyone knows that the weather affects how we feel. What is less obvious is that this phenomenon can affect judgments that we make, even when we are quite unaware of it. In a classic study (Schwartz and Clore, 1983), respondents to a telephone survey allegedly being conducted from a remote city were asked to rate their life satisfaction on either the first warm spring day, or the first cold, cloudy, rainy day following the first warm spring day. Respondents on the first warm spring day reported high life-satisfaction ratings (around 7.5 on a 9-point scale), and these ratings were independent of whether respondents were incidentally prompted about the weather at the beginning of the conversation. Specifically, half of the respondents were casually asked how the weather was in their location and half were not.

Similar mean ratings were recorded for (different) respondents being called on the cold rainy day, but only if they were queried with the weather remark. Respondents on that day who were not reminded of the unpleasant weather reported significantly (about 2 scale points) lower life-satisfaction ratings. Schwartz and Clore explained this finding in terms of their "affect as information" theory wherein respondents unwittingly interpret their pre-existing feelings (in this case, negative feelings on the cold rainy day) as a reaction to the target unless the informational value of those feelings for the judgment at hand (life-satisfaction) is made salient (as it is when they are reminded about the unpleasant weather).

These studies are but three examples of the pervasive influence that affect has on what people think and do, and it is not hard to tell a story as to why, in general, these influences are likely to be beneficial. However, the point here is not so much to tell such a story as to simply emphasize the fact that affect matters, and at the most general level, it is undifferentiated affect conceived of as pure undifferentiated positive or negative feelings (as opposed to specific emotions) that is the fundamental driving force. These two kinds of feelings—positive feelings about something here and now deemed to be in one way or another, good, and negative feelings about something deemed to be bad—are the bedrock of emotion.

Central to my view, however, is the idea that with the incorporation of cognition these undifferentiated forms begin to break apart into conditions that look increasingly like emotions. For example, a positive feeling about a potential good goes beyond the here and now and requires the organism to be able to conceptualize a possible future, and in doing so, we could argue that what was originally just an undifferentiated positive feeling now looks more like a primitive form of hope. And perhaps more compelling, the incorporation of a representation of a possible future into a negative feeling about a potentially bad thing is the minimal requirement for a primitive form of fear. In this view, the transition from undifferentiated affect to

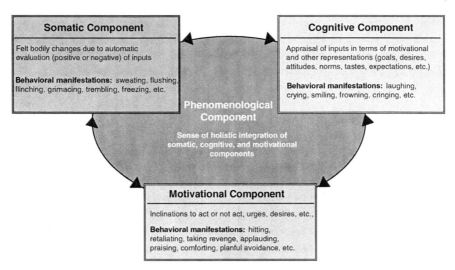

Fig. 2.2 Components of a typical "full-blown" emotion.

"full-blown" emotions emerges through the addition of cognitive content so that one can think of emotions as cognitively elaborated good and bad feelings ultimately involving all four modes of processing, affect, cognition, motivation, and behavior, as illustrated in Figure 2.2.

2.2.2 Representing Affect and Emotions in Agents

The Cognitive Component

The cognitive component has to do with appraising the world in terms of concerns. Elsewhere, in what has come to be called the OCC model (Ortony, Clore, and Collins, 2005), my colleagues and I proposed three classes of emotions emanating from three kinds of concerns or sources of value: goals, standards, and tastes. We have already seen how a rudimentary form of fear emerges when minimal cognitive content is added to undifferentiated affect to generate a negative feeling about a potentially bad thing. Potentially bad things, which pertain to goals, can be further elaborated cognitively in terms of related outcomes, thus generating more specific emotions that can be characterized as (1) a negative feeling because a potentially bad thing happened (fears confirmed) or (2) a positive feeling because a potentially bad thing didn't happen (relief). Similarly, further elaboration of a positive feeling about a potentially good thing (hope), gives rise to (3) a positive feeling because a potentially good thing happened (satisfaction), or (4) a negative feeling because a potentially good thing didn't happen (disappointment).

Notice that what we are doing here is to characterize the way in which the world is evaluated by the agent in terms of concerns, in these cases, goals. This is a central tenet of the OCC model, and it is decidedly not the same thing as attempting to define emotion words. Thus, for example, whereas we refer to the type of negative feelings that arise because one perceives the world in terms of a potentially good thing that didn't happen as "disappointment" emotions, we view this type of emotion to be given by the specification of the way in which the negative feeling is cognitively elaborated rather than by the emotion word. In fact the question of which, if any, of the linguistic expressions (including individual words) of a language that refer to emotional states can be accommodated by the type specification is itself an interesting question.

In the case of this particular example, apart from "disappointment," "dashed hopes," "despair," "frustration," "upset," "heartbroken," and so on can all be used in a way that is compatible with the type specification. However, the fact that, for example, "upset" can be used in many other ways as well (e.g., to refer to an angry state) illustrates why it is that we prefer to specify emotion types without direct reference to emotion words. Because some emotional states (anger, fear, etc.) have many associated linguistic tokens, whereas others (e.g., relief) have only one, and yet others (e.g., fears-confirmed) have none, words are not the place to start.

Behavioral Manifestations

Earlier I suggested, as illustrated in Figure 2.2, that the principal components of emotions—affect, cognition, and motivation—all have behavioral manifestations. The idea that these behavioral manifestations could be effectively modeled is certainly an appealing one. Unfortunately, matters are not so simple, for whereas the emotion–cognition linkage seems to be quite orderly and easy to specify, this is not true of the emotion–behavior linkage. Observable behaviors are often highly ambiguous unless disambiguated by contextual information. For example, a face that appears to exhibit excruciating pain might in fact be reflecting uncontrollable joy, as can be seen in Figure 2.3, which is the facial expression of Jana Novotna at the moment of winning Wimbledon in 1998, her first Grand Slam title in 45 tries.

When all we see is a "raw" behavior such as a person running, the running behavior alone (i.e., in the absence of context) is generally insufficient to tell us whether it is a manifestation of, say, love (e.g., trying to catch up with a romantic interest), or fear (e.g., trying to escape from a perceived threat), or neither (simply running for exercise). There are many reasons for the low diagnosticity of emotion-relevant behaviors, but there are at least two particularly obvious reasons, each relating to important determinants of such behaviors: the intensity of affect, and the coping potential of the agent.

First, if the intensity of affect is very low one might expect little or no observable behavioral manifestation at all, so sometimes affective states have no observable behavioral correlates. Clearly, one would not expect the same behavioral signs from an individual who was slightly nervous or worried about something as one would

Fig. 2.3 Extreme distress?

from that same individual who was in the grip of extreme fear. So, although our theoretical position is that fear emotions are fear emotions, with all, from nervousness to terror, sharing a common cognitive foundation, nevertheless they can differ radically in other respects, one of which is the way in which they manifest themselves in behavior as a function of intensity.

Second, within the same emotion type, an agent's expectations about coping potential are also a major determinant of emotion-relevant behavior. If I see no prospect of running away from a perceived threat, I might deem it more prudent to "play dead." Along with fleeing and fighting, freezing is, of course, one of nature's ways of coping with threat. Thus, again, the same emotion type can have radically different behavioral manifestations. In addition to these kinds of sources of variation in the behavioral aspects of emotions, there is the important fact that individuals vary greatly too. Some people are much more labile than others.

The conclusion to be drawn from these facts is that the kinds of generalizations that can be made about the relation between emotions and observable behavior are quite limited. Nevertheless, if one chooses the right level of specificity, it does seem possible to find some systematicity. For example, one might propose a taxonomy along the lines of the one illustrated in Figure 2.4. One thing this taxonomy suggests is, moving from left (somatic) to right (motivational), a general increase in the planfulness of behavioral manifestations. The idea here is that the behavioral manifestations associated with the somatic component tend to be immediate, spontaneous, and reactive, whereas those associated with the motivational component

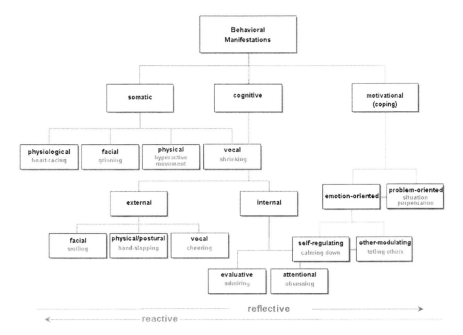

Fig. 2.4 Proposed structure of behavioral manifestations.

are often more deliberate, planned, and reflective. The figure also indicates (in bold type) proposed subcategories, with the leaf nodes having associated with them examples of the kinds of particular manifestations that might be expected in the case of a positive emotion such as joy.

Life is full of trade-offs. So although we can search for some systematicity in characterizations of the emotion–behavior connection, we need to guard against rigidity. Perhaps the best way to think about the issue is that as we move from emotion to emotion, the typical associated behaviors (and the constraints that govern them) change. We can see how this might work by comparing what look like reasonable proposals for the behaviors typically associated with joy emotions (Table 2.1) with those typically associated with anger emotions (Table 2.2).

Exactly what the typical behaviors are is an empirical question and to the best of my knowledge, there has been no comprehensive work on this topic. However, some researchers have studied particular emotions in great detail and in that context have collected data on what people tend to do when in those emotional states. One of the most carefully studied and best documented cases is Averill's (1982) detailed study of anger, which I took as the source for the proposals for anger emotions indicated in Table 2.2.

The fact that for each emotion type there is a range of possible behavioral manifestations raises the question of which particular behaviors are selected in any particular case. The general answer to this, as already indicated, is that it depends

Table 2.1 Behavioral Manifestations of Joy Emotions

Behavioral Manifestations of Joy Emotions		
SOMATIC	physiological	heart racing/pounding
	facial	grinning
	physical	exaggerated, hyperactive, movements
	vocal	shrieking, screaming
EXTERNAL **COGNITIVE** **INTERNAL**	facial	smiling
	physical/postural	opening out, jumping for joy, "high-fiving"
	vocal	cheering, laughing
	evaluative	admiring/liking perceived facilitators
	attentional	obsessing about how it happened/what it means
MOTIVATIONAL	emotion: self-regulating	sharing the news, telling others
	emotion: other-regulating	soliciting praise/congratulations from others
	problem-oriented	maintaining/preserving cause, reaffirmation

Table 2.2 Behavioral Manifestations of Anger Emotions

Behavioral Manifestations of Anger Emotions		
SOMATIC	physiological	shaking, flushing
	facial	baring of teeth
	physical	clenching of teeth or hands, body tense
	vocal	raising of voice
EXTERNAL **COGNITIVE** **INTERNAL**	facial	scowling, glaring
	physical/postural	throwing, banging, hitting
	vocal	shouting, swearing, sarcastic/sulky remarks, refusing to speak
	evaluative	disliking offender
	attentional	obsessing about event, ruminating about how and why
MOTIVATIONAL	emotion: self-regulating	calming down, getting a grip, talking it over
	emotion: other-regulating	causing distress to offender (direct aggression, denial of benefits)
	problem-oriented	preventing continuation or recurrence of problem

partly on the motivational component, with considerations of capacity, time, and prudence often playing an important role at the more planful (reflective) end. At the more somatic (reactive) end, the manifestations will be primarily determined by intensity issues. For example, an intense joy emotion is more likely to be accompanied by some sort of spontaneous vocal manifestation such as shrieking than is a mild one, and so on.

I would be the first to admit that these proposals are very vague and preliminary; they are only offered as a starting point, a way, perhaps, to think about the problem. Clearly, if they are to have any utility, they will need to be worked out in much greater detail. Thus, it should be borne in mind that they are offered as a suggested way of approaching the problem, not as a solution. Unless and until they can be specified sufficiently precisely to be formalizable, there is not much that can be done with them, but then, one has to start somewhere, and this is where I am proposing we start.

2.3 Conclusion

In this chapter, I have suggested a way of thinking about the complex interactions of affect, motivation, cognition, and behavior, and I have suggested that the evident role and value of affect and emotion in effective functioning in humans justifies their incorporation in at least some kinds of computational artifacts. I then made some suggestions about how to incorporate at least (nonphysiological/somatic) aspects of relations among emotion, cognition, and motivation and behavior into the design of such artifacts, acknowledging that the kind of work that remains to be done on the behavioral aspects is likely to be more challenging than the work that has already been done on the cognitive aspects because the linkage between emotions and behavior is so much weaker than that between emotions and cognition.

References

Averill, J. R. (1982). *Anger and aggression: An essay on emotion*. New York: Springer-Verlag.

Clore, G. L., & Ortony, A. (2000). Cognition in emotion: Always, sometimes, or never? In L. Nadel, R. Lane, & G. L. Ahern (Eds), *The cognitive neuroscience of emotion*. New York: Oxford University Press.

Gasper, K., & Clore, G. L. (2002). Attending to the big picture: Mood and global versus local processing of visual information. *Psychological Science, 13*, 34–40.

Isen, A. M., & Levin, P. F. (1972). Effect of feeling good on helping: Cookies and kindness. *Journal of Personality and Social Psychology, 21*, 384–388.

Ortony, A., Clore, G. L., & Collins, A. (1988). *The cognitive structure of emotions*. New York: Cambridge University Press.

Ortony, A., Norman, D. A., & Revelle, W. (2005). Affect and proto-affect in effective functioning. In J. M. Fellous & M. A. Arbib (Eds.), *Who needs emotions: The brain meets the robot*. New York: Oxford University Press.

Schwartz, N., & Clore, G. L. (1983). Mood, misattribution, and judgment of well-being: informative and directive functions of affective states. *Journal of Personality and Social Psychology, 45*, 513–523.

Simon, H. A. (1967). Motivational and emotional controls of cognition. *Psychological Review, 74*, 29–39.

Sloman, A., & Croucher, M. (1981). You don't need a soft skin to have a warm heart: Towards a computational analysis of motivation and emotions. *Cognitive Science Research Paper, CSRP 004*, Sussex University.

Chapter 3
Cognitive Emotion Modeling in Natural Language Communication

Valeria Carofiglio, Fiorella de Rosis, and Nicole Novielli

Abstract This chapter describes some psychological theories that are at the foundation of research on cognitive models of emotions, and then reviews the most significant projects in this domain in recent years. The review is focused on probabilistic dynamic models, due to the key role of uncertainty in the relationships among the variables involved: the authors' experience in this domain is discussed by outlining open problems. Two aspects are discussed in particular: how probabilistic emotion models can be validated and how the problem of emotional–cognitive inconsistency can be dealt with in probabilistic terms.

3.1 Introduction

Computer science recently began, with success, to endow natural language dialogues with emotions, by mainly relying on the OCC theory. More recent works went beyond this classification, to consider categories of emotions that occur frequently in human–computer communication (Carberry & de Rosis, 2008). This chapter describes how emotion activation and interpretation theories may contribute to build affective state representations of human and artificial agents, which are the problems in building and validating these models.

Section 3.2 is focused on describing the affective states that may influence natural language communication. Section 3.3 briefly reviews some psychological theories of emotions: as appraisal theories are best suited to cognitive modeling, essential aspects of these theories are considered in particular. In Section 3.4, the main requirements of cognitive models that combine rational with emotional mental state components are discussed.

V. Carofiglio (✉), F. de Rosis, and N. Novielli
Department of Informatics, Via Orabona 4, 70124 Bari, Italy
e-mail: carofiglio@di.uniba.it

J.H. Tao, T.N. Tan (eds.), *Affective Information Processing*,
© Springer Science+Business Media LLC 2009

Previous experiences in this area are analyzed briefly in Section 3.5, with special focus on models considering uncertainty and time-dependency in emotion activation and decay. In the same section, the authors' own formalism for emotion modeling is then introduced and compared with these models.

A general method for validating these probabilistic models is outlined in Section 3.6, with an example of application. Finally, Section 3.7 reflects critically on the problem of cognitive–emotional inconsistency and how this may be dealt with in probabilistic models.

3.2 Affective States Relevant in NL Communication

The term "affective state" includes several aspects that vary in their degree of stability and in their "object-oriented specificity." In this contribution, the following aspects are considered in particular (Cowie, 2006).

- *Personality traits*: Stable, dynamic, and organized set of characteristics of a person that uniquely influence his or her cognitions, motivations, and behaviors in various situations.
- *Interpersonal stance*: A relatively short-lived state where feeling towards another person comes to the fore and inclines you to behave in a particular way towards him or her.
- *Emotions*: Typically complex, episodic, dynamic, and structured events. They are complex in that they typically involve many different elements: perceptions, thoughts, feelings of various kinds, bodily changes, dispositions to experience further emotional episodes. They are episodic and dynamic in that, over time, the elements can come and go, depending on all sorts of factors. They are structured in that they constitute part of an unfolding sequence of actions and events, thoughts and feelings, in which they are embedded.

3.3 Theories Behind Cognitive Emotion Models: Which Ones Best Fit?

Psychologists worked at decoding emotions for decades, by focusing on two main questions: how can emotions be classified and what their functioning is (i.e., how are they triggered)? How do they affect behavior? What role is played by cognition? Two points of view prevailed: the first one assumes that a limited set of basic emotions exists, and the second one considers emotions as a continuous function of one or more dimensions; see, for example, the "circumplex model" of affect (Russell, 2003).

Theories following the "discrete trend" agree on the idea that a limited set of basic emotions exists, although consensus about the nature and the number of these basic emotions has not been reached. Ekman (1999) defines a basic emotion as having specific feelings, universal signals, and corresponding physiological changes; emotions may be triggered by either an automatic (very quick) or extended (slow, deliberate, and conscious) appraisal mechanism. Plutchik (1980) defines discrete emotions as corresponding to specific adaptive processes: reproduction, safety, and so on.

In Izard's "differential emotion theory," distinct discrete emotions are triggered by neural activation, which induces a specific experience and influences behavior and cognition (Izard, 1993). Lazarus (1991) describes nine negative (anger, anxiety, guilt, shame, sadness, envy, jealousy, disgust) and six positive (joy, pride, love, relief, hope, compassion) emotions, with their appraisal patterns: positive emotions are triggered if the situation is congruent with one of the individual's goals; otherwise, negative emotions are triggered.

Some physiological theories assume that stimuli produce a physiological activation that creates emotions, with no cognitive intervention (James, 1984). Evolutionary theories assume that emotions were inherited during evolution and are automatically triggered with no cognitive intervention (Ekman, 1999). On the other side, cognitive theories assume that cognition is essential in the triggering of emotion.

Among the cognitive theories of emotions, "appraisal theories" assume that emotions are triggered by the evaluation of a stimulus, using different criteria. To Arnold (1960) "appraisal" is the process for determining the significance of a situation for an individual, that is, if a given situation is good or bad for himself or herself. Appraisal triggers an emotion that induces an "action tendency" of attraction or repulsion, with a corresponding physiological change (to favor the individual's adaptation to the environment).

Ortony, Clore, and Collins (1988) focus their theory on the cognitive elicitors of emotions. They postulate that emotions represent valenced reactions to perceptions of the world. Thus, one can be pleased or not about the consequences of an event; one can endorse or reject the actions of an agent or can like or dislike aspects of an object. Lazarus assumes that the human emotional process is made up of two separated processes: appraisal (which characterizes the person's relationship with her environment) and coping (which suggests strategies for altering or maintaining this relationship). Cognition informs both these processes; it informs appraisal by building mental representations of how events relate to internal dispositions such as beliefs and goals, and informs coping by suggesting and exploring strategies for altering or maintaining the person–environment relationship (Lazarus, 1991).

These theories show several advantages for cognitive modeling.

- *A fine-grained differentiation among emotions*: Cognitive appraisal theories assume that emotions result from the evaluation of stimuli. Thus each distinct emotion corresponds to a particular appraisal pattern, that is, a particular combination of appraisal criteria.
- *A differentiation (at various levels) among individuals in felt emotions*: In the same situation, several individuals can feel different emotions. Different evaluations of the situation represent cognitive mediation between the stimulus and the

felt emotion. These may be linked to individual personality traits or to mental representations of how events relate to internal dispositions such as beliefs and goals.

- *A temporal differentiation of felt emotions by an individual*: The same individual can appraise differently the same situation at different moments, and thus feel different emotions, depending on the context.

3.3.1 Relationship Between Emotions and Goals

A general consensus exists on the hypothesis that emotions are a biological device aimed at monitoring the state of reaching or threatening our most important goals (Oatley & Johnson-Laird, 1987). In Lazarus's primary appraisal, the relevance of a given situation to the individual's relevant goals is assessed (Lazarus, 1991). At the same time, emotions activate goals and plans that are functional to re-establishing or preserving the well-being of the individual, challenged by the events that produced them (secondary appraisal; Lazarus (1991)).

There is a strong relationship, then, between goals and emotions: goals, at the same time, cause emotions and are caused by emotions. They cause emotions because, if an important goal is achieved or threatened, an emotion is triggered: emotions are therefore a feedback device that monitors the reaching or threatening of our high-level goals. At the same time, emotions activate goals and action plans that are functional for re-establishing or preserving the well-being of the individual who was challenged by the events that produced them (Poggi, 2005). As personality traits may be viewed in terms of weights people put on different goals, the strength of the relationship between goals and emotions also depends on personality traits. These considerations suggest the following criteria for categorizing emotions (Poggi, 2005).

- *The goals the emotion monitors:* For instance, "Preserving self from—immediate or future—bad" may activate distress and fear; "achieving the—immediate or future—good of self," may activate joy and hope. "Dominating others" may activate envy. "Acquiring knowledge and competence" activates the cognitive emotion of curiosity. Altruistic emotions such as guilt or compassion involve the goal of "defending, protecting, helping others." Image emotions such as gratification involve the goal of "being evaluated positively by others." Self-image emotions such as pride involve the goal of "evaluating oneself positively," and so on.
- *The level of importance of the monitored goal:* This may be linked to the type of goal but is also an expression of some personality traits (e.g., neuroticism).
- *The probability of threatening/achieving the monitored goal:* Some emotions (joy, sadness) are felt when the achievement or thwarting is certain, others (hope, fear), when this is only likely.
- *The time in which the monitored goal is threatened/achieved:* Some emotions (joy, sadness) are felt only after goal achievement or thwarting, others (enthusiasm) during or before goal pursuit.

- *The relevance of the monitored goal with respect to the situation:* If a situation is not relevant to any individual's goal, then it cannot trigger any emotion in the individual.
- *The relationship between the monitored goal and the situation in which an individual feels an emotion:* This is linked to the emotion valence, but also to its intensity. Some emotions belong to the same "family" but differ in their intensity (disappointment, annoyance, anger, fury).

Once an emotion is felt by an individual, an evaluation of the actions he may perform and their envisaged effects on the situation occurs. Coping potential is a measure of how individuals can change their goals, to restore a good relationship with the environment (Lazarus, 1991).

3.3.2 Relationship Between Emotions and Beliefs

Emotions are biologically adaptive mechanisms that result from evaluation of one's own relationship with the environment. However, not all appraisal variables are translated into beliefs: some of them influence emotion activation without passing through cognitive processing, whereas others do it. These cognitive appraisals are beliefs about the importance of the event, its expectedness, the responsible agent, the degree to which the event can be controlled, its causes, and its likely consequences: in particular (as said) their effect on goal achievement or threatening. Different versions of this assumption can be found in various cognitive appraisal theories of emotion (Arnold, 1960; Lazarus, 1991; Ortony et al., 1988; Scherer et al., 2004). In individual emotions, cognitive appraisals are first-order beliefs whereas in social emotions second-order beliefs occur as well.

Beliefs therefore influence activation of emotions and are influenced by emotions in their turn (Frijda & Mesquita, 2000). They may trigger emotions either directly (as emotion antecedents) or through the activation of a goal (Miceli de Rosis, & Poggi, 2006). On the other hand, psychologists agree in claiming that emotions may give rise to new beliefs or may strengthen or weaken existing beliefs.

Classical examples are jealousy, which strengthens perception of malicious behaviors, or fear, which tends to increase perception of the probability or the amount of danger of the feared event (see Section 3.7). As events that elicit emotions may fix beliefs at the same time, this effect may strengthen the cyclical process of belief holding —emotion activation—belief revision: when you hear on TV about a plane crash, your fear strengthens your beliefs about the risks of flying. These beliefs may be temporary, and last for as long as the emotion lasts. But they may become more permanent, as a result of a "rumination and amplification" effect: in this case, for instance, feeling fearful after looking at the TV service may bring one to detect more fearful stimuli in the news, which increase fear in their turn.

Finally, emotions may influence beliefs indirectly, by influencing thinking: they are presumed to play the role of making human behavior more effective, by activating goals and orienting thinking towards finding a quick solution to achieving them. They hence influence information selection by being biased towards beliefs that support emotional aims.

3.4 Applying These Theories to Build Emotion Models

The lesson from the psychological theories mentioned so far is that, in trying to formalize a computationally tractable model of emotion, researchers have to deal with a very complex reality. Individuals can experience several emotions at the same time, each with a different intensity, which is due to the importance of the goal, the likelihood of the impact of the perceived event on that goal, the level of surprise about the event, the measure of how probable it is that the event will occur, and the level of involvement in the situation that leads to emotion triggering. Once activated, emotions can decay over time with a trend that depends on the emotion and its intensity; duration is also influenced by personality traits and social aspects of the interaction. Hence, the following factors may be listed as aspects to necessarily include in a computational model of emotions.

3.4.1 Appraisal Components of Emotions

How is it that two persons report feeling different emotions in the same situation? Clearly, the main source of difference is due to the different structure of beliefs and goals of the two individuals: the goals they want to achieve, the weights they assign to achieving them, and the structure of links between beliefs and goals. Differences among experienced emotions may be due to the link between situation characteristics (e.g., which event, together with its consequences, which social aspects, role of individuals involved in the situation, their relationship, and which individual's personality traits) and emotion components (appraisal variables but also other internal dispositions, beliefs, and goals). They may be due, as well, to the mutual links between emotion components themselves (van Reekum & Scherer, 1997).

3.4.2 Influence of Personality Factors

Individual differences can alter experienced emotions. Some personality traits may be viewed in terms of the general "propensity to feel emotions" (Poggi & Pelachaud, 1998; Plutchik, 1980). Picard (1997) calls this subset of personality traits "temperament," whereas other authors relate them directly to one of the factors in the "Big-Five" model (Mc Crae & John, 1992), for instance, neuroticism.

These traits imply, in a sense, a lower threshold in emotion feeling (Ortony et al., 1988). For instance, a "shy" person is keener to feel "shame," especially in front of unknown people. "Proud" persons attribute a high weight to their goal of self-esteem, in particular to the subgoal of not depending on other people. So, every time one of these goals is achieved, the proud person will feel the emotion of pride; conversely, every time these goals are threatened (if, for instance, one is obliged to ask for help), the person will feel the opposite emotion, shame. A personality trait (proud) is therefore related to attaching a higher weight to a particular goal (self-esteem, autonomy), and, because that goal is important to that kind of person, the person will feel the corresponding emotion (pride or shame) with a higher intensity.

3.4.3 Emotion Intensity and Decay/Duration

In the OCC theory (Ortony et al., 1988), desirability, praiseworthiness, and appealingness are key appraisal variables that affect the emotional reaction to a given situation, as well as their intensity: they are therefore called local intensity variables. For example, the intensity of prospect-based and confirmation emotions is affected by the likelihood that the prospective event will happen, the effort (degree of utilization of resources to make the prospective event happen or to prevent it from happening), and the realization (degree to which the prospective event actually happens).

The intensity of fortune-of-others emotions is affected by desirability for the other (how much the event is presumed to be desirable for the other agent), liking (has the individual appraising the situation a positive or a negative attitude toward the other?), and deservingness (how much the individual appraising the situation believes that the other individual deserved what happened to him).

Some global intensity variables also affect the intensity of emotions: sense of reality measures how much the emotion-inducing situation is real; proximity measures how much the individual feels psychologically close to the emotion-inducing situation; unexpectedness measures how much the individual is surprised by the situation; and arousal measures how much the individual was excited before the stimulus.

Some of the systems that follow the OCC theory define a measure for emotion intensity in terms of some mathematical function combining the previously mentioned variables. In (Prendinger, Descamps, and Ishizuka, 2002) "emotion-elicitation rules" some of these variables are selected, and emotion intensities depend on the logarithm of the sum of their exponentials. The intensity of joy, for instance, coincides with the desirability of the triggering event; the intensity of happy-for is a function of the interlocutor's happiness and of the "degree of positive attitude" of the agent towards the interlocutor.

In Elliot and Siegle's (1993) emotion-eliciting condition, the intensity of emotions also depends on a combination of some variables, in a set of 22 possible ones (e.g., importance, surprisingness, temporal proximity, etc.). A limit of this method may be in the combination of several heterogeneous measures in a single function: when different scales are employed, the effect of their combination cannot be foreseen precisely.

In addition, the range of variability of the function may go outside the range of the variable that this function should measure, with the need of normalizing the obtained value or of cutting off values out of this range.

A second approach adopts a probabilistic representation of the relationships among the variables involved in emotion triggering and display. These are usually dynamic models that represent the transition through various emotional states during time. Intensity of emotions is calculated by applying utility theory (see, e.g., Conati (2002) and de Rosis, Pelachaud, Poggi, De Carolis & Carofiglio (2003)). This approach is further analyzed in Section 3.5.

3.4.4 Emotion Mixing

In her book on affective computing, Rosalind Picard (1997) proposes two metaphors for describing the way emotions may combine: in a "microwave oven" metaphor, juxtaposition of two or more states may occur even if, at any time instant, the individual experiences only one emotion. In this type of mixing, emotions do not truly co-occur but the affective state switches among them in time: this is, for instance, the case of love–hate. In the "tub of water" metaphor, on the contrary, the kind of mixing allows the states to mingle and form a new state: this is, for instance, the case of feeling wary, a mixture of interest and fear. Different emotions may coexist because an event produced several of them at the same time or because a new emotion is triggered and the previous ones did not yet completely decay.

Picard evokes the generative mechanism as the key factor for distinguishing between emotions that may coexist (by mixing according to the tub of water metaphor) and emotions that switch from each other over time (by mixing according to the microwave oven metaphor). She suggests that co-existence may be due, first of all, to differences in these generative mechanisms. But it may be due, as well, to differences in time decay among emotions that were generated by the same mechanism at two distinct time instants: for instance, "primary" emotions, such as fear, and cognitive ones, such as anticipation.

3.4.5 Role of Uncertainty

To represent triggering of emotions and also the two ways in which emotions may mix, the modeling formalism adopted should be able to represent their generative mechanism, the intensity with which they are triggered and the way this intensity decays over time. Logical models are probably inappropriate to handle all the parameters mentioned above. Due to the presence of various sources of uncertainty (static/dynamic), belief networks (BNs/DBN) or dynamic decision networks (DDNs) are probably more appropriate to achieve these goals. A BN is a graphical model whose nodes represent discrete random variables and whose arcs represent dependencies between variables in terms of conditional probabilities (Pearl, 1988).

DBNs are an extension of BNs, to enable modeling temporal environments (Nicholson & Brady, 1994). A DBN is made up of interconnected time slices of usually structurally identical static BNs; previous time slices are used to predict or estimate the nodes' state in the current time slice. The conditional probability distributions of nodes with parents in different time slices are defined by a state evolution model, which describes how the system evolves over time. Finally, DDNs (Russell & Norvig, 1995) extend DBNs to provide a mechanism for making rational decisions by combining probability and utility theory within changing environments: in addition to nodes representing discrete random variables over time, the networks contain utility and decision nodes.

In the following, the power of DBNs in representing the dynamic arousal, evolution, and disappearing of emotions is discussed, together with the way these phenomena are influenced by personality factors and social context. The logic behind the DBN-based modeling method is illustrated in a paper in which the advantages the method offers in driving the affective behavior of an embodied conversational agent are also discussed (de Rosis et al., 2003). Due to the importance of uncertainty in emotion activation and interpretation, the next section is focused on some remarkable probabilistic emotion models.

3.5 Some Remarkable Experiences in Emotion Modeling

In a first attempt (Ball & Breese, 2000), a simple model was proposed: emotional state and personality traits were characterized by discrete values along a small number of dimensions (valence and arousal, dominance and friendliness). These internal states were treated as unobservable variables in a Bayesian network model. Model dependencies were established according to experimentally demonstrated causal relations among these unobservable variables and observable quantities (expressions of emotion and personality) such as word choice, facial expression, speech, and so on. EM (Reilly, 1996) simulated the emotion decay over time for a specific set of emotions, according to the goal that generated them. A specific intensity threshold was defined for each emotion to be triggered.

The Affective Reasoner (Elliott & Siegle, 1993) was a typical multiagent model. Each agent used a representation of both itself and the interlocutor's mind, evaluated events according to the OCC theory, and simulated a social interactive behavior by using its knowledge to infer the other's mental state. Emile (Gratch & Marsella, 2001) extended the Affective Reasoner by defining emotion triggering in terms of plan representation: the intensity of emotions was strictly related to the probability of a plan to be executed, which was responsible for the agents' goal achievement.

Conati (2002) proposed a model based on dynamic decision networks to represent the emotional state induced by educational games and how these states are displayed. The emotions represented in this model (reproach, shame, and joy) were a subset of the OCC classification; some personality traits were assumed to affect the student's goals. The grain size of knowledge representation in this model was not very fine: among the various attitudes that may influence emotion activation (first- and second-order beliefs and goals, values, etc.), only goals were considered in the model. Subsequently, the same group (Conati & McLaren, 2005) described how they refined their model by adding new emotions and learning parameters from a dataset collected from real users. In Prendinger and Ishizuka (2005) work, an artificial agent empathizes with a relaxed, joyful, or frustrated user by interpreting physiological signals with the aid of probabilistic decision networks: these networks include representation of events, agent's choices, and utility functions.

In the next sections, the authors briefly describe their work on Bayesian affective models. This was oriented in two directions: in a first model (emotional-mind), they advocated for a fine-grained cognitive structure in which the appraisal of what happens in the environment was represented in terms of its effects on the agent's system of beliefs and goals, to activate one or more individual emotions in the OCC classification (Carofiglio et al., 2008). They subsequently (with social-mind) worked at representing how social emotions (in particular, the social attitude of users towards an Embodied Advice-Giving Agent) can be progressively recognized from the user's linguistic behavior (de Rosis et al., 2007).

3.5.1 Emotional-Mind

As anticipated, the starting point of the model is that emotions are activated by the belief that a particular important goal may be achieved or threatened (Carofiglio & de Rosis, 2005). So, the simulation is focused on the change in the belief about the achievement (or threatening) of the goals of an agent A, over time. In this monitoring system, the cognitive state of A is modeled at the time instants $\{T_1, T_2, \ldots, T_i, \ldots\}$. Events occurring in the time interval $[T_i, T_i + 1]$ are observed to construct a probabilistic model of the agent's mental state at time $T_i + 1$, with the emotions that are eventually triggered by these events. The intensity of emotions depends on the parameters: (1) the uncertainty in the agent's beliefs about the world and, in particular, about the possibility that some important goal will be achieved or threatened, and (2) the utility assigned to this goal.

Figure 3.1 shows an example of application of this model. Here, M (a mother) is observing her little child C who just learned to bicycle. Happy-for and fear may be activated at consecutive time slices (T_1 and T_2), because of positive and negative consequences of this event occurring or just imagined by M, in two distinct time intervals $[T_0, T_1]$ and $[T1, T_2]$: the child is growing up (GrowsUp-C) and might be at risk in a more or less near future (Ev-AtRisk-C).

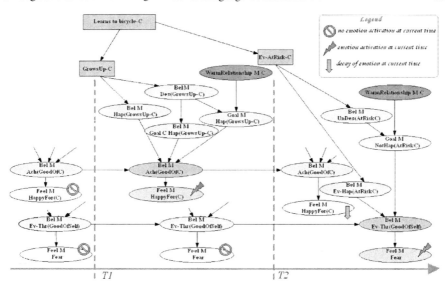

Fig. 3.1 An example application of emotional-mind to activation of happy-for and fear according to the "microwave oven" metaphor. Square boxes represent an event and its consequences in the intervals $[T_0,T_1]$ and $[T_1,T_2]$. Circular boxes represent appraisal variables, internal dispositions (beliefs, goals), and emotions at the current time. At every time slice, triggered emotions with the associated goals are highlighted (respectively, in light blue and light green).

Let us first consider the positive consequence of C learning to bicycle: as M is in a warm relationship with her child (`WarmRelationship M C`), happy-for will be triggered after believing that C is growing up (`Bel M Hap(GrowsUp-C)`), that this is a desirable event to C (`Bel M Des(GrowsUp-C)`), and hence that this is what M desires (`Goal M Hap(GrowsUp-C)`) and what M believes that C desires as well (`Bel M Goal C Happ(GrowsUp-C)`). In this situation, the goal of "getting the good of others" is achieved (`Bel M Ach(GoodOfC)`). The intensity of this emotion depends on how much this probability varies when evidence about the mentioned desirable event is propagated in the network. It depends, as well, on the weight M attaches to achieving that goal which is, in its turn, a function of the agent's personality.

Let us now consider the negative consequence of the same event. The figure shows that fear may also be activated in M by the belief that C might fall down by cycling because of his lack of experience: (`Bel M Ev-Hap(AtRisk-C)`) and (`Bel M UnDes(AtRisk-C)`). In this example, the affective state of M switches among the two emotions in time.

3.5.2 Social-Mind

In this model, DBNs are employed to represent how the social attitude of users towards a human or artificial agent evolves during dialogic interaction. The definition of social attitude applied is based on Andersen and Guerrero's concept (1998) of interpersonal warmth as "the pleasant, contented, intimate feeling that occurs during positive interactions with friends, family, colleagues and romantic partners. . . ." The main idea is to combine linguistic and acoustic features of the user move at time T with information about the context in which the move was uttered at $T - 1$, to dynamically build an image of the user's social attitude towards the agent, as a function of its value at time $T - 1$ and of the characteristics of the user move at time T.

Rather than focusing on individual emotions, social-mind is conceived to model interpersonal stances, that is, long-lasting and gradually evolving affective states. In particular, the model allows representing how the "social attitude" of users towards the application smoothly changes during interaction, by collecting evidence about a set of "signs" displayed by the user and conveyed by language features. Signs can be detected with a Bayesian classifier based on spotting of domain-relevant linguistic features or general semantic categories of salient (sequences of) words.

The categories are defined according to psycholinguistic theories (Andersen & Guerrero, 1998; Polhemus, Shih, & Swan, 2001), and the Bayesian classification enables computing, for every string, a value of a posteriori probability for every sign of social attitude. Figure 3.2 shows the version of the model in which the observable variables (leaf nodes of the oriented graph) are the semantic categories that characterize the presence of a sign of "warm" attitude: personal address and acknowledgment, feeling, paralanguage, humor, social sharing, social motivators, negative responses, and self-disclosure.

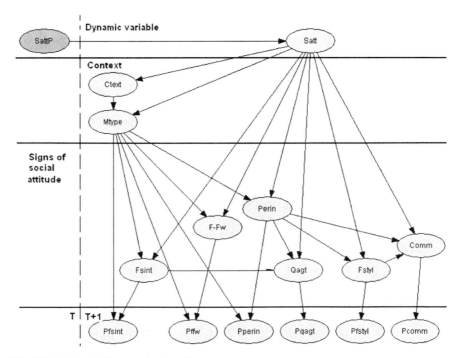

Fig. 3.2 Social-mind: a generic time slice.

Evidence about these signs, deriving from linguistic analysis of the user moves, is combined with information about the user's personality traits, the context, and the previous move of the agent. The model is employed to guess how the social attitude of the user evolves during a dialogue by also considering the dialogue history. The conversational agent's behavior is adapted accordingly as follows.

- At the beginning of interaction, the model is initialized by propagating evidence about stable user features.
- Every time a new user move is entered, its linguistic features are analyzed and the resulting evidence is introduced and propagated in the network, together with evidence about the context.
- The new probabilities of the signs of social attitude are read and contribute to formulating the next agent move; the probability of the dynamic variable representing social attitude supports revising high-level planning of the agent's behavior, according to the goal of adopting a successful persuasion strategy. More details about this model and about its extension to acoustic signs of social attitude can be found in Carofiglio et al. (2005) and de Rosis, Batliner, Novielli and Steidl (2007).

Social-mind has some similarities with the work described in Shaikh et al. (this volume): in that system, semantic parsing techniques are combined with a set of rules derived from the OCC classification of emotions (Ortony et al., 1988) to "sense affective information" from texts. The semantic parser produces a computational data model for every sentence in the form of triplets: this output is used for setting the value of the cognitive variables that act as antecedents of rules describing emotion triggering. The method allows sensing the affective content carried by every sentence that is provided as an input for the system.

In Figure 3.3, emotional-mind and social-mind are compared with the models by Ball & Breese (2000) and Conati and MacLaren (2005): the figure shows that the

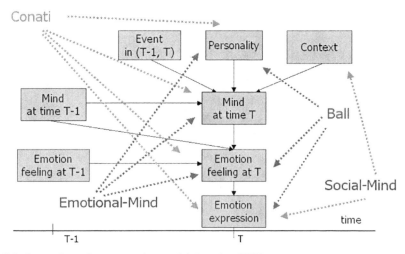

Fig. 3.3 Comparison of some emotion models based on DBNs.

four models differ in the aspects of the "emotion activation and expression" cycle they consider and in the grain size of knowledge represented. Some peculiarities make emotional-mind and social-mind two models of some value, especially in the context of affective dialogues. In particular: their ability to represent the role of personality and social relationship in emotion activation and time decay, the ability of emotional-mind to represent the various ways in which emotions may combine with different intensities, and, finally, its potential of being used, as well, for interpreting the reasons why an emotion is displayed (Carofiglio & de Rosis, 2005).

3.6 Problems in Building Emotion Models as DBNs

The problem of how to estimate parameters when building probabilistic models is still a matter of discussion. In particular, in probabilistic emotion triggering models, the following questions, among others, are raised. What is the probability of an event? How life-threatening is this event to me? How important is it to me to avoid this risk?

Similar considerations apply to defining variables involved in the recognition process. BN parameters can be estimated by learning them from a corpus of data (frequentist approach) or according to subjective experience or common sense (neo-Bayesian approach). To validate probabilistic emotion activation and expression models in emotional-mind, for example, a parameter sensitivity analysis (PSA) can be performed. This analysis investigates the effect of uncertainty in the estimates of the network's parameters on the probability of one or more nodes of interest, and discovers critical parameters that significantly affect the network's performance. Its purpose is to guide experts in making more precise assessments of the few parameters identified as "critical," in tuning the network. Some notations are as follows.

- X and Z denote a node and its parent, x and z the states they (respectively) assume, and $p = P(X = x | Z = z)$ a conditional probability associated with the arc connecting them.
- h denotes a node or a subset subBN of nodes in the BN, and ε is evidence propagated in this node or in a subBN.
- $f(P(h|\varepsilon),p)$, $f.(P(h, \varepsilon),p)$, $g(P(\varepsilon),p)$ are functions describing probability distributions when p is varied in the $(0,1)$ interval.

PSA is based on the observation that the probability of ε is a linear function of any single parameter (conditional probability distribution) in the model; hence $g(P(\varepsilon),p)$ has the simple form $y = \alpha p + \beta$, where α, β are real numbers. This implies that the conditional probability distribution of a hypothesis given some evidence, when the considered parameter is varied, is the following.

$$f(P(h|\varepsilon), p) = f'(P(h,\varepsilon), p)/g(P(\varepsilon), p) = \gamma p + \delta / \alpha p + \beta. \qquad (3.1)$$

The coefficients of this linear function can be determined from the values it takes for two different value assignments to p. The two function values can be computed by propagating the evidence twice in the network (once for every value of p).

According to the method suggested by Coupé and Van der Gaag (2002), given a Bayesian network model with its parameters, a hypothesis (node of interest with its state), and a set of evidence, the task of sensitivity analysis is to determine how sensitive the posterior probability of the hypothesis is to variations in the value of some predefined parameters. This analysis can be simplified by considering changes in the value of a single parameter.

Hence, given one of the BNs of emotional-mind, if the model is used in a prognostic mode, the aim is to investigate which emotion is felt in a given situation. In this case:

- The hypothesis is the node that represents the felt emotion at time T (e.g., node (Feel M HappyFor(C)) in Figure 3.1).
- The observed nodes are an appropriate combination of the emotional state at time $T - 1$, intrinsic variables, influencing factors, and context-related variables.
- PSA may be applied, for example, to the activation of HappyFor in Figure 3.1 (subnetwork during the time interval $[T_1,T_2]$), where:
- The hypothesis is (Feel M HappyFor(C)) and the evidence set is ε ={(Bel M Hap(GrowsUp-C)),(WarmRelationship M C)}.
- The parameter of interest is:
  p1 =P((Bel M Ach(GoodOfC))|(Bel M Hap(GrowsUp-C)),(Bel M (Goal C Hap(GrowsUp-C)),(Goal M Hap(GrowsUp-C))).

That is, the goal is to estimate the posterior probability that M is feeling happy-for after observing that her lovely little child C is able to cycle by himself, depending on the initial assessment of the variables that are intrinsic to triggering the happy-for: M's belief and goal that her child is growing up, together with her belief that the mentioned goal is a valid one also for her child.

Figure 3.4a shows the sensitivity function $f(P(h|\varepsilon),p)$ for this example.[1] This function is used to compute a belief value for the two states of the hypothesis variable: (Feel M HappyFor(C)) = *yes/no*. The two lines represent how sensitive the states of this variable are to changes in the value of the parameter p_1. The graph shows that the most likely state of the hypothesis variable changes when $p_1 = .6$. It shows, as well, that the probability $P($ (Feel M HappyFor(C)) $|\varepsilon)$ is rather sensitive to variations in the value of p_1, as one would expect; this reflects the fact that this parameter involves variables (with their states) that are intrinsic to triggering happy-for.

If the model is used in a diagnostic mode, to interpret the reason why an emotion was displayed, then:

- The hypothesis is one of the nodes that represents an intrinsic variable, an influencing factor or a context-related variable.
- The observed node is the felt emotion.

---

[1] The graph is plotted with Hugin. www.hugin.com.

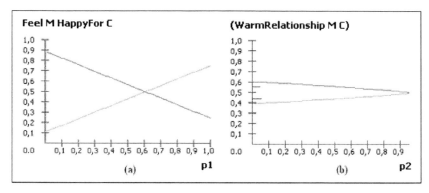

Fig. 3.4 Parameter sensitivity analysis for the happy-for model: in **a**, the BN is used in a prognostic mode; in **b**, it is used in a diagnostic mode.

Figure 3.4b shows the sensitivity function $f(P(h|\varepsilon),p)$ when the hypothesis is (WarmRelationship M C) and the initial evidence set is $\varepsilon = \{$(Feel M HappyFor(C))$\}$. This time, we are interested in the posterior probability of a (hypothesized) cause of the observed emotion of happy-for in M. In this case, $p_2 = P(($Bel M Goal C Hap(GrowsUp-C))$|$(Bel M Des(GrowsUp-C)$))$ is the parameter of interest. The sensitivity function computes a probability value for the two states of the hypothesis variable, (WarmRelationship M C) = yes/no. The graph shows that the probability (P(WarmRelationship M C)$|\varepsilon$) is rather insensitive to variations in the value of p_2.

In the discussed example, if the BN is used in a diagnostic mode the results of propagating evidence are rather insensitive to variations in the value of the considered parameter of the model. This is due to the structure of the network and also to its use (which observed nodes, which nodes of interest). If, on the contrary, the BN is used in a prognostic mode, sensitivity analysis helps in discovering parameters with a significant impact on the network's performance.

This analysis leaves room for further investigation about the quality of emotion models, by applying evidence sensitivity analysis (Coupé & Van der Gaag, 2002). The analysis is aimed at answering questions such as the following. What are the minimum and the maximum probabilities produced in the hypothesis when observing a variable? Which evidence acts in favor of or against a given hypothesis? Which evidence discriminates a hypothesis from an alternative one, and what if a given variable had been observed with a different value? Knowing the answers to these and similar questions may help to explain and understand the conclusions reached by the model as a result of probabilistic inference, and hence to evaluate the predictive value of emotion models.

3.7 An Open Problem: Cognitive Inconsistency

Irrespective of the formalism adopted and of the grain size in knowledge representation, computational models of emotions are built on the hypothesis of consistency among the variables included in the model: variables that represent appraisal of the environment (occurred, occurring, or future events), cognitive aspects that translate these variables into "attitudes" (first- and second-order beliefs, goals, values, etc.), and emotions that are presumably activated. Various psychological studies, however, seriously discuss this consistency hypothesis. In the following, two of them are considered, each giving a slightly different interpretation of this phenomenon.

Goldie (2008) denotes with misleading emotions the emotions that are not useful in picking up saliences in the environment and enabling quick and effective action, as (on the contrary) emotions are presumed to do. To Brady (2007), recalcitrant emotions are those emotions that involve a conflict between an emotional perception and an evaluative belief: the subject perceives her situation to be thus-and-so, while believing that it is not thus-and-so. For instance, a recalcitrant bout of fear is one where someone is afraid of something, despite believing that it poses little or no danger: he may believe both that flying is dangerous and that it is perfectly safe or (in the mother–child example introduced in Section 3.5), that running with a bike is safe while believing that it is not.

Interpretation of the reasons for this contradiction differ in the two authors. Goldie follows the "dual process" theory (Sloman, 1996), according to which our perception and response to emotional situations would be processed through two routes: (i) a fast and frugal route (also called intuitive thinking) which involves imagination, operates fast, and uses limited resources and speed of processing, and (ii) a more complex, slower route (also called deliberative thinking), whose function would be to operate as a check or balance on intuitive thinking. The dual process theory acknowledges the possibility that the two routes do not work in perfect agreement: therefore, it may happen that some emotions resulting from intuitive thinking mislead us, and that deliberative thinking does not succeed in correcting them.

Goldie's hypothesis is that intuitive thinking would be performed through some heuristics that were built after environmental situations humans had to face in their past history. Changes in environmental conditions (that he calls "environmental mismatches") would then be responsible for producing misleading emotions, which conflict with deliberative thinking, and that this complex and slower route is not able to detect and correct. Rather than accepting the hypothesis of recalcitrant emotions as "irrational," Brady proposes a positive role for this contradiction as a means to facilitate the processing of emotional stimuli: even if our deliberative thinking recognizes the felt emotional state as "unreasonable," our emotional system would ensure that our attention remains fixed on the dangerous objects and events, thus checking them and facilitating a more accurate representation of the danger (or the insult, the loss, for emotions different from fear). In this interpretation, the excessive and recalcitrant emotion of fear in the mother–child example (Section 3.5) is functional to her checking carefully that her child does not adopt a dangerous attitude in cycling.

This contradiction between the emotional and cognitive state is one of the cases of cognitive dissonance that was originally described by Festinger (1957). To this author, "cognitions" are elements of knowledge, such as beliefs, attitudes, values, and feelings (about oneself, others, or the environment); dissonance may occur among any of these attitudes. His definition of dissonance is quite strong, as cognitions are said to be "dissonant with one another when they are *inconsistent* with each other or *contradict* one another," therefore, a logical view of contradiction. In Brady and in Goldie, on the contrary, "weak" contradictions may also occur, as they may involve (again, for instance, in the case of fear) the estimation of a degree of dangerousness that influences a degree of inconsistency or incongruence with other attitudes.

Festinger's theory, subsequently elaborated by Harmon Jones (2000), was focused on the study of the (negative) emotions that result from becoming aware of a state of cognitive dissonance, and on how these negative effects can be reduced. In the context of this chapter, this theory is evoked in order to highlight that influential psychological theories exist, according to which the human mind cannot be assumed to be internally consistent. And this problem should not be ignored in building computational models of emotion activation, irrespective of the formalism employed.

The following alternatives then arise in building these models: (a) don't make room for the possibility of conflict: but then an important part of emotional life is eliminated; (b) make room for the possibility of conflict: but then the problem should be considered of how to emulate such a kind of representational state. The second alternative might be implemented by representing the dual process with two separate models, one for intuitive and one for reflective thinking (as envisaged in Cañamero (2005)). In this case, the cognitive component should represent the ability to correct errors introduced by fast and frugal intuitive algorithms; however, it should leave space, at the same time, for the occurrence of misleading or recalcitrant emotions and should deal with them. This is a quite demanding and still not tackled challenge.

Emotion models that deal with uncertainty, however, do enable representing cognitive-emotional contradictions, although in a quite simplified way. Several typical examples of weak contradiction between cognition and negative emotions may be found in the ISEAR Databank.[2] In the following, one of these examples, a case of fear, is taken as the starting point for further reasoning.

> If I walk alone in the night, it might happen that I will be attacked. I feel fearful, even though I don't believe that it is likely that I will be attacked.

In this example, the situation is hypothetical (or was possibly experienced in the past): fear is felt in spite of a low or very low danger. ("It is not likely that I will be attacked;" "It might happen.")

---

[2] In the 1990s, a large group of psychologists collected data in a project directed by Klaus R. Scherer and Harald Wallbott (Geneva University). Student respondents, both psychologists and nonpsychologists, were asked to report situations in which they had experienced all seven major emotions (joy, fear, anger, sadness, disgust, shame, and guilt). The final dataset thus contained reports on these emotions by close to 3000 respondents in 37 countries on all five continents. http://www.unige.ch/fapse/emotion/databanks/isear.html.

If:

- A denotes the agent on which reasoning is performed.
- `WalkAloneInTheNight-A` is the considered event occurring to A.
- `Attacked(A)`, `BadConsequences(A)`, are formulas denoting the state of the world after the event occurred (A is attacked, bad consequences occur to A).
- $\Rightarrow$? denotes an "uncertain implication."

The activation of fear may be represented (in probabilistic terms) as follows.[3]

`WalkAloneInTheNight-A`$\Rightarrow$? `Bel A Attacked(A)`, with:

$P((\text{Bel A Attacked(A)})\,|\,\text{WalkAloneInTheNight-A}) = p_1$, probability that A believes she will be attacked when walking alone in the night.

`Bel A (Attacked(A)` $\Rightarrow$? `BadConsequences(A))`, with:

$P(\text{BadConsequences(A)}\,|\,\text{Attacked(A)}) = p2$, probability that A associates with bad consequences of being attacked; degree of danger of these consequences $= d$.

`(Bel A BadConsequences(A))`$\Rightarrow$? `(Bel A Thr(GoodOfSelf))`, with $P((\text{Bel A Thr(GoodOfSelf)})\,|\,(\text{Bel A BadConsequences(A)})) = p_3$, probability that A perceives her goal of self-preservation as threatened, when bad consequences of being attacked occur; $w =$ weight attached by A to GoodOfSelf.

`(Bel A Thr(GoodOfSelf))`$\Rightarrow$? `(Feel A Fear)`, with

$P((\text{Feel A Fear})\,|\,(\text{Bel AThr(GoodOfSelf)}))\,p_3$, probability that A feels fearful after perceiving her goal of self-preservation as threatened; the intensity of fear will be a function of p_3 but also of w.

In applying this model to different situations and different subjects, it may happen that the intensity of fear felt by A is not too low, although A considers unlikely to be attacked (when p_1 is low but p_2, p_3, d, and w are high): this will simulate a case of mild cognitive inconsistency. There will be, however, also cases in which, in the same situation (same value of p_1), A will not feel fear, if p_2, p_3, d, and w are low: for instance, if A is persuaded that attacks in the area in which she is walking are not very dangerous and if she is a brave person. In these cases, cognitive inconsistency will not occur.

Overall, weak contradictions may therefore be produced by the following factors.

(i) *Overestimating conditional likelihoods* (p_1, p_2, and p_3 in our example): as Kahneman, Slovic, and Tversky (1982) pointed out, in subjectively estimating probabilities humans apply some "quick-and-dirty" heuristics that are usually very effective, but may lead them to some bias in particular situations. "How dark is the place in which I'm walking," "Whether there is some unpleasant noise," or "Whether I'm nervous," are examples of factors that may bias this estimate.

(ii) *Overweighting of the losses due to the negative event* (d in the example above): the "risk aversion" effect may bring the subject to overweight the losses and to be distressed by this perspective.

---

[3] In this model, A's attitudes that bring her to feeling fear are represented with a slightly different formalism than in Figure 3.1.

(iii) *Overweighting the goal of self-preservation* (*w* in the example above), due to personality factors.

These contradictions can be represented in emotion models by trying to emulate the way humans make inferences about unknown aspects of the environment. Uncertainty will be represented, in this case, with some algorithm that makes near-optimal inferences with limited knowledge and in a fast way, such as those proposed by Gigerenzer and Goldstein (1996). Alternatively, as in the representation considered in this chapter, they can be built on probability theory. In this case, models will have to include consideration of context variables that might bring the subject to over- or underestimate conditional likelihoods, and losses or gains due (respectively) to negative or positive events. That is, rather than assigning fixed parameters to the dynamic belief networks (as happens in emotional-mind), conditional probability distributions should be driven by selected context variables. This is another reason for including context in emotion activation models, a direction followed in Emotional-Mind and Social-Mind (Section 3.5).

Acknowledgments This work was financed, in part, by HUMAINE, the European Human-Machine Interaction Network on Emotions (EC Contract 507422). The authors owe many of the ideas about cognitive-emotional contradiction, and their role in emotion modeling, to Professor Peter Goldie (University of Manchester), with which one of them had interesting and enlightening discussions in the scope of HUMAINE.

References

Andersen, P. A., & Guerrero, L. K. (1998). The bright side of relational communication: Interpersonal warmth as a social emotion. In P. A. Andersen & L. K. Guerrero (Eds.), *Handbook of Communication and emotions. Research, theory, applications and contexts*. New York: Academic.

Arnold, M. B. (1960). *Emotion and personality*. New York: Columbia University Press.

Ball, G., & Breese, J. (2000). Emotion and personality in a conversational agent. In S. Prevost, J. Cassell, J. Sullivan, & E. Churchill (Eds.), *Embodied conversational agents* (pp. 89–219). Cambridge, MA: MIT Press.

Brady, M. (2007). Recalcitrant emotions and visual illusions. *American Philosophical Quarterly 44*, 3: 273–284.

Cañamero, L. (Coordinator) (2005). *Emotion in cognition and action*. Deliverable D7d of the HUMAINE NoE.

Carberry, S., & de Rosis, F. (2008). Introduction to the Special Issue of *UMUAI* on Affective Modeling and Adaptation *18*(1–2): 1–9.

Carofiglio, V., & de Rosis, F. (2005). In favour of cognitive models of emotions. In *Proceedings of the Workshop on 'Mind Minding Agents'*, in the context of AISB05.

Carofiglio, V., de Rosis, F., & Grassano, R. (2008). Dynamic models of mixed emotion activation. In L. Canamero & R. Aylett (Eds.), *Animating expressive characters for social interactions*. John Benjamin.

Carofiglio, V., de Rosis, F., & Novielli, N. (2005) Dynamic user modeling in health promotion dialogues. In J. Tao, T. Tan, and R. W. Picard (Eds), *Affective computing and intelligent interaction, first international conference*, ACII 2005 (pp. 723–730), LNCS 3784, New York: Springer.

Conati, C. (2002). Probabilistic assessment of user's emotions in educational games. *Applied Artificial Intelligence*, Special Issue on merging cognition and affect in HCI, 16: 555– 575.

Conati, C., & MacLaren, H. (2005). Data-driven refinement of a probabilistic model of user affect. In L. Ardissono, P. Brna, & A. Mitrovic (Eds.), *User modeling* (pp. 40–49), LNAI 3538. New York: Springer.

Coupé, V. M. H., & Van der Gaag, L. C. (2002). Properties of sensitivity analysis of Bayesian belief networks. *Ann Math Artif Intell*, *36*(4): 323–356.

Cowie, R. (2006). Emotional life, terminological and conceptual clarifications. Available at the HUMAINE Portal: http://emotion-research.net/deliverables/D3i final.pdf.

de Rosis, F., Batliner, A., Novielli, N., & Steidl, S. (2007). "You are sooo cool Valentina!" Recognizing social attitude in speech-based dialogues with an ECA. In A. Paiva, R. Prada, & R. W. Picard (Eds.), *Affective Computing and Intelligent Interaction, Second International Conference*, ACII (pp. 179–190), LNCS 4738. New York: Springer.

de Rosis, F., Pelachaud, C., Poggi, I., De Carolis, B., & Carofiglio, V. (2003). From Greta's mind to her face: Modelling the dynamics of affective states in a conversational embodied agent. In *International Journal of Human-Computer Studies 59*(1/2): 81–118.

Ekman, P. (1999). Basic emotions. In T. Dalgleish and T. Power (Eds.), *The handbook of cognition and emotion* (pp. 45–60). Sussex, UK: John Wiley & Sons.

Elliott, C., & Siegle, G. (1993). Variables influencing the intensity of simulated affective states. In *Reasoning about mental states – Formal theories & applications*. Papers from the *1993 AAAI Spring Symposium* [Technical Report SS–93–05] (pp. 58–67). Menlo Park, CA: AAAI Press.

Festinger, L. (1957). *A theory of cognitive dissonance*. Stanford, CA: Stanford University Press.

Frijda, N. H., & Mesquita, B. (2000). The influence of emotions on beliefs. In N. H. Frijda, A. S. R. Manstead, & S. Bem (Eds.), *Emotions and beliefs: How feelings influence thoughts*. Cambridge, UK: Cambridge University Press.

Gigerenzer, G., & Goldstein, D. G. (1996). Reasoning the fast and frugal way: Models of bounded rationality. *Psychological Review*, *103*(4): 650–669.

Goldie, P. (2008). Misleading emotions. In D. G. Brun, U. Doguolu, & D. Kuenzle (Eds.), *Epistemology and emotions*, Ashgate, University of Zürich, Switzerland.

Gratch, J., & Marsella, S. (2001). Tears and fears: Modelling emotions and emotional behaviors in synthetic agents. In *Proceedings of the 5th International Conference on Autonomous Agents* (pp. 278–285). New York: ACM Press.

Harmon Jones, E. (2000). A cognitive dissonance theory perspective on the role of emotion in the maintenance and change of beliefs and attitudes. In N. H. Frijda, A. S. R. Manstead, & S. Bem (Eds.), *Emotions and beliefs. How feelings influence thoughts* (pp. 185–211). Cambridge, UK: Cambridge University Press.

Izard, C. E. (1993). Four systems for emotion activation: Cognitive and non cognitive processes. *Psychological Review 100*(1): 68–90.

James, W. (1984). What is an emotion? *Mind 9*: 188–205.

Kahneman, D., Slovic, P., & Tversky, A. (1982). *Judgment under uncertainty, heuristics and biases*. Cambridge, UK: Cambridge University Press.

Lazarus, R. S. (1991). *Emotion and adaptation*. New York: Oxford University Press.

Mc Crae, R., & John, O. P. (1992). An introduction to the five-factor model and its applications. *Journal of Personality 60*: 175–215.

Miceli, M., de Rosis, F., & Poggi, I. (2006). Emotional and non emotional persuasion. *Applied Artificial Intelligence: An International Journal*, *20*(10): 849–879.

Nicholson, A. E., & Brady, J. M. (1994). Dynamic belief networks for discrete monitoring. *IEEE Transactions on Systems, Men and Cybernetics*, *24*(11): 1593–1610.

Oatley, K., & Johnson-Laird, P. N. (1987). Towards a cognitive theory of emotions. *Cognition and Emotion. 13*: 29–50.

Ortony, A., Clore, G. L., & Collins, A. (1988). *The cognitive structure of emotions*. Cambridge UK: Cambridge University Press.

Pearl, J. (1988) *Probabilistic reasoning in intelligent systems: Networks of plausible inference*. San Francisco: Morgan Kaufmann.

Picard, R. W. (1997). *Affective computing*. Cambridge, MA: MIT Press.

Plutchik, R. (1980). A general psycho-evolutionary theory of emotion. In R. Plutchik & H. Kellerman (Eds.), *Emotion: Theory, research, and experiences* (pp.1:3–33). New York: Academic Press.

Poggi, I. (2005). The goals of persuasion. *Pragmatics and Cognition. 13*(2): 297–336.

Poggi, I., & Pelachaud, C. (1998). Performative faces. *Speech Communication, 26*: 5–21.

Polhemus, L., Shih, L. F., & Swan, K. (2001) Virtual interactivity: The representation of social presence in an on line discussion. *Annual Meeting of the American Educational Research Association*.

Prendinger, H., Descamps, S., & Ishizuka, M. (2002). Scripting affective communication with life-like characters. *Applied Artificial Intelligence*, Special Issue on Merging cognition and affect in HCI, *16*(7–8): 519–553.

Prendinger, H., & Ishizuka, M. (2005). The empathic companion. A character-based interface that addresses users' affective states. *AAI, 19*: 267–285.

Reilly, N. (1996). Believable social and emotional agents. PhD dissertation, School of Computer Science, Carnegie Mellon University, Pittsburgh, PA.

Russell, J. A. (2003). Core affect and the psychological construction of emotion. *Psychological Review, 110*:145–172.

Russell, S., & Norvig, P. (1995). *Artificial intelligence: A modern approach*. San Francisco: Morgan-Kaufman.

Scherer, K. R., Wranik, T., Sangsue, J., Tran, V., & Scherer, U. (2004). Emotions in everyday life: Probability of occurrence, risk factors, appraisal and reaction pattern. *Social Science Informatics: 43*(4):499–570.

Sloman, S. A. (1996). The empirical case for two systems of reasoning. *Psychological Bulletin, 119*(1): 3–22.

van Reekum, C. M., & Scherer, K. R. (1997) Levels of processing in emotion-antecedent appraisal. In G. Matthews (Ed.), *Cognitive science perspectives on personality and emotion* (pp. 259–300). Amsterdam: Elsevier Science.

Chapter 4
A Linguistic Interpretation of the OCC Emotion Model for Affect Sensing from Text

Mostafa Al Masum Shaikh, Helmut Prendinger, and Mitsuru Ishizuka

Abstract Numerous approaches have already been employed to 'sense' affective information from text; but none of those ever employed the OCC emotion model, an influential theory of the cognitive and appraisal structure of emotion. The OCC model derives 22 emotion types and two cognitive states as consequences of several cognitive variables. In this chapter, we propose to relate cognitive variables of the emotion model to linguistic components in text, in order to achieve emotion recognition for a much larger set of emotions than handled in comparable approaches. In particular, we provide tailored rules for textural emotion recognition, which are inspired by the rules of the OCC emotion model. Hereby, we clarify how text components can be mapped to specific values of the cognitive variables of the emotion model. The resulting linguistics-based rule set for the OCC emotion types and cognitive states allows us to determine a broad class of emotions conveyed by text.

4.1 Introduction

Research on *Affective Computing* (Picard 1997) investigates foundations of human emotions and applications based on the recognition of emotions. Early work in Affective Computing emphasized the physiological and behavioral aspects of emotion,

M.A.M. Shaikh (✉)
Department of Information and Communication Engineering, University of Tokyo,
7-3-1 Hongo, Bunkyo-ku, 113-8656 Tokyo, Japan
e-mail: mostafa@mi.ci.i.u-tokyo.ac.jp

H. Prendinger
Digital Contents and Media Sciences Research Division, National Institute of Informatics,
2-1-2 Hitotsubashi, Chiyoda-ku, 101-8430 Tokyo, Japan
e-mail: helmut@nii.ac.jp

M. Ishizuka
Department of Information and Communication Engineering, University of Tokyo,
7-3-1 Hongo, Bunkyo-ku, 113-8656 Tokyo, Japan
e-mail: ishizuka@i.u-tokyo.ac.jp

J.H. Tao, T.N. Tan (eds.), *Affective Information Processing*,
© Springer Science+Business Media LLC 2009

for instance, by analyzing biometric sensor data, prosody, posture, and so on. More recently, the 'sensing' of emotion from text gained increased popularity, because textual information provides a rich source of the expression of the human affective state. Specifically, research has been devoted to exploring different techniques to recognize positive and negative opinion, or favorable and unfavorable sentiments towards specific subjects occurring in natural language texts.

Application areas for such an analysis are numerous and varied, ranging from newsgroup flame filtering, news categorization, and augmenting the responses of search engines on the basis of analysis of general opinion trends, emotional responses, and customer feedback regarding the querying product, service, or entity. For many of these tasks, recognizing the manner of the expression as generally positive or negative is an important step and significant results have been reported in Hatzivassiloglou & McKeown (1997), Hatzivassiloglou & Wiebe (2000), Kamps & Marx (2002), Pang, Lee, and Vaithyanathan (2002), Turney & Littman (2003), Turney (2002), and Wiebe (2000). The research direction of this chapter can be seen as a continuation of these research works.

A core feature of our approach is to provide a more detailed analysis of text, so that named individual emotions can be recognized, rather than dichotomies such as positive–negative. From a technical viewpoint, there are four main factors that distinguish our work from other methods of textual emotion sensing.

First, we have integrated semantic processing on the input text by functional dependency analysis based on semantic verb frames. Second, we utilize cognitive and commonsense knowledge resources to assign prior valence or semantic orientation (SO; Hatzivassiloglou & McKeown, 1997) to a set of words that leverages scoring for any new words. Third, instead of using any machine-learning algorithm or corpus support, a rich set of rules for calculating the contextual valence of the words has been implemented to perform word-level sentiment (i.e., positive, negative, or neutral) disambiguation. Finally, we apply a cognitive theory of emotions known as the OCC model (Ortony, Clore, & Collins, 1988) which is implemented to distinguish several emotion types identified by assessing valanced reactions to events, agents or objects, as described in text.

Sentiment or opinion (i.e., bad or good) described in text has been studied widely, and at three different levels: word, sentence, and document level. For example, there are methods to estimate positive or negative sentiment of words (Esuli & Sebastiani, 2005; Pennebaker, Mehl, & Niederhoffer, 2003), phrases and sentences (Kim & Hovy, 2006; Wilson, Wiebe, & Hoffmann, 2005), and documents (Wilson et al., 2005; Pang & Lee, 2005).

On the other hand, research on affect sensing from text has hitherto received less attention in affective computing research (e.g., Liu, Lieberman, & Selker,2003; Mihalcea & Liu, 2006; Riloff, Wiebe, & Wilson, 2003). The focus of this chapter is thus to provide a set of rules for emotions as defined by the OCC emotion model, and to show how the rules can be implemented using natural language processing (NLP).

We use the words 'sentiment' (e.g., good or bad) and 'opinion' (e.g., positive or negative) synonymously, and consider sentiment sensing as a task that precedes the task of 'affect' or 'emotion' (e.g., happy, sad, anger, hope, etc.) sensing. In other words, affect sensing or emotion recognition from text is the next step of sentiment recognition or opinion assessment from text. Emotion sensing requires a significantly more detailed analysis, inasmuch as ultimately, it strives to classify 22 emotion types rather than two categories (such as 'positive' and 'negative').

The remainder of this chapter is organized as follows. Section 4.2 describes related investigations regarding the recognition of affective information from text. Section 4.3 discusses the OCC emotion model from the perspective of a linguistic implementation, which forms the basis of this chapter. Section 4.4 is the core part of the chapter, where we first briefly describe the linguistic resources being employed, and subsequently show how the linguistically interpreted rules of the OCC model implement emotion recognition from text. This procedure is illustrated by examples. Section 4.5 discusses our primary experiment. Finally, Section 4.6 concludes the chapter.

4.2 Affect Sensing from Text

Research on affect sensing from text addresses certain aspects of subjective opinion, including the identification of different emotive dimensions and the classification of text primarily by the opinions (e.g., negative or positive) expressed therein, or the emotion affinity (e.g., happy, sad, anger, etc.) of textual information. Emotions are very often expressed in subtle and complex ways in natural language, and hence there are challenges that may not be easily addressed by simple text categorization approaches such as n-gram, lexical affinity, or keyword identification based methods. It can be argued that analyzing affect in text is an 'NLP'-complete problem (Shanahan, Qu, & Wiebe, 2006) and interpretation of text varies depending on audience, context, and world knowledge.

4.2.1 Existing Approaches

Although various conceptual models, computational methods, techniques, and tools are reported in Shanahan et al. (2006), we argue that the current work for sensing affect communicated by text is incomplete and available methods need improvement. The assessment of affective content is inevitably subjective and subject to considerable disagreement. Yet the interest in sentiment- or affect-based text categorization is increasing with the large amount of text becoming available on the Internet. Different techniques applied to sense sentiment and emotion from the text are briefly described in the following paragraphs.

Keyword Spotting, Lexical Affinity, Statistical, and Hand-Crafted Approaches

According to a linguistic survey (Pennebaker et al., 2003), only 4% of the words used in written texts carry affective content. This finding shows that targeting affective lexicons is not sufficient to recognize affective information from texts. Usually these approaches have a tagging system that splits the sentence into words and checks through the tagged dictionary to find each word and the corresponding tag category. If a word is not found in the dictionary, the engine will undergo a suffix and prefix analysis. By examining the suffix and prefix of the word, the assumed tag may be derived. The output of the tagging system includes the words and corresponding affect categories. Thus an input text is classified into affect categories based on the presence of fairly unambiguous affect words like "distressed", "furious", "surprised", "happy", etc. Ortony's Affective Lexicon (Ortony, 2003) provides an often-used source of affect words grouped into affective categories. The weaknesses of this approach lie in two areas: poor recognition of affect when negation is involved, and reliance on surface features. About its first weakness: while the approach will correctly classify the sentence, "*John is happy for his performance,*" as being happy, it will likely fail on a sentence like "*John isn't happy for his performance.*" About its second weakness: the approach relies on the presence of obvious affect words which are only surface features of the prose. In practice, a lot of sentences convey affect through underlying meaning rather than affect adjectives. For example, the text: "*The employee, suspecting he was no longer needed, he might be asked to find another job*" certainly evokes strong emotions, but use no affect keywords, and therefore, cannot be classified using a keyword spotting approach. In Liu et al. (2003) the authors provided detailed criticisms of these approaches and concluded that they are not very practical for sensing affect from a text of smaller size (e.g., a sentence).

Commonsense-Based Approach

The latest attempt, for example, Liu et al. (2003), can categorize texts into a number of emotion groups such as the six so-called 'basic' emotions (i.e., happy, sad, anger, fear, disgust, and surprise) based on 'facial expression variables' proposed by Paul Ekman. In our view, this emotion set is not optimal for classifying emotions expressed by textual information. Most important, those 'expression'-based emotion types do not consider the cognitive antecedents of human emotions, or their relation to humans' beliefs, desires, and intentions (by reference to the well-known BDI model for autonomous agents).

In Liu et al. (2003) the authors utilize a knowledge-base of commonsense that represents a semantic network of real-world concepts associated with the basic emotion categories. Hence, for the input, 'My husband just filed for divorce and he wants to take custody of my children away from me,' the system outputs it as a 'sad' sentence, but it fails to sense the emotion correctly from input such as 'It is very difficult to take a bad picture with this camera,' and classifies it as a 'sad' sentence as well.

The limitation of this approach is that it does not consider the semantic relationship between the linguistic components of the input text and the context in which the words occur.

Fuzzy Logic

Fuzzy logic assesses an input text by spotting regular verbs and adjectives, without processing their semantic relationships. Here, the verbs and adjectives have pre-assigned affective categories, centrality, and intensity (for details see Subasic & Huettner (2001)). As with lexical affinity-based approaches, this method cannot adequately analyze smaller text units such as sentences, for instance, 'The girl realized that she won't be called for the next interview,' where no affective word occurs.

Knowledge-Based Approach

The knowledge-based approach in Fitrianie & Rothkrantz (2006) investigates how humans express emotions in face-to-face communication. Based on this study, a two-dimensional (pleasant/unpleasant, active/passive) affective lexicon database and a set of rules that describes dependencies between linguistic contents and emotions is developed (for details see Fitrianie & Rothkrantz (2006)). In our opinion, this approach is very similar to keyword-spotting and therefore not suitable for sentence-level emotion recognition.

Machine Learning

Sentences typically convey affect through underlying meaning rather than affect words, and thus evaluating the affective clues is not sufficient to recognize affective information from texts. However, machine-learning approaches (e.g., Kim & Hovy, 2006; Strapparava, Valitutti, & Stock, 2007) typically rely on affective clues in analyzing a corpus of texts. This approach works well when a large amount of training data of a specific domain of interest (e.g., movie reviews) is given. It requires, however, special tuning on datasets in order to optimize domain-specific classifiers.

Although some researchers (e.g., Hu & Liu, 2004; Polanyi & Zaenen, 2004; Valitutti, Strapparava, & Stock, 2004; Wiebe, 2000) proposed machine-learning methods to identify words and phrases that signal subjectivity, machine learning methods usually assign predictive value to obvious affect keywords. Therefore these are not suitable for sentence-level emotion classification for not incorporating emotion-annotation for other non-affective lexical elements which may have affective connotation. Moreover, machine-learning-based approaches fail to incorporate rule-driven semantic processing of the words (e.g., contextual valence) used in a sentence.

Valence Assignment

A number of researchers have explored the possibility of assigning prior valence (i.e., positive or negative value) to a set of words (e.g., Polanyi & Zaenen, 2004; Shaikh, Prendinger, & Ishizuka, 2007; Wilson, Wiebe, & Hoffmann, 2005). By contrast, the system in Shaikh et al. (2007) begins with a lexicon of words with prior valence values using WordNet (Fellbaum, 1999) and ConceptNet (Liu & Singh, 2004), and assigns the contextual valence (e.g., Polanyi & Zaenen, 2004) of each semantic verb-frame by applying a set of rules.

Kim & Hovy (2006) and Wilson et al. (2005) count the prior polarities of clue instances of the sentence. They also consider local negation to reverse valence; yet they do not use other types of features (e.g., semantic dependency) contained in the approach mentioned by Shaikh et al. (2007). Nasukawa and Yi (2003) compute the contextual valence of sentiment expressions and classify expressions based on manually developed patterns and domain-specific corpora. Because a valence assignment approach focuses on the contextual aspects of linguistic expressions of attitude, it is suitable for sentence-level sentiment sensing (i.e., good or bad) from texts of any genre with higher accuracy.

4.2.2 Motivation for a New Approach

Although different types of emotions are expressed by text, research efforts so far have been mostly confined to the simplifying case of recognizing positive and negative sentiment in text. (Observe that from a more general perspective, all emotions can be seen as positive or negative). A recent attempt described in Liu et al. (2003) goes beyond the positive/negative dichotomy by aiming to sense six emotions. This is achieved by detecting associations between an event/concept and emotions, using commonsense knowledge of everyday life.

In our opinion, the emotion recognition capacity of this system is limited in the following aspects.

- It does not incorporate any semantic assessment of text (i.e., the contextual meaning of text).
- It does not consider the appraisal structure of emotions (i.e., the cognitive antecedent of a particular emotion.
- It does not consider the variety of cognitive emotions that can be expressed by text (e.g., hope, love, etc.).

To summarize, none of the models and techniques we have encountered thus far has ever considered the cognitive structure of individual emotions. On the other hand, an emotion model that considers emotions as valenced reactions to the consequences of events, actions of agents, and different aspects of objects as explained by the theory of emotion in Ortony et al. ((1988); the OCC model) has the potential to detect a large number of differences from text. By way of example, it can detect the user's attitude towards events or objects as described in email, chat, blogs, and so on.

The approach described in this chapter can be considered as the extension of existing research for assessing sentiment of text by applying the valence assignment approach (Shaikh et al., 2007). We assume that a particular emotion a person experiences or describes in text on some occasion is determined by the way she construes the world. Thus the attempt of using only commonsense knowledge without considering the cognitive structure of emotions and a semantic interpretation of the words used in a sentence will fail to successfully recognize the emotion and the intensity of emotion.

Therefore, the goal of this chapter is to describe a linguistic implementation of the OCC emotion model. This paradigm of content analysis allows sensing emotions from texts of any genre (e.g., movie or product review, news articles, blogs, posts, etc.).

4.3 The OCC Model

In 1988, Ortony, Clore, and Collins published the book titled *The Cognitive Structure of Emotions*, which explores the extent to which cognitive psychology could provide a viable foundation for the analysis of emotions. Taking the first letters of the authors' names their emotion model is now commonly referred to as the OCC model. It is presumably the most widely accepted cognitive appraisal model for emotions. The authors propose three aspects of the environment to which humans react emotionally: events of concern to oneself, agents that one considers responsible for such events, and objects of concern.

These three classes of reactions or emotion-eliciting situations lead to three classes of emotions, each based on the appraisal of different kinds of knowledge representation. They set forth the model to characterize a wide range of emotions along with the factors that influence both the emotion-eliciting situations and intensity of each emotion, that is, cognitive variables. According to the OCC model, all emotions can be divided into three classes, six groups, and 22 types as shown in Figure 4.1. The model constitutes a systematic, comprehensive, and computationally tractable account of the types of cognition that underlie a broad spectrum of human emotions.

4.3.1 Why the OCC Model?

The core motivation for choosing the OCC model is that it defines emotions as a valanced reaction to events, agents, and objects, and considers valenced reactions as a means to differentiate between emotions and nonemotions. This approach is very suitable for affect sensing from text, also in view of the valence assignment approach mentioned above.

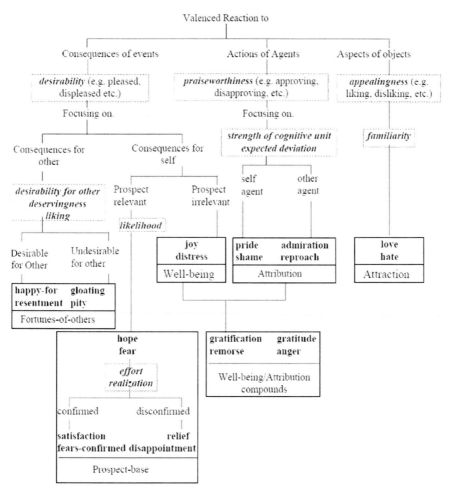

Fig. 4.1 The OCC emotion model: ***bold-italic*** phrases indicate variables and **bold** phrases indicate emotion types. This figure has been reproduced by considering two original models (Ortony et al.,1988), and are provided here for easier reference.

Moreover, the OCC model constitutes a goal-, standard-, and attitude-oriented emotion appraisal structure. As such, it provides an opportunity for applying natural language processing (NLP) to the identification of emotion-inducing situations (e.g., event/action), the cognitive state of the user (usually expressed by adjectives and adverbs), and the variables causing emotion (e.g., real-world knowledge about something or somebody etc.).

In our search for relevant literature, we did not find any research that implements the OCC emotion model for the purpose of affect sensing from text. Yet, by incorporating intelligent text processing and semantic analysis, we can uncover the values that are needed as input to the antecedents of the rules for emotion recognition.

The OCC model is widely used in intelligent user interfaces employing embodied lifelike agents, in order to process feedback from the interaction partner (e.g., the user or another lifelike agent), and to generate an appropriate emotional reaction (Bartneck, 2003; Chengwei & Gencai, 2001; Prendinger & Ishizuka, 2005).

However, we did not find any implementation of the OCC emotion model in the linguistic domain. In fact, the rule-based approach of the OCC emotion types and a rich set of linguistic tokens to represent those emotions, offer a sophisticated methodology and 'can do' approach for a computer program to sense the emotions expressed by textual descriptions. Hence this chapter describes how to apply an NLP method for emotion sensing based on the OCC emotion model.

4.3.2 Characterization of the OCC Emotions

The cognitive and appraisal structure of the OCC emotion types can be characterized by specific rules and their interplay with several variables. The variables and rules are listed, respectively, in Tables 4.1 and 4.2. They directly relate to the OCC emotion model shown in Figure 4.1. The names of the variables are mostly self-explanatory. Some of them are discussed in detail.

The Variables

There are two kinds of variables, namely, *emotion-inducing variables* (event-, agent-, and object-based) and *emotion intensity variables*. For our purpose, we

Table 4.1 The Variables (i.e., Cognitive Variables) of the OCC Emotion Model

Variables for the OCC Emotion Types		
Type	Variable Name	Possible Enumerated Values
Agent-based	agent_fondness (af)	liked, not liked
	direction_of_emotion (de)	self, other
Object-based	object_fondness (of)	liked, not liked
	object_appealing (oa)	attractive, not attractive
Event-based	self_reaction (sr)	pleased, displeased
	self_presumption (sp)	desirable, undesirable
	other_presumption (op)	desirable, undesirable
	prospect (pros)	positive, negative
	status (stat)	unconfirmed, confirmed, disconfirmed
	unexpectedness (unexp)	true, false
	self_appraisal (sa)	praiseworthy, blameworthy
	valenced_reaction (vr)	true, false
Intensity	event_deservingness (ed)	high, low
	effort_of_action (eoa)	obvious, not obvious
	expected_deviation (edev)	high, low
	event_familiarity (ef)	common, uncommon

Table 4.2 The Definitions (from 'Self' Perspective) of the Rules for the OCC Emotion Types

Defining the OCC Emotion Types Using the OCC Emotion Variables	
Emotion	Definition
Joy	Pleased about a Desirable event
Distress	Displeased about an Undesirable event
Happy-for	Pleased about an event Desirable for a Liked agent
Sorry-for	Displeased about an event Undesirable for a Liked agent
Resentment	Displeased about an event Desirable for another agent who is a Not Liked agent
Gloating	Pleased about an event Undesirable for another agent who is a Not Liked agent
Hope	Pleased about Positive Prospect of a Desirable Unconfirmed event
Fear	Displeased about Negative Prospect of an Undesirable Unconfirmed event
Satisfaction	Pleased about Confirmation of Positive Prospect of a Desirable event
Fears-Confirmed	Displeased about Confirmation of Negative Prospect of a Undesirable event
Relief	Pleased about Disconfirmation of Negative Prospect of an Undesirable event
Disappointment	Displeased about Disconfirmation of Positive Prospect of a Desirable event
Shock	Distress emotion with Unexpected Undesirable event
Surprise	Joy emotion with Unexpected Desirable event
Pride	Pleased for Praiseworthy action/event of Self
Shame	Displeased for Blameworthy action/event of Self
Admiration	Pleased for Praiseworthy action/event of Other
Reproach	Displeased for Blameworthy action/event of Other
Gratification	Higher Joy emotion with higher Pride emotion
Remorse	Higher Distress emotion with higher Shame emotion
Gratitude	Higher Joy with higher Admiration
Anger	Higher Distress with higher Reproach
Love	Liking an Attractive entity (e.g., agent or object)
Hate	Disliking an Unattractive entity

characterize some of the variables slightly differently from their definition in the OCC emotion model. The *event-based variables* are calculated with respect to the event, which is typically a verb–object pair found in the sentence. For example, the simple sentence, '*John bought Mary an ice-cream,*' describes an event of the form (buy, ice-cream). The abbreviations of variables are represented by bold italic letters in Table 4.1. In general we can call these variables 'cognitive variables.'

The Rules for Emotion Types

The OCC emotion model specifies 22 emotion types and two cognitive states. Table 4.2 enlists the definitions of the 22 emotion types and the two cognitive states according to the OCC emotion model by employing the values of the variables mentioned in Table 4.1. The definitions are given in verbal form (rather than formalized form) for easier explanation and intuitive understanding of the emotion rules. In formalized form, these definitions are rules (Horn clauses), whereby the cognitive variables constitute the antecedent, and the emotion type is represented as the consequent (or head) of the rule.

From a computational point of view, emotion recognition consists in inferring the set of emotions by rule application. Depending on whether states expressed by certain cognitive variables hold or do not hold, multiple emotions can be inferred from a given situation; that is, the cognitive variables of one rule antecedent can be a proper subset of the antecedent of another rule (as, e.g., for 'Joy' and 'Happy-for' in Table 4.2). This computational feature of the OCC rules is in accord with our intuition that text may express more than one type of emotion.

Here we briefly explain the idea for one emotion type (which is explained in more detail below). 'Happy-for' is characterized as an agent a (actor in the sentence) senses *'Happy-for'* emotion towards someone/object x, for an event e, with respect to an input text *txt*, if (1) there are found explicit affective lexicon(s) for 'Joy' emotion type without any negation in the input text *txt* or (2) there is a valanced reaction (i.e., a certain degree of negative or positive sentiment, θ) to trigger emotion from *txt*, and the values of the associated cognitive variables (represented by bold-face) are: a's **self-reaction** for e in *txt* is 'pleased', **other-presumption** (i.e., x's self-presumption) for e in *txt* is 'desirable', **agent-fondness** is 'Liked' (i.e., a Likes x in the context of *txt*), and **direction-of-emotion** is 'other' (i.e., a and x are not the same entity).

4.4 Implementation of the Rules

In order to implement the rules, first, we have to devise how the values of the cognitive variables could be assigned by applying NLP techniques and tools. In this section, we explain how such values can be assigned to the cognitive variables of the emotion rules.

4.4.1 Linguistic Resources

In this subsection, we explain the different linguistic resources being utilised. They partly rely on other reliable sources.

Semantic Parser

We have created a semantic parser using machinese syntax (2005) that produces XML-formatted syntactic output for the input text. For example, for the input sentence, 'My mother presented me a nice wristwatch on my birthday and made deli-

Table 4.3 Semantic Verb-Frames Output by the Semantic Parser for "My Mother Presented Me a Nice Wrist Watch on My Birthday and Made Delicious Pancakes."

	Tuple Output of Semantic Parser
Triplet 1	[['Subject Name:', 'mother', 'Subject Type:', 'Person', 'Subject Attrib:', ['PRON PERS GEN SG1:i']], ['Action Name:', 'present', 'Action Status:', 'Past ', 'Action Attrib:', ['time: my birthday', 'Dependency: and']], ['Object Name:', 'watch', 'Object Type:', 'N NOM SG', 'Object Attrib:', ['Determiner: a', 'A ABS: nice', 'N NOM SG: wrist', 'Goal: i']]]
Triplet 2	[['Subject Name:', 'mother', 'Subject Type:', 'Person', 'Subject Attrib:', []], ['Action Name:', 'make', 'Action Status:', 'Past ', 'Action Attrib:', []], ['Object Name:', 'pancake', 'Object Type:', 'N NOM PL', 'Object Attrib:', ['A ABS: delicious']]]]

cious pancakes,' the output tuples of the semantic parser are shown in Table 4.3. It outputs each semantic verb-frame of a sentence as a triplet of 'subject–verb–object.' So the parser may output multiple triplets if it encounters multiple verbs in a sentence. A triplet usually indicates an event encoding the information about 'Who is doing what and how.' The output given in Table 4.3 has two triplets, which are mutually dependent, as indicated by the 'dependency' keyword in the action attribute of Triplet 2. This semantic parser outputs the computational data model for each sentence.

These two triplets indicate two events *(present, watch)* and *(make, pancake)*. The actor for both the events is 'mother'. In this case, the triplets also contain additional attributes that give more information about the events.

Scored List of Action, Adjective, and Adverb

Initially eight judges have manually counted the number of positive and negative senses of each word of a list of verbs, adjectives, and adverbs according to the contextual explanation of each sense found in WordNet 2.1 (Fellbaum, 1999). The results are maintained in a database of prior valence of the listed words[1] using Equation (4.1).

A rater's score of a verb is stored in the following format: verb-word [Positive Sense Count, Negative Sense Count, Prospective Value, Praiseworthy Value, Prior Valence]. For example, for the word 'attack', WordNet 2.1 outputs six senses as a verb, and of these senses, one may consider five senses as negative and one as positive. Thus we collected the scores for the listed words, and the following equations (range of −5 to 5) are used to assign the prior valence, and prospective and praiseworthy values to each action word. Adjectives and adverbs have valence values only.

Our notion of 'prior valence' is sometimes called 'semantic orientation' (SO; Turney & Littman, 2003). SO refers to a real number measure of the positive or negative sentiment expressed by a word or phrase. We are aware of the procedures

---

[1] http://www.englishclub.com/vocabulary/.

mentioned in Pang, Lee, and Vaithyanathan (2002) and Turney & Littman (2003) that employed the hit-result of search engines to assign different semantic axes (i.e., positive or negative, excellent or bad, etc.) to words. Instead of using the traditional approach, we are motivated (due to some limitations of the SO approach mentioned in Turney & Littman (2003) and Turney (2002)) to devise a new method by incorporating WorldNet-based manual scoring for verbs and adjectives, commonsense knowledge to score nouns, and Opinmind[2] to score named-entities as mentioned in the following subsections.

$$\text{prior valence} = \text{Average}(((\text{Positive-Sense Count} - \text{Negative-Sense Count})/ \text{Total Sense Count})^*5.0) \quad (4.1)$$

$$\text{prospect polarity} = (\text{Positive-Sense Count} > \text{Negative-Sense Count})?1:-1 \quad (4.2)$$

$$\text{prospective value} = \text{Average}(\max(\text{Positive-Sense Count}, \text{Negative-Sense Count})/ \text{Total Sense Count})^*5.0^*\text{Prospect Polarity})$$

$$\text{praiseworthy value} = \text{Average}(\text{prior valence} + \text{prospective value}) \quad (4.3)$$

The interagreement among the raters for the assignment task for scoring 723 verbs, 205 phrasal verbs, 237 adjectives related to shape, time, sound, taste/touch, condition, appearance, 711 adjectives related to emotional affinity, and 144 adverbs is reliable (i.e., the Kappa value is 0.914). The prior valence and prospective and praiseworthy values indicate the lexical affinity of a word with respect to 'good or bad', 'desirable or undesirable', and 'praiseworthiness or blameworthiness', respectively. The 'prospective value' and 'praiseworthy value' of a verb/action word are necessary to evaluate an event according to the OCC emotion model.

Scored-List of Nouns and Named Entities

Because manual scoring is a tedious job and the number of nouns is presumably higher than in the above list, we devised an automatic approach to assign prior valence to nouns by employing ConceptNet (Liu & Singh, 2004). ConceptNet is a semantic network of commonsense knowledge containing 1.6 million edges connecting more than 300,000 nodes by an ontology of 20 semantic relations encompassing the spatial, physical, social, temporal, and psychological aspects of everyday life.

A value between -5 to 5 is assigned as the valence for an unrated noun or concept as follows. To assign a prior valence to a concept, the system collects all semantically connected entities that ConceptNet can find for that input concept. The returned entries are separated into two groups of semantic relations. In the first group all the entries for the relations such as 'IsA', 'DefinedAs', 'MadeOf', 'part of', and so on are listed, and the second group enlists the entries for the relations such as 'CapableOf', 'UsedFor', 'CapableOfReceivingAction', and so on.

---

[2] Opinmind, Discovering Bloggers (2006), http://www.opinmind.com/.

Of the two lists, the first one basically enlists noun words representing other associated concepts with the input concept, and the second one indicates the actions that the input concept can either perform or receive. The first list is recursively searched for any matching concept in the already scored list of nouns. If it fails to assign a nonzero value, the first five unique verbs of the second list are matched with the already scored verb list, and an average score for those verbs is retuned as the prior valence (Shaikh et al., 2007; Wilson et al., 2005). For example, to obtain the prior valence for the noun 'rocket', the system failed to find it in the existing knowledgebase, but from the second list the system returned the value 4.112 by averaging the scores of the verbs 'carry (4.438)', 'contain (4.167)', 'fly (3.036)', 'launch (5.00)', and 'go (3.917)'.

We also maintain a list called 'named-entity list' that contains the prior valence of named entities. We did not use any named entity recognizer to identify a named entity, and hence make the simplifying assumption that anything for which ConceptNet fails to assign a nonzero value (as mentioned above) is a named entity. For example, for the sentence, 'President George Bush spoke about the "Global War on Terror",' the system signals 'George Bush' as a named entity because it failed to assign a nonzero valence using ConceptNet. While storing the prior valence of a named entity the value of an attribute named 'general-sentiment' is also stored. The 'general-sentiment' attribute contains either a negative (i.e., -1) or a positive (i.e., $+1$) value based on the value of the prior valence obtained for the named entity.

To assign 'general-sentiment' as well as prior valence we have developed a tool that can extract sentiment from Opinmind.[3] Opinmind is a Web search engine that has a sentiment scale named 'Sentimeter' that displays the relative number of positive and negative opinions expressed by people on many topics including users' views on politics and current events. It also finds what people think about products, brands, and services by mining the opinion-bearing texts of people's blogs.

Opinmind exercises no editorial judgment when computing 'Sentimeter' values. For example, ConceptNet fails to assign a valence to 'George Bush' or 'Discovery'. From Opinmind we obtain 37% positive and 63% negative opinion about the named entity 'George Bush'. Similarly for 'Discovery' we obtain 82% positive and 18% negative opinions. From the obtained values we set the 'general-sentiment' and 'prior valence' as -1 and -3.15 (the maximum vote in the scale of 5) for 'George Bush', and similarly for 'Discovery' the values are $+1$ and $+4.1$. Initially a list of 2300 entries is manually created and scored using Opinmind. This list grows automatically whenever the system detects a new named entity.

SenseNet

SenseNet (Shaikh et al., 2007) calculates the contextual valence of the words using rules and prior valence values of the words. It outputs a numerical value ranging from -15 to $+15$ flagged as the 'sentence-valence' for each input sentence. As

---

[3] Opinmind, Discovering Bloggers, (2006), http://www.opinmind.com/.

examples, SenseNet outputs -11.158 and $+10.466$ for the inputs, 'The attack killed three innocent civilians' and 'It is difficult to take a bad photo with this camera,' respectively. These values indicate a numerical measure of negative and positive sentiments carried by the sentences.

The accuracy of SenseNet to assess sentence-level negative/positive sentiment has been shown as 82% in an experimental study (Shaikh et al., 2007). In this work (Shaikh et al., 2007), SenseNet's output for each sentence is considered as the 'valenced reaction' (vr) which is the triggering variable to control the mechanism of emotion recognition to branch towards either positive or negative groups of emotion types or signal neutrality.

4.4.2 Assigning Values to the Variables

In this subsection we describe the cognitive variables listed in Table 4.2 and explain how the enumerated values can be assigned to those variables using the aforementioned linguistic resources. The notion of 'self' refers to the computer program or the system itself which senses the emotion from the text. We assume that the system usually has a positive sentiment towards a positive concept and vice versa. For example, in general the events 'pass examination' and 'break up friendship' give 'positive' and 'negative' sentiments, respectively, and the system also considers those as 'positive' and 'negative' events. Moreover we consider the system as a positive valenced actor or entity while assessing an event from the 'self' perspective.

Self Presumption (sp) and Self Reaction (sr)

According to the appraisal structure of an event after the OCC model, the values for the variables self_presumption (sp) and self_reaction (sr) are 'desirable' or 'undesirable', and 'pleased' or 'displeased', respectively. These variables are assessed with respect to the events. For example, for the events 'buy ice-cream', 'present wristwatch', 'kill innocent civilians' referred to in the example sentences, SenseNet returns the contextual valence as $+7.83$, $+8.82$, and -8.46, respectively. According to the SenseNet scoring system, the valence range for an event (i.e., verb, object pair) lies between -10 to $+10$.

Thereby we decide that for an event, if the valence is positive (e.g., 'buy ice-cream'), sp and sr are set as 'desirable' and 'pleased', and in the case of negative valence (e.g., 'kill innocent civilian') both sp and sr are set to 'undesirable' and 'displeased', respectively. But for the sentences such as 'I like romantic movies' and 'She likes horror movies', the positive action 'like' is associated with a positive concept (i.e., romantic movie) and negative concept (i.e., horror movie) that eventually give 'desirable & pleased' and 'undesirable & displeased' assessments for the events, respectively. But both events are conveying positive sentiment because positive affect is being expressed by the word 'like'. In order to deal with such cases, SenseNet has a list of positive and negative affective verbs (e.g., love, hate, scare, etc.) that deals with the heuristic that if a positive affect is expressed by an event, the event is considered as positive irrespective of the polarity of the object and vice versa. Thus for the events, *'loathe violence'* and *'loathe shopping'* are assessed as 'undesirable' and 'displeased' due to the negative affective verb 'loathe'.

Other Presumption (*op*)

As above, the values for other_presumption (*op*) could be set 'desirable' or 'undesirable' while assessing the event from the perspective of the agent pertaining to an event being assessed.

We explain the heuristic of assigning value to this variable by using several examples. For the sentence 'A terrorist escaped from the jail,' the value of *op* (for the event 'escape from jail') is presumably 'desirable' for the agent 'terrorist' because the contextual valence of the event 'escape from jail' is negative (i.e., -6.715) which is associated with a negative valenced actor 'terrorist' (i.e., -3.620). For simplicity, we assume that a negative actor usually desires to do negative things. Thus the event 'escape from jail' is usually 'desirable' by the actor 'terrorist' under this simplified assumption. But for the same event, it is 'undesirable' and 'displeased' for *sp* and *sr* because of negative valence (i.e., -6.715). Thus in this case, we set *op* as 'desirable' because of having a negative valenced event associated with a negative valenced agent. Similarly we provide the following simple rules to assign the values to *op* for other cases.

- If a positive valenced event is associated with a positive valenced agent, *op* is set to 'desirable'; for example, 'The teacher was awarded the best-teacher award. John bought a new car.' The first sentence is a passive sentence where the actor is 'someone' according to the output of Semantic Parser and the object is 'teacher' having attribute 'best-teacher award'. The agent 'someone' has the positive valence (i.e., $+4.167$) and the event 'award teacher best-teacher award' also has positive valence (i.e., $+8.741$), hence the event's *op* value is 'desirable' with respect to the agent. For the second sentence, 'John' is the actor associated with a positive event (i.e., 'buy new car'), and hence the *op* value for the event is 'desirable' considering 'John' as a positive named-entity.
- If a negative valenced event is associated with a positive valenced agent, *op* is set to 'undesirable'; e.g., 'Boss sacked the employee from the job. Teacher punished the boy for breaking the school rule.' For, the first sentence the negative valenced event (i.e., -7.981) 'sack employee from job' is associated with a positive valenced actor (i.e., $+3.445$) 'Boss', hence the *op* value for the event is 'undesirable' for 'Boss'. Similarly, for the second sentence the *op* value for the event 'punish boy for breaking the school rule' is also 'undesirable' for 'Teacher'.
- If a positive valenced event is associated with a negative valenced agent, *op* is set 'undesirable'. For example, in the sentence 'The kidnapper freed the hostage', a negative valenced actor (i.e., -4.095) 'kidnapper' is associated with a positive valenced event (i.e, $+5.03$) 'free the hostage' and hence the *op* value for this

event is set 'undesirable'. This simplified rule may produce peculiarities; for example, 'The murderer lived in this town' or 'The criminal loved a girl' sentences have positive valenced events 'live in this town' and 'love a girl' associated with negative valenced actors 'murderer' and 'criminal', respectively. According to the rule for both of these events, the *op* value will be set to 'undesirable' for the agents. For simplicity we assume that any positive event is not expected for a negative role actor. But in the future, we would like to deal with such cases more deeply.

Direction of Emotion (*de*)

Depending on whether the agent that experiences some emotion is reacting to consequences of events for itself or to consequences for others, the system sets the value of the variable 'Direction of Emotion' *(de)* as either 'self' or 'other'. If 'other' is set the emotion being recognized belongs to the 'fortune-of-others' emotion group and the recognized emotion is anchored to the author or the subject of the event. This value for *de* is set as 'other' if the object or the predicate of the event described in the text is a person (e.g., John) or a personal pronoun (e.g., I, he) according to the triplet output given by the Semantic Parser; otherwise it is set as 'self'. For the sentences, 'Mary congratulates John for having won a prize.', and 'I heard Jim having a tough time in his new job,' the value of *de* is set 'other' for having 'John' and 'Jim' as the 'person' objects detected by Semantic Parser. Thus the value of *de* being set as 'other' makes our system recognize an emotion from the 'fortunes-for-other' emotion group and eventually emotions such as 'happy-for', 'sorry-for' would be recognized from the given sentences anchored to the author for the objects of the events. Additionally the system will also recognize that the authors/agents of the events (e.g., 'Mary' and 'I') are with 'joy' and 'distress' while considering the 'well-being' emotion group. But, for the sentence, 'Susan won the million dollar lottery', 'It is a very interesting idea', the value of *de* is set 'self' which eventually indicates that the sensed emotion is anchored to the author himself and the system will not proceed to recognize any 'fortunes-of-others' emotion types.

Prospect (*pros*)

According to the OCC model, the prospect of an event involves a conscious expectation that it will occur in the future, and the value for the variable prospect (*pros*) can be either positive or negative. Following the aforementioned Equation (4.2) in Section 4.4.1, SenseNet considers either the positive or negative sense-count (whichever is the maximum for a verb) to calculate prospective value. The heuristic behind this score is to know the semantic orientation (SO) of a verb with respect to optimism and pessimism. According to the equation, if a verb has more positive senses than negative senses, the verb is more close to optimism and has positive prospective value; otherwise, the verb gets a negative prospective value.

Because of some limitations (Turney & Littman, 2003; Turney, 2002) of applying other SO methods, we applied this heuristic and plan to compare our result to other methods as a future work. In order to assign *pros* value to an event, we consider the 'prospective value' of the verb instead of 'prior-valence' of that verb. Empirically we have set that if the valence of some event is higher than or equal to $+3.5$, the *pros* value of that event is set 'positive.' Similarly, if the valence is less than or equal to -3.5, the *pros* value for the event is 'negative.' Otherwise, *pros* value is set to 'neutral.' For example, for the events 'admit to university,' 'kill innocent people,' and 'do it,' SenseNet returns $+9.375$, -8.728, and $+2.921$ as the valence values for the events, respectively, and according to the values, *pros* values of the events are set to 'positive,' 'negative,' and 'neutral,' respectively.

Status (*stat*)

The variable status (*stat*) has values such as 'unconfirmed,' 'confirmed,' and 'disconfirmed.' If the tense of the verb associated with the event is present or future or modal, the value is set to 'unconfirmed' for the event. For examples, 'I am trying to solve it. He will come. The team may not play,' the tenses of the verbs are 'present,' 'future,' and 'modal,' respectively, and hence the *stat* value of the events is 'unconfirmed.' If the verb of the event has positive valence and the tense of the verb (with or without a negation) is past, *stat* is set 'confirmed' (e.g., 'I succeeded. He didn't come. The team played well.'). Again, if the verb of the event has negative valence and the tense of the verb is past without a negation, the value of *stat* is also set 'confirmed' (e.g., 'The hostage was killed. The team defeated its opponent.'). But if the verb of the event has negative valence and the tense of the verb is past with a negation, *stat* is set 'disconfirmed' (e.g., 'I didn't fail. He didn't hit the boy. The team couldn't defeat its opponent.').

Agent Fondness (*af*)

If the valence of the agent or object associated with the event is positive, "liked" is set to the variables agent_fondness (*af*) and object_fondness (*of*); otherwise 'not-liked' is set. For example, for the sentences, 'The hero appeared to save the girl', and 'A terrorist escaped from the jail,' *af* for 'hero' and 'terrorist' is set to 'liked' and 'not-liked,' respectively, because of positive and negative valence returned by SenseNet. In the same manner the value of *of* is set "liked" and "not-liked" for the objects 'girl' and 'jail', respectively.

Self Appraisal (*sa*)

According to the appraisal structure of an event mentioned in the OCC model, the value for self_appraisal (*sa*) can be either 'praiseworthy' or 'blameworthy.' In the aforementioned Equation (4.3) in Section 4.4.1, SenseNet takes the average of 'prior valence' and 'prospective value' of a verb to assign the praiseworthy value of that verb. The praiseworthy value is considered as the semantic orientation score of a verb with respect to 'praise' and 'blame.'

To assign the *sa* value to an event, the 'praiseworthy value' of the verb is considered instead of its 'prior-valence.' Empirically we have set that if an event's valence is more than or equal to $+4.5$, the *sa* value of that event is set 'praiseworthy.' Similarly, if the valence is less than or equal to -4.5, the *sa* value for the event is 'blameworthy.' Otherwise the *sa* value is set to 'neutral.' For example, let's consider these events, 'pass final exam,' 'forget friend's birthday,' and 'kick ball.' For these events SenseNet returned $+7.95$, -9.31, and -3.87, respectively. Thereby for the events discussed above, the value for *sa* is set 'praiseworthy,' 'blameworthy,' and 'neutral,' respectively.

Object Appealing (*oa*)

The value of object_appealing (*oa*) indicates whether an object is 'attractive' or 'not attractive.' In order to assign a value to *oa* for an object, we consider two scores, namely, 'object valence' and 'familiarity valence' with the following heuristic. The value 'attractive' is set if the object has a positive 'object valence' with a 'familiarity valence' less than a certain threshold. Conversely 'not attractive' is set if the object has a negative 'object valence' with a 'familiarity valence' above a certain threshold.

The 'familiarity valence' is obtained from ConceptNet by calculating the percentage of nodes (out of 300,000 concept nodes) linking to and from the given object/concept. For example, the 'familiarity valence' for the object/concept 'restaurant,' 'thief,' and 'diamond ring' are 0.242%, 0.120%, and 0.013%, respectively. Empirically we kept the value 0.10% as the threshold value to signal familiarity and unfamiliarity of an object. Basically the 'familiarity valence' indicates how common or uncommon the input object is with respect to the commonsense knowledge-base corpus. According to our heuristic an object that is relatively uncommon and bears a positive sense is usually 'attractive.' On the contrary, an object that is relatively common and shows a negative concept is usually 'not attractive.' Thus 'diamond ring' and 'thief' appear to be 'attractive' and 'not attractive,' respectively, but 'restaurant' receives the value 'neutral' due to being positive and too common.

Valenced Reaction (*vr*)

The value for valenced_reaction (*vr*) is set either 'true' or 'false' in order to initiate further analysis to sense emotions or decide the sentence(s) as expressing a neutral emotion. We consider *vr* to be 'true' if the 'sentence-valence' returned by SenseNet is either above 3.5 or less than -3.5. For example, 'I go,' does not lead to further processing (i.e., sentence-valence is $+3.250$) but 'I go to gym everyday,' yields an emotion classification because of the higher 'sentence-valence' (i.e., $+7.351$). This value indicates the negative or positive sentiment of the input sentence numerically. Thus we call this variable the trigger for a further emotion analysis process.

Unexpectedness (*unexp*)

In the English language, there are some words that express suddenness of an event. The variable *unexp* indicates whether an event (either positive or negative) is described in an abrupt orsudden manner. The value to the variable *unexp* is set 'true' if there is a linguistic token to represent suddenness (e.g., abruptly, suddenly, etc.) of the event in the input sentence; otherwise 'false' is set. We have a list of such tokens to indicate suddenness. For example, the sentences, 'I met my friend unanticipatedly at the bar,' and 'The storm hit the city without warning,' indicate two events 'meet friend' and 'hit city' expressed with a kind of suddenness represented by two of our listed linguistic clue words namely, 'unanticipatedly' and 'without warning.' Hence the value for *unexp* is set true for both events.

Event Deservingness (*ed*)

The OCC model has several variables to signal emotional intensity. Event deservingness is one of them. It indicates the degree to which 'self' desires the event for 'oneself' as well as for 'others.' Actually there are two types of variables: 'Event Deservingness for Self' and 'Event Deservingness for Other.' In this case we assign the same value obtained towards an event for 'Event Deservingness for Self' to the variable 'Event Deservingness for Other.' This implies that which someone deserves for oneself, to the same extent that event is deserved for other by that someone. For that reason our model is not able (i.e., designed not to be able) to infer 'resentment' and 'gloating' type ill-will emotions. In the model, the value for the intensity variable event_deservingness (*ed*) is set 'high' for an event having a higher positive valence (i.e., above +7.0) or 'low' for higher valence in thenegative scale (i.e., less than −7.0). The values are set empirically.

Effort of Action (*eoa*)

According to the OCC model, when effort is a factor, the greater the effort invested, the more intense the emotion. It is difficult to answer a question such as, 'Has any effort been realized for the event?' from a single sentence. However, we make the simplified assumption that, if an action is qualified with an adverb (except the exceptional adverbs such as hardly, rarely listed in SenseNet), for example, 'He worked very hard,' or target object qualified with an adjective (e.g., 'I am looking for a quiet place') without a negation, the value for effort_of_action (*eoa*) is set 'obvious,' otherwise 'not obvious.'

Expected Deviation (*edev*)

The variable called expected_deviation (*edev*) indicates the difference between the event and its actor in terms of expectancy of the event being associated with the actor. For example, in the sentence 'The police caught the criminal finally,' the actor 'police' and the event 'catch criminal' do not deviate because the action is presumably expected by the actor. We set the value for *edev* to 'low' if ConceptNet can find any semantic relationship between the actor and event; otherwise 'high' is set. For example, for the sentence 'A student invented this theory,' *edev* is set 'high' because ConceptNet doesn't return any relationship between 'student' and 'invent.' On the contrary, for the sentence, 'The scientist invented the theory,' the value of edev is 'low' because ConceptNet finds a conceptual relationship between the action 'invent' and actor 'scientist.'

Event Familiarity (*ef*)

The values 'common' or 'uncommon' are set for event_familiarity (*ef*) according to the average familiarity valence obtained from ConceptNet for the action and object of the event. For example, for the events 'eat sushi' and 'buy diamond ring,' we obtain the familiarity score for 'eat' as 0.205, 'sushi' as 0.062, 'buy' as 0.198, and 'diamond ring' as 0.013. This gives the familiarity score for the events as 0.134 and 0.106, respectively. Empirically we have set the value less than 0.15 to set 'uncommon,' else 'common' as the value of *ef* for the event.

4.4.3 The Rules of the OCC Emotion Types

In Section 4.3.2 we illustrated how a rule for an emotion defined in the OCC model (e.g., happy-for) can be characterized using the values of the associated cognitive variables, and in Section 4.4.2 we explained how specific values can be assigned to the cognitive variables. Now we list the rules for emotion types from the OCC model. Although in input text, *txt*, there might be multiple events, *e*, described and we also deal with such cases to receive the resultant emotion types from *txt*, the following rules are described for a single event, *e*. We provide an example involving multiple events in Section 4.4.4. Hence, the rules for the OCC emotion types are given assuming an event *e* described in text *txt*.

By way of example, the actor or author of an event *e* feels the emotion 'Joy' if the following condition is true.

[Linguisitc_Token_found_for_Joy(*txt*) and No_Negation_Found (*txt*)] or [*vr* = true and *sr* = 'pleased' and *sp* = 'desirable'] (i.e., literally 'Joy' means that the author or the agent of the event is 'pleased about the event which is desirable.')

Because we have the token words for each emotion type, we omit the first condition in the subsequent rules due to space limitations.

The rules for the emotion are listed as follows.

- If (vr = true & sr = 'displeased' & sp = 'undesirable' & de = 'self'), 'distress' is true.
- If (vr = true & sr = 'displeased' & op = 'undesirable' & af = 'liked' & de = 'other'), 'sorry-for' is true.
- If (vr = true & sr = 'displeased' & op = 'desirable' & af = 'not liked' & de = 'other'), 'resentment' is true.
- If (vr = true & sr = 'pleased' & op = 'undesirable' & af = 'not liked' & de = 'other'), 'gloating' is true.
- If (vr = true & sr = 'pleased' & $pros$ = 'positive' & sp = 'desirable' & $status$ = 'unconfirmed' & de = 'self'), 'hope' is true.
- If (vr = true & sr = 'displeased' & $pros$ = 'negative' & sp = 'undesirable' & $status$ = 'unconfirmed' & de = 'self'), 'fear' is true.
- If (vr = true & sr = 'pleased' & $pros$ = 'positive' & sp = 'desirable' & $status$ = 'confirmed' & de = 'self'), 'satisfaction' is true.
- If (vr = true & sr = 'displeased' & $pros$ = 'negative' & sp = 'undesirable' & $status$ = 'confirmed' & de = 'self'), 'fears-confirmed' is true.
- If (vr = true & sr = 'pleased' & $pros$ = 'negative" & sp = 'undesirable & $status$ = 'disconfirmed' & de = 'self'), 'relief' is true.
- If (vr = true & sr = 'displeased' & $pros$ = 'positive' & sp = 'desirable' & $status$ = 'disconfirmed' & de = 'self'), 'disappointment' is true.
- If (vr = true & sr = 'pleased' & sa = 'praiseworthy' & sp = 'desirable' & de = 'self'), 'pride' is true.
- If (vr = true & sr = 'displeased' & sa = 'blameworthy' & sp = 'undesirable' & de = 'self'), 'shame' is true.
- If (vr = true & sr = 'pleased' & sa = 'praiseworthy' & op = 'desirable' & de = 'other'), 'admiration' is true.
- If (vr = true & sr = 'displeased' & sa = 'blameworthy' & op =
- 'undesirable' & de = 'other'), 'reproach' is true.
- If (vr = true & sp = 'desirable' & sr = 'pleased' & of = 'liked' & oa = 'attractive' & event valence = 'positive' & de = 'other'), 'love' is true.
- If (vr = true & sp = 'undesirable' & sr = 'displeased' & of = 'not liked' & oa = 'not attractive' & event valence= 'negative' & de= 'other'), 'hate' is true.

The OCC model has four complex emotions, namely, 'gratification,' 'remorse,' 'gratitude,' and 'anger.' The rules for these emotions are as follows.

- If both 'joy' and 'pride' are true, 'gratification' is true.
- If both 'distress' and 'shame' are true, 'remorse' is true.
- If both 'joy' and 'admiration' are true, 'gratitude' is true.
- If both 'distress' and 'reproach' are true, 'anger' is true.

The cognitive states 'shock' and 'surprise' are ruled as follows.

- If both 'distress' and $unexp$ are true, 'shock' is true (e.g., the bad news came unexpectedly).
- If both 'joy' and $unexp$ are true, 'surprise' is true (e.g., I suddenly met my school friend in Tokyo University).

4.4.4 Walk-Through Example for Emotion Recognition from Text

Like Liu et al. (2003), we also believe that a statement may express more than one emotion type. According to the OCC model, the 22 emotion types and two cognitive states are grouped into seven groups, namely, well-being emotion, fortune of other emotion, prospect-based emotion, cognitive state, attribution emotion, attraction emotion, and compound emotion. Hence an input sentence may contain one of the emotion types from each group. In the following, we provide a detailed analysis of emotion recognition from an example text.

Our example sentence is: 'I didn't see John for the last few hours; I thought he might miss the flight but I suddenly found him on the plane.'

The output from the Semantic Parser is given below.

Triplet 1: [['Subject Name:', 'i', 'Subject Type:', 'Person', 'Subject Attrib:', []], ['Action Name:', 'see', 'Action Status:', 'Past', 'Action Attrib:', ['negation', 'duration: the last few hours ', 'dependency: and']], ['Object Name:', 'john', 'Object Type:', 'Person', 'Object Attrib:', []]]

Triplet 2: [['Subject Name:', 'i', 'Subject Type:', 'Self', 'Subject Attrib:', []], ['Action Name:', 'think', 'Action Status:', 'Past', 'Action Attrib:', ['dependency: to']], ['Object Name:', ' ', 'Object Type:', ' ', 'Object Attrib:', []]]

Triplet 3: [['Subject Name:', 'john', 'Subject Type:', 'Person', 'Subject Attrib:', []], ['Action Name:', 'miss', 'Action Status:', 'Modal Infinitive ', 'Action Attrib:', ['dependency: but']], ['Object Name:', 'flight', 'Object Type:', 'Entity', 'Object Attrib:', ['Determiner: the']]]

Triplet 4: [['Subject Name:', 'i', 'Subject Type:', 'Person', 'Subject Attrib:', []], ['Action Name:', 'find', 'Action Status:', 'Past ', 'Action Attrib:', ['ADV: suddenly', 'place: on the plane']], ['Object Name:', 'john', 'Object Type:', 'Person', 'Object Attrib:', []]]

According to the output, Triplet 2 has a 'dependency: to' relationship with Triplet 3. Then these two triplets are considered as a combined event. Hence there are three events as indicated below.

- $e1$: 'not see john the last few hours,' [agent: I, tense: 'Past', 'dependency: and']
- $e2$: 'think <no obj>, might miss flight' [agent: John, object: flight, tense: 'Modal', dependency: but]
- $e3$: 'find john on the plane' [agent: I, tense: 'Past']

In event $e2$, there are two subevents and for simplicity we consider the second subevent's subject as the agent, action status as the status, and object as the object of the event while assigning values to the cognitive variables for this event. However, while assessing the event valence the subevents are treated individually, and SenseNet has implemented specific rules to assign contextual valence for the triplets having a 'dependency: to' relationship to the other (Shaikh et al., 2007). The rest of the analysis is summarized in Table 4.4.

Table 4.4 Recognizing the OCC Emotions from the Sentence "I didn't see John for the last few hours; I thought he might miss the flight but I suddenly found him on the plane."

Analysis of the Recognition of OCC Emotions for the Given Example Sentence		
Events	e1	e2	e3
Event Dependency	dependency: and	dependency: but	
SenseNet Value (returned for each event)	event valence: −9.33 prospect value: −9.11 praiseworthy val: −9.22 agent valence: +5.0 object valence: +4.2	event valence: −8.69 prospect value: −7.48 praiseworthy val: −8.09 agent valence: +4.2 object valence: +2.72	event valence: +9.63 prospect value: +8.95 praiseworthy val: +9.29 agent valence: +5.0 object valence: +4.2
ConceptNet Value	familiarity valence: john' 0.059% 'see' 0.335% action-actor deviation: 'I-see': null	familiarity valence: 'flight' 0.113% 'miss' 0.14% action-actor deviation: "john-miss": null	familiarity valence: 'john' 0.059% 'find' 0.419% action-actor deviation: "I-find": null
Values of Cognitive Variables	of: liked de: other oa: attractive sr: displeased sp: undesirable pros: negative stat: confirmed unexp: false sa: blameworthy vr: true ed: low eoa: not obvious edev: low ef: common	of: liked af: liked de: self oa: neutral sr: displeased sp: undesirable op: undesirable pros: negative stat: unconfirmed unexp: false sa: blameworthy vr: true ed: low eoa: not obvious edev: low ef: uncommon	of: liked de: other oa: attractive sr: pleased sp: desirable pros: positive stat: confirmed unexp: true sa: praiseworthy vr: true ed: high eoa: obvious edev: low Ef: common
Apply Rules Phase 1	distress, sorry-for, fears-confirmed, reproach	distress, fear, shame	joy, happy-for, satisfaction, admiration
Apply Rules Phase 2	fears-confirmed, sorry-for, anger	fear, remorse	happy-for, satisfaction, gratitude
Apply 'and'-logic		sorry-for, fears-confirmed, anger	happy-for, satisfaction, gratitude
Apply 'but'-logic		happy-for, relief, gratitude	

The values of the cognitive variables are set according to the explanation given in Section 4.4.2 on the basis of the values obtained from SenseNet and Concept-Net modules. Phase 1 shows the list of emotions for each event after applying the rules for simple OCC emotions. Phase 2 shows more refined sets of emotions after applying the rules for complex OCC emotions.

Because the first event is having an 'and' relationship with the second one, 'add'-logic is applied to the set of emotions resolved from the events e1 and e2. The rule of applying 'add'-logic is to simplify two emotions and keep one of the two emotions by applying the following rules. The rules are developed from the motivation explained in Ortony et al. (2003) where one of the authors of the OCC model described regarding the collapsing of OCC-defined emotions into five specializations of generalized good and bad feelings.

- 'Hope' and 'satisfaction' are collapsed to 'satisfaction.'
- 'Fear' and 'fear-confirmed' are collapsed to 'fear-confirmed.'
- 'Pride' and 'gratification' are collapsed to 'gratification.'
- 'Shame' and 'remorse' are collapsed to 'remorse.'
- 'Admiration' and 'gratitude' are collapsed to 'gratitude.'
- 'Reproach' and 'anger' are collapsed to 'anger.'
- 'Gratitude' and 'gratification' are collapsed to 'gratitude.'
- 'Remorse' and 'anger' are collapsed to 'anger.'

At this stage, we find all the possible emotions that the sentence is expressing. We believe that a part of a sentence (i.e., in a complex sentence) may express a negative emotion while the other part may express positive emotion and vice versa. So we can say that the example sentence is expressing this set of emotions: {fears-confirmed, sorry-for, anger, happy-for, satisfaction, gratitude}. Yet we proceed further by applying the 'but'-logic for the emotion. Our rules in this case are:

- 'Negative emotion' but 'positive emotion', accept 'positive emotion.'
- 'Positive emotion' but 'negative emotion', accept 'negative emotion.'

We also extended this rule to some of the emotion types.

- If 'fears-confirmed' or 'fear' but 'satisfaction' is found, then output 'relief.'
- If 'hope' but 'fears-confirmed' or 'fear' is found, then output 'disappointment.'
- If 'anger' but 'gratification' or 'gratitude' is found, then output 'gratitude.'
- If 'remorse' but 'gratification' or 'gratitude' is found, then output 'gratitude.'
- If 'gratification' but 'anger' or 'remorse' is found, then output 'anger.'
- If 'gratitude' but 'anger' or 'remorse' is found, then output 'anger.'

Hence, applying the above rules, eventually yields 'happy-for,' 'relief,' and 'gratitude' emotions sensed by the agent/subject (in this case "I" or the author himself) with respect to the object(s) of the given example sentence. In the same evaluation process, for the sentence 'I suddenly got to know that my paper won the best paper award,' the emotions are 'gratification' and 'surprise.' The sentence 'She failed to pass the entrance examination,' outputs 'anger' and 'disappointment' emotions. For sentences such as (1) 'I saw that Mary had a great experience to ride on the roller coaster,' and (2) 'John noticed that Mary could not ride the roller coaster,' the system recognizes "happy-for" and "sorry-for" emotions, respectively. The recognized emotions are anchored to the author of the sentence (in (1)), and to John (in (2)), because the value of the direction of emotion (*de*) variable is set to 'other' in these cases.

4.5 Evaluation and Discussion

Currently, our system is able to perform sentence-level affect sensing. By implementing the OCC model, our system is the first system capable of sensing a broad range of emotions from the text. A system similar to ours is the *EmpathyBuddy* described in Liu et al. (2003). That system is also based on a commonsense knowledgebase (i.e., ConceptNet; Liu and Singh (2004)), and it seems to be the best performing system for sentence-level affect sensing that senses happy, fear, sad, anger, disgust, and surprise emotions. For each sentence it calculates a vector containing the percentage value afferent to each emotion.

By way of example, we provide input and output for *EmpathyBuddy* and our system.

Input: I avoided the accident luckily.

Output of *EmpathyBuddy*: fearful (26%), happy (18%), angry (12%), sad (8%), surprised (7%), disgusted (0%).

Output of ours: sentence valence +11.453; emotions: [gratification, relief, surprise].

We evaluated our system to assess the accuracy of sentence-level affect sensing when compared to human-ranked scores (as the 'gold standard') for 200 sentences. The sentences were collected from Internet-based sources for reviews of products, movies, news, and email correspondence. Five human judges assessed each sentence. In the experimental setup we have two systems, Our System and *EmpathyBuddy*. Each judge received the output from both systems for each of the sentences from the list of 200 sentences. Upon receiving the output a judge could accept both outputs or either of the two or reject both.

For example, for the input sentence 'She is extremely generous, but not very tolerant with people who don't agree with her,' three judges out of five accepted the output of our system, two accepted the output of *EmpathyBuddy*. Because the majority of the judges accepted the output of our system, a vote for this sentence was counted for our system. Similarly for a given sentence if the majority of the judges accepted both outputs of the two systems, vote for that sentence was counted for both systems. In this manner the vote for each sentence was counted and a gold standard score prepared. This experimentation yielded the result reported in Table 4.5. Because predefined classifications of the sentences by the human judges had not been done, we cannot calculate recall and precision based on the predefined scoring or separated emotion classes.

Table 4.5 Preliminary Experimental Result of the Two Systems

Dataset of 200 Sentences				
	Our System	EmpathyBuddy	Both	Failed to Sense
Number of Sentences accepted to be correct	41	26	120	13
Total number of Sentences correctly sensed	161	146		
Accuracy	80.5%	73%		

To measure interagreement among judges, we used Fleiss' kappa statistic. The obtained kappa value (i.e., $\kappa = 0.82$) indicates that the overall agreement among the judges for scoring the sentences by the two systems are reliable. Those who collected data from different sources and the judges who scored the sentences were not aware of the architecture and working principle of the systems.

The approach adopted by *EmpathyBuddy* is well-founded because from a given textual description concept(s) are extracted and mapped to already annotated concepts where the annotated concept(s) are created by using large-scale real-world commonsense knowledge. The annotated concepts usually have an inherent affective connotation (e.g., happy or sad, etc.). An approach that is based on first extracting concepts from text, and then linking concepts to emotional affinity works well when the sentence(s) are semantically simple and descriptive. But it fails for the sentences such as, 'You will hardly get a bad shot with this camera.' Such an approach fails because it does not consider the semantic structure of the sentence.

4.6 Conclusions

In this chapter, we described how the OCC emotion model can be implemented using linguistic tools for the task of affect recognition from the text. The OCC emotion model explains 22 emotion types and two cognitive states by interplaying among several cognitive variables. Several heuristics are proposed to assign values to those cognitive variables, and emotion rules based on them are defined in accord with the OCC emotion rules. An initial experimental result of sensing different OCC-defined emotions from the input text obtained an accuracy of 80.5% when compared to the result from human judges as the gold standard.

Our approach overcomes problems of other similar approaches because we consider the semantic structure of sentences. Our approach is more robust and superior to the commonsense-based approach for the following reasons.

- Employs a commonsense knowledge base to assign words either a negative or positive score
- Considers the semantic structure of the sentence
- Applies rules to assign the contextual valence of the so-called concepts (i.e., semantic verb-frame in this case) described in the sentence
- Senses emotions according to the cognitive theory of emotions having explicit reasons for the particular emotions being detected from the input text

We believe that a linguistic approach would strengthen human–computer interaction for various applications such as developing socially intelligent user interfaces for various applications, including intelligent text processing for informative augmentation of search engine responses to analysis of public opinion trends and customer feedback, socially and emotionally intelligent applications, and so on. In order to facilitate further testing, we plan to implement a Web-based user interface so that any user can input a chunk of text and receive output from our system and that of other competing systems for emotion recognition from text.

References

Bartneck, C. (2003) Interacting with and embodied emotional character, In *Proceedings of DPPI* (pp. 55–60). Pittsburgh.

Chengwei, Y., & Gencai, C. (2001). An emotion development agent model based on OCC model and operant conditioning, In *Proceedings of ICII* (pp. 246–250).

English Vocabulary, http://www.englishclub.com/vocabulary/.

Esuli, A., & Sebastiani, F. (2005). Determining the semantic orientation of terms through gloss analysis. In *Proceedings of CIKM* (pp. 617–624).

Fellbaum, C. (Ed.) (1999). *WordNet: An electronic lexical database*, Cambridge, MA: MIT Press.

Fitrianie, S., & Rothkrantz, L. J. M. (2006). Constructing knowledge for automated text-based emotion expressions, In *Proceedings of CompSysTech*, Tarnovo, Bulgaria.

Hatzivassiloglou, V., & McKeown, K. R. (1997). Predicting the semantic orientation of adjectives, In *Proceedings of the 35th Annual Meeting on Association for Computational Linguistics*, Madrid (pp. 174–181).

Hatzivassiloglou, V., & Wiebe, J. M. (2000). Effects of adjective orientation and grabability on sentence subjectivity. In *Proceedings of the 18th International Conference on Computational Linguistics*.

Hu, M., & Liu, B. (2004). Mining and summarizing customer reviews. In *Proceedings of KDD* (pp. 168–177).

Kamps, J., & Marx, M. (2002). Words with attitude. In *Proceedings of the First International Conference on Global WordNet*, Mysore, India.

Kim, S. M., & Hovy, E. H. (2006). Identifying and analyzing judgment opinions. In *Proceedings of HLT-NAACL*, ACL (pp. 200–207).

Liu, H., Lieberman, H., & Selker, T. (2003). A model of textual affect sensing using real-world knowledge, In *Proceedings of IUI*, Miami (pp. 25–132). New York: ACM Press.

Liu, H., & Singh, P. (2004). ConceptNet: A practical commonsense reasoning toolkit. *BT Technology Journal*, 22(4): 211–226.

Machinese Syntax (2005). The official Website, http://www.connexor.com/connexor/.

Mihalcea, R., & Liu, H. (2006). A corpus-based approach to finding happiness, Computational approaches for analysis of weblogs, In *Proceedings of the AAAI Spring Symposium*.

Nasukawa, T., & Yi, J. (2003). Sentiment analysis: Capturing favorability using natural language processing, In *Proceedings of K-CAP* (pp. 70–77). New York: ACM Press.

Opinmind (2006). Discovering bloggers, http://www.opinmind.com/

Ortony, A. (2003). On making believable emotional agents believable. In R. Trappl, P. Petta, & S. Payr (Eds.), *Emotions in humans and artifacts* (pp. 189–211). Cambridge, MA: MIT Press.

Ortony, A., Clore, G. L., & Collins, A. (1988). The cognitive structure of emotions, Cambridge University Press, New York, USA.

Pang, B., & Lee, L. (2005). Seeing stars: Exploiting class relationships for sentiment categorization with respect to rating scales. In *Proceedings of ACL* (pp. 115–124).

Pang, B., Lee, L., & Vaithyanathan, S. (2002). Thumbs up? Sentiment classification using machine learning techniques. In *Proceedings of the Conference on Empirical Methods in Natural Language Processing (EMNLP)* (pp. 79–86).

Pennebaker, J. W., Mehl, M. R., & Niederhoffer, K. (2003). Psychological aspects of natural language use: Our words, our selves. *Annual Review of Psychology 54*: 547–577.

Picard, R. W. (1997). *Affective computing*. Cambridge, MA: MIT Press.

Polanyi, L., & Zaenen, A. (2004). Contextual valence shifters. In J. Shanahan, Y. Qu, & J. Wiebe (Eds.), Computing attitude and affect in text: Theory and applications, *The Information Retrieval Series 20*: 1–10.

Prendinger, H., & Ishizuka, M. (2005). The empathic companion: A Character-based interface that addresses user's affective states. *Journal of Applied Artificial Intelligence, 19*(3–4): 267–285.

Riloff, E., Wiebe, J., & Wilson, T. (2003). Learning subjective nouns using extraction pattern bootstrapping. In *Proceedings of CoNLL*.

Shaikh, M. A. M., Ishizuka, M., & Prendinger, H. (2007). Assessing sentiment of text by semantic dependency and contextual valence analysis. In *Proceedings of the International Conference on Affective Computing and Intelligent Interaction* Lisbon (pp. 191–202, LNCS 4738, New York: Springer.

Shaikh, M. A. M, Prendinger, H., & Ishizuka, M. (2007). SenseNet: A linguistic tool to visualize numerical-valance based sentiment of textual data. In *Proceedings of ICON*, Hyderabad, India (pp. 147–152).

Shanahan, J. G., Qu, Y., & Wiebe, J. (Eds.) (2006). *Computing attitude and affect in text: Theory and applications*. The Netherlands: Springer.

Strapparava, C., Valitutti, A., and Stock, O. (2007). Dances with words. In *Proceedings of IJCAI*, Hyderabad, India. New York: Springer, pp. 1719–1724.

Subasic, P., & Huettner, A. (2001). Affect analysis of text using fuzzy semantic typing, *IEEE Transactions on Fuzzy Systems* 9(4): 483–496.

Turney, P. D. (2002). Thumbs up or thumbs down? Semantic orientation applied to unsupervised classification of reviews. In *Proceedings of the 40th Annual Meeting on Association for Computational Linguistics*, Pennsylvania (pp. 417–424).

Turney, P. D., & Littman, M. L. (2003). Measuring praise and criticism: Inference of semantic orientation from association. *ACM Transactions on Information Systems (TOIS)*, *21*(4): 315–346.

Valitutti, A., Strapparava, C., & Stock, O. (2004). Developing affective lexical resources. *Psychology Journal 2*(1): 61–83.

Wiebe, J. (2000). Learning subjective adjectives from corpora. In *Proceedings of the 17th National Conference on Artificial Intelligence and 12th International Conference on Innovative Applications of Artificial Intelligence,* Texas (pp. 735–740).

Wiebe, J., and Mihalcea, R. (2006). Word sense and subjectivity. In *Proceedings of ACL–06* (pp. 1065–1072).

Wilson, T., Wiebe, J., & Hoffmann, P. (2005). Recognizing contextual polarity in phrase-level sentiment analysis. In *Proceedings of HLT/EMNLP,* ACL (pp. 347–354). http://www.zoesis.com/mrbubb/ (Mr. Bubb in Space).

Chapter 5
Affective Agents for Education Against Bullying

Ruth Aylett, Ana Paiva, Joao Dias, Lynne Hall, and Sarah Woods

Abstract In this chapter, we give an overview of the FearNot! virtual drama system constructed for use in education against bullying. The motivation for the system is discussed and the chapter considers issues relating to believability. It describes the emotionally driven architecture used for characters as well as the management of the overall story and finally considers issues relating to evaluation of systems like this.

5.1 Introduction

There are a number of different ways of thinking about affective interfaces. One might be as a mechanism for capturing the affective state of the human doing the interacting in order to adjust the functionality behind the interface in some appropriate way. This relates well to a model of information services in which information is

R. Aylett (✉)
Mathematics and Computer Science, Heriot-Watt University, Edinburgh, EH14 4AS, UK
e-mail: ruth@macs.hw.ac.uk

A. Paiva
INESC-ID, TagusPark, Av. Prof. Dr. Cavaco Silva, 2780-990 Porto Salvo, Portugal
e-mail: ana.paiva@inesc-id.pt

J. Dias
NESC-ID, TagusPark, Av. Prof. Dr. Cavaco Silva, 2780-990 Porto Salvo, Portugal
e-mail: joao.assis@tagus.ist.utl.pt

L. Hall
School of Computing and Technology, University of Sunderland, Sunderland, SR6 0DD, UK
e-mail: lynne.hall@sunderland.ac.uk

S. Woods
Psychology Department, University of Hertfordshire, Hatfield, Herts, AL10 9AB, UK
e-mail: s.n.woods@herts.ac.uk

J.H. Tao, T.N. Tan (eds.), *Affective Information Processing,* tailored to a perceived affective state. In an educational context, this approach would lead to affective tutoring systems in which knowledge would be presented in a way sensitive to the affective engagement of the user (Heylen, Vissers, op den Akker, & Nijholt, 2004).

However, not all education is based on the transmission of knowledge in this way. Most educational systems are also concerned with socially acceptable behaviour, an area known in the United Kingdom as Personal and Social Education (PSE), or, for example, in China, as Political and Moral Education. Here, educational objectives are tied much more closely to attitudes and emotional responses to social situations, and rather than capturing the user's affective state, the issue is one of shaping it in a much more active way. The emphasis of an affective interface in this domain is one of evoking emotion in the interaction partner, and the appropriate model is closer to drama than to information systems. Indeed, Theatre-in-Education (TiE) is, in the United Kingdom, an accepted approach to PSE, using story, character, and situation as a way of creating affective engagement.

Creating this sort of active affective interface puts the emphasis on the modelling of affective state on the computer side and its embodiment in believable graphical characters. In order to reach the pedagogical objectives, the system then draws on human empathic responses to involve the user in the dramatic situations portrayed by the characters. This raises issues of what constitutes believability in the characters, and how suitably dramatic situations can be created.

In this chapter we discuss how these issues were addressed in the context of a specific system that uses virtual drama, acted out by intelligent affective characters, for a particular aspect of PSE, that of education against bullying. Further discussion of some of the more technical aspects can be found in other material (e.g., Paiva, Dias, Aylett, Woods, Hall, & Zoll, 2005; Aylett et al., 2006a; Aylett, Dias, & Paiva, 2006b; Figueiredo, Dias, Paiva, Aylett, & Louchart, 2006; Hall, Woods, & Aylett, 2006a; Hall, Woods, Aylett, & Paiva, 2006b; Hall, Woods, Dautenhahn, & Wolke, 2007; Ho, Dias, Figueiredo, & Paiva, 2007).

5.2 Using Characters to Create Affect

Two somewhat different approaches can be seen in the use of characters to produce affective states in the user. One focuses on internal aspects of the character, modelling affective state as the basis for selecting appropriate actions through which to interact with the user or with other characters. Work here draws on cognitive modelling and artificial intelligence. The other concentrates more on the externals, the character's expressive behaviour, and is concerned more deeply with graphical animation. Both draw on work in psychology.

Seminal work on the use of characters for dramatic purposes was carried out by the Oz project in the early 1990s. This was an early and influential use of affective architectures as a means of generating dramatically appropriate behaviour that would engage users emotionally (Mateas, 1999). Its focus was artistic, rather than educational, but its artistic aims required characters for which users were prepared to 'suspend their disbelief' and it pioneered the concept of believable characters discussed below.

The architecture used in their work was based on the concept, taken from psychology, of cognitive appraisal. This argues that humans do not carry out 'blank sheet' perception but continuously evaluate sensory data for its significance in relation to their own goals. The concept was originally popularised in the field of synthetic characters by the work of Elliot (1992) who drew on the taxonomy of 22 emotions proposed by Ortony, Clore, and Collins (1988) to construct the Affective Reasoner. Each emotion was associated with a type of appraisal rule linking it to events, objects, or other characters, formulated in relation to the specific domain of a synthetic character. The approach has been widely implemented since and has become known as the OCC system as a result.

Perhaps the earliest system to use an affective architecture for specifically educational purposes was the Mission Rehearsal Environment (MRE; Swartout et al., 2001). Here, a dramatic dilemma was presented to the user, assumed to be a soldier carrying out training on issues relating to peace-keeping missions. The scenario involved a child being run over by a military vehicle as help was being rushed to forward units under attack, and forced the user to resolve an emotional as well as an operational conflict.

Closest to FearNot! was Carmen's Bright IDEAS (Marsella, Johnson, & LaBore, 2000). This explicitly invoked empathy between the user and a graphical character for educational purposes in a scenario concerning the treatment of young cancer patients. Framed as a dialogue between the mother of such a patient and a psychiatrist, its purpose was to teach a cognitive behavioural therapy approach to dealing with the emotional and practical problems a mother in this situation faces. The user, a real mother in the situation depicted in the scenario, could choose among three responses framed as the thoughts of the character.

As well as the use of OCC-based cognitive appraisal, MRE and Carmen made use of a second idea from psychology, that of coping behaviour (Lazarus & Folkman, 1984). This links appraisal to action through mechanisms that deal with the emotions aroused by appraisal either externally in the world through action or internally in the mind by adjustment of goals and plans. Thus if one were insulted by a stranger in the street, external coping behaviour for the anger this would arouse might involve the use of aggressive language. On the other hand, internal coping behaviour might involve reasoning that the stranger was mentally disturbed and ought not to be taken literally, thus defusing the emotion of anger.

Early work in the dramatic use of synthetic characters with a more graphical focus was aimed at virtual theatre, in which the user could act as a high-level director of virtual actors, at most semi-autonomous (Rousseau & Hayes-Roth, 1998; Perlin & Goldberg, 1996). Here, expressive animations were required and the internal architecture was designed to interface with the requirements of the user rather than with any internal goals of the character.

Influential work on expressive movement drew on Laban Movement Analysis (Bishko, 1992), originating in the context of choreography for dance, to build the

EMOTE model (Chi, Costa, Zhao, & Badler, 2000). This used the Laban effort and shape parameters to modify a specific animation in expressive ways that could be characterised by adverbs, such as 'slowly', 'tiredly'. This work was taken further using the Embodied Conversational Agent Greta (Bevacqua, Mancini, Niewiadomski, & Pelachaud, 2007) to produce specifically emotional expressive behaviour. Here, naturalism rather than drama has been the guiding principle, however, because this work has focused on conversational interaction between a user and a character rather than dramatic interaction between characters.

5.3 An Overview of FearNot!

Bullying is a serious social problem that can have very negative effects on its victims, having an impact not only on their academic success but also their whole emotional well-being, with examples in different countries of victims driven to suicide. It can be distinguished from other forms of aggressive behaviour because it is persistent, planned, and involves an inequality of strength, power, or status. Not all languages recognize these distinctions: there is no specific word in German or in Portuguese for this behaviour, although there is in English and in Chinese. In the words of one of the earliest researchers of bullying in schools (Olweus 1978):

> A student is being bullied or victimised when he or she is exposed *repeatedly* and *over time* to *negative action* on the part of one or more other students. (Olweus 1991)

Hitting, punching, blackmail, threats, and spiteful behaviour, including stealing or damaging possessions, may all occur. This is known as *direct bullying*. *Verbal bullying* includes insults, mockery, and the spreading of lies, sometimes in actual words, sometimes in writing such as by passing notes or now in so-called cyberbullying, using email, comment on Web 2.0 social spaces, or texting to mobiles.

A sometimes less-recognised type of bullying is known as *relational bullying* in which social exclusion is used: 'The purposeful damage and manipulation of peer relationships and feelings of social exclusion' (Crick & Grotpeter, 1995).

Examples might include refusing to sit next to someone, or excluding them from group activities, both in the school environment and outside social contexts. Wolke, Woods, Schulz, and Stanford, 2001, in a study carried out in the United Kingdom and Germany in the period 1996–1998, showed that 24% of U.K. school students aged 9–11 said they were bullied every week, whereas between 12% and 17% of the sample admitted to bullying others at least four times in the previous term. Similar figures have been found in many other countries.

One of many problems associated with dealing with bullying is that no specific strategy, or coping behaviour, will always be successful. This makes it impossible to educate against bullying by communicating a single course of action to take. The standard advice, 'Tell someone you trust; don't suffer in silence,' is generally agreed to be sensible, but this too is not guaranteed to succeed. Parents may often suggest fighting back, advice strongly opposed by teachers. Fighting in fact succeeds rarely, and only in direct bullying cases, but because of its dramatic effect, success may well be over-reported.

FearNot! – Fun with Empathic Agents Reaching Novel Outcomes in Teaching – is software aimed at education against bullying inspired by the existing use of dramatic performance. A Theatre in Education (TiE) company typically performs a number of dramatic scenarios in a school and then smaller workshop-based discussions take place, often including role-play as well as relating the scenarios to the everyday experience of the children involved. The affective engagement of the audience with the characters and their situations as portrayed in the performance is seen as crucial to the ability to transfer lessons to real-world experience.

That such TiE experiences are collective is both an advantage and a disadvantage. It facilitates discussion and sharing of experience, as well as the construction of a social norm against bullying behaviour, but in any group of children involved in this process, fieldwork shows that some will be bullying others in the group. A motivation for the development of FearNot! was the wish to supplement TiE, which is also expensive and complex to run, with an experience that was still dramatic in intent but supported individual interaction.

FearNot! was specifically inspired by the Forum Theatre of Augusto Boal (1999), and developed to allow the active discussion of political and social issues in a dramatic context. The audience is divided into groups, and each group is allocated an actor who plays one of the characters in the drama, staying in role all of the time. The drama divides into segments in which the characters interact with each other as in a normal drama, and segments in which each character interacts with his or her group, taking advice about what to do next and discussing what has already happened.

FearNot! follows a similar form, structured as a short introduction, followed by an episode in which bullying takes place. At the end of the episode, an interaction session takes place in which the victimised character asks the child to suggest a way of dealing with the bullying. This advice will affect the emotional state modelled inside the character and thus indirectly change the response in the following episode. It is important to note that the child cannot intervene directly in the episode, but acts as an invisible friend to the victim.

Input in the interaction section is through typed free text (Figure 5.1) rather than through speech, but speech has been incorporated into the dramatic episodes, with a version in both UK English and German (Weiss et al., 2007).

The pedagogical effect is based on the ability of the child to explore social scenarios and reactions and specifically on the establishment of empathic relations between the child and the character, so that the child cares what happens to the character and is engaged with the advice offered in dealing with it. The issue of believability is seen as crucial to the creation of empathy and was thus a key issue for the project.

John:What should I do?
Mark:hit him in the face
John:So you think I should hit him back?

Fig. 5.1 The FearNot! interaction screen.

5.4 Believability

Believability is a central concept in relation to synthetic characters as used in FearNot! but is at the same time very hard to define precisely. It derives from traditional animation in which cartoon characters were created so as to give 'the illusion of life' (Johnston & Thomas, 1995). As discussed above, it was a central concern of the Oz project (Bates, 1994). If one considers the intentional stance, it might be defined as a long-lasting attribution of intentional stance to the character, such that it feels as if it has an autonomous internal affective state of its own.

5.4.1 Believability and Naturalism

Believability is not at all the same as the graphic realism or naturalism sought in many computer games. Traditional animated characters were intentionally not naturalistic. Basic principles of traditional animation included exaggeration for dramatic effect, and in cartoon worlds, that characters are flattened by large weights, leave body-shaped holes in walls, and literally steam with rage, are well-understood non-naturalistic conventions. One is able to suspend disbelief in the animation context and engage emotionally with the characters and the story in spite of knowing that this is not real life. The real tears wept by whole cinemas of children at the death of Simba's father in the Disney film, *The Lion King*, did not depend on believing that these were real lions. It is unclear whether the graphically realistic characters of computer games have ever made anyone cry.

Not only is believability a quite different concept from graphic realism, as the comparison just made between the impact of *The Lion King* and most computer games suggests, graphic realism may actually undermine believability and the basis for empathic engagement. This potentially negative relationship was first hypothesized by a Japanese researcher, Mori (1982), in relation to humanoid robots.

Mori suggested that as a robot became more 'like us' in appearance, it would be viewed more favourably up to the point where it was very close to realistic. However at this point, acceptability would suddenly fall and actually become negative, with a feeling of repulsion being generated. This big drop, labelled by Mori 'the uncanny valley' has indeed been observed in practice in both humanoid robots and graphical characters. The rationale seems to be that as a character becomes closer to naturalism, the expectations brought to it by a human interaction partner rise very steeply, making it harder and harder to suspend disbelief in the face of inconsistencies between appearance and behaviour.

At some point the jolt to the feeling of belief this generates, creates a negative affective state in the user, often the feeling that the character is like a zombie, somehow alive but dead at the same time. In the current state-of-the-art, it is not feasible to endow a character that has a very human appearance with equally human behaviour, so that attempts at photorealism can all too easily invoke the uncanny valley effect.

Thus there are two strong reasons why the characters designed for FearNot! were designed to be cartoonlike in appearance as can be seen in Figures 5.1 and 5.2. It was consistent with the use of dramatic exaggeration, very useful in clearly communicating the emotional state of the characters, and it also allowed the characters to avoid the uncanny valley.

With these characters, simple methods of generating expressive behaviour could be used, very important given the need to be able to run the system on school computers of limited power. Rather than trying to create realistic facial expressions

Fig. 5.2 The FearNot! UK characters.

Fig. 5.3 Use of visemes for simple lip synchronization in FearNot!.

with a complex polygonal mesh and a Facial Action Coding System approach (Ekman & Friesen, 1978), stereotypical emotional expressions were designed as textures and simply switched to match the dominant emotional state generated by the internal architecture of the character. With morphing between expressions, this is surprisingly effective. In the same way, sophisticated synchronization of lips with speech is not expected of cartoonlike characters, although even small errors in lip synchronization are very obvious in photorealistic characters. A simple move between a small set of mouth expressions (visemes) works well with the FearNot! characters, as seen in Figure 5.3.

5.4.2 FatiMA, an Architecture for Believable Characters

However, as argued above, believability is not only to do with appearance; neither is it only to do with expressive behaviour. Consistency between physical appearance and behaviour can be thought of as a necessary but not a sufficient condition for believability; in order for the user to believe in the internal state of the character it has be responsive to its environment and the other characters around it. In an emotionally driven drama, all action can be thought of as expressing the inner state of the characters because it is interpreted through the empathic relationship between the child user and the victim character, mediated by the dramatic situation. The link between internal character state and selected action must be appropriate in order to produce coherent interaction between the characters.

It is in relation to responsiveness that scripted actions are so destructive of believability as soon as the user realises the character is 'doing what it is told' by an authoring system and not deciding anything for itself. A key element in giving the FearNot! characters' believability lies in taking an agent-centred approach and giving each character its own sense–reflect–act cycle using events generated by the underlying ION framework on which it is built as a sensing mechanism.

Figure 5.4 shows FatiMA (Dias & Paiva, 2005), the architecture driving each individual character, giving it the ability to autonomously select actions dispatched at the right of the diagram in response to perception data arriving at the left of the diagram from the ION framework.

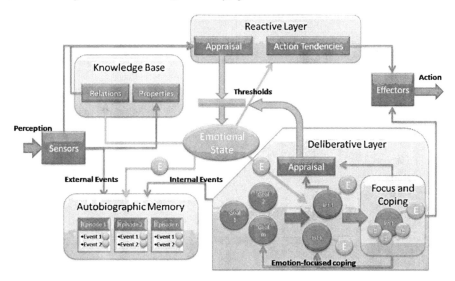

Fig. 5.4 The architecture of a FearNot! character: FatiMA.

It can be seen that the emotional state of the character plays a central role, and this is generated by the Appraisal boxes in the Reactive and the Deliberative Layer components. The appraisal carried out in the Reactive Layer component applies the OCC taxonomy described above, and results in reactive action tendencies, which might, for example, include a character crying if its level of distress were high.

The Deliberative Layer component carries out appraisal as part of a continuous planning process, with the emotions hope and fear, both related in the OCC taxonomy to prospective or future events, being involved internally in the appraisal cycle. This component implements the concept of *coping behaviour*, discussed above, as the means through which planned actions – as distinct from reactions – are related to emotional state. Problem-focused coping takes place when the character tries to deal with its emotions by planning actions to be carried out in the world; for example, the victimised character might deal with the emotion of anger aroused by the bully's attack by planning to hit him back. Emotion-focused coping on the other hand adjusts internal state, so that one might deal with a feeling of anger by denying that the action that caused it was at all important.

This layer makes a distinction between goals, which are generic, and intentions, which instantiate concrete realizations of goals. Goals can be seen on the left of this component and intentions on their right. Thus the generic goal of eating might be activated when the character is hungry and sees something it can eat. If what it sees is an apple, a specific intention to eat the apple and not something else will be created.

Initial hope and fear emotions based on the intention's probability and the goal's importance are created and stored with the intention and these are used as part of the mechanism for selecting between competing intentions and possible coping

Fig. 5.5 Using autobiographic memory to communicate with the user.

strategies. Planning is carried out for the intentions with the most intense associated emotions, but the process of planning itself has the effect of updating the hope and fear emotions depending on the probability of success or failure. A victim character may abandon the plan to hit the bully back if the fear of getting hurt as a result is high, and it is these feelings that may be influenced by the advice of the child user.

FatiMA also includes two specific types of memory. The Knowledge Base component in Figure 5.4 holds world knowledge, for example about objects and their properties. The Autobiographical Memory component is a novel (Ho, Dias, Figueiredo, & Paiva, 2007) episodic memory in which a character holds the events that have affected it emotionally. It allows the character to tell the child user in the interaction section how it felt about the events of the dramatic episodes, contributing to believability. Figure 5.5 shows an example of such recall.

5.5 Creating Dramatic Situations

We have argued above that scripting character behaviour is at some point likely to fatally undermine the believability of the characters because it makes it clear that the character's internal state is only an illusion. For this reason, and also because of the branching factor on the number of possible coping responses that can be suggested by the user, a generative approach has been taken to narrative, using interaction between characters to create dramatic incident on the fly. This forms an example of *emergent narrative* (Aylett & Louchart, 2003).

Thus it is the actions each character chooses in response to its own goals, emotional state, and the event that has just happened that determines how the story develops. If the bully character and the victim character encounter each other, then the goal of the bully to hurt the victim will produce a bullying action. The resulting emotional state of the victim will determine how it responds.

This does not, however, remove the need for some degree of story management or facilitation. We have seen that FearNot! is organized into dramatic episodes separated by interaction sessions. Some mechanism has to be in place to initialize a dramatic episode, deciding where it takes place and what characters and props are present. Equally, in an emergent narrative, some mechanism has to decide when an episode has finished. Finally, a standard introduction of the characters and the scene is needed to familiarise the user with the overall application, and such a segment has itself to be invoked at the correct point.

FearNot! has a Story-Facilitator (SF) for all these purposes (Figueiredo, Dias, Paiva, Aylett, & Louchart, 2006). Figure 5.6 shows the state machine traversed by the SF, which is implemented as a separate agent within the ION framework. Figure 5.7 shows the overall FearNot! architecture and the position of the SF in relation to the FatiMA instantiations driving each character. In the version discussed here, the visualisation engine being used is the Ogre3D opensource games engine.

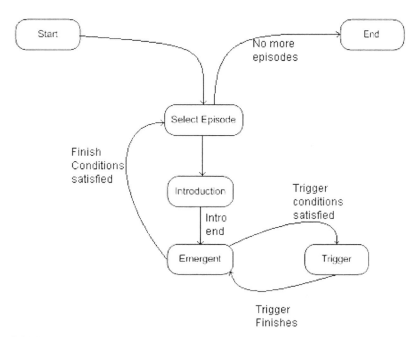

Fig. 5.6 The Story Facilitator (SF) State Transtion Machine.

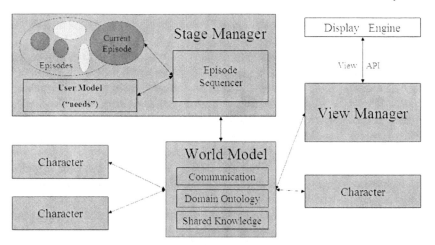

Fig. 5.7 The FearNot! overall architecture using the ION framework.

The SF receives and monitors all the messages exchanged between characters and ION as well as all the messages generated by ION and returned to the characters. This allows the SF to know everything that happens in the virtual world and to make decisions based on the actions the agents intend to execute as well as the ones they have executed.

The SF has a repertoire of narrative actions that affect the environment, each with preconditions allowing for it to be triggered. It is these actions that are currently used for the selection and setup of episodes, as well as their termination. The SF is also involved in 'off-stage' episodes that are not shown in the graphical world. These are episodes in which the character implements the coping advice to tell his parents or a teacher about the bullying. This advice is basically sound but like all other pieces of advice it does not in the real world always work. However, showing unsympathetic parents or teachers on screen seemed to the project team likely to cause negative responses from both, and for this reason the outcome of such an episode is reported by a character in the next visualized episode: for example, the bully may call the victim a 'grass' for telling the teacher.

In order to make FearNot! ready for a longitudinal evaluation in schools in the United Kingdom and Germany, held in the autumn of 2007, it was necessary to equip the SF with a large number of potential episodes. These were split into episodes relating to direct bullying, featuring male characters, and episodes featuring relational bullying featuring female characters. This division was made in response to earlier evaluations showing a very clear gender divide in the impact of the characters on the target age-group (Hall, Woods, Dautenhahn, & Wolke, 2007). There was indeed some evidence that in the target age-range of 9–11, boys found it hard to understand that relational bullying was in fact bullying because of their generally less-developed social skills at this age. Some 40 episodes in total have been developed, where an episode is defined by the setting, the characters present, and the type of action that is likely to take place in it. Many of the scenarios used as the basis for these episodes were collected from children themselves in a user-centred design process (Hall, Woods, & Aylett, 2006a).

Because of the emergent nature of the narrative, however, exactly what happens in an episode is a little unpredictable, as it will depend on the internal states of the characters at the time, and this will be influenced by interaction with the users and the order in which the SF had invoked the episodes for a particular child. The end result should be that each user has a somewhat different experience, reinforcing the believability of the characters and allowing each child to bring different experiences with the software to other classroom activities on the topic, such a collective discussion. FearNot! is not intended to displace these other activities, but to reinforce them, just as a TiE production is not used as a substitute for other pedagogical elements.

5.6 Conclusions

Evaluation of affective interfaces clearly raises issues over and above the usual usability criteria, and is itself a research area (Ruttkay & Pelachaud, 2004). FearNot! itself has been evaluated so far along a number of different dimensions and with a number of different methods, ranging from conventional questionnaires to the use of classroom discussion forums, in which small group discussion by child users is facilitated by members of the research team (Hall et al., 2006a,b, 2007).

FearNot! intends to achieve the pedagogical objective of educating against bullying by creating empathy between the child user and the victimized character, which therefore forms an affective interface. This mechanism is itself a hypothesis: one can imagine creating empathy successfully while not creating any long-lasting change in attitudes towards bullying, and one could also imagine changing attitudes towards bullying even without successfully creating empathy, although this does seem less likely.

The issue is further complicated by the varying status of the children using the system in relation to bullying. Some subjects may themselves be what are known as 'pure bullies', bullying other children but not themselves being victimised; some may be pure victims; some may be what are known as 'bully–victims', being both bullied and bullying other children; some may be bystanders who see bullying but do not intervene; some may be helpers who will try to stop bullying if they see it happening. The cognitive status of these categories of children may well be systematically different; for example, there is evidence that pure bullies are able to understand the emotional pain they cause to their victims but do not care. The mechanism through which they experience empathy may therefore be different from say, bully–victims.

It is for this reason that such a wide range of methods has been applied in evaluating FearNot!, including assessing the 'Theory of Mind' of child users, their ability to understand the cognitive processes of others (Hall et al. 2006b). Results so far have shown that empathy is successfully created with characters, although there is a substantial gender variation (Hall et al. 2006a) and this is based on a short exposure of 30–60 mins to the software. This suggests that the measures taken to support the believability of the characters are successful.

The pedagogical aims of the system can really only be tested with a much longer exposure to FearNot! and in the normal school setting, where it would be used if it were to form a regular part of the curriculum. Such a longitudinal evaluation was run in the autumn of 2007 and will be to the knowledge of the research team the first such evaluation of intelligent autonomous characters in a school setting.

In conclusion, one should not underestimate the effort involved in creating competent affective interfaces that can be evaluated for success. FearNot! is, however, an innovative approach to educating against bullying and could be extended into other areas of personal and social education; the approach could also be used for therapeutic applications. It represents an early instance of the attempt to apply affective interfaces in areas in which conventional knowledge-based applications are insufficient.

Acknowledgements The work on *FearNot!* discussed was partially supported by the European Community (EC) under the Information Society Technology (IST) RTD programme in the project VICTEC IST-2001-33310-victec (www.victec.net) and is currently funded by the eCIRCUS project IST-4-027656-STP (www.e-circus.org). The authors are solely responsible for the content of this publication. It does not represent the opinion of the European Community, and the European Community is not responsible for any use that might be made of data appearing therein.

References

Aylett, R., Dias, J., & Paiva, A. (2006b). *An affectively driven planner for synthetic characters. ICAPS 2006*, California: AAAI Press, 2–10.

Aylett, R., & Louchart, S. (2003) Towards a narrative theory of VR. Special issue on storytelling. *Virtual Reality Journal, 7*, 2–9.

Aylett, R. S., Louchart, S., Dias, J., Paiva, A., Vala, M., Woods, S., & Hall, L. (2006a) Unscripted narrative for affectively driven characters. *IEEE Journal of Graphics and Applications*, May/June 26:(3), 42–52.

Bates, J. (1994). The role of emotion in believable agents. *Communications of the ACM, 37*(7), 122–125.

Bevacqua, E., Mancini, M., Niewiadomski, R., & Pelachaud, C. (2007). An expressive ECA showing complex emotions. *AISB'07 – Artificial and Ambient Intelligence*. Newcastle upon Tyne, UK: Newcastle University.

Bishko, L. (1992) Relationships between Laban movement analysis and computer animation. In *Dance and Technology I: Moving Toward the Future*.

Boal, A. (1999). *Legislative theatre: Using performance to make politics*. New York: Routledge.

Chi, D., Costa, M., Zhao, L., & Badler, N. (2000) The EMOTE model for effort and shape. In *Proceedings of SIGGRAPH 2000, ACM Computer Graphics Annual Conference*, New Orleans, LA, 23–28 July (pp. 173–182).

Crick, N. R., & Grotpeter, J. K (1995). Relational aggression, gender, and social-psychological adjustment. *Child Development, 66*, 710–722.

Dias, J., & Paiva, A. (2005). Feeling and reasoning: A computational model. *12th Portuguese Conference on Artificial Intelligence, EPIA* (pp. 127–140). New York: Springer.

Ekman, P., & Friesen, W. V (1978). *Manual for the facial action coding system*. Palo Alto, CA: Consulting Psychology Press.

Elliot C. (1992). The affective reasoner: A process model of emotions in a multi-agent system. PhD Thesis, Illinois..

Figueiredo, R., Dias, J., Paiva, A., Aylett, R., & Louchart, S. (2006) Shaping emergent narratives for a pedagogical application. In *NILE - Narrative and Interactive Learning Environments*, Aug. (pp. 27–36).

Hall, L., Woods, S., & Aylett, R., (2006a) FearNot! Involving children in the design of a virtual learning environment. *International Journal of AI in Education, 16* (Oct.), 327–351.

Hall, L., Woods, S., Aylett, R., & Paiva, A., (2006b) Using theory of mind methods to investigate empathic engagement with synthetic characters. *International Journal of Virtual Humanoids, 3*(3), 351–370.

Hall, L., Woods, S., Dautenhahn, K., & Wolke, D. (2007). Implications of gender differences for the development of animated characters for the study of bullying behavior. *Computers in Human Behavior, 23*(3), 770–786..

Heylen, D., Vissers, M., op den Akker, R., & Nijholt, A. (2004). Affective feedback in a tutoring system for procedural tasks. In E. Andre, L. Dybkjaer, W. Minker, & P. Heisterkamp (Ed.), *Affective dialogue systems*, Kloster Irsee, Germany, June 14–16, . *Tutorial and Research Workshop ADS*, LNCS 3068/2004 (pp. 244–253), Heidelberg: Springer-Verlag.

Ho, W. C., Dias, J., Figueiredo, R., & Paiva, A. (2007) Agents that remember can tell stories: Integrating autobiographic memory into emotional agents. In *Proceedings of Autonomous Agents and Multiagent Systems (AAMAS)*, New York: ACM Press.

Johnston, O., & Thomas, F. (1995). *The illusion of life: Disney animation*. New York: Hyperion Press.

Lazarus, R. S., & Folkman, S. (1984). *Stress, appraisal and coping*. New York: Springer.

Louchart, S., & Aylett, R. S. (2007). Evaluating synthetic actors. In *Proceedings, AISB Symposia*, April (pp. 439–445). University of Newcastle.

Marsella, S., & Gratch, J. (2003) Modeling coping behavior in virtual humans: Don't worry, be happy. In *AAMAS 2003* (pp. 313–320). New York: ACM Press.

Marsella, S., Johnson, L. W., & LaBore, C. (2000). *Interactive pedagogical drama, International Conference on Autonomous Agents*. Barcelona, Spain, pp. 301–308.

Mateas, M. (1999) An Oz-centric review of interactive drama and believable agents. In M. Wooldridge and M. Veloso (Eds.), *AI today: Recent trends and developments*, LNAI 1600. Berlin: Springer.

Mori, M. (1982). *The Buddha in the robot*. Boston: Charles E. Tuttle.

Olweus, D. (1978). *Aggression in schools: Bullies and whipping boys*. Washington, DC: Hemisphere.

Olweus, D. (1991). Bully/victim problems among schoolchildren: Basic facts and effects of a school-based intervention programme. In D. Pepler & K. Rubin (Eds.), *The development and treatment of childhood aggression* (pp. 411–438). Hillsdale, NJ: Erlbaum.

Ortony, A., Clore, G., & Collins, A. (1988). *The cognitive structure of emotions*. Cambridge: Cambridge University Press.

Paiva, A., Dias, J., Aylett, R., Woods, S., Hall, L., & Zoll, C. (2005). Learning by feeling: Evoking empathy with synthetic characters. *Applied Artificial Intelligence, 19*, 235–266.

Perlin, K., & Goldberg, A. (1996). Improv: A system for scripting interactive actors in virtual worlds. *Computer Graphics, 29*(3), 205–216.

Rousseau, D., & Hayes-Roth, B. (1998). A social-psychological model for synthetic actors. In *Proceedings of the Second International Conference on Autonomous Agents (Agents'98)*.

Ruttkay, Z., & Pelachaud. C. (Eds.). (2004). *From brows to trust: Evaluating embodied conversational agents*. Dordrecht: Kluwer. Swartout, W., Hill, R. W., Jr., Gratch, J., Johnson, L. W., Kyriakakis, C., LaBore, C., Lindheim, R., Marsella, S., Miraglia, D., Moore, B., Morie, J. F., Rickel, J., Thiébaux, M., Tuch, L., & Whitney, R. (2001). Toward the holodeck: Integrating graphics, sound, character and story. In J. P. Muller, E. Andre, S. Sen, & C. Frasson (Eds.), *Proceedings of 5th International Conference on Autonomous Agents* (pp. 409–416). New York: ACM Press.

Weiss, C., Oliveira, L. C., Paulo, S., Duarte Mendes, C. M., Dias Mestre Figueira, L. A., Vala, M., Sequeira, P., Paiva, A. Vogt, T., Andre, E. (2007). ECIRCUS: Building Voices for Autonomous Speaking Agents. In *Sixth Speech Synthesis Workshop, ISCA*, August. Wolke, D., Woods, S., Schulz, H., & Stanford, K. (2001). Bullying and victimisation of primary school children in South England and South Germany: Prevalence and school factors. *British Journal of Psychology, 92,* 673–696.

Part II
Affect in Speech

Chapter 6
Emotion Perception and Recognition from Speech

Chung-Hsien Wu, Jui-Feng Yeh, and Ze-Jing Chuang

Abstract With the increasing role of speech interfaces in human–computer interaction applications, automatically recognizing emotions from human speech becomes more and more important. This chapter begins by introducing the correlations between basic speech features such as pitch, intensity, formants, MFCC, and so on, and the emotions. Several recognition methods are then described to illustrate the performance of the previously proposed models, including support vector machine (SVM), K-nearest neighbors (KNN), neural networks, and the like.

To give a more practical description of an emotion recognition procedure, a new approach to emotion recognition is provided as a case study. In this case study, the Intonation Groups (IGs) of the input speech signals are first defined and extracted for feature extraction. With the assumption of linear mapping between feature spaces in different emotional states, a feature compensation approach is proposed to characterize the feature space with better discriminability among emotional states. The compensation vector with respect to each emotional state is estimated using the Minimum Classification Error (MCE) algorithm. The IG-based feature vectors compensated by the compensation vectors are used to train the Gaussian Mixture Models (GMMs) for each emotional state. The emotional state with the GMM having the maximal likelihood ratio is determined as the emotion state output.

C.-H. Wu (✉)
Department of Computer Science and Information Engineering, National Cheng Kung University, Tainan,
e-mail: chwu@csie.ncku.edu.tw

J.-F. Yeh
National Chia-Yi University, Chia Yi

Z.-J. Chuang
Department of Computer Science and Information Engineering, National Cheng Kung University, Tainan

J.H. Tao, T.N. Tan (eds.), *Affective Information Processing*,
© Springer Science+Business Media LLC 2009

6.1 Introduction

Intact perception and experience of emotion is vital for communication in the social environment. Emotion perception in humans is associated with affective factors especially in communication (Borod & Madigan, 2000; Picard, Vyzas, & Healey, 2001). Scientists have found that emotional skills can be an important component of intelligence, especially for human–human interaction (Pantic & Rothkrantz, 2003). Human–machine interface technology has been investigated for several decades. Although human–computer interaction is different from human–human communication, some theories have shown that human–computer interaction essentially follows the basics of human–human interaction (Reeves & Nass, 1996). Speech technologies have expanded the interaction modalities between humans and computer-supported communicational artifacts, such as robots, PDAs, and mobile phones.

Recent advances in speech recognition and synthesis have gradually redefined the computer's position with regard to humans and consequently the human's position with regard to computers. Communication of emotion has been a major focus of many in the speech research community over recent years. However, limited analysis has been presented on how the voice source varies in emotional speech. A true understanding of how emotion is encoded and communicated through the parameters of speech should be carefully considered. Emotions have some mechanical effects on physiology, which in turn have effects on the intonation of the speech. This is why it is possible in principle to predict some emotional information from the prosody of a sentence. Recognition of emotions in speech is a complex task that is further complicated by the fact that there is no unambiguous answer to what the "correct" emotion is for a given speech sample.

Emotion-aware speech recognition will improve the spontaneous speech recognition result. By capturing the emotional status of speakers, the dialogue systems and interactive voice response systems can detect the speech act and the user's response more exactly. Students interacting with an emotion-enabled ITSpoke (Litman & Silliman, 2004), are able to report quantitatively the results of emotion modeling, and can obtain better learning efficiency compared to conventional tutoring systems. Affect-sensitive e-learning systems such as AutoTutor developed by MIT have shown that emotion detection is one of the future trends in intelligent educational systems (D'Mello, Picard, & Graesser, 2007).

Emotion recognition can be applied to essential services in digital life. Emotional information extracted from speech can monitor the status of the elderly who are alone and children in homecare service. Emotionally reactive television will provide more affective benefits; it became one of the new trends in interactive television. Morrison, Wang, and De Silva (2007) used the MultiClassifier System (MCS) approaches to spoken emotion recognition in Customer Service Representative (CSR) call centers.

Devillers, Vidrascu, and Lamel (2005) presented a new annotation scheme allowing the annotation of emotion mixtures for real-life speech such as financial customer service call center dialogues and medical emergency call center dialogues.

The multilevel emotion and context annotation scheme consists of context annotation at the dialogue level and emotion annotation at the segment level. In addition, emotional feedback will increase the enjoyment for cartoons and toys such as Sony's robotic dog AIBO (Shami & Kamel, 2005).

Because emotion is an essential attribute of humanity, affective communicative intent in robot development is vital (Breazeal & Aryananda, 2002). Emotional state is one of the important speech attributes to improve the performance of traditional speech recognition (Shriberg, 2005; Lee et al., 2007). Emotion perception and recognition from speech are important because of their substantial applicability and usefulness for automated systems that are based on the user's perception of its intelligence and receptiveness.

Among emotion categories that exist, two groups of emotions are considered, adult-to-adult acted vocal expressions of common types of emotions such as happiness, sadness, and anger and adult-to-infant vocal expressions of affective intents also known as "motherese" (Shami & Verhelst, 2007). Ortony and Turner (1990) collected research about the definition and identification of basic emotions. Parrott (2001) categorized emotions into a hierarchical tree structure with three levels. He defined the primary emotions as love, joy, surprised, anger, sadness, and fear at the first branch.

Murray and Arnott (1993) classified the emotions in speech into two categories: primary and secondary emotions. Primary emotions mean the basic emotions that are experienced by social mammals and have particular manifestations. Fear, anger, joy, sadness, and disgust are included in primary emotions. Secondary emotions are derived emotions that are variations or combinations of primary emotions such as pride, gratitude, sorrow, tenderness, irony, and surprise.

In recent years, speech corpora involving people in various natural emotional states in response to real situations have been collected, which will, it is hoped, allow the development of more sophisticated systems for recognizing the relevant emotional states in such data. Considering the labeling of the speech corpus, there are three emotion categories: approval, attention, and prohibition, defined in BabyEars (Slaney and McRoberts, 2003). Different from BabyEars, Kismet (Breazeal & Aryananda, 2002) contains two extra emotion categories: soothing and neutral. The emotional classes: anger, sadness, happiness, neutral, fear, boredom, and disgust are employed to tag speech in the corpus-Berlin (Paeschke & Sendlmeier, 2000). There are four emotion categories: angry, sad, happy, neutral, and surprised used in Danish (Engberg & Hansen, 1996). The Linguistic Data Consortium (LDC) defined 14 emotion categories for emotional prosody description.[1]

In addition to the above description of the reports, a large amount of work has been described in the neurobiology literature on how the human brain recognizes emotional states (e.g., Damasio, 1994). There are also numerous psychological studies and theories on perception and production models of emotion (Scherer, 1999).

Although emotion has attracted the interest of researchers in many disciplines of neurosciences and psychology, this chapter focuses on how to represent and

---

[1] (http://www.ldc.upenn.edu/Catalog/docs/LDC2002S28/Emotion_Categories.pdf).

automatically detect a subject's emotional state in speech. In the following sections, we first describe the acoustic and prosodic features generally adopted for emotion recognition. Then we illustrate some recognition models and their performance. Finally, a new approach with discriminative feature extraction and recognition is described to present the detailed recognition procedure of emotion recognition from speech.

6.2 Feature Analysis

An important problem for all emotion recognition systems from speech is the selection of the set of relevant features to be used with the most efficient recognition models. In recent research, many different feature sets and recognition models have been used. However, there is no consistent conclusion for the best feature set and the most efficient models from the reported results, which show that they appear to be data-dependent.

For emotion detection of natural speech, prosodic features, such as pitch, energy, and speaking rate, are classical features and mainly used in research systems. However, lexical, disfluency, and discourse cues are also important features and should be included in the feature set. Acoustic features, such as zero-crossing, spectrum, formants, MFCC, and so on have also been studied but have not yet obtained significant improvements. Because there is no common agreement on a best feature set and the feature choice seems to be data-dependent, some approaches tried to use as many features as possible even if many of the features are redundant, and to optimize the choice of features with the recognition algorithm (Devillers et al., 2005).

Previous studies have focused on a number of different aspects of the emotion recognition problem. Some studies focus on finding the most relevant acoustic features of emotions in speech. Pitch, intensity, and speech rate-related features are classical features used to detect the emotion states in asegment-based approach (Shami & Verhelst, 2007). Using a segment-based approach, AIBO divided the feature set into three categories: acoustic features, the derived series, and statistics of acoustic features (Shami & Kamel, 2005).

Short time Log Frequency Power Coefficients (LFPC) outperformed the Linear Prediction Cepstral Coefficients (LPCC) and Mel-Frequency Cepstral Coefficients (MFCC) in emotion recognition from speech by Hidden Markov Model (HMM; Nwe et al., 2003). For emotion recognition, Kwon, Chan, Hao, and Lee (2003) selected pitch, log energy, formant, mel-band energies, and mel-frequency cepstral coefficients as the base features, and added velocity/acceleration of pitch and MFCCs to form feature streams. Fernandez and Picard (2005) used three categories of discriminative features associated with modeling loudness, intonation, and voice quality for affect recognition from speech. Cichosz & Slot (2005) used low-dimensional feature space derivation of acoustic features for emotion recognition (Liscombe, Riccardi, & Hakkani-Tr (2005)). Oudeyer also selected the 20 best attributes according to the information gain they provided (Kwon et al., 2003).

In addition to the generally used prosodic and acoustic features, some special features are also applied for this task, such as TEO-based features (Rahurkar & Hansen, 2003). Contextual features composed of prosodic context, lexical context, and discourse context are used for emotion classification of speech in spoken dialogue systems (Liscombeet al., 2005).

Table 6.1 summarizes the correlations between basic speech features and the emotions from previous reports (Morrison, Wang, & De Silva, 2007; Oudeyer, 2003; Pantic & Rothkrantz, 2003). In addition to conventional features, the disfluency features and nonlinguistic event features are used to form the paralinguistic feature set. Morrison et al. found that the pause duration in disfluency and the voice in nonlinguistic events such as mouth noise, laughter, and crying with essential information are useful to recognize emotion from the speech signal. In addition, Devillers et al. (2005) reported that lexical and paralinguistic scores can be combined to detect emotion state in speech.

Table 6.1 Correlations Among Basic Speech Features and Emotions

	Anger	Happiness	Sadness	Surprise	Disgust	Fear	Comfort
Pitch/F0 mean	Increased	Increased	Decreased	Normal or increased	Decreased	Increased or decreased	Increased but less than happiness
Pitch/F0 range	Wider	Wider	Narrower	Wider	Wider or narrower	Wider or narrower	—
Energy/ Intensity	Increased	Increased	Decreased	—	Decreased or normal	Normal	
Speaking rate(Duration)	High	High/slow tempo	Low	Normal	Higher	High or low	Low
Formants	F1 mean increased; F2 mean higher or lower, F3 mean higher	F1 mean decreased; F1 bandwidth increased	F1 mean increased; F1 bandwidth decreased; F2 mean lower	—	F1 mean increased; F1 bandwidth decreased; F2 mean lower	F1 mean increased; F1 bandwidth decreased; F2 mean lower	—
Pitch contour	Descending line, stressed syllables ascend frequently and rhythmically, irregular up and down inflection.	Descending line	Descending line	—	—	Disintegration in pattern and great number of changes in the direction.	—
Accented syllables	A lot of syllables, the last one word is not accented	Few, the last one word is accented	Very few, the last one word is not accented	—	—	—	Very few, the last one word is accented

Source: Morrison et al. (2007), Oudeyer (2003), and Pantic & Rothkrantz (2003).

6.3 Recognition Models

Several pattern recognition methods, using acoustic signal information, have been explored for automatic emotion recognition from speech. The recognition models used for emotion detection include decision trees, Neural Network (NN; Bhatti, Wang, & Guan, 2004; Fragopanagos & Taylor, 2005), Hidden Markov Model (HMM) (New et al., 2003; Inanoglu & Caneel, 2005), Support Vector Machine (SVM; Chuang & Wu, 2004), and so on. Ten Bosch (2003) presented the relationship between emotion detection and the speech recognition framework. Cichosz and Slot (2007) used binary decision trees to recognize emotion in speech signals.

Kwon et al. (2003) compared the emotion recognition performances of the methods using SVM, LDA, and QDA classifiers. Oudeyer (2003) illustrated machine-learning algorithms to classify emotions such as KNN, decision tree-C4.5, decision rules, kernel density, K Star, linear regression, locally weighted regression, voted perceptrons, support vector machine, voted features interval, M5PRime regression method, and naive Bayes. In addition to the utterance level approaches (Oudeyer, 2003; Cichosz & Slot, 2005), segment-level approaches were recently proposed to model the acoustic contours (Shami & Verhelst, 2007; Katz, Cohn, & Moore, 1996). Lee and Narayanan (2005) used the combination of acoustic, language, and discourse information by averaging the outputs from each information stream by Linear Discriminant Analysis (LDA) and k-Nearest Neighbor classifiers (k-NN). Table 6.2 illustrates the recognition performances for several algorithms based on speech corpus NATURAL and the SONY acted corpus (Morrison et al., 2007; Pierre-Yves, 2003).

According to the experimental results for the corpus NATURAL, the best recognition model is the support vector machine with the Radial Basis Function (RBF)

Table 6.2 Performance of Recognition Algorithms

Algorithm	Accuracy (%)	
	NATURAL (Morrison et al., 2007)	Sony acted corpus (Pierre-Yves, 2003)
SVM (non-polynomial)	76.93(RBF kernel)	91.5 (Gaussian kernel)
KNN ($K = 5$)	75.85	85.2
Artificial neural networks	74.25 (Multilayer perception)	85.2 (Radial Basis Function)
Random forest	71.98	—
K^*	70.67	81
Naïve Bayes	69.56	89.8
SVM (Polynomial)	69.50	92.1 (degree 1)
C4.5 decision tree	67.47	94.1
Random tree	60.05	—

Source: Morrison et al. (2007) and Pierre-Yves (2003).

kernel. The random forest, the multilayer perception (artificial neural network), K^*, and K-nearest neighbors with $K = 5$ can also achieve better performance with accuracies higher than 70%. For the SVM, the RBF kernel showed a significant improvement over the polynomial kernel. However, the results for the SONY acted corpus are different from those for NATURAL. Decision tree and support vector machines with polynomial kernels are able to achieve better performance compared to K-nearest neighbors and artificial neural networks. The algorithms for some recognition models with good performance are described in the following.

Support vector machines are a set of related supervised learning methods used for classification and regression in machine learning introduced by Vapnik (1995). By maximizing the margin, a hyperplane is used to separate two classes of the training samples. A Sequential Minimal Optimization (SMO) algorithm to implement SVM is provided in WEKA (Waikato Environment for Knowledge Analysis: http://www.cs.waikato.ac.nz/~ml/weka/). The polynomial and radial basis function kernels are commonly used, and take the form of Equations (6.1) and (6.2).

$$K(x_i, y_j) = (x_i \cdot y_j)^d, \tag{6.1}$$

and

$$K(x_i, y_j) = \exp\left(-\gamma \|x_i - y_j\|^2\right), \quad \gamma > 0, \tag{6.2}$$

where d is the order of the polynomial and γ is the width of the radial basis function.

K-nearest neighbors (KNNs) is an instance-based method for classifying objects based on closest training examples in the feature space (Cover & Hart, 1967). A test sample is classified by a majority vote of its neighbors, with the sample being assigned to the class most common amongst its k nearest neighbors. Because of comparable performance and simplicity, KNN is employed to recognize vocal emotion (Yacoub, Simske, Lin, & Burns, 2003).

Artificial neural networks (ANNs) are traditionally used as classifiers by training the numerical weights of those interconnect nodes in the different layers using supervised learning. Specifically, multilayer perceptions (MLPs) based on the back-propagation algorithm for training neural networks can achieve good performance in emotion recognition from speech (Huber, Noth, Batliner, Buckow, Warnke, & Niemann, 1998; Petrushin 2000).

Random forest, developed by Leo Breiman (2001), is an ensemble of tree predictors such that each tree depends on the values of a random vector sampled independently and with the same distribution for all trees in the forest. Random forest is more robust with respect to noise. Actually, random forest, composed of decision trees, is a classifier in machine-learning algorithms. The output of the classifier depends on the output from the individual tree. That is to say, a random forest is formed after a large number of trees have been generated and they vote for the most popular one. The classification trees are $h_1(x), h_2(x), \ldots, h_k(x)$ with a random training set drawn at random from the distribution of random vector Y, X. To obtain a discriminative classification result, the margin functions are used to measure the extent to which the average number of votes at X, Y for the right class succeeds the average vote for any other class. Herein, the margin function is formulated as

$$mgf(X,Y) = ave_k I(h_k(X) = Y) - \max_{j \neq Y} ave_k I(h_k(X) = j), \qquad (6.3)$$

where I means the indicator function and $ave(\cdot)$ denotes the average function that estimates the mean value of the observation events. The larger the margin is leads to the more confidence there is in the classification. Furthermore, the generalization error is defined as

$$PE^* = P_{X,Y}(mgf(X,Y) < 0), \qquad (6.4)$$

where $P_{X,Y}(\cdot)$ is the probability over the X,Y feature space.

6.4 Case Study

For providing more detailed illustration about emotion recognition from speech, a case study is introduced in this section. Despite the many features and recognition models that have been tested in previous work, large overlaps between the feature spaces for different emotional states are rarely considered. Also, the pretrained emotion recognition model is highly speaker-dependent.

Considering the above questions, this case study presents an approach to emotion recognition based on feature compensation. The block diagram of the approach is shown in Figure 6.1. In order to identify the most significant segment, the Intonation Groups (IGs) of the input speech signals are first extracted. Following the feature extraction process (Deng, Droppo, & Acero, 2003), the prosodic feature sets are estimated for the IG segments. Then all the feature vectors compensated by compensation vectors are modeled by a Gaussian Mixture Model (GMM). Finally, the

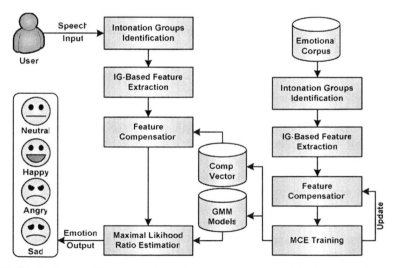

Fig. 6.1 Block diagram of the proposed emotion recognition approach in the case study.

Minimum Classification Error (MCE) training method (Wu & Huo, 2002) iteratively estimates all the model parameters. Herein, four common emotion categories— neutral, happy, angry and sad—are employed as the system output.

6.4.1 Feature Extraction

It is possible to achieve the goal only if there are some reliable acoustic correlates of emotion/affect in the acoustic characteristics of the signal. It has been suggested that acoustic correlates of emotion can be described using pitch contour, utterance timing, and voice quality. The intonation group, also known as a breath-group, tone-group, or intonation phrase, is usually defined as the segment of an utterance between two pauses. In this chapter, the intonation group is adopted as the basic segment for feature extraction and classification. Besides, some pitch patterns are especially significant for the discrimination of emotional states. Therefore, the definition of the intonation group is adopted for feature extraction.

6.4.1.1 Intonation Group Extraction

The intonation group identification process starts from pitch detection and smoothing. In order to retain the special pattern of emotional pitch contour, the original pitch contour is presegmented according to some predefined characteristics of the parts with no pitch or rapid change. Inside each segmented part, the smoothing process is only done on the part with pitch.

As shown in Figure 6.2, the intonation group is identified by analyzing the smoothed pitch contour (the thick gray line in the figure). Three types of smoothed pitch contour patterns are defined as the intonation group:

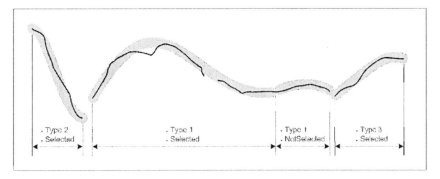

Fig. 6.2 An illustration of the definition and extraction of intonation groups. Four IGs are extracted from the smoothed pitch contour (thick gray line), but only three IGs (first, second, and forth IGs) are selected for feature extraction.

- *Type 1:* A complete pitch segment that starts from the point of a pitch rise to the point of the next pitch rise
- *Type 2:* A monotonically decreasing pitch segment
- *Type 3:* A monotonically increasing pitch segment

From the experimental investigation, it can be found that there are some emotion-dependent occurrences of pitch contour patterns. For example, the monotonic decreasing pitch contour pattern frequently appears in sad but rarely appears in neutral emotion. This investigation can help IG selection and feature extraction. In our approach, only the following kinds of IGs are used for feature extraction.

- The complete IGs with the largest pitch range or duration
- The monotonically decreasing or increasing IGs with the largest pitch range or duration
- The monotonically decreasing or increasing IGs at the start or end of a sentence

As shown in Figure 6.2, only three IGs are selected for feature extraction.

6.4.1.2 IG-Based Feature Extraction

Emotional state can be characterized by many speech features, such as pitch, energy, or duration (Ververidis, Kotropoulos, & Pitas, 2005). Deciding appropriate acoustic features is a crucial issue for emotion recognition. This study adopts pitch and energy features and their derivatives. In addition, trembling speech, unvoiced speech, speech duration, and hesitation contain useful characteristics for emotion detection. These features are also extracted in the related study. In total, the following 64 prosodic features are employed as the input features for emotion recognition.

- Speaking rate and relative duration (2 values). The relative duration is normalized with respect to the length of the input sentence.
- Pause number and relative pause duration (2 values). The relative duration is normalized with respect to the length of the intonation group.
- Average and standard deviation of pitch, energy, zero-crossing-rate, and F1 values (8 values).
- Average and standard deviation of jitter (for pitch) and shimmer (for energy) (4 values).
- Maximum and minimum of pitch, energy, zero-crossing-rate, and F1 values (8 values).
- Relative positions at which the maximal pitch, energy, zero-crossing-rate, and F1 value occur (4 values).
- Relative positions at which the minimal pitch, energy, zero-crossing-rate, and F1 value occur (4 values).
- Fourth-order Legendre parameters of pitch, energy, zero-crossing-rate, and F1 contours of the whole sentence (16 values).
- Fourth-order Legendre parameters of pitch, energy, zero-crossing-rate, and F1 contours of the segment during the positions of maximum and minimum values (16 values).

The definitions of jitter and shimmer are given in Levity, Huberz, Batlinery, & Noeth (2001). Jitter is a variation of individual cycle lengths in pitch-period measurement. Similarly, shimmer is the measure for energy values. The calculation of jitter contour is shown as follows.

$$J_i = \frac{\sum_{u=0}^{m} f_i - ug_u}{f_i}, \quad g = \frac{1}{4}\{-1,3,-3,1\}, \tag{6.5}$$

where variable f_i indicates the ith pitch value. The mean and standard deviation of jitter are calculated by Equations (6.6) and (6.7), respectively.

$$J_{avg} = \frac{\sum_{J_i < J_\theta} J_i}{\#_{J_i < J_\theta} J_i}, \tag{6.6}$$

$$J_{dev} = \sqrt{\frac{\sum_{J_i < J_\theta} (J_i - J_{avg})^2}{\#_{J_i < J_\theta} J_i}}. \tag{6.7}$$

In order to remove the discontinuities in the contour, pitch and energy features are smoothed by a window method.

6.4.2 Compensation Vector Estimation Using MCE

The goal of feature compensation is to move the feature space of an emotional state to a feature space more discriminative to other emotional states. Given is a sequence of the training data $X^e = \{x_n^e\}_{n=1}^N$, where x_n^e indicates the nth feature vector that belongs to emotional state E_e. The feature vector extracted for each intonation group contains the prosodic features mentioned above. With the assumption of linear mapping between feature spaces in different emotional states, the vector compensation function is defined as

$$\tilde{x}_n^{e \to f} = x_n^e + p(E_e | x_n^e) r_{e \to f}, \tag{6.8}$$

where $r_{e \to f}$ is a compensation vector of emotional state E_e with respect to the reference emotional state E_f. The basic concept for feature vector compensation is shown in Figure 6.3.

The conditional probability of the emotional state E_e given the input feature vector x_n^e is estimated as

$$p(E_e | x_n^e) = \frac{p(x_n^e | E_e) p(E_e)}{\sum_i p(x_n^e | E_i) p(E_i)}. \tag{6.9}$$

Minimum classification error training based on the generalized probabilistic descent (GPD) method is applied in this chapter. It is assumed that the probability of a

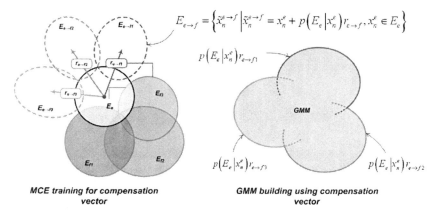

$$E_{e\to f} = \left\{ \tilde{x}_n^{e\to f} \middle| \tilde{x}_n^{e\to f} = x_n^e + p\left(E_e \middle| x_n^e\right) r_{e\to f}, x_n^e \in E_e \right\}$$

MCE training for compensation
vector

GMM building using compensation
vector

Fig. 6.3 Illustration of feature vector compensation.

mapped feature vector $\tilde{x}_n^{e\to f}$ given an emotional state E_c follows the distribution of a mixture of Gaussian density function:

$$g_c\left(\tilde{x}_n^{e\to f}\right) \equiv p\left(\tilde{x}_n^{e\to f} \middle| E_c\right) = \sum_m w_m^c \cdot N\left(\tilde{x}_n^{e\to f}; \mu_m^c, \delta_m^c\right), \qquad (6.10)$$

where $N\left(\cdot; \mu_m^c, \delta_m^c\right)$ denotes the normal distribution with mean μ_m^c and diagonal covariance matrix δ_m^c, and w_m^c is the mixture weight. To estimate the mapping coefficients and GMM parameters jointly by MCE training, the misclassification measure is defined as

$$D_e \equiv D\left(\mathbf{X}_e\right) = -g_e\left(\mathbf{X}_e\right) + \frac{1}{\eta} \log\left[\frac{1}{\mathbf{C}-1} \sum_{c\neq e} \exp\left(\eta \cdot g_c\left(\mathbf{X}_e\right)\right)\right], \qquad (6.11)$$

where X_e denotes a set of data compensated from the emotional state E_e, $X_e = \left\{\tilde{x}_n^{e\to f}\right\}_{f\neq e}$, $\mathbf{C}$ is the number of emotional state, and η is a penalty factor. The function $g_c\left(\mathbf{X}_e\right)$ is the average likelihood estimated by the GMM of the emotional state E_c given $\mathbf{X}_e$. Based on the GPD iterative theory, the parameters will approximate the global optimization using the iterative equation:

$$\Theta_{t+1} = \Theta_t - \varepsilon \cdot \nabla l. \qquad (6.12)$$

The loss function is defined as a sigmoid function of the misclassification measure. And the gradient of loss function ∇l is the partial differential to the updated parameter. Using the chain rule, the gradient of loss function can be divided into three components. The first component can be derived to a closed form $a \cdot l_e \cdot (1 - l_e)$, and the second component is defined as

$$\frac{\partial D_e}{\partial g_c} = \begin{cases} -1, & e=c \\ 1, & e\neq c \end{cases}. \qquad (6.13)$$

Because there are four different parameters that need to be updated, the last component of the gradient with respect to each parameter is obtained as

$$\frac{\partial g_e}{\partial r_{e\to f}} = \frac{-1}{N(C-1)} \sum_n \sum_m \frac{w_m^e \left(\tilde{x}_n^{e\to f} - \mu_m^e \right) p(E_e | x_n^e)}{(\delta_n^e)^2} N(x_n^e; \mu_m^e, \delta_n^e), \quad (6.14)$$

$$\frac{\partial g_e}{\partial w_m^e} = \frac{1}{N(C-1)} \sum_n \sum_r N\left(\tilde{x}_n^{e\to f}; \mu_m^e, \delta_m^e \right), \quad (6.15)$$

$$\frac{\partial g_e}{\partial \mu_m^e} = \frac{1}{N(C-1)} \sum_n \sum_r \left[w_m^e \left(\tilde{x}_n^{e\to f} - \mu_m^e \right) (\delta_m^e)^{-2} N\left(\tilde{x}_n^{e\to f}; \mu_m^e, \delta_m^e \right) \right], \quad (6.16)$$

$$\frac{\partial g_e}{\partial \delta_m^e} = \frac{1}{N(C-1)} \sum_n \sum_e \left[w_m^e \left(\left(\tilde{x}_n^{e\to f} - \mu_m^e \right)^2 - (v_m^e)^2 \right) (v_m^e)^{-3} N\left(\tilde{x}_n^{e\to f}; \mu_m^e, \delta_m^e \right) \right],$$

$$(6.17)$$

Given an input feature vector y, the recognized emotional state E_e^* is determined according to the following equation.

$$E_e^* = \arg\max_e \left[\sum_{i\neq e} g_e\left(y + p(E_e|y)r_{e\to i}\right) \middle/ \sum_{j\neq e} g_j\left(y + p(E_j|y)r_{j\to e}\right) \right]. \quad (6.18)$$

6.4.3 Experimental Results

For system evaluation, in order to obtain the real emotional state from natural speech signals, the training corpus was collected from a broadcast drama. There are 1085 sentences in 227 dialogues from the leading man and 1015 sentences in 213 dialogues from the leading woman. The emotional states of these sentences were manually tagged. The result of emotion tagging is listed in Table 6.3. The outside test was performed with an extra corpus collected from different chapters of the drama. There are in total 400 sentences in 51 dialogues in this corpus. The system has been implemented on a personal computer with Pentium IV CPU and 512 MB memory. A preprocessing step including endpoint detection and DC bias elimination was applied to all recorded sentences before emotion recognition process.

Table 6.3 Statistics of the Tagged Emotion Sentences in the Test Corpus

	Number of Tagged Sentences	
	Male	Female
Happiness	126	121
Sadness	121	92
Anger	98	80
Neutral	1617	1530

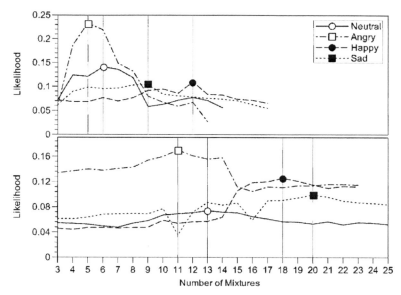

Fig. 6.4 The likelihood contours of GMMs with increasing mixture number. The upper part is the plot using prosodic features, and the lower part is the plot using MFCC features.

6.4.3.1 Mixture Number Determination

The number of mixtures in the GMM is first determined for each emotional state. Assuming that the number of mixtures is greater than 3, the average likelihood of all training data given the GMM with different mixture numbers is calculated. Figure 6.4 shows the plot of GMM likelihoods using both prosodic and MFCC features. Accordingly, the number of mixtures using prosodic features is set to 6, 5, 12, and 9 for neutral, angry, happy, and sad emotions, respectively. To evaluate the performance of MFCC features, the number of mixtures was also evaluated using the same method. The contours of the likelihood using MFCC features are also shown in Figure 6.4, and the mixture numbers for neutral, angry, happy, and sad emotions are set to 13, 11, 18, and 20, respectively.

6.4.3.2 Experiments on Emotion Recognition

In addition to the proposed prosodic features, the recognition rate for MFCC features was also evaluated, which is generally used in speech recognition tasks. To investigate the performance of the proposed method, both the proposed method and a baseline system, which is a GMM emotion recognition system, were tested without any preprocessing before feature extraction. Table 6.4 shows the results of the first experiment, which is the performance of a system without feature compensation. In this table, Outside–Open (OO) represents that the test data are from

Table 6.4 The Emotion Recognition Result of a System Without Feature Compensation[a]

Rec. App.	PROS (%)	MFCC (%)	PROS+IG (%)	MFCC+IG (%)
Without FC (In)	74.33	99.96	76.32	99.24
Without FC (OO)	49.78	35.15	51.07	35.01
Without FC (OC)	55.95	37.22	59.90	42.13

[a]In indicates the result of Inside test. OO and OC indicate the results of Outside–Open and Outside–Close tests, respectively.

Table 6.5 Emotion Recognition Results of the Feature Compensation Method

Rec. App.	PROS (%)	MFCC (%)	PROS+IG (%)	MFCC+IG (%)
With FC (In)	80.72	95.12	83.94	91.32
With FC (OO)	55.19	41.27	60.13	49.10
With FC (OC)	61.03	41.03	67.52	52.86

different speakers, and Outside–Close (OC) denotes that the test data are from the same speakers but not used for training.

Although the MFCC feature outperforms the prosodic feature in the inside test, the prosodic feature has better performance in both outside–open and outside–close tests. The reason for this result is that the MFCC features contain much acoustic information and are sensitive to the speech content and speaker. Modeling the emotional state using MFCC features turns out to model the speech content and speaker. Therefore, a GMM can perfectly model the distribution of MFCC vectors, but cannot predict the unseen vectors well.

In the second experiment, the recognition rate of the proposed feature compensation method was tested. The result is shown in Table 6.5.

In Table 6.5, although the MFCC features remain its higher recognition rate in the inside test, the proposed method with prosodic feature achieved the best overall performance.

From the above two experiments, we demonstrate the performance for the approach based on IG-based feature extraction and feature compensation. The increase of recognition rate without and with IG-based feature extraction is about 5% to 10%, and the improvement on feature compensation is about 10%.

6.4.3.3 Summary of Case Study

In this case study, the feature analysis and models employed to recognize emotion from speech are presented. An overall sample of emotion recognition from speech signals is illustrated. In order to obtain crucial features, the IG-based feature extraction method is used. After feature extraction, the feature vector compensation approach and MCE training method are applied to increase the discriminability among emotional states. The experiments show that it is useful to integrate IG-based feature extraction and feature compensation to emotion recognition. The result of emotion recognition using the proposed approaches is 83.94% for the inside test and 60.13% for the outside–open test. It demonstrated that the prosodic feature is more suitable for emotion recognition than the acoustic MFCC features in a speaker-independent task.

6.5 Conclusion

This chapter reviews some basic features and recognition algorithms for emotion recognition from speech. A case study is introduced to give a more practical description of emotion recognition. In this case study, the intonation groups of the input speech signals are first selected. A feature compensation approach is proposed to characterize the feature space with better discriminability among emotional states. The IG-based feature vectors compensated by the compensation vectors are used in the GMM for emotional state modeling.

Considering the existing features and methods, there are some important issues that should be considered. How can the recognition be improved in accuracy for outside data? How to deal with the variances in speaking styles of spontaneous speech? Future work includes adaptive recognition and incremental learning methods for emotion recognition from speech. Instead of recognizing the emotion in a single utterance, discourse analysis and emotion state transition will be one of the mainstreams in affective computing. For some applications in practice, personalized emotion recognition approaches will be an essential research issue in the near future.

References

Bhatti, M. W., Wang, Y., & Guan, L. (2004). A neural network approach for human emotion recognition in speech. *IEEE International Symposium on Circuits and Systems*, Vancouver, Canada (pp. 181–184).

Borod, J. C., & Madigan, N. K. (2000). Neuropsychology of emotion and emotional disorders: An overview and research directions. In J. C. Borod (Ed.), *The Neuropsychology of Emotion* (pp. 3–28). New York: Oxford University Press.

Breazeal, C., & Aryananda, L. (2002). Recognition of affective communicative intent in robot-directed speech. *Autonomic Robots, 12*, 83–104.

Breiman, L. (2001). Random forests. *Machine Learning, 45*, 5–32.

Chuang, Z. J., & Wu, C. H. (2004). Multi-modal emotion recognition from speech and text. *International Journal of Computational Linguistics and Chinese Language Processing, 9*(2), 1–18

Cichosz, J., & Slot, K. (2005). Low-dimensional feature space derivation for emotion recognition. In *Interspeech 2005*, Lisbon, Portugal (pp. 477–480).

Cichosz, J., & Slot, K. (2007). Emotion recognition in speech signal using emotion-extracting binary decision trees. *ACII* 2007. http://www.di.uniba.it/intint/DC-ACII07/Chicosz.pdf

Cover, T. T., & Hart, P. E. (1967). Nearest neighbour pattern classification. *IEEE Transactions on Information Theory, 13*, 21–27.

Damasio, A. (1994). *Descartes' error: Emotion, reason and the human brain*. New York: Grosset/Putnam.

Deng, L., Droppo, J., & Acero, A. (2003). Recursive estimation of nonstationary noise using iterative stochastic approximation for robust speech recognition. *IEEE Transactions on Speech and Au-dio, 11*(6), 568–580.

Devillers, L., Vidrascu, L., & Lamel, L. (2005). Challenges in real-life emotion annotation and machine learning based detection. *Neural Networks, 18*, 407–422.

D'Mello, S. Picard, R. W. & Graesser, A. (2007). Towards an affect-sensitive autotutor. *IEEE Intelligent Systems*, Special issue on intelligent educational systems, 53–61.

Engberg, I. S., & Hansen, A. V. (1996). Documentation of the Danish emotional speech database (DES). Internal AAU Report, Center for Person Kommunikation, Denmark.

Fernandez, R., & Picard, R. W. (2005). Classical and novel discriminant features for affect recognition from speech. In *Interspeech 2005*, Lisbon, Portugal (pp. 473–476).

Fragopanagos, N. & Taylor, J. G. (2005). Emotion recognition in human-computer interaction. *Neural Networks, 18*(4), 389–405.

Huber, R., Noth, E., Batliner, A., Buckow, J., Warnke, V., & Niemann, H. (1998). You beep machine - emotion in automatic speech understanding systems. In *Proceedings of the Workshop on Text, Speech, and Dialog*. Masark University (pp. 223–228).

Inanoglu, Z., & Caneel, R. (2005). Emotive alertHMM-based emotion detection in voicemail messages. In *IEEE Intelligent User Interfaces '05*, San Diego (pp. 251–253).

Katz, G., Cohn, J., & Moore, C. (1996). A combination of vocal F0 dynamic and summary features discriminates between pragmatic categories of infant-directed speech. *Child Development, 67*, 205–217.

Kwon O., Chan K., Hao J., & Lee T. (2003). Emotion recognition by speech signals. In *Proceedings of Eurospeech 2003*, Geneva (pp. 125–128).

Lee, C.-H., Clements, M., Dusan, S., Fosler-Lussier, E., Johnson, K., Juang, B.-H., & Rabiner, L. (2007). An overview on automatic speech attribute transcription (ASAT). In *Proceedings of Interspeech 2007*, August 27–31, Antwerp, Belgium (pp. 1825–1828).

Lee, C. M., & Narayanan, S. S. (2005). Toward detecting emotions in spoken dialogs. *IEEE Transactions on Speech and Audio Processing, 13*(2), 293–303.

Levity, M., Huberz, R., Batlinery, A., & Noeth, E. (2001). Use of prosodic speech characteristics for automated detection of alcohol intoxication. In *Prosody in Speech Recognition and Understanding*, Molly Pitcher Inn, Red Bank, NJ.

Liscombe, J., Riccardi, G., & Hakkani-Tr, D. (2005). Using context to improve emotion detection in spoken dialogue systems. In *Proceedings of Interspeech*, Lisbon, Portugal (pp. 1845–1848).

Litman D., & Silliman, S. (2004). Itspoke. An intelligent tutoring spoken dialogue system. In *Proceedings of the 4th Meeting of HLT/NAACL (Companion Proceedings)*, Boston, May (pp. 233–236).

Morrison, D., Wang, R., & De Silva, L. C. (2007). Ensemble methods for spoken emotion recognition in call-centres. *Speech Communication, 49*, 98–112.

Murray, I. R., & Arnott, J. L. (1993). Towards the simulation of emotion in synthetic speech: A review of the literature on human vocal emotion. *Journal of the Acoustic Society of America, 93*(2), 1097–1108.

Nakatsu, R., Solomides, A., & Tosa, N. (1999). Emotion recognition and its application to computer agents with spontaneous interactive capabilities. In *Proceedings of the IEEE International Conference on Multimedia Computing and Systems (ICMCS '99)* (vol. 2; pp. 804–808).

Nwe, T., Foo, S., & De Silva, L. (2003). Speech emotion recognition using hidden Markov models. *Speech Communications, 41*(4), 603–623.

Ortony, A., & Turner, T. J. (1990). What's basic about basic emotions? *Psychological Review, 97*, 315–331.

Oudeyer, P. (2003). The production and recognition of emotions in speech: features and algorithms. *International Journal of Human–Computer Studies, 59*, 157–183.

Paeschke, A., & Sendlmeier, W. (2000). Prosodic characteristics of emotional speech: Measurements of fundamental frequency movements. In *Proceedings of ISCA ITRW on Speech and Emotion*, Belfast (pp. 75–80).

Pantic, M., & Rothkrantz, L. J. K. (2003). Toward an affect-sensitive multimodal human–computer interaction. *Proceedings of the IEEE, 91*(9), 1370–1390

Parrott, W. (2001). *Emotions in social psychology*, Philadelphia: Psychology Press.

Petrushin, V. (2000). Emotion recognition in speech signal: Experimental study, development, and application. In *Proceedings of the Sixth International Conference on Spoken Language Processing (ICSLP 2000)*, Beijing (pp. 222–225).

Petrushin, V. A. (1999). Emotion in speech recognition and application to call centers. In *Proceedings of Artificial Neural Networks In Engineering (ANNIE 99)* (pp. 7–10).

Picard, R. W., Vyzas, E., & Healey, J. (2001). Toward machine emotional intelligence: analysis of affective physiological state. *IEEE Transactions on Pattern Analysis and Machine Intelligence, 23*(10), 1175–1191

Pierre-Yves, O. (2003). The production and recognition of emotions in speech: Features and algorithms. *International Journal of Human-Computer Studies, 59*, 157–183

Rahurkar, M. A., & Hansen, J. H. L.(2003). Frequency distribution based weighted sub-band approach for classification of emotional/stressful content in speech. In *Eighth European Conference on Speech Communication and Technology*, Geneva (pp. 721–724).

Reeves, B., & Nass, C. (1996). *The media equation: How people treat computers, television, and new media like real people and places*. University of Chicago Press, Chicago.

Scherer, K. R. (1999). Appraisal theory. In T. Dalgleish, & M. Power (Eds.), *Handbook of cognition and emotion* (pp. 637–663). New York: John Wiley.

Shami, M., & Kamel, M. (2005). Segment-based approach to the recognition of emotions in speech. In *IEEE Conference on Multimedia and Expo (ICME05)*, Amsterdam, The Netherlands. http://ieeexplore.ieee.org/iel5/10203/32544/01521436.pdf?tp=&isnumber=&arnumber=1521436

Shami, M., & Verhelst, W. (2007). An evaluation of the robustness of existing supervised machine learning approaches to the classification of emotions in speech. *Speech Communication 49*, 201–212.

Shriberg, E. (2005). Spontaneous speech: How people really talk and why engineers should care. In *Eurospeech 2005*, Lisbon, Portugal.

Slaney, M., & McRoberts, G. (2003). A recognition system for affective vocalization. *Speech Communication 39*, 367–384.

Ten Bosch, L. (2003). Emotions, speech and the ASR framework. *Speech Communication 40*(1–2), 213–225.

Vapnik, V. (2005). *The nature of statistical learning theory*. New York: Springer-Verlag.

Ververidis, D., Kotropoulos, C., & Pitas, I. (2005). Automatic emotional speech classification. In *IEEE International Conference on Acoustics, Speech, and Signal Processing*, Montreal (pp. 593–596).

Wu, J., & Huo, Q. (2002). An environment compensated minimum classification error training approach and its evaluation on aurora2 database. In *Seventh International Conference on Spoken Language*, Denver (pp. 453–456).

Yacoub, S., Simske, S., Lin, X., & Burns, J. (2003). Recognition of emotion in interactive voice systems. In: *Proceedings of Eurospeech 2003, Eighth European Conference on Speech Communication and Technology*, Geneva (pp. 729–732).

Chapter 7
Expressive Speech Synthesis: Past, Present, and Possible Futures

Marc Schröder

Abstract Approaches towards adding expressivity to synthetic speech have changed considerably over the last 20 years. Early systems, including formant and diphone systems, have been focused around "explicit control" models; early unit selection systems have adopted a "playback" approach. Currently, various approaches are being pursued to increase the flexibility in expression while maintaining the quality of state-of-the-art systems, among them a new "implicit control" paradigm in statistical parametric speech synthesis, which provides control over expressivity by combining and interpolating between statistical models trained on different expressive databases. The present chapter provides an overview of the past and present approaches, and ventures a look into possible future developments.

7.1 Introduction

Synthetic speech nowadays is mostly intelligible; in some cases, it also sounds so natural that it is difficult to distinguish it from human speech. However, the flexible and appropriate rendering of expressivity in a synthetic voice is still out of reach: making a voice sound happy or subdued, friendly or empathic, authoritative or uncertain are beyond what can be done today. Indeed, even though quite some research has been carried out on the issue of adding any kind of recognisable expressivity to synthetic speech, the question of its "appropriateness" in a given communicative situation has barely been touched upon.

This chapter aims to give an overview of the work in the area in the past and in present work, and points to some types of developments that may bring substantial contributions to the area in the future.

Adding expressivity to a synthetic voice has two aspects: being able to realise an expressive effect, that is, having the technological means to control the acoustic

M. Schröder
DFKI GmbH, Saarbrücken, Germany
e-mail: schroed@dfki.de

J.H. Tao, T.N. Tan (eds.), *Affective Information Processing*,
© Springer Science+Business Media LLC 2009

111

realisation, and having a model of how the system's realisation, should sound in order to convey the intended expression. We show that some progress has been made on both of these levels, but that neither the technological means of control nor the models of expressivity in state-of-the-art systems are anywhere close to what would be needed for truly natural expressive speech synthesis. Nevertheless, it is interesting to look at existing approaches to understand the challenges involved.

The chapter is structured in terms of technologies as they evolve over time. Through that structure, it will become clear that the technologies are not independent of the approach chosen for modelling expressivity, but that each technology has its favourite and natural control model: "explicit control" and "playback" in early times, and "implicit control" in some of the current works.

7.2 A Short History of Expressive Speech Synthesis

Work on emotional expressivity in synthetic speech goes back to the end of the 1980s. As technology evolved, different technologies have been used, each with their strengths and weaknesses. The following sections provide a concise overview of the range of techniques employed over time; for more details, see Schröder (2008).

7.2.1 Formant Synthesis

Rule-based formant synthesis, the oldest speech synthesis technique, predicts the acoustic realisation of speech directly using a set of rules, usually designed carefully by experts. As these rules tend not to capture the complexity of natural human speech, the synthetic speech sounds unnatural and 'robotlike'. By its very nature, however, formant synthesis allows for control over a broad range of parameters, including glottal as well as supraglottal aspects of speech production. Many of these parameters are potentially relevant for modelling expressive speech.

The first emotionally expressive speech synthesis systems were created based on the commercial formant synthesiser DECTalk: both Cahn's (1990) Affect Editor and Murray and Arnott's (1995) HAMLET added emotion-specific acoustic modification modules on top of that system. For each emotion category, they implemented an explicit model for the acoustic realisation, drawing on the existing literature and fine-tuning the rules in a trial-and-error procedure.

In a more recent study, Burkhardt and Sendlmeier (2000) used formant synthesis to systematically vary acoustic settings in order to find perceptually optimal values for a number of emotion categories. A first coarse exploration of a five-dimensional acoustic space was followed by an optimisation phase adding parameters based on the literature in order to increase the specificity of emotion patterns.

Examples for the kinds of explicit emotion models implemented in these systems are listed in Table 7.1.

Table 7.1 Examples of Successful Explicit Prosody Rules for Emotion Expression in Synthetic speech

Emotion Study Language Rec. Rate	Parameter Settings
Joy Burkhardt & Sendlmeier (2000) German 81% (1/9)	**F0 mean**: +50% **F0 range**: +100% **Tempo**: +30% **Voice Qu.**: modal or tense; "lip-spreading feature": F1/F2 +10% **Other**: "wave pitch contour model": main stressed syllables are raised (+100%), syllables in between are lowered (−20%)
Sadness Cahn (1990) American English 91% (1/6)	**F0 mean**: "0", reference line "−1", less final lowering "−5" **F0 range**: "−5", steeper accent shape "+6" **Tempo**: "−10", more fluent pauses "+5", hesitation pauses "+10" **Loudness**: "−5" **Voice Qu.**: breathiness "+10", brilliance "−9" **Other**: stress frequency "+1", precision of articulation "−5"
Anger Murray & Arnott's (1995) British English	**F0 mean**: +10 Hz **F0 range**: +9 s.t. **Tempo**: +30 wpm **Loudness**: +6 dB **Voice Qu.**: laryngealisation +78%; F4 frequency −175 Hz **Other**: increase pitch of stressed vowels (2ary: +10% of pitch range; 1ary: +20%; emphatic: +40%)
Fear Burkhardt & Sendlmeier (2000) German 52% (1/9)	**F0 mean**: " + 150%" **F0 range**: "+20%" **Tempo**: "+30%" **Voice Qu.**: falsetto
Surprise Cahn (1990) American English 44% (1/6)	**F0 mean**: "0", reference line "−8" **F0 range**: "+8", steeply rising contour slope "+10", steeper accent shape "+5" **Tempo**: "+4", less fluent pauses "−5", hesitation pauses "−10" **Loudness**: "+5" **Voice Qu.**: brilliance "−3"
Boredom Mozziconacci (1998) Dutch 94% (1/7)	**F0 mean**: end frequency 65 Hz (male speech) **F0 range**: excursion size 4 s.t. **Tempo**: duration rel. to neutrality: 150% **Other**: final intonation pattern 3C, avoid final patterns 5&A and 12

From Schröder (2001).
Recognition rates are presented with chance level for comparison. Sadness and Surprise: Cahn uses parameter scales from −10 to +10, 0 being neutral; Boredom: Mozziconacci indicates intonation patterns according to a Dutch grammar of intonation; see Mozziconacci (1998) for details.

7.2.2 Diphone Concatenation

In the early 1990s, a fundamentally different synthesis technology gained popularity: synthesis by concatenation, that is, by resequencing small pieces of human speech recordings. The early systems recorded one example of each "diphone" – the piece of a speech signal going from the middle of one phone to the middle of the next phone – usually at monotone pitch. By reordering these, any phone sequence in a given language can be generated. Through signal-processing techniques such as pitch-synchronous overlap-add (PSOLA; Charpentier & Moulines, 1989), different F0 contours and duration patterns could be realised at the price of a certain degree of distortion. The resulting quality is usually quite a bit better than formant synthesis; however, it is important to note that the voice quality (tense, creaky, lax, etc.) is fixed, determined by the rendition of the speaker during diphone recordings.

Therefore, when using diphone synthesis for expressive speech, it is a crucial question whether it is acceptable not to modify voice quality, that is, whether F0 and duration alone can create a desired expressive effect. Interestingly, different studies have come to different conclusions on this matter. A majority (e.g., Vroomen, Collier, & Mozziconacci, 1993; Edgington, 1997; Montero, Gutiérrez-Arriola, Colás, Enríquez, & Pardo, 1999) report at least some degree of success in conveying various emotions; some, however, report recognition rates close to chance level (Heuft, Portele, & Rauth, 1996; Rank & Pirker, 1998). Indeed, by cross-combining voice quality and prosody of different expressive styles, Montero et al. (1999) and Audibert, Vincent, Aubergé, and Rosec (2006) found that for a given speaker, the relative contribution of prosody and voice quality depends on the emotion expressed. However, there is not yet a clear picture which emotions predominantly rely on voice quality and which can be recognised based on prosody. Indeed, it may be (Schröder, 1999) that different speaker strategies exist to express the same emotion, relying to various extents on voice quality and on prosody.

In the absence of explicit parametric control over voice quality, one approach is to record the diphone inventory with the same speaker's voice in different voice qualities (Schröder & Grice, 2003); in order to change the voice quality, one needs to switch to a different diphone inventory from the same speaker.

7.2.3 Explicit Prosody Control

The synthesis methods described above require explicit settings for prosodic parameters in order to convey emotional expressivity. How are these settings determined?

A straightforward approach to control the acoustic correlates of a given emotion is to copy a natural rendition, the so-called 'copy synthesis' (e.g., Bulut, Narayanan, & Syrdal, 2002): the parameters that can be controlled in the synthesizer (e.g., F0 and duration) are measured in an expressive recording, and used directly as the input to a synthesizer. This method is appropriate for testing to which extent a given synthesis method can reproduce the same auditory impression as a human speech sample; however, the generalisability is obviously low.

A general text-to-speech setting requires an automatic way of computing the acoustic correlates of an expression from a representation of an emotion. With formant and diphone synthesis, such a model needs to link explicitly the emotion with its acoustics, in the sense that the parameters through which the emotion is expressed are clearly listed and the respective effect is explicitly stated. As we show below, this contrasts with the implicit modelling introduced in recent statistical synthesis approaches.

Explicit prosody models have been formulated based on various sources of information. Usually, rules are based on effects reported in the literature (e.g., Cahn, 1990), on analyses of own data (e.g., Iriondo et al., 2000), or on perception studies (e.g., Burkhardt & Sendlmeier, 2000), and are fine-tuned in a manual trial-and-error procedure. Clearly, such rules can only be as good as the quality of the literature reports, data analysed, and the analysis and control parameters studied.

Table 7.1 lists some examples of explicit prosody rule sets as described in the literature, for a typical selection of emotional states modelled (from Schröder, 2001).

Systems vary with respect to the underlying representation of the "predictor" variables, for example, emotions: although most studies used emotion categories or other distinct states, it is also possible to use the emotion dimensions arousal, valence, and power (Schröder, 2006).

It is worth pointing out that even the relevant set of acoustic parameters is a research issue, and is far from being resolved. All studies in the area seem to agree on the importance of global prosodic settings, such as F0 level and range, speech tempo, and possibly loudness. Some studies try to go into more detail about these global settings, modelling for example, steepness of the F0 contour during rises and falls, distinguishing between articulation rate and the number and duration of pauses, or modelling additional phenomena such as voice quality or articulatory precision. A further step is the consideration of interactions with linguistic categories, such as further distinguishing between the speech tempo of vowels and consonants, of stressed and unstressed syllables, or the placement of pauses within utterances. The influence of linguistic prosodic categories, such as F0 contours, is only rarely taken into account, although these have been shown to play an important role in emotion recognition (Mozziconacci & Hermes, 1999; Burkhardt & Sendlmeier, 2000).

7.2.4 Unit Selection

In the mid-1990s, the concept of concatenative synthesis was developed further: instead of using just one example of each diphone recorded with a flat pitch, several versions of a diphone unit are recorded in natural speech. Through a sophisticated selection method, the most suitable chain of such units is determined for any given target sentence, hence the name *unit selection* synthesis. If suitable units are available in the recordings, no or very little signal processing is needed, and the resulting synthesized speech can sound highly natural, sometimes difficult to distinguish from natural human speech.

For expressive speech, the strength of the method – interfering with the recorded speech as little as possible – is also its main weakness: only the speaking style recorded in the database can be generated, and little or no control is available over prosody and voice quality.

Nevertheless, it is of course possible to generate expressive speech within the unit selection framework, in what could be called a "playback" approach: in order to generate speech in style X, a database in style X is recorded. In this way, Iida & Campbell (2003) have produced a system capable of speaking with the same person's voice in each of three emotions: happy, angry, and sad. To achieve the effect, the authors had to record three databases: one consisting of utterances spoken in a happy tone, one spoken in an angry tone, and one spoken in a sad tone. A given emotion was generated by selecting units only from the corresponding subset of the recordings.

Johnson, Narayanan, Whitney, Das, Bulut, and LaBore (2002) pursued a similar approach. They employed limited domain synthesis for the generation of convincing expressive military speech, in the framework of the Mission Rehearsal Exercise project. The styles, each recorded as an individual limited domain speech database, were shouted commands, shouted conversation, spoken commands, and spoken conversation.

Along the same line of thought, Pitrelli, Bakis, Eide, Fernandez, Hamza, and Picheny (2006) recorded full unit selection databases for a 'good news' versus a 'bad news' expressive voice by the same speaker.

7.3 Current Trends in Expressive Speech Synthesis

It becomes clear from this short historic overview of formant, diphone, and unit selection synthesis that these technologies form a dichotomy between flexibly parameterisable systems on the one hand, requiring explicit acoustic models of expressivity which are difficult to formulate, and natural-sounding but inflexible "playback" systems.

In recent times, a range of approaches is being pursued to overcome this separation, by adding more control to data-driven synthesis methods in various ways. This section reviews some of the major trends.

7.3.1 Expressivity-Based Selection of Units

In unit selection synthesis, the notion of a 'target' is central; units that are similar to the given target are likely to be selected. Originally, this target is defined in purely linguistic terms: phone identity, context, position in the sentence, and so on. Some systems also employ acoustic targets, in the sense of prosodic models trained on the synthesis database.

One important step towards flexible expressivity in unit selection synthesis would therefore be the use of expressivity-related targets in the selection process itself.

Such targets can be of two kinds: symbolic and acoustic. A symbolic target can be a label identifying the intended speaking style; strictly enforced, it amounts to the same kind of separation between expressive subsets as used in earlier works. However, it can be complemented with a cost matrix, which for a given target style allows for the selection of a unit with a different style at a cost. For example, it would be possible to allow both 'angry' and 'neutral' units for a 'sad' target, but to discourage the use of 'angry' units by giving them a high penalty. This approach was used in recent work by Fernandez and Ramabhadran (2007).

Acoustic expressive targets, on the other hand, rely on acoustical models of expressive styles to identify units that could be suitable for the targeted expressive style. A major attraction of this approach is that it could be used with unlabelled or only partially labelled databases.

The first attempt in this sense seems to have been published by Campbell and Marumoto (2000). They used parameters related to voice quality and prosody as emotion-specific selection criteria. Three emotion-specific databases (Iida & Campbell, 2003) were combined into one database. Different kinds of selection criteria were tested, including hidden Markov models trained on the emotion-specific subsets, and hand-crafted prosody rules. Recognition results in listening tests indicated a partial success: anger and sadness were recognised with up to 60% accuracy, whereas joy was not recognised above chance level.

Fernandez and Ramabhadran (2007) explored a semi-automatic recognition of emphasis for synthesis. A statistical acoustic model of emphasis was trained on a manually labelled database consisting of approximately 1,000 sentences; this model was then used to identify emphasised words in a larger unlabelled database consisting of about 10,000 sentences. Different symbolic labels were assigned for manually versus automatically labelled emphasis; in a cost matrix, for a target style 'emphasis,' manually labelled emphasis units were slightly favoured over automatically labelled ones. In a listening test, the authors could show that the automatic annotation in the large corpus increased the number of sentences where emphasis was perceived as intended, even if the total level stayed very low (at 51% in a two-class setup).

In the context of generating expressive synthetic speech from the recordings of an audio book, Wang, Chu, Peng, Zhao, and Soong (2007) have prepared the ground for future work by identifying a suitable perceptual annotation scheme for the speech material. Out of the 18,000 utterances of the audio book, a representative sample of 800 expressive utterances was annotated using auditory ratings of pitch, vocal effort, voice age, loudness, speaking rate, and speaking manner. In addition, similarity ratings of utterance pairs were obtained. A set of nine perceptually homogeneous speaking styles was determined by growing a classification tree, using similarity ratings between sentences as an impurity criterion and auditory ratings as decision nodes. The next step in their work is to train acoustic classifiers on the nine utterance clusters, and to use those classifiers to annotate the full database, which would allow for expressive unit selection in a way similar to that of Fernandez and Ramabhadran.

7.3.2 Unit Selection and Signal Modification

Signal modification, traditionally used in diphone synthesis, is usually avoided in unit selection because of the deteriorating effect on the overall speech quality. Nevertheless, it is possible to apply the same techniques, such as PSOLA, on unit selection output, modifying pitch and duration according to emotional prosody rules (Zovato, Pacchiotti, Quazza, & Sandri, 2004). As for diphone synthesis, this approach has the disadvantage of not being able to modify voice quality, and of creating audible distortions for larger modifications.

Research is underway to improve on that state of things. Working towards an explicit control of the voice source, d'Alessandro and Doval (2003) have proposed a method for modifying the glottal source spectrum, described by the parameters glottal formant and spectral tilt. They decompose the speech signal into a periodic and an aperiodic part, and recombine these after modifying them separately.

One of the main problems in model-based modification of voice quality is the reliable automatic estimation of voice source parameters from the speech signal. Avoiding the problem of inverse filtering, Vincent, Rosec, and Chonavel (2005) have proposed an analysis by synthesis method for the joint estimation of glottal source and vocal tract filter coefficients: for each speech frame, they try out all examples of a codebook of glottal source configurations, and use the one with which a linear predictive coding (LPC) analysis yields the smallest residual error. The method has been applied to the analysis of emotional speech (Audibert, et al., 2006) and could potentially be used for signal modification.

A data-driven alternative to such explicit modelling attempts is to use voice conversion techniques with expressive speech. The main difference is that in voice conversion, a source and a target need to be defined by datasets. The aim is to define a mapping function that can convert a large, high-quality source (e.g., a large neutral unit selection voice) into a target style for which only a small amount of recordings would be required. Carrying out research in this direction, Matsui and Kawahara (2003) converted one emotional recording of a speaker into a different emotion uttered by the same speaker. They achieved good recognition rates, but anchor points in the time–frequency plane had to be set manually. Ye and Young (2004) used voice morphing for converting one speaker's voice into another speaker's, by means of linear transformations in a sinusoidal model. The same technology could be used to convert a given speaker's voice expressing one emotion into the same speaker's voice expressing another emotion.

A further step towards flexible control in the data-driven framework is the use of interpolation technology, the creation of a mixed speech signal out of two different speech streams. A method for interpolating the spectral envelope of a source and a target voice was proposed by Turk, Schröder, Bozkurt, and Arslan (2005). They used diphone voices with different vocal effort (Schröder & Grice, 2003), and created intermediate voices. In a perception test, these were rated as intermediate in vocal effort to the respective source and target voices. The method can be incorporated into unit selection (Schröder, 2007), allowing for the continuous interpolation between a source and a target synthesis voice. The principle of interpolation is the same whether the target voice is recorded as in the 'playback' approaches described above, or whether it is the result of a mapping process in a voice conversion framework.

7.3.3 HMM-Based Parametric Speech Synthesis

A new synthesis technology is establishing itself as a serious alternative to unit selection synthesis: statistical parametric synthesis based on hidden Markov models. The method became very well known when it became the surprise winner of the first Blizzard speech synthesis competition in 2005 (Zen & Toda, 2005).

In essence, the method works as follows. Context-dependent HMMs are trained on a speech database; the spectrum, F0, and duration are modelled separately. The context-dependent models are organised in a decision tree; at run-time, for a given "target" context to be realised, the tree yields the appropriate HMM state sequence corresponding to that context, describing mean and standard deviation of the acoustic features. A vocoding technique is used to generate an audio signal from the acoustic features, resulting in a very intelligible, but muffled-sounding speech output.

By nature, the approach is an interesting hybrid between data-driven and parametrisable synthesis approaches: similarly to unit selection, the approach is relatively natural-sounding because it is trained on natural speech data, but unlike unit selection, the speech is generated from a parametric representation which can potentially be controlled if a suitable "handle" to the parameters is provided.

As in unit selection, the simplest approach to expressive speech with HMMs is to train models on speech produced with different speaking styles. Yamagishi, Onishi, Masuko, and Kobayashi (2003) trained HMM-based voices from four different speaking styles: 'reading', 'rough', 'joyful', and 'sad'. In addition to creating fully separate voices for each style, they also built a combined voice in which the style was part of the context description. For both kinds of voices, very high recognition rates were obtained in a perception test, showing that the basic technology can reproduce the style.

Although in theory it would be possible to influence the parametric representation generated by the HMMs in the sense of explicit models similarly to formant and diphone synthesis, work on flexible style control with HMM-based synthesis has pursued a different method. It could be called an 'implicit modelling approach,' because landmarks for interpolation are defined from data rather than by explicitly characterising them as acoustic configurations. In this line of thought, Miyanaga, Masuko, and Kobayashi (2004) presented a method to control speaking style by training style-specific HMM models and interpolating between them using a 'style vector.' Experiments were carried out that demonstrated, also for intermediate style values, a gradual effect on perceived style, for models trained on reading, joyful, rough, and sad speaking styles.

A further strength of HMM-based synthesis is that speaker-specific or style-specific voices can also be created by adaptation rather than training. While in training, a style-specific voice requires several hundreds of sentences spoken in a given speaking style, the adaptation of an average voice to a specific style can be performed with as little as a few dozen sentences. Yamagishi, Kobayashi, Tachibana, Ogata, and Nakano (2007) compared various adaptation techniques both in objective terms (objective distance to the target speech) and in terms of subjective similarity. Interestingly, they found that when creating a voice by adapting spectrum, F0, and duration of an average voice to 100 sentences from a target speaker, it sounded more similar to that target speaker than a voice trained on 453 sentences from that speaker. This is probably due to the greater robustness of the average voice model, trained on several thousands of sentences from various speakers. Note that from the point of view of technology, the terms 'speaker' and 'style' can be used interchangeably: if it is possible to adapt an average voice to a range of different speakers, it is very likely that it is also possible to adapt it to various speaking styles of one speaker.

In summary, even though this approach requires style-specific recordings as in unit selection, the resulting flexibility is greater. Because of the parametric representation, interpolation between the styles is possible, enabling the expression of low-intensity emotions by interpolation between a neutral speaking style and a high-intensity emotional speaking style. Similarly, blends of emotions can be generated by interpolating between two emotional speaking styles.

Table 7.2 summarises the approaches to parameterisation of expressive speech as found in current research on speech synthesis.

7.3.4 Nonverbal Vocalisations

As research on expressive speech is moving towards conversational speech, it is becoming clear that read speech is an insufficient basis. Expressive conversational speech does not result from applying suitable prosody modifications to read speech. Indeed, as Campbell (2007) showed, a large proportion of everyday vocalisations are nonverbal: laughs, speech 'grunts,' and other small sounds which are highly communicative but which are not adequately described as 'text plus prosody.'

To illustrate the point, Campbell (2005) has produced a conversational speech synthesizer which uses a huge database of everyday speech as the unit selection database. With adequate annotation of speech units and careful manual selection, this system can produce conversational speech of unprecedented naturalness. However, the subtleties of meaning produced and perceived by humans with respect to the meaning of nonverbal vocalisations in context are still far beyond the reach of current automatic selection algorithms.

The difficulty of identifying 'suitable' nonverbal expressions for the use with synthetic speech was illustrated by Trouvain and Schröder (2004). They inserted laughter sounds of different intensity into a short dialogue, and asked listeners to rate their appropriateness. The result clearly showed that the lowest-intensity laughs

Table 7.2 Current Approaches to the Parameterisation of Expressivity in State-of-the-Art Speech Synthesis

	Unit Selection		HMM-Based
	Selection of Units	**Signal Modification**	**Synthesis**
Explicit acoustic models	Hand-crafted prosody rules as targets (Campbell and Marumoto, 2000)	PSOLA with explicit rules (Zovato et al., 2004) Explicit control of glottal spectrum (d'Alessandro and Doval, 2003) Brute-force estimation of glottal source parameters (Vincent et al., 2005) (potentially usable for modification)	
Playback	Recording separate expressive voice databases (Iida and Campbell, 2003; Johnson et al., 2002) Manually labelled symbolic targets (Fernandez and Ramabhadran, 2007)		Train models on style-specific speech data (Yamagishi et al., 2003) Adapt models to style-specific speech data (Yamagishi et al., 2007)
Implicit acoustic models	HMM models as targets (Campbell and Marumoto, 2000) Automatically trained symbolic targets (Fernandez and Ramabhadran, 2007), potentially (Wang et al., 2007)	Voice conversion between emotional recordings of same speaker (Matsui and Kawahara, 2003), potentially (Ye and Young, 2004) Interpolation between recorded or converted voices (Turk et al., 2005; Schröder, 2007)	Interpolate between style-specific models (Miyanaga et al., 2004)

were perceived as most suitable. In a similar line of research, Schröder, Heylen, and Poggi (2006) investigated the suitability of various affect bursts (short emotional interjections, see Schröder (2003) for details) as listener feedback in a short natural language interaction. Suitability ratings were interpreted in terms of social appropriateness, of 'display rules' (Ekman, 1977), to be obeyed by a listener in a conversation.

From these works, it becomes clear that research on the use of nonverbal vocalisations in human–machine communication is still in its infancy, but further work will be inevitable if truly natural conversational speech synthesis is the goal.

7.4 Possible Future Directions for Expressive Speech Synthesis

So where is research on expressive speech synthesis heading? Will there be methods developed that are able to combine high quality with flexible control? Will they provide explicit or implicit control, in the sense of the words introduced above? Although of course it is impossible to predict the future, there are some tendencies visible or emerging today, which are worth having in mind when thinking about future developments.

One of the promising extensions of today's research is the improvement of vocoding algorithms for HMM-based speech synthesis. With more natural speech-generation methods, parametric systems would become a real competitor to concatenative systems, and would have the built-in advantage of providing implicit control over expressivity.

In the concatenative framework, improvements in selection, voice conversion, and interpolation may also lead to more expressive systems. The main challenge on this level is the instability of the synthesis quality in the face of missing data, and the degradation of signal quality incurred by signal modification.

Alternatively, it may be that statistical and concatenative approaches are becoming more similar. Already now, a 'hybrid' system that uses HMM-based statistical models to predict the target for unit selection was among the best ones in the Blizzard Challenge 2007 (Ling et al., 2007).

A promising avenue for explicit models seems to be opening up on the level of articulatory speech synthesis. Birkholz (2007) has proposed a sophisticated system capable of generating intelligible speech from a 'score' representation of articulator movements. Studies such as the one by Wollermann and Lasarcyk (2007), investigating the use of articulatory speech synthesis for emotional expression, are starting to appear. The tremendous potential of this method is given by the fact that an explicit model of physiological effects of emotions on the articulators could be specified, and its acoustic correlates can be computed through the articulatory model. Things such as the tension of the vocal folds, the absorption ratio of the walls of the vocal tract, or the precision of articulation, whose relations to emotions have been described in detail in the psychological literature on emotional speech (Scherer, 1986), can be modelled in an explicit way. The main shortcoming of the approach for the nonexpert is that there is not yet a fully working Text-to-Speech mode for this system; a considerable amount of expert knowledge is still required to design the articulator score from the text.

One major area where progress is direly needed is the (explicit or implicit) model of suitable expressions. Manually tuned rules tend to be overly simplified and exaggerated, so that some doubts are due whether purely manmade rules will be most successful. Machine-learning methods, on the other hand, depend crucially on suitable models and on large amounts of data. Models must describe not only the acoustics (the predictee), but also the causing factors serving as predictors; emotion, mood, communicative situation, social stance, physiological state, and so on must be expected to interact in producing the acoustic effect, and are likely to be used by a human listener when interpreting the meaning of an acoustic configuration in speech. Large-scale data collections such as the one by Campbell (2007) will help shed light on these effects if they are supplemented with suitable annotations of predictors.

Another interesting contribution to this area may come from cognitive systems that use the speech synthesizer as an actuator for interacting with their environment, such as Moore's PRESENCE model (Moore, 2007). Through a feedback mechanism, such a cognitive system can learn how to express itself appropriately in a given situation. Feedback can include, for example, proprioception (e.g., hearing oneself), explicit evaluation and correction by a human user, or success at performing a given task. Situationally adequate 'communication strategies' involving expressive speech may emerge from such systems that cannot be predicted today.

7.5 Summary and Conclusion

This chapter has attempted to trace the development of expressive speech synthesis since its beginnings, with formant synthesis, via early concatenative systems relying on explicit models of expressive prosody and 'playback' models, to current challenges in the area, which all seem to address the same issue from different angles: how to combine a high degree of naturalness with a suitable level of control over the expression. Based on the current state of affairs, the chapter also ventures some speculation about future developments, pointing out promising aspects in statistical, concatenative, and articulatory synthesis, and the challenge of learning appropriate rules, which may see some interesting 'fresh air' from the area of cognitive systems entering the field of speech synthesis.

Acknowledgements The preparation of this chapter has received funding from the EU project HUMAINE (IST-507422), the DFG project PAVOQUE, and from the European Community's Seventh Framework programme (FP7/2007-2013) under grant agreement no. 211486 (SEMAINE).

References

Audibert, N., Vincent, D., Aubergé V., & Rosec, O. (2006). Expressive speech synthesis: Evaluation of a voice quality centered coder on the different acoustic dimensions. In: *Proceedings of Speech Prosody*, Dresden, Germany.

Birkholz, P. (2007). Control of an articulatory speech synthesizer based on dynamic approximation of spatial articulatory targets. In: *Proceedings of Interspeech*, Antwerp, Belgium.

Bulut, M., Narayanan, S.S., & Syrdal, A.K. (2002). Expressive speech synthesis using a concatenative synthesiser. In: *Proceedings of the 7th International Conference on Spoken Language Processing*, Denver.

Burkhardt, F., & Sendlmeier, W.F. (2000). Verification of acoustical correlates of emotional speech using formant synthesis. In: *Proceedings of the ISCA Workshop on Speech and Emotion*, Northern Ireland, pp. 151–156.

Cahn, J.E. (1990). The generation of affect in synthesized speech. *Journal of the American Voice I/O Society*, 8, 1–19.

Campbell, N. (2005). Developments in corpus-based speech synthesis: Approaching natural conversational speech. IEICE *Transactions on Information and Systems* 88(3), 376–383.

Campbell, N. (2007). Approaches to conversational speech rhythm: Speech activity in two-person telephone dialogues. In: *Proceedings of the International Congress of Phonetic Sciences*, Saarbrücken, Germany, pp. 343–348.

Campbell, N., & Marumoto, T. (2000). Automatic labelling of voice-quality in speech databases for synthesis. In: *Proceedings of the 6th International Conference on Spoken Language Processing*, Beijing.

Charpentier, F., & Moulines, E. (1989). Pitch-synchronous waveform processing techniques for text-to-speech synthesis using diphones. In: *Proceedings of Eurospeech*, Paris, pp. 13–19.

d'Alessandro, C., & Doval, B. (2003). Voice quality modification for emotional speech synthesis. In: *Proceedings of Eurospeech 2003*, Geneva, Switzerland, pp. 1653–1656.

Edgington, M. (1997). Investigating the limitations of concatenative synthesis. In: *Proceedings of Eurospeech 1997*, Rhodes/Athens.

Ekman, P. (1977) Biological and cultural contributions to body and facial movement. In: J. Blacking (Ed.) *The anthropology of the body*, London: Academic Press, pp. 39–84.

Fernandez, R., & Ramabhadran, B. (2007). Automatic exploration of corpus-specific properties for expressive text-to-speech: A case study in emphasis. In: *Proceedings of the 6th ISCA Workshop on Speech Synthesis*, Bonn, Germany, pp. 34–39.

Heuft, B., Portele, T., & Rauth, M. (1996). Emotions in time domain synthesis. In: *Proceedings of the 4th International Conference of Spoken Language Processing*, Philadelphia.

Iida, A., & Campbell, N. (2003). Speech database design for a concatenative text-to-speech synthesis system for individuals with communication disorders. *International Journal of Speech Technology* 6, 379–392.

Iriondo, I., Guaus, R., Rogríguez, A., Lázaro, P., Montoya, N., Blanco, J. M., Bernadas, D., Oliver, J. M., Tena, D., & Longhi, L. (2000). Validation of an acoustical modelling of emotional expression in Spanish using speech synthesis techniques. In: *Proceedings of the ISCA Workshop on Speech and Emotion*, Northern Ireland, pp. 161–166.

Johnson, W.L., Narayanan, S.S., Whitney, R., Das, R., Bulut, M., & LaBore, C. (2002). Limited domain synthesis of expressive military speech for animated characters. In: *Proceedings of the 7th International Conference on Spoken Language Processing*, Denver.

Ling, Z. H., Qin, L., Lu, H., Gao, Y., Dai, L. R., Wang, R. H., Jiang, Y., Zhao, Z. W., Yang, J. H., Chen, J., Hu, G. P. (2007). The USTC and iFlytek speech synthesis systems for Blizzard Challenge 2007. In: *Proceedings of Blizzard Challenge*, Bonn, Germany.

Matsui, H., & Kawahara, H. (2003). Investigation of emotionally morphed speech perception and its structure using a high quality speech manipulation system. In: *Proceedings of Eurospeech 2003*, Geneva, Switzerland, pp. 2113–2116.

Miyanaga, K., Masuko, T., & Kobayashi, T. (2004). A style control technique for HMM-based speech synthesis. In: *Proceedings of the 8th International Conference of Spoken Language Processing*, Jeju, Korea.

Montero, J. M., Gutiérrez-Arriola, J., Colás, J., Enríquez, E., Pardo, J. M. (1999). Analysis and modelling of emotional speech in Spanish. In: *Proceedings of the 14th International Conference of Phonetic Sciences*, San Francisco, pp. 957–960.

Moore, R. K. (2007). Spoken language processing: Piecing together the puzzle. Speech Communication, 49, 418–435

Mozziconacci, S.J. L. (1998). Speech variability and emotion: Production and perception. PhD thesis, Technical University Eindhoven

Mozziconacci, S. J. L., & Hermes, D. J. (1999). Role of intonation patterns in conveying emotion in speech. In: *Proceedings of the 14th International Conference of Phonetic Sciences*, San Francisco, pp. 2001–2004.

Murray I. R., & Arnott, J. L. (1995). Implementation and testing of a system for producing emotion-by-rule in synthetic speech. *Speech Communication*, 16, 369–390

Pitrelli, J. F., Bakis, R., Eide, E. M., Fernandez, R., Hamza, W., & Picheny, M. A. (2006). The IBM expressive text-to-speech synthesis system for American English. *IEEE Transactions on Audio, Speech and Language Processing* 14(4):1099–1108.

Rank, E., & Pirker, H. (1998). Generating emotional speech with a concatenative synthesizer. In: *Proceedings of the 5th International Conference of Spoken Language Processing*, Sydney, Australia, vol 3, pp. 671–674.

Scherer, K. R. (1986). Vocal affect expression: A review and a model for future research. *Psychological Bulletin* 99,143–165

Schröder, M. (1999). Can emotions be synthesized without controlling voice quality? Phonus 4, Research Report of the Institute of Phonetics, University of the Saarland, pp. 37–55.

Schröder, M. (2001) Emotional speech synthesis: A review. In: *Proceedings of Eurospeech 2001*, Aalborg, Denmark (vol 1, pp. 561–564).

Schröder, M. (2003). Experimental study of affect bursts. *Speech Communication Special Issue Speech and Emotion* 40(1–2), 99–116.

Schröder, M. (2006). Expressing degree of activation in synthetic speech. *IEEE Transactions on Audio, Speech and Language Processing* 14(4),1128–1136

Schröder, M. (2007). Interpolating expressions in unit selection. In: *Proceedings of the second International Conference on Affective Computing and Intelligent Interaction (ACII'2007)*, Lisbon, Portugal.

Schröder, M. (2008). Approaches to emotional expressivity in synthetic speech. In: K. Izdebski (Ed.) *The emotion in the human voice*, vol 3, Plural, San Diego.

Schröder, M., & Grice, M. (2003). Expressing vocal effort in concatenative synthesis. In: *Proceedings of the 15th International Conference of Phonetic Sciences*, Barcelona.

Schröder, M., Heylen, D., & Poggi, I. (2006). Perception of non-verbal emotional listener feedback. In: *Proceedings of Speech Prosody 2006*, Dresden, Germany.

Trouvain, J., & Schröder, M. (2004). How (not) to add laughter to synthetic speech. In: *Proc. Workshop on Affective Dialogue Systems*, Kloster Irsee, Germany, pp 229–232.

Turk, O., Schröder, M., Bozkurt, B., & Arslan, L. (2005). Voice quality interpolation for emotional text-to-speech synthesis. In: *Proceedings of Interspeech 2005*, Lisbon, Portugal, pp. 797–800.

Vincent, D., Rosec, O., & Chonavel, T. (2005). Estimation of LF glottal source parameters based on an ARX model. In: *Proceedings of Interspeech*, Lisbon, Portugal, pp. 333–336.

Vroomen, J., Collier, R., & Mozziconacci, S. J. L. (1993). Duration and intonation in emotional speech. In: *Proceedings of Eurospeech 1993*, Berlin, Germany, vol 1, pp. 577–580.

Wang, L., Chu, M., Peng, Y., Zhao, Y., & Soong, F. (2007). Perceptual annotation of expressive speech. In: *Proceedings of the sixth ISCA Workshop on Speech Synthesis*, Bonn, Germany, pp. 46–51.

Wollermann, C., & Lasarcyk, E. (2007). Modeling and perceiving of (un-)certainty in articulatory speech synthesis. In: *Proceedings the sixth ISCA Speech Synthesis Workshop*, Bonn, Germany, pp. 40–45.

Yamagishi, J., Kobayashi, T., Tachibana, M., Ogata, K., & Nakano, Y. (2007). Model adaptation approach to speech synthesis with diverse voices and styles. In: *Proceedings of ICASSP*, Hawaii, vol. IV, pp. 1233–1236.

Yamagishi, J., Onishi, K., Masuko, T., & Kobayashi T. (2003) Modeling of various speaking styles and emotions for HMM-based speech synthesis. In: *Proceedings of Eurospeech, Geneva, Switzerland*, pp. 2461–2464.

Ye, H., & Young, S. (2004). High quality voice morphing. In: *Proceedings of ICASSP 2004*, Montreal.

Zen, H., & Toda, T. (2005). An overview of Nitech HMM-based speech synthesis system for Blizzard Challenge 2005. In: *Proceedings of Interspeech*, Lisbon, Portugal, pp. 93–96.

Zovato, E., Pacchiotti, A., Quazza, S., & Sandri, S. (2004). Towards emotional speech synthesis: A rule based approach. In: *Proceedings of the fifth ISCA Speech Synthesis Workshop*, Pittsburgh, PA, pp 219–220.

Chapter 8
Emotional Speech Generation by Using Statistic Prosody Conversion Methods

Jianhua Tao and Aijun Li

Abstract The chapter introduces prosody conversion models for emotional speech generation by using a Gaussian Mixture Model (GMM), and a Classification And Regression Tree (CART) model. Unlike the rule-based or linear modification method, the GMM and CART models try to map the subtle prosody distributions between neutral and emotional speech. A pitch target model that is optimized to describe Mandarin F0 contours is also introduced. For all conversion methods, a Deviation of Perceived Expressiveness (DPE) measure is created to evaluate the expressiveness of the output speech. The results show that the GMM method is more suitable for a small training set, whereas the CART method gives the better emotional speech output if trained with a large context-balanced corpus. The methods discussed in the chapter indicate ways to generate emotional speech in speech synthesis. The objective and subjective evaluation processes are also analyzed. These results support the use of a neutral semantic content text in databases for emotional speech synthesis.

8.1 Introduction

In Chapter 7 we discussed many rule-based, unit selection-based, HMM-based methods for expressive speech synthesis. This chapter introduces another method by using prosody conversion methods that aim at the transformation of the prosodic parameters, for example, F0, duration and intensity of the given utterance, to generate emotional speech. Although the conversion method has been widely used for

J.H. Tao (✉)
National Laboratory of Pattern Recognition, Institute of Automation, Chinese Academy of Sciences, Beijing
e-mail: jhtao@nlpr.ia.ac.cn

A.J. Li
Institute of Linguistic, Chinese Academy of Social Science, Beijing
e-mail: liaj@cass.org.cn

J.H. Tao, T.N. Tan (eds.), *Affective Information Processing*,
© Springer Science+Business Media LLC 2009

research on voice conversion, the methods discussed in this chapter provide a new way to produce emotional speech synthesis.

Compared to the unit selection method which can keep the original expressiveness for speech synthesis results but has to use a very large corpus, the conversion methods are based on only the limited training set. In this chapter, we introduce two conversion methods, the Gaussian Mixture Model (GMM) method and Classification And Regression Tree (CART) method, to solve the problem. The GMM method attempts to map the prosody feature distribution from a "neutral" state to the various emotions, and the CART model links linguistic features to the prosody conversion. The emotions are classified into 12 patterns (four emotions with three degrees, "strong," "medium," and "weak" are used).

The chapter is composed of seven major parts. Section 8.2 analyzes the F0 features for prosody conversion and describes it by using a pitch target model. Sections 8.3 and 8.4 introduce the GMM and CART methods which convert the prosody features from "neutral" to emotional speech. In Section 8.5, the chapter provides experiments and analysis for the conversion methods. A perception correlation calculation method is also introduced for the evaluation of expressiveness in the synthesized emotions. In Section 8.6, some discussion on methods comparing context influences for emotional speech is provided for the model analysis. The conclusion is also provided in this section.

8.2 F0 Representation

The underlying meaning of the mapping is to establish a relation between two sets of multidimensional vectors, which correspond to the source speech and the converted speech, respectively. To use a more complex conversion model, it is difficult to deal with the raw F0 contour. A suitable parametric model for describing contours is needed. In this chapter, we use Mandarin speech as the sample to describe our work.

Mandarin is a typical tonal language, in which a syllable with different tone types can represent different morphemes. There are four tone types referred to as "high," "rising," "low," and "falling" (Xu & Wang, 2001). They are mainly manifested by the F0 contours. There have been numerous studies on the tones and intonation of Mandarin. Several quantitative representations have been proposed to describe continuous F0 contours, such as the Fujisaki model (Fujisaki & Hirose, 1984), The Soft Template Mark-Up Language (Stem-ML) model (Kochanski & Shih, 2000), and the pitch target model (Xu & Wang, 2001).

The Fujisaki model is a command–response model for F0 contours. It uses two types of commands: the impulse-shaped phrase commands giving rise to the phrase-level component for global intonation, and the pedestal-shaped accent commands giving rise to accent components for local undulation due to word accent. The Soft Template Mark-Up Language proposed by Bell Labs is a tagging system, in which F0 contours are described by mark-up tags, including both stress tags for local tone shapes and step and slope tags for global phrase curves. Both models have the ability

Fig. 8.1 Pitch target model
(Xu & Wang, 2001).

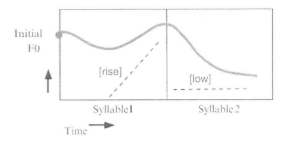

of representing F0 contours in Mandarin. Their common problem is that it is difficult to establish the relation among the model commands (or tags) of different utterances.

In the pitch target model, variations in surface F0 contours result not only from the underlying pitch units (syllables for Mandarin), but also from the articulatory constraints. Pitch targets are defined as the smallest operable units associated with linguistically functional pitch units, and these targets may be static (e.g., a register specification, [high] or [low]) or dynamic (e.g., a movement specification, [rise] or [fall]). Among these models, the features of the pitch target model are quite suitable for prosody conversion.

Figure 8.1 gives a schematic illustration of hypothetical pitch targets (dashed lines) and their surface realization (solid curved line). The three vertical lines represent the boundaries of the two consecutive pitch target-carrying units. The level dashed line on the right of the figure represents a static pitch target [low]. The oblique dashed line on the left represents a dynamic pitch target [rise]. In both cases, the targets are asymptotically approximated.

The implementation rules are based on possible articulatory constraints on the production of surface F0 contours. The production of surface F0 contours is a process of continuous approximations of the targets throughout tone-carrying syllables. When the syllable boundary is reached, it starts the new approximation for the next syllable with the new pitch target.

Let the syllable boundary be $[0, D]$. The pitch target model uses the following equations (Sun, 2002).

$$T(t) = at + b \qquad (8.1)$$

$$y(t) = \beta \exp(-\lambda t) + at + b \qquad (8.2)$$

$$0 \leq t \leq D, \lambda \geq 0,$$

where $T(t)$ is the underlying pitch target, and $y(t)$ is the surface F0 contour. The parameters a and b are the slope and intercept of the underlying pitch target, respectively. These two parameters describe an intended intonational goal of the speaker, which can be very different from the surface F0 contour. The coefficient β is a parameter measuring the distance between the F0 contour and the underlying pitch target at $t = 0$. λ describes how fast the underlying pitch target is approached. The greater the value of λ is, the faster the speed. A pitch target model of one syllable can be represented by a set of parameters (a, b, β, λ).

As described by (Sun, 2002), (a, b, β, λ) can be estimated by a nonlinear regression process with expected-value parameters at initial and middle points of each syllable's F0 contour. The Levenberg–Marquardt algorithm (Sun, 2002) is used for estimation as a nonlinear regression process.

8.3 GMM-Based Prosody Conversion

Gaussian mixture models have proved to be very useful in the research of voice conversion (Moulines & Sagisaka, 1995). They work particularly well in spectrum smoothing, which assumes the probability distribution of the observed parameters to take the following form,

$$p(x) = \sum_{q=1}^{Q} \alpha_q N(x; \mu_q; \Sigma_q), \sum_{q=1}^{Q} \alpha_q = 1, \alpha_q \geq 0, \tag{8.3}$$

where Q is the number of Gaussian components, α_q is the normalized positive scalar weight, and $N(x; \mu_q; \Sigma_q)$ denotes a D-dimensional normal distribution with mean vector μ_q and covariance matrix Σ_q, and can be described as

$$N(x) = \frac{1}{(2\pi)^{D/2} |\Sigma_q|^{1/2}} \exp[-\frac{1}{2}(x - \mu_q)^T \Sigma_q^{-1}(x - \mu_q)]. \tag{8.4}$$

The parameters (α, μ, Σ) are estimated with the expectation-maximization (EM) algorithm (McLachlan & Krishnan, 1997).

The conversion function can be found using the regression

$$F(x) = \sum_{q=1}^{Q} p_q(x)[\mu_q^Y + \Sigma_q^{YX}(\Sigma_q^{XX})^{-1}(x - \mu_q^X)], \tag{8.5}$$

where $p_q(x)$ is the conditional probability of a GMM class q by given x,

$$p_q(x) = \frac{\alpha_q N(x; \mu_q^X; \Sigma_q^X)}{\sum_{p=1}^{Q} \alpha_p N(x; \mu_p^X; \Sigma_p^X)}. \tag{8.6}$$

Here, $\Sigma_q = \begin{bmatrix} \Sigma_q^{XX} & \Sigma_q^{YX} \\ \Sigma_q^{XY} & \Sigma_q^{YY} \end{bmatrix}; \mu_q = \begin{bmatrix} \mu_q^X \\ \mu_q^Y \end{bmatrix}.$

$N(x; \mu_q^X; \Sigma_q^X)$ denotes a normal distribution with mean vector μ_q and covariance matrix Σ_q.

The parameters of the conversion function are determined by the joint density of source and target features (Xu & Wang, 2001). In Kain's (2001) work it was shown that the joint density performs better than the source density. It can lead to a more judicious allocation of mixture components and avoids certain numerical problems (Kain, 2001). For each pitch target parameter a, b, β, and λ, source and

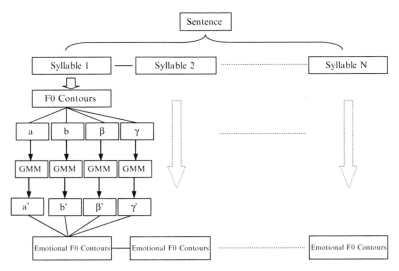

Fig. 8.2 The framework of GMM-based emotional prosody conversion.

target parameters are assumed to be Gaussian distributed, and then the combination of source (marked as x) and target (marked as y) vectors $Z_k = [X_k \ Y_k]^T, k = 1,...,N$ is used to estimate the GMM parameters.

Figure 8.2 shows the framework of the GMM-based prosody conversion.

A GMM was trained for the conversion from "neutral" to each of the four emotions at three levels. This method facilitates continuous and smooth conversion without discontinuities with incremental learning, but it is a pure numerical algorithm; in other words, the GMM mapping method fails to incorporate any linguistic information.

8.4 CART-Based Model

Classification and regression trees have been successfully used in prosody prediction, such as duration, prosody phrase boundaries, and so on. They efficiently integrate the contextual information into prediction (Shuang, Wang, Ling, & Wang, 2004). In our research, the framework of the CART-based prosody conversion is shown in Figure 8.3.

In this model, the input parameters of the CART contain:

- Tone identity (including current, previous, and following tones, with 5 categories)
- Initial identity (including current and following syllables' initial types, with 8 categories)
- Final identity (including current and previous syllables' final types, with 4 categories)

Fig. 8.3 The framework of CART-based emotional prosody conversion.

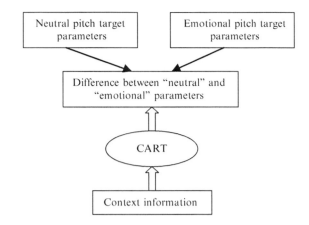

- Position in sentence
- Part of speech (including current, previous, and following words, with 30 categories)

The output parameters are the differences of pitch target parameters a, b, β, and λ between "neutral" and emotional parameters.

The Wagon toolkit,[1] with full CART function, was used in our work. Similar to the GMM method in training procedure, source and target pitch contours from the parallel corpus are aligned according to labeled syllable boundaries, and then pitch target parameters are extracted from each syllable's pitch contour, finally mapping functions of parameters a, b, β, and λ are estimated using the CART regression. Again, there were a total of 12 CART models trained with different "neutral" and emotion mappings. For conversion, the pitch target parameters estimated from source pitch contours are transformed by the mapping functions obtained in the training procedure and then the converted pitch target parameters generate new pitch contours associated with the target characteristics.

8.5 Experiments and Analysis

8.5.1 Corpus

To create the model, a corpus containing 1500 sentences was produced by searching the appropriate data from newspapers and magazines. Each utterance in our database contains at least 2 phrases. There were 3649 phrases and 14,453 syllables in total.

After the corpus was designed, each sentence was recorded in five emotions, "neutral", "happiness", "sadness", "fear", and "anger", by a professional actress

---

[1] http://festvox.org/docs/speech_tools-1.2.0/x3475.htm

in a professional recording studio with a large membrane microphone. A Laryn-gograph signal was also recorded in parallel to obtain accurate pitch information. Two persons assisted in the recording. One accompanied the speaker to provide hints on how to speak. One was outside the recording space for technical control. The speaker was asked to simulate the emotions based on her own experience. The accompanying person made the final judgment. Recording was not stopped until satisfactory results were obtained. After the recording, all the utterances were seg-mentally and prosodically annotated with break index and stress index information (Li, 2002). The F0 values were also processed and manually checked.

We presented the sentences in a randomized order to a group of 15 subjects, graduate students of engineering who were asked to participate in the experiment. Each sentence was played back to the subjects twice with a three-second interval. The subjects were asked to annotate the perceived emotion with four levels, "strong" (degree 3), "medium" (degree 2), "weak" (degree 1), and "unlike" (degree 0).

Different listeners perceived different aspects of emotion realized by the speech and it was difficult to reach a consensus. One useful representation of the labeling results is the mean emotion degree over all subjects. The mean degrees were rounded off into integer values, and thus corresponded to the four degrees, that is, "strong", "medium", "weak", and "unlike".

Out of the 1500 sentences in the corpus, 1200 were used for analysis or training and the remaining 300 were used for testing.

Figure 8.4 shows the scatterplots of the mapping from "neutral" to "strong hap-piness" for the four F0 model parameters. The correlation coefficient of (a, b, β, λ)

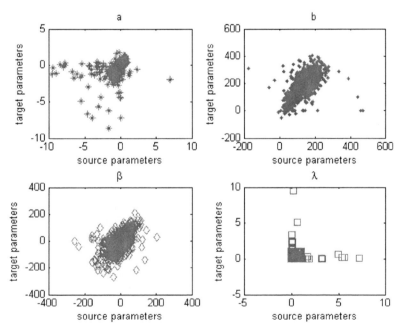

Fig. 8.4 The scatterplots of four pitch target parameters in "neutral" to "strong happiness" conversion.

between "neutral" to "strong happiness" is (0.3592, 0.5282, 0.3564, 0.0676). It can be observed that a, b, and β exhibit more correlation between source speech and target speech than λ.

8.5.2 Accuracy Analysis of the GMM and CART methods

In the testing set (300 utterances), all of the transform patterns are applied to convert the "neutral" speech into emotional speech via a synthesizer which uses STRAIGHT (Kawahra & Akahane-Yamada, 1998) as the acoustic processing model. The results are compared to the corresponding natural recording.

An example of prosody conversion is given in Figure 8.5, in which the "neutral" pitch contours are converted into the "strong happiness" with the GMM method and the CART method.

To get more statistical information of conversion results, four emotional conversions (marked as "neutral – strong happiness", "neutral – strong anger", "neutral – strong sadness", and "neutral – strong fear") were conducted in the experiment. To compare the GMM and CART mapping methods, root mean square errors are shown in Table 8.1.

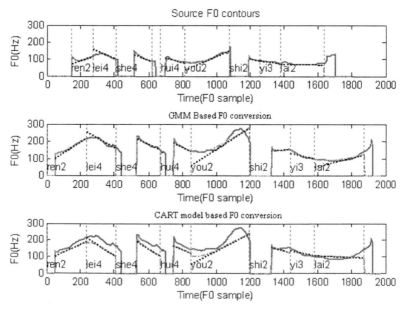

Fig. 8.5 An example of F0 conversion using the pitch target model in "neutral" to "strong happiness" conversion.

Table 8.1 Mapping Errors of GMM and CART Methods

Methods	Neutral – Strong Happiness	Neutral – Strong Anger	Neutral – Strong Sadness	Neutral – Strong Fear
GMM a	1.96	2.59	1.70	1.92
b	105.60	71.03	79.64	46.09
β	43.03	29.93	42.93	27.04
CART a	2.71	3.25	2.54	2.84
b	101.02	98.23	106.71	82.45
β	53.74	47.86	56.74	45.47

From the table, the performance of the GMM method has better results than that of the CART method. However, the conventional GMM-based conversion tends to generate overly smoothed prosody.

8.5.3 Combined with Spectral Conversion

Although it is commonly believed that the prosody features are very important for emotional speech classification, the modification of prosody features alone might not be sufficient to generate an expected emotion. An emotional speech utterance differs from a neutral one not only in prosodic features but also in spectral features. Parameters describing laryngeal processes on voice quality were also taken into account (Gobl & Chasaide, 2003; Tato, Santos, Kompe, & Pardo, 2002).

It has been pointed out that strong feelings often literally distort the physical vocal tract (Petrushin, 2000). For example, "anger" often involves a physical tension that can be felt throughout the body and certainly has an effect on the tenseness of the speech organs, which in turn creates a distinct acoustic effect. Similarly, "happiness" might involve a less total physical change, often just a smile which is "talked through." Spectral conversion is necessary to implement an emotional conversion especially from "neutral" to "negative" emotions. There are a lot of mapping methods available, such as codebook mapping (Shuang et al., 2004; Arslan & Talkin, 1997), Linear Multivariate Regression (LMR; Mizuno & Abe, 1995), neural networks (Watanabe et al., 2002), GMM (Chen & Chu, 2003; Toda, Black, & Tokuda, 2005), and Hidden Markov Models (HMM) (Stylianou et al., 1998). Among these mapping methods, codebook mapping and GMM methods are two representative and popular mapping algorithms.

In our work, we integrate GMM and codebook mapping (Kang, Shuang, Tao, Zhang, & Xu, 2005). This method encodes the basic spectral envelope using GMM and converts spectral details using an offset codebook mapping method. By this means, the problems of smoothing and discontinuity can be counteracted.

8.5.4 Deviation of Perceived Expressiveness (DPE)

Traditionally, an ABX test is commonly used for performance evaluation of voice conversion methods (Kain, 2001). In an ABX test, the listener is required to judge whether the unknown speech sample X sounds closer to the reference sample A or B. For the evaluation of expressiveness in emotional speech, an ABX test is not easy to use because an emotion state cannot be easily defined, especially with the distinction among "strong", "medium", and "weak" degrees. The forced one-to-one match is also unsuitable. To evaluate emotional simulation results, we therefore proposed a Deviation of Perceived Expressiveness (DPE) method.

The error rate of a certain emotion simulation is measured by

$$\Delta_{n,i} = \sum_{i=0}^{I} (\bar{d}_{n,i} - \bar{d}'_{n,i}), \tag{8.7}$$

where n denotes the emotion state, that is, "fear", "sadness", "anger", and "happiness"; i indexes the emotion level, that is, "strong", "medium", and "weak". $\bar{d}_{n,i}$ represents the mean level labeled for the synthesized emotion, and $\bar{d}'_{n,i}$ is the mean level labeled for the original speech.

The DPE experiment involved the same group of 15 subjects who took part in the emotion labeling process. The subjects were asked to annotate 3600 synthesized utterances (300 test sentences with four emotions at three levels) by using the same method as described in Section 8.2. With the integration of prosody conversion and spectral conversion, more results of DPE tests are shown in Tables 8.2 and 8.3.

Here, $\bar{\Delta}_i$ denotes the mean errors of emotion level i. Tables 8.2 and 8.3 seem to confirm that the GMM mapping method is better than the CART method, although the DPE tests didn't show much difference. The results are not consistent with the previous analysis that the prosody patterns of emotions are closely related to content and linguistic features. A possible reason might be that the training data in the

Table 8.2 Expressiveness Deviation Based on GMM-Based Prosody Conversion

Degrees	Emotions	$\bar{d}_{n,i}$	$\bar{d}'_{n,i}$	$\Delta_{n,i}$	$\bar{\Delta}_i$
Strong	Fear	1.71	2.81	−1.10	
	Sadness	2.53	2.69	−0.16	−0.56
	Anger	2.34	2.91	−0.57	
	Happiness	2.50	2.89	−0.39	
Normal	Fear	1.51	1.87	−0.36	
	Sadness	1.40	1.99	−0.59	
	Anger	1.92	2.11	−0.19	−0.29
	Happiness	1.99	2.01	−0.02	
Weak	Fear	0.61	1.01	−0.40	
	Sadness	0.82	1.11	−0.29	
	Anger	1.02	1.23	−0.21	−0.23
	Happiness	1.00	1.02	−0.02	

Table 8.3 Expressiveness Deviation from CART-Based Prosody Conversion

Degrees	Emotions	$\bar{d}_{n,i}$	$\bar{d}'_{n,i}$	$\Delta_{n,i}$	$\bar{\Delta}_i$
	Fear	2.01	2.81	−0.80	
	Sadness	2.23	2.69	−0.46	−0.60
Strong	Anger	2.56	2.91	−0.35	
	Happiness	2.11	2.89	−0.78	
	Fear	1.32	1.87	−0.55	
	Sadness	1.41	1.99	−0.58	−0.43
Normal	Anger	2.02	2.11	−0.09	
	Happiness	1.53	2.01	−0.48	
	Fear	0.58	1.01	−0.43	
	Sadness	0.78	1.11	−0.33	−0.27
Weak	Anger	1.12	1.23	−0.11	
	Happiness	0.83	1.02	−0.19	

experiment were not enough to cover most linguistic information when using the CART method. The GMM method was applied purely on prosody features, The CART method may obtain better results with a larger training corpus, which still needs to be confirmed in our future research.

8.6 Discussion and Conclusion

The chapter proposed using a GMM method and a CART method to map the subtle prosody distributions between neutral and emotional speech. Whereas GMM just uses the acoustic features, the CART model allows us to integrate linguistic features into the mapping. A pitch target model that was designed to describe Mandarin F0 contours was also introduced.

Although a good result has been got, it's still limited by the performed speech. For real spontaneous speech, the acoustic distributions are notoriously various among different emotions. Even for the same emotion there are still various expression methods. One speaker may increase F0 jitter for "happiness", rather than increasing the overall pitch level. The locations of sentence stress in "anger" utterances can also vary according to differences in content and linguistic emphasis. In most cases, it is located in the word that the speaker wants to emphasize. These various methods of emotional expression increase our difficulties in emotion simulations, because the acoustic features can be widely distributed.

Figure 8.6 shows the perceived stress patterns among five "strong" emotions. "I" means the sentence stress is located in the first word of the utterance, whereas "F" means the final word, and "M" means any middle words. We found that the stress shifts in the sentence among different emotions. In our corpus, the shifting amplitude is pertinent to the emotional states, from big to small: "anger" > "sadness" > "fear" > "happiness".

Fig. 8.6 Perceived stress
pattern.

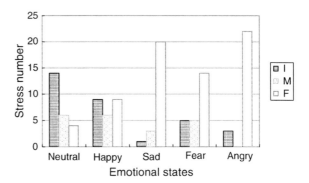

Although stresses might be shifted among emotions, the stress distribution varies
with different content, different situations, and different people. Sometimes, the
stress in "happiness" keeps the stress pattern as in the "neutral" states. Also, when a
sentence stress is sentence-medial, the corresponding stress in other emotions might
be shifted to the sentence-final words.

From this point, context information from linguistic features is very important
for emotion expression. Sometimes it is not necessary to change any prosodic parameters to express the emotion, if some functional emotinal keyword was inserted
into the utterance (Tao, 2003). For example, "I'm really angry about what you did,"
sufficiently shows the "anger" emotion by use of the functional word "angry" alone.

Also, emotion may mislead the listener into perceiving a different sentence act
if the context is not provided. Sometimes, the listeners may perceive some "happy"
voices with a raising end intonation as an echo question, as shown in Figure 8.7.
Here the high boundary tone (with a final stressed pattern) is used to express a
"happy" emotion. Because the high boundary tone is one of the major features of
an interrogative sentence, it is not strange for the listener to recognize an emotional
statement as a question, without context.

In this chapter, we tried to integrate some of these linguistic features to predict
the emotional prosody, but the results were still far from our expectations. Emotional functional words were analyzed in our previous work for emotion control
(Tao, 2003), but were not considered here because we didn't collect a large enough
training set for the CART model. Otherwise, we can consider the functional emotional keywords as a kind of special part of speech.

We have combined the prosody conversion and spectral conversion for emotion
simulation. The work does enhance the expressiveness of emotions, especially for
"happiness". When Ladd described the relations between paralanguage and intonation (Petrushin, 2000), he described the relations between paralinguistic and linguistic features and pointed out that lexical tone was also affected by paralinguistic
expression. In fact, intonational and tonal ambiguities are caused by the stress patterns in expressing certain strong emotions or attitudes. The influences on stress
patterns, tones, and intonations from paralinguistic features should also be consid-

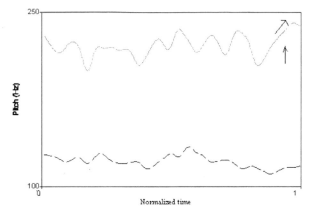

Fig. 8.7 F0 contours of a "happy" statement (upper curve) and its neutral counterpart (lower dashed curve). The utterance is "xi1 an1 bo1 yin1 qi1 san1 qi1 fei1 ji1." The happy statement is perceived as an echo question because both the contour and the register of the final syllable "ji1", bearing a high-level tone HH, are raised.

ered in future work, otherwise, the utterance will not be able express emotions or attitudes as naturally as possible.

We also proposed a DPE method in the chapter to evaluate the conversion results. Unlike the traditional ABX test which is normally used for voice conversion evaluation, but is hardly to be used for an uncertain judgment, the DPE method uses different degrees for perception, such as "strong", "medium", and "weak". The degrees give more flexibility in comparing among the emotions. In addition, the DPE method adopted the advantage of the MOS test, with the mean scores of the degrees from many listeners.

References

Amir, N. (2001). Classifying emotions in speech: A comparison of methods. Holon Academic Institute of Technology. In *Eurospeech2001*, Scandinavia.

Arslan, L. M., & Talkin, D. (1997). Voice conversion by codebook mapping of line spectral frequencies and excitation spectrum. In *Eurospeech'97*, Rhodes, Greece.

Cahn, J.E. (1990). The generation of affect in synthesized speech. *Journal of the American Voice I/O Society, 8*, 1–19.

Campbell, N. (2004). Perception of affect in speech – Towards an automatic processing of paralinguistic information in spoken conversation. In *ICSLP2004*, Jeju, Korea.

Campbell, N. (2004). Synthesis units for conversational speech – Using phrasal segments, IEICE Trans., 87, 497–500.

Chen, Y., & Chu, M. et al. (2003). Voice conversion with smoothed GMM and map adaptation. In *Eurospeech*, Geneva, Switzerland (pp. 2413–2416).

Chuang, Z., & Wu, C. (2002). Emotion recognition from textual input using an emotional semantic network. In *International Conference on Spoken Language Processing, ICSLP 2002*, Denver.

Eide, E., Aaron, A., Bakis, R., Hamza, W., Picheny, M., & Pitrelli, J. (2002). A corpus-based approach to <ahem/> expressive speech synthesis. In *IEEE Speech Synthesis Workshop*, Santa Monica

Fujisaki, H., & Hirose, K. (1984). Analysis of voice fundamental frequency contours for declarative sentence of Japanese. *Journal of the Acoustic Society of Japan. (E) 5*(4), 233–242.

Gobl C., & Chasaide, A. (2003). The role of voice quality in communicating emotion, mood and attitude. *Speech Communication, 40*, 189–212.

Hayes, B. (1995). *Metrical stress theory: Principles and case studies.* Chicago: University of Chicago Press

Kain, A. B. (2001). High resolution voice transformation. PhD thesis, Oregon Health and Science Unitversity.

Kang, Y., Shuang, Z., Tao, J., Zhang, W., & Xu, B. (2005). A hybrid GMM and codebook mapping method for spectral conversion. In *The First International Conference on Affective Computing and Intelligent Interaction*, Beijing, pp. 303–310.

Kawahra, H., & Akahane-Yamada, R. (1998). Perceptual effects of spectral envelope and f0 manipulations using STRAIGHT method. *Journal of the Acoustic Society of America, 103*(5, Pt.2), 1aSC27: 2776.

Kochanski, G. P., & Shih, C. (2000). Stem-ML: Language independent prosody description. In *ICSLP2000*, Beijing.

Li, A. (2002). Chinese prosody and prosodic labeling of spontaneous speech. In *International Conference on Speech Prosody*, Aix-en-Provence, France, pp. 39–46.

Li, A. and Wang, H. (2004). Friendly speech analysis and perception in standard Chinese. *ICSLP2004*, Korea, pp. 897–900.

McGilloway, S., Cowie, R., Doulas-Cowie, E., Gielen, S., Westerdijk, M., & Stroeve, S. (2000). Approaching automatic recognition of emotion from voice: A rough benchmark, In *Proceedings of the ISCA workshop on Speech and Emotion*, pp. 207–212.

McLachlan, G., & Krishnan, T. (1997). *The EM algorithm and extensions.* Wiley series in probability and statistics. New York: John Wiley & Sons.

Mizuno, H., & Abe, M. (1995). Voice conversion based on piecewise linear conversions rules of formant frequency and spectrum tilt. *Speech Communication, 16*, 153–164.

Moulines, E., & Sagisaka, Y. (1995). Voice conversion: State of the art and perspectives. *Speech Communication, 16*(2), 125–126.

Mozziconacci, S. J. L., & Hermes, D. J. (2000). Expression of emotion and attitude through temporal speech variations. In *ICSLP2000*, Beijing.

Murray, I., & Arnott, J. L. (1993). Towards the simulation of emotion in synthetic speech: A review of the literature on human vocal emotion. *Journal of the Acoustic Society of America, 1993*, 1097–1108.

Ortony, A., Clore, G. L., & Collins A. (1990). *The cognitive structure of emotions.* Cambridge, UK: Cambridge University Press.

Petrushin, V. A. (2000). Emotion recognition in speech signal: Experimental study, development and application. In *ICSLP 2000*, Beijing.

Rank, E., & Pirker, H. (1998). Generating emotional speech with a concatenative synthesizer. In *ICSLP98*.

Santen, J. P. H., Sproat, R. W., Olive, J. P., & Hirschberg, J. (Eds.) (1997). *Progress in speech synthesis.* New York: Springer.

Schröder, M., & Breuer, S. (2004). XML Representation languages as a way of interconnecting TTS modules. In *ICSLP2004* Jeju, Korea, pp. 1889–1892.

Shuang, Z., Wang, Z., Ling, Z., & Wang, R. (2004). A novel voice conversion system based on codebook mapping with phoneme-tied weighting. In *ICSLP*, Jeju, Korea, pp. 1197–1200.

Stibbard, R. M. (2001). Vocal expression of emotions in non-laboratory speech: An investigation of the reading/leeds emotion in speech project annotation data. PhD thesis. University of Reading, UK.

Stylianou, Y. et al. (1998). Continuous probabilistic transform for voice conversion. *IEEE Transactions on Speech and Audio Processing, 6*(2), 131–142.

Sun, X. (2002). The determination, analysis, and synthesis of fundamental frequency. PhD thesis, Northwestern University, Evanston, IL.

Tao, J. (2003). Emotion control of Chinese speech synthesis in natural environment. In *Eurospeech2003* (pp. 2349–2352).

Tato, R., Santos, R., Kompe, R., & Pardo, J. M. (2002). Emotional space improves emotion recognition. In *ICSLP2002*, Denver.

Toda, T., Black, A. W., & Tokuda, K. (2005). Spectral conversion based on maximum likelihood estimation considering global variance of converted parameter. In *ICASSP* (pp. 9–12).

Watanabe, T. et al. (2002). Transformation of spectral envelope for voice conversion based on radial basis function networks. In *ICSLP*, Denver (pp. 285–288).

Xu, Y. & Wang, Q. E. (2001). Pitch targets and their realization: Evidence from mandarin Chinese. *Speech Communication, 33*, 319–337.

Part III
Affect in Face

Chapter 9
Why the Same Expression May Not Mean the Same When Shown on Different Faces or Seen by Different People

Ursula Hess and Pascal Thibault

A man's face is his autobiography. A woman's face is her work of fiction.
Oscar Wilde

Abstract This somewhat sexist quote by Oscar Wilde points nonetheless to two important issues about faces. First, faces seem to tell us about who the other person is, and second, we may be misled by them. The present chapter has the goal to present some findings about the importance of faces in the context of emotion communication. Most research on emotion considers the face as if it were a blank canvas with no meaning of its own. However, as we show, faces convey information relevant to the interpretation of emotion expressions and they have a meaning of their own which interacts with the facial expression shown.

Because faces tell us about who the other person is, we may also not use the same cues when interpreting the facial expressions of different people. That is, when it comes to interpreting emotional facial expressions it really matters who shows what to whom and in which context (Hess, Beaupré, & Cheung, 2002). This in turn has relevance for the use of emotion expressions in human–machine interfaces. Agents are made to express emotions so as to facilitate communication by making it more like human–human communication (Koda & Maes, 1996; Pelachaud & Bilvi, 2003). However, this very naturalness may mean that an agent may fail to convey the intended message because of the way it looks and the biases in perception and interpretation that this may entrain. It is therefore important to not only focus on creating believable expressions but also to keep in mind that the face on which these expressions appear is not an empty canvas. In what follows we present two examples of

U. Hess
Department of Psychology, University of Quebec at Montreal, PO Box 8888, station A, Montreal
Qc. H3C3P8
e-mail: Hess.Ursula@uqam.ca

P. Thibault
Department of Psychology, McGill University, Montreal, Canada
e-mail: pascal.thibault@videotron.ca

J.H. Tao, T.N. Tan (eds.), *Affective Information Processing*,
© Springer Science+Business Media LLC 2009

how faces interact with emotion expressions and how information transmitted by faces may change the way facial cues are interpreted.

9.1 What Information Do Faces Provide?

Research on personality judgments at zero levels of acquaintance suggests that overall people can and do draw conclusions about a person's personality from no more information than provided by the face, even though accuracy varies widely and is dependent on both encoder and decoder personality (e.g., Ambady, Hallahan, & Rosenthal, 1995). However, more important in the present context, faces tell us who our interaction partner is. If we do not know the person we interact with, faces tell us the sex, age, and race of the other person. This information is important for the decoding of facial expressions. Specifically, the decoding of emotion displays can be based on either or both of two important sources of information: the sender's emotion displays and knowledge about the sender. It is with regard to this second source of information that the information that faces provide becomes relevant.

If the sender and the receiver know each other well, the receiver usually is aware of the sender's personality, beliefs, preferences, and emotional style. This knowledge permits the receiver to take the perspective of the sender and to deduce which emotional state the sender most likely experiences in the given situation. For example, a given expression of happiness in a person we know to be very gregarious may be interpreted as suggesting less happiness than would the same expression when shown by a person known to be very timid.

This may indeed be the most effective approach to the decoding of emotion displays in many situations (see e.g., Wiggers, 1984) and studies on emotion communication between interaction partners who know each other well, for example, in marital interactions, underscore the importance of previous knowledge for emotion communication (e.g., Guthrie, & Noller, 1988). Yet, when interaction partners do not know each other this knowledge can be replaced with knowledge and beliefs about the groups to which the interaction partners belong (Karniol, 1990; Kirouac & Hess, 1999). In fact, we have very strong beliefs about the likely emotional reactions of others, based simply on their ethnic background, gender, and age.

9.2 Beliefs About Emotions

9.2.1 Beliefs About the Emotions of Members of Different Ethnic Groups

People in fact hold beliefs about the emotionality of a variety of members of other cultures. In a questionnaire study we found, for example, that people from Quebec consider members of their own group to be not very likely (21%) to react with antagonistic emotional behaviors to a negative emotional event, but they consider

North-African women to be even less likely (12%), whereas South-American men are perceived to be more likely (46%) to do so.

Beliefs about different ethnic groups' emotional behavior have been most consistently studied in the context of research on decoding rule differences between collectivist Japanese and individualist U.S. American decoders (Matsumoto, 1992; Matsumoto, Kasri, & Kooken, 1999; Matsumoto & Kudoh, 1993; Yrizarry, Matsumoto, & Wilson-Cohn, 1998). Decoding rules (Buck, 1984) are the flip side of display rules. Display rules in turn are culturally learned rules that define when to show what emotion and how to show it (Ekman & Friesen 1971). Conversely, people who are aware of such rules will adjust their interpretation of the emotional expressions of others in function. For example, U.S. Americans are usually encouraged to show emotions, especially positive emotions and tend to show emotion more intensely than warranted by the underlying feeling state. This is not the case in Japan. Consequently, U.S. Americans attribute less intense underlying emotions to expressions of the same intensity than do Japanese (Matsumoto et al., 1999); that is, they "correct" their estimate of a person's feeling state based on the decoding rule that people are likely to exaggerate their expressions.

9.2.2 Beliefs About the Emotions of Persons of Different Age

People also have beliefs about age and emotionality. In a recent study we showed participants photos of individuals from four different age groups (18–29; 30–49; 50–69; 70+) and asked them to indicate how likely they thought it that the person shown in the photo would express each of four emotions (happiness, sadness, anger, and fear) in everyday life. The responses differed with regard to both sex and age. Thus, as they get older, men were perceived to be less likely to show anger whereas the reverse was the case for women. Men were also perceived as more likely to show sadness as they get older.

9.2.3 Beliefs About Men's and Women's Emotionality

As mentioned above, beliefs about emotionality are strongly influenced by the sex of the expresser. In fact, one of the best-documented gender stereotypes regards men's and women's emotionality. Thus, women are generally believed to be more expressive of all emotions except anger, which is perceived to be more typical for men (Fischer, 1993). These expectations are socialized early and can have dramatic consequences for the perception of emotion in others. For example, even children as young as five years tend to consider a crying baby as 'mad' when the baby is purported to be a boy but not when it is purported to be a girl (Haugh, Hoffman, & Cowan, 1980). Thus, the 'knowledge' that the baby was a boy or a girl biased the perception of the otherwise ambiguous emotion display.

These beliefs can also lead people to expect different emotional behaviors from men and women, even when they do not expect them to actually feel differently about a situation. For example, when presented with a vignette that describes a person who just learned that his or her car was vandalized, participants rated the person as very likely to be angry, regardless of whether the person was described as a man or a woman (Hess, Adams, & Kleck, 2005). Yet, whereas a man is then expected to show this anger, a woman is expected to show sadness instead.

However, in this case we also found a second – and opposite – stereotype at work: a stereotype based on the perception of the person as high versus low dominant. Specifically, if the woman was described as highly dominant she was expected to show anger to the same degree as a man. In a similar vein, men are expected to show less happiness unless they are described as high in affiliation, in which case they are expected to smile even more than women. In sum, the judgement of the appropriateness of showing anger or happiness was heavily dependent on the perceived dominance and affiliation of the protagonist, and not just the product of gender category membership per se.

This latter observation is very relevant to the present argument because one important source of information about a person's dominance and also affiliativeness is the human face (Hess, Adams, & Kleck, 2004; Keating, 1985; Senior, Phillips, Barnes, & David, 1999). That is, just seeing a person's face provides information on dominance, affiliation, age, and gender, all of which moderate expectations as to how the person will react in a given situation and may thereby bias the perception of ambiguous expressions (Kirouac & Hess, 1999). This can have a pervasive influence on interaction with quasi-strangers because most spontaneous facial expressions tend to be somewhat ambiguous (Motley & Camden, 1988) and only group-based additional information is available.

9.2.4 Facial Expressions Signal Dominance and Affiliation

However, the situation is further complicated by the fact that emotional facial expressions also are powerful signals of dominance and affiliation. Specifically, drawing the eyebrows together in anger leads to increased attributions of dominance, whereas smiling leads to increased attributions of affiliation (Hess et al., 2000a; Knutson, 1996). At the same time, anger expressions are perceived as threatening (e.g., Aronoff, Barclay, & Stevenson, 1988), whereas smiles are perceived as warm, friendly, and welcoming (see, e.g., Hess, Beaupré, & Cheung, 2002). Similarly, it has been argued that fear expressions elicit affiliative reactions in conspecifics (Bauer and Gariépy, 2001; Marsh, Adams, and Kleck, 2005). Recent work using connectionist modeling also provides evidence for a perceptual overlap between the physical cues of babyfacedness versus maturity and the meanings derived from them along the dominance and affiliation continua on one hand and facial expressions. In fact, objective indices of babyfaceness partially mediated impressions of the emotion expressions (Zebrowitz, Kikuchi, & Fellous, 2007). For a review of related work using principal components analyses see also Calder and Young (2005).

This suggests that emotional expressive behavior can serve to mimic or simulate certain morphological traits linked to size or juvenescence that are important for social species including humans and thus confer an evolutionary advantage (Marsh et al., 2005). Consistent with this line of reasoning, there is evidence that humans tend to confuse morphological with expressive traits (Malatesta et al. 1987a,b).

9.3 Functional Equivalence Hypothesis

Darwin (1872/1965) first noted the equivalence between certain emotional behaviors in animals and more enduring morphological appearance characteristics. Importantly in the present context, he proposed that piloerection and the utterance of harsh sounds by 'angry' animals are 'voluntarily' enacted to make the animal appear larger and hence a more threatening adversary (see, e.g., pp. 95 and 104).

Taking up this notion, Hess, Adams, and Kleck, (2007) proposed that some aspects of facial expressive behavior and morphological cues to dominance and affiliation are equivalent in both their appearance and their effects on emotional attributions. Such a functional equivalence between morphology and expression also implies that there are important interactions between facial expressions and facial morphology in the decoding of expressions of emotion. Specifically, persons with dominant-appearing faces may not only be perceived as particularly capable of anger but also when anger is expressed on such a face it should be seen as quite intense. Likewise a more affiliative-appearing face displaying happiness may be seen as happier than would a less affiliative face displaying the identical facial movement.

We initially tested the functional equivalence hypothesis by examining differences in the attribution of emotions to men and women (Hess et al., 2004, 2005). As mentioned above, individuals attribute higher levels of emotional expressivity to women than to men with the exception of anger, which is seen as more frequent in men (see, e.g., Fischer, 1993). This pattern is also found when participants are presented with vignettes describing a specific emotion-eliciting event (Hess et al., 2000b). These stereotypical expectations regarding men and women's emotionality seem to be strongly normative (Hess et al., 2005).

And indeed men's and women's faces differ in ways that make men appear more dominant and women appear more affiliative. As mentioned above, we postulate that facial expressions can also make faces appear more dominant and affiliative and thereby more or less male or female. This is because smiling enhances the appearance of the roundness of the face, a female sex marker and a marker of baby-facedness, which signals warmth and affiliative intent. Conversely, those aspects of the face that make a face appear both dominant and masculine are made more salient by anger expressions. Specifically, the tightening of the lips in anger makes the mouth region appear more square and the drawing together of the eyebrows enhances the apparent thickness of the eyebrows. Thus, these expressions resemble both the morphological markers for the perceived behavioral intentions of dominance and affiliation. In addition, they are among the markers for sex.

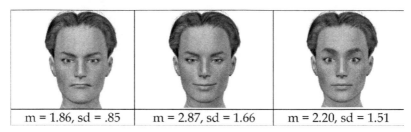

| m = 1.86, sd = .85 | m = 2.87, sd = 1.66 | m = 2.20, sd = 1.51 |

Fig. 9.1 Rated likelihood that 'this person is a woman' for an avatar showing anger, smiling, and a fearful expression.

In fact, this relation among emotion expression, dominance and affiliation, and gender is so strong that it can reverse bias; that is, the facial expression shown by an androgynous face can bias the assignation of gender to this face, such that in a recent study we found that an avatar who shows a happy or fearful expression is perceived as more likely to represent a woman and an avatar who looks angry is considered to be less likely to represent a woman (see Figure 9.1).

And in fact, this perceptual overlap seems to explain the beliefs that people have about men's and women's emotionality. Specifically, Hess et al. (2005) asked separate groups of participants to rate men's and women's neutral faces either with regard to how dominant or affiliative they appeared or with regard to the likelihood that the person in the photo would show a series of emotions in everyday life. They found that as expected, actor sex was related to dominance and affiliation such that men were perceived as more dominant and women as more affiliative. After statistically controlling for the influence of actor sex, perceived dominance was significantly positively related to the disposition to show anger, disgust, and contempt, and significantly negatively related to the actors' perceived disposition to show fear and sadness. However, perceived dominance was not related to the disposition to show surprise or happiness. Conversely, and again after controlling for the effect of actor sex, perceived affiliativeness was significantly positively related to the perceived disposition to show happiness, surprise, and fear and significantly negatively related to the perceived disposition to show anger, disgust, and contempt.

Mediational analyses showed that the tendency to perceive women as more likely to show happiness, surprise, sadness, and fear was in fact mediated by their higher perceived affiliation and lower perceived dominance, respectively. The tendency to perceive men as more prone to show anger, disgust, and contempt was partially mediated by both their higher level of perceived dominance and their lower level of perceived affiliation (see Figure 9.2). That is, if men and women were perceived to be equal on these dimensions, then we would not expect observers to rate their emotionality differently.

More recently, we could show that this also is the case for the beliefs about age and sex mentioned above. That is, the notion that men are less prone to anger as they get older and women more so, with the converse for happiness, is mediated through the fact that as they get older men appear less dominant and more affiliative, whereas women appear more dominant and less affiliative.

Fig. 9.2 Mediation of expectations regarding men's and women's emotionality via perceptions of facial dominance and affiliation.

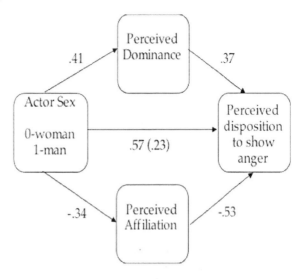

Actor Sex

0-woman
1-man

Perceived Dominance

Perceived Affiliation

Perceived disposition to show anger

.41

.37

.57 (.23)

-.34

-.53

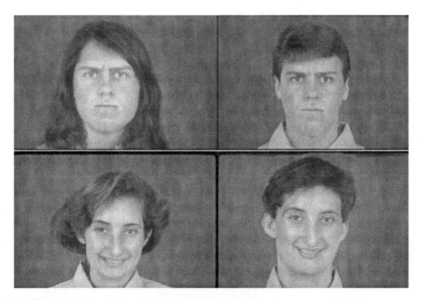

Fig. 9.3 Changing hairstyles to change perceived gender.

With regard to gender this notion could also be tested experimentally. Specifically, the interior of the face contains markers of dominance and affiliation (i.e., square jaw, heavy eyebrows), whereas hairstyle is a very potent marker of sex but not of social motives. Thus, by combining androgynous interior faces with male and female hairstyles, apparent men and women with identical facial appearance can be created (see Figure 9.3).

For both neutral faces and posed emotion displays (Adams et al., 2007, Study 4; Hess et al., 2004, Study 2) parallel findings obtained such that for ratings of anger and happiness, a pattern opposite to the gender stereotypical pattern was found. That is, when equated for facial appearance, apparent women were seen as more likely to show anger and less likely to show happiness than were apparent men. Similarly, expressions of anger by apparent women were rated as more intense and their expressions of happiness as less intense than when the identical expressions appeared on the faces of apparent men.

This reversal demands an explanation as it suggests that intrinsically, facial appearance being equal, women are perceived as more anger prone and less likely to be happy than are men. We propose that this reversal is due to the equivalence between morphological and expressive cues of dominance and affiliation, which leads to an interaction between these two sets of cues. That is, anger expressions emphasize some of the features that make a face appear dominant (e.g., the mouth region often appears especially square, and frowning reduces the distance between eyebrows and eyes). Conversely, smiling enhances the appearance of roundness of the face that is associated with perceived affiliation motivation and babyishness.

Due to the manner in which the present stimuli were constructed, the expressive cues for anger and happiness were not 'compensated for' by gender typical appearance (the faces were chosen specifically because they were androgynous and were credible as either male or female). In some ways one could say that by depriving the interior of the face of clear gender cues we actually amplified the expressive cues to anger in women and happiness in men, which are normally 'obscured' or reduced by the gender typical facial appearance which also conveys dominance and affiliation. This notion that anger on a male face presents a clearer and less ambiguous anger signal than anger on a female face and the converse, that happiness on a female face, is a clearer signal of happiness has recently been confirmed by Hess, Adams, and Kleck, (2007).

To reiterate, we are arguing that facial morphology and certain emotional expressions are parallel messaging systems with regard to the emotion inferences they generate. However, to the degree that both morphology and expression have to use the same 'canvas' to communicate, there is a possibility of perceptual interference. Specifically, some of the same facial features that signal dominance and affiliation are used in expressive behavior and hence change appearance. In this process the facial appearance cues can either enhance or attenuate the perceived intensity of the expression. The implications of these findings for more general person perception processes should be obvious.

Hess, Adams, and Kleck, (2007) also report the results of an experiment designed to assess the relative contributions of gender, the gender role stereotype, and facial appearance on men and women's perceived emotionality. The findings suggest that even though both of the latter do influence these perceptions, gender per se does not. This implies that knowledge about gender roles and the perceptual effects of facial morphology combine to make men appear more anger prone and their expressions more angry whereas women are seen as more likely to smile and their smiles to be indicative of greater happiness.

In sum, emotional facial expressions via their shared signal value with morphological trait cues signal behavioral intentions to perceivers. In turn, the morphological cues contained in the face tend to bias the decoding of emotion expressions in a manner consistent with those cues. Thus, men's anger and women's smiles are stronger signals for these specific affects because they are supported by an underlying facial morphology consistent with each of those expressions. Conversely, women's anger and men's smiles are partially veiled by the morphological context in which they are shown.

The research by Hess et al. (2004, 2005, 2007) serves to highlight the influence of facial morphology on the perception and interpretation of emotional facial expressions. In a similar vein, Marsh, Adams, and Kleck, (2005) found evidence for functional equivalence between mature versus babyfacedness and the signal value of angry versus fear faces. Yet, it is clear that not all traits that may be attributed to a person on the basis of facial appearance have a functional equivalence in expressive displays. There is no evidence, for example, that facial expressions lead to such trait attributions as trustworthiness or conscientiousness even though these are also traits of great relevance to a social species.

Overall the research presented above outlines the impact that a face has on the perception of facial expressions. This applies also to the avatars and agents used in human–computer interfaces. Thus an agent with a very square masculine face may not be a good choice if warmth and care are to be transmitted.

However, as mentioned above, the face on which an expression appears may also determine the cues that are used for the interpretation of the expression. In what follows we present data suggesting that the authenticity of a smile is evaluated differently depending on who shows the smile.

9.4 Authentic Smiles

In Western society smiling is a highly valued behavior. People who smile are generally perceived more positively. This effect was first reported by Thornton (1943) who found that smiling individuals tend to be rated higher in kindliness, honesty, and sense of humor. Numerous studies have found similar effects for other positive personality traits. For example, people who smile are perceived as more pleasant (Mueser, Grau, Sussman, & Rosen, 1984), sincere, sociable, and competent (Reis, Wilson, Monestere, & Bernstein, 1990) as well as more honest (Ruback, 1981). According to Deutsch, LeBaron, and Fryer, (1987) smiling individuals are perceived not only as happier, but also as more carefree, more relaxed, and more polite. Furthermore, the frequency of smiling by an individual affects the amount of warmth perceived by others (Bayes, 1972; Deutsch et al., 1987; Lau, 1982). In addition, smiling increases ratings of attractiveness (McGinley, McGinley, & Nicholas, 1978; Mueser et al., 1984; Reis et al., 1990). Sandow (1997) found that eight- to ten-year-olds draw both 'nice people' and 'clever people' as smiling. Smiling also elicits greater leniency towards an individual accused of an academic transgression, even

Fig. 9.4 Duchenne smile.

though the smiling transgressor is not judged as less guilty than the nonsmiling transgressor (LaFrance & Hecht, 1995). By contrast the absence of smiling is often perceived as hostile or indicative of negative intent.

However, for a smile to have these positive effects it has to be perceived as authentic (Bugental, Kaswan, & Love, 1970). Research on smiles has shown that smiles that are perceived as authentic or "felt" differ systematically from smiles that are not so perceived (Duchenne, 1862/1990; Ekman, Davidson, & Friesen, 1990; Ekman, Hager, & Friesen, 1981; Frank, & Ekman, 1993) Authentic and inauthentic smiles differ in terms of timing parameters (Hess, Kappas, McHugo, Kleck, & Lanzetta, 1989; Hess & Kleck, 1990, 1994), degree of left–right asymmetry (Ekman et al., 1981) and in particular, the presence and absence of the so-called Duchenne marker, the activation of *Orbicularis Oculi*, which creates wrinkles around the eye, in addition to *Zygomaticus Major*, which pulls up the corners of the mouth (Duchenne, 1862/1990; Ekman et al., 1990) (see Figure 9.4).

However, recently Thibault, Thibault, Levesque, Gosselin, and Hess, (2007) noted that the research on smile authenticity had been restricted to Western countries and questioned whether the same cues would be used in other cultural contexts. This notion was based on nonverbal dialect theory, which proposes the presence of cultural differences in the use of emotional expressions that are subtle enough to allow accurate communication across cultural boundaries in general, yet substantive enough to result in a potential for miscommunication (Elfenbein, & Ambady, 2002, 2002; Marsh, Elfenbein, & Ambady, 2003).

Thibault et al., (2007) showed smiles that differed in intensity as well as in the presence and absence of the Duchenne marker shown by individuals from Quebec, Gabon, and Mainland China to members of these same three groups and asked them to specify how authentic each smile appeared to them. The results were most interesting. In what follows we focus on the perception of three types of smiles, a weak smile without Duchenne marker and medium intensity smiles with and

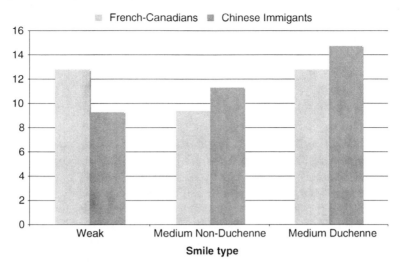

Fig. 9.5 Perceived authenticity of smiles shown by Quebeçois models as a function of decoder ethnicity.

without Duchenne marker shown by members of a western culture and evaluated by members of the same culture or by immigrants from Mainland China.

As Figure 9.5 shows, the two groups did not evaluate the smiles in the same way. French Canadians rate a medium intense smile without a Duchenne marker as quite inauthentic compared to either a weak smile or a medium intense smile with the marker. In other words they penalized for the absence of an authenticity marker. By contrast, the Chinese immigrants rated a smile as more authentic to the degree that it showed the authenticity marker. This use of the Duchenne marker is closer to how this marker is usually referred to when people talk about the twinkle in the eyes, or laughing wrinkles as signs of true enjoyment and seems therefore suggestive of the application of a culturally transmitted rule.

In fact, the degree to which the Duchenne marker was used as a marker of the authenticity of smiles shown by the members of the host cultures was correlated with the perceivers' length of stay in the culture. Interestingly, when rating the smiles of Chinese models, the Chinese immigrants did not use the Duchenne marker as a sign of authenticity at all; in fact, they rated the Duchenne and the non-Duchenne smiles as exactly equal in authenticity.

This study shows that the impact of one of the most commonly used facial expressions in humans and most commonly implemented features in facial animation is dependent on the ethnicity of both observer and actor. That is, within a Western cultural context, smiles of a certain intensity must include the Duchenne marker in order to be perceived as authentic, and this generalizes to immigrants from other cultures who will quite rapidly learn to use this marker as well (albeit in a subtly different way). However, members of other cultures seem to base their perception on other indices; the Gabonese participants as well did not use the Duchenne marker as a cue to authenticity. Hence there may be the danger that a smile is recognized but perceived as inauthentic and hence does not have the hoped-for positive effect on the interaction when used in non-Western contexts.

9.5 Conclusion

In sum, ample research has shown that human interactions are generally accompanied by emotional facial expressions. Humans also translate this into human–machine interactions by reacting facially to computer agents (King, 1997). Hence a believable agent needs to show believable emotion expressions. (Pelachaud & Bilvi, 2003). The present manuscript had the aim of pointing to some recent findings from research on human–human interaction, which suggest that this may require more than just the implementation of believable movement patterns. Rather it seems important to consider the appearance of the agent and the types of beliefs that people unconsciously associate with the appearance and that may bias their perception.

References

Adams, R. B., Jr., Hess, U., & Kleck, R. E. (2007). Emotion in the Neutral Face: The Influence of Gender-emotion Stereotypes and Gender-related Facial Appearance. Manuscript submitted for publication.

Ambady, N., Hallahan, M., & Rosenthal, R. (1995). On judging and being judged accurately in zero-acquaintance situations. *Journal of Personality and Social Psychology, 69*, 518–529.

Aronoff, J., Barclay, A. M., & Stevenson Aronoff, J., Barclay, A. M., & Stevenson, L. A. (1988). The recognition of threatening facial stimuli. *Journal of Personality and Social Psychology, 54*, 647–665.

Bauer, D. J., & Gariépy, J. L. (2001). The functions of freezing in the social interactions of juvenile high-and low-aggressive mice. *Aggressive Behavior, 27*, 463–475.

Bayes, M. A. (1972). Behavioral cues of interpersonal warmth. *Journal of Consulting and Clinical Psychology, Oct. 39*(2), 333–339.

Bulk, R. (1984). Nonverbal receiving ability. In R. Buck (Ed.), *The communication of emotion* (pp. 209–242). New York: Guilford Press.

Bugental, D. E., Kaswan, J. W., & Love, L. R. (1970). Perception of contradictory meanings conveyed by verbal and nonverbal channels. *Journal of Personality and Social Psychology, 16*, 647–655.

Calder, A. J., & Young, A. W. (2005). Understanding the recognition of facial identity and facial expression. *Nature Reviews Neuroscience, 6*, 641–651.

Darwin, C. (1872/1965). *The expression of the emotions in man and animals.* Chicago: The University of Chicago Press. (Originally published, 1872).

Deutsch, F. M., LeBaron, D., & Fryer, M. M. (1987). What is in a smile? *Psychology of Women Quarterly, sep. vol. 11*(3), 341–351.

Duchenne, G. B. (1862/1990). *The mechanism of human facial expression.* R. A. Cuthbertson (Ed. and Trans.). Cambridge, UK: Cambridge University Press.

Ekman, P., Davidson, R. J., & Friesen, W. V. (1990). The Duchenne smile: Emotional expression and brain physiology II. *Journal of Personality and Social Psychology, 58*, 342–353.

Ekman, P., & Friesen, W. V. (1971). Constants across cultures in the face and emotion. *Journal of Personality and Social Psychology, 17*, 124–129.

Ekman, P., Hager, J. C., & Friesen, W. V. (1981). The symmetry of emotional and deliberate facial actions. *Psychophysiology, 18*(2), 101–106.

Elfenbein, H. A., & Ambady, N. (2002). On the universality and cultural specificity of emotion recognition: A meta-analysis. *Psychological Bulletin, 128*, 203–235.

Elfenbein, H. A., & Ambady, N. (2003). When familiarity breeds accuracy: Cultural exposure and facial emotion recognition. *Journal of Personality and Social Psychology, 85*, 276–290.

Fischer, A. H. (1993). Sex differences in emotionality: Fact or stereotype? *Feminism & Psychology, 3*, 303–318.

Frank, M. G., & Ekman, P. (1993). Not all smiles are created equal: The differences between enjoyment and nonenjoyment smiles. Special issue: Current issues in psychological humor research. *Humor: International Journal of Humor Research, 6*, 9–26.

Guthrie, D. M., & Noller, P. (1988). Spouses' perception of one another in emotional situations. In P. Noller & M. A. Fitzpatrick (Eds.), *Perspectives on marital interaction* (pp. 153–181). Clevedon and Philadephia: Multilingual Matters.

Haugh, S. S., Hoffman, C. D., & Cowan, G. (1980). The eye of the very young beholder: Sex typing of infants by young children. *Child Development., 51*, 598–600.

Hess, U., Adams, R. B., Jr., & Kleck, R. E. (2004). Facial appearance, gender, and emotion expression. *Emotion, 4*, 378–388.

Hess, U., Adams, R. B., Jr., & Kleck, R. E. (2005). Who may frown and who should smile? Dominance, affiliation, and the display of happiness and anger. *Cognition and Emotion, 19*, 515–536.

Hess, U., Beaupré, M. G., & Cheung, N. (2002). Who to whom and why – Cultural differences and similarities in the function of smiles. In M. Abel & C. H. Ceia (Eds.), *An empirical reflection on the smile* (pp. 187–216). New York: Edwin Mellen Press.

Hess, U., Blairy, S., & Kleck, R. E. (2000a). The influence of expression intensity, gender, and ethnicity on judgments of dominance and affiliation. *Journal of Nonverbal Behavior, 24*, 265–283.

Hess, U., Kappas, A., McHugo, G. J., Kleck, R. E., & Lanzetta, J. T. (1989). An analysis of the encoding and decoding of spontaneous and posed smiles: The use of facial electromyography. *Journal of Nonverbal Behavior, 13*(2), 121–137.

Hess, U., & Kleck, R. E. (1990). Differentiating emotion elicited and deliberate emotional facial expressions. *European Journal of Social Psychology, 20*, 369–385.

Hess, U., & Kleck, R. E. (1994). The cues decoders use in attempting to differentiate emotion elicited and posed facial expressions. *European Journal of Social Psychology, 24*, 367–381.

Hess, U., Adams, R. B., Jr., & Kleck, R. E. (2007). When two do the same it might not mean the same: The perception of emotional expressions shown by men and women. In U. Hess & P. Philippot (Eds.), *Group Dynamics and Emotional Expression* (pp. 33–52). New York, NY: Cambridge University Press.

Hess, U., Senécal, S., Kirouac, G., Herrera, P., Philippot, P., & Kleck, R. E. (2000b). Emotional expressivity in men and women: Stereotypes and self-perceptions. *Cognition and Emotion, 14*, 609–642.

Karniol, R. (1990). Reading people's minds: A transformation rule model for predicting others' thoughts and feelings. *Advances in Experimental Social Psychology, 23*, 211–247.

Keating, C. F. (1985). Human dominance signals: The primate in us. In S. L. Ellyson & J. F. Dovidio (Eds.), *Power, dominance, and nonverbal communication* (pp. 89–108). New York: Springer Verlag.

King, J. (1997). Human computer dyads? A survey of nonverbal behavior in human–computer systems. In *Proceedings of the Workshop on Perceptual User Interfaces (PUI '97)* (pp. 54–55). Banff, Canada, Oct. 19–21: Los Alamitos, CA: IEEE Computer Society Press.

Kirouac, G., & Hess, U. (1999). Group membership and the decoding of nonverbal behavior. In P. Philippot, R. Feldman & E. Coats (Eds.), *The social context of nonverbal behavior* (pp. 182–210). Cambridge, UK: Cambridge University Press.

Knutson, B. (1996). Facial expressions of emotion influence interpersonal trait inferences. *Journal of Nonverbal Behavior, 20*, 165–182.

Koda, T., & Maes, P. (1996). Agents with faces: The effects of personification of agents. In *Proceedings of Human–Computer Interaction '96*. August, London, UK.

LaFrance, M., & Hecht, M. A. (1995). Why smiles generate leniency. *Personality and Social Psychology Bulletin, 21*(3), 207–214.

Lau, S. (1982). The effect of smiling on person perception. *Journal of Social Psychology, Jun. 117*(1), 63–67.

Malatesta, C. Z., Fiore, M. J., & Messina, J. J. (1987a). Affect, personality, and facial expressive characteristics of older people. *Psychology and Aging, 2*, 64–69.

Malatesta, C. Z., Izard, C. E., Culver, C., & Nicolich, M. (1987b). Emotion communication skills in young, middle-aged, and older women. *Psychology and Aging, 2*, 193–203.

Marsh, A. A., Adams, R. B., Jr., & Kleck, R. E. (2005). Why do fear and anger look the way they do? Form and social function in facial expressions. *Personality and Social Psychological Bulletin, 31*, 73–86.

Marsh, A. A., Elfenbein, H. A., & Ambady, N. (2003). Nonverbal "accents": Cultural differences in facial expressions of emotion. *Psychological Science, 14*, 373–376.

Matsumoto, D. (1992). American-Japanese differences in the recognition of universal facial expressions. *Journal of Cross-Cultural Psychology, 23*, 72–84.

Matsumoto, D., Kasri, F., & Kooken, K. (1999). American-Japanese cultural differences in judgements of expression intensity and subjective experience. *Cognition & Emotion, 13*, 201–218.

Matsumoto, D., & Kudoh, T. (1993). American-Japanese cultural differences in attribution of personality based on smiles. *Journal of Nonverbal Behavior, 17*, 231–243.

McGinley, H., McGinley, P., & Nicholas, K. (1978). Smiling, body position, and interpersonal attraction. *Bulletin of the Psychonomic Society., Jul. 12*(1), 21–24.

Motley, M. T., & Camden, C. T. (1988). Facial expression of emotion: A comparison of posed expressions versus spontaneous expressions in an interpersonal communications setting. *Western Journal of Speech Communication, 52*, 1–22.

Mueser, K. T., Grau, B. W., Sussman, S., & Rosen, A. J. (1984). You're only as pretty as you feel: Facial expression as a determinant of physical attractiveness. *Journal of Personality and Social Psychology, 46*(2), 469–478.

Pelachaud, C., & Bilvi, M. (2003). Computational model of believable conversational ahgents. In M.-P. Huget (Ed.), *Communication in multiagent systems: Agent communication languages and conversation policies* (pp. 300–317). Heidelberg, Germany: Springer.

Reis, H. T., Wilson, I. M., Monestere, C., & Bernstein, S. (1990). What is smiling is beautiful and good. *European Journal of Social Psychology, May–Jun, 20*(3), 259–267.

Ruback, R. B. (1981). Perceived honesty in the parole interview. *Personality and Social Psychology Bulletin, 7*, 677–681.

Sandow, S. (1997). The good King Dagobert, or clever, stupid, nice, nasty. *Disability and Society, 12*, 83–93.

Senior, C., Phillips, M. L., Barnes, J., & David, A. S. (1999). An investigation into the perception of dominance from schematic faces: A study using the World-Wide Web. *Behavior Research Methods, Instruments and Computers, 31*, 341–346.

Thibault, P., Levesque, M., Gosselin, P., & Hess, U. (2007). *Wrinkles around the eyes or not? A cultural dialect for smile authenticity*: Manuscript submitted for publication.

Thornton, G. R. (1943). The effect upon judgements of personality traits of varying a single factor in a photograph. *Journal of Social Psychology, 18*, 127–148.

Wiggers, M. (1984). Emotion recognition in children and adults. Unpublished dissertation, University of Nijmegen.

Yrizarry, N., Matsumoto, D., & Wilson-Cohn, C. (1998). American-Japanese differences in multiscalar intensity ratings of universal facial expressions of emotion. *Motivation and Emotion, 22*, 315–327.

Zebrowitz, L. A., Kikuchi, M., & Fellous, J.-M. (2007). Are effects of emotion expression on trait impressions mediated by babyfaceness? Evidence from connectionist modeling. *Personality and Social Psychological Bulletin, 33*, 648–662.

Chapter 10
Automatic Facial Action Unit Recognition by Modeling Their Semantic And Dynamic Relationships

Yan Tong, Wenhui Liao, and Qiang Ji

Abstract A system that could automatically analyze the facial actions in real-time has applications in a wide range of different fields. The previous facial action unit (AU) recognition approaches often recognize AUs or certain AU combinations individually and statically, ignoring the semantic relationships among AUs and the dynamics of AUs. Hence, these approaches cannot always recognize AUs reliably, robustly, and consistently due to the richness, ambiguity, and the dynamic nature of facial actions. In this work, a novel AU recognition system is proposed to systematically account for the relationships among AUs and their temporal evolutions based on a dynamic Bayesian network (DBN). The DBN provides a coherent and unified hierarchical probabilistic framework to represent probabilistic relationships among various AUs and to account for the temporal changes in facial action development. Within the proposed system, robust computer vision techniques are used to obtain AU measurements. And such AU measurements are then applied as evidence to the DBN for inferring various AUs. The experiments show that the integration of AU relationships and AU dynamics with AU measurements yields significant improvement of AU recognition, especially under realistic environments including illumination variation, face pose variation, and occlusion.

Y. Tong
General Electric Global Research Center, Schenectady, NY
e-mail: tongyan@ge.com

W. Liao
The Thomson Corporation, Eagan, MN
e-mail: wenhui.liao@thomson

Q. Ji (✉)
Department of Electrical, Computer and Systems Engineering, Rensselaer Polytechnic Institute, Troy, NY
e-mail: qji@ecse.rpi.edu

J.H. Tao, T.N. Tan (eds.), *Affective Information Processing*,
© Springer Science+Business Media LLC 2009

10.1 Introduction

Facial expression is one of the most important nonverbal interactive signals for human communication (Pantic & Bartlett, 2007). The Facial Action Coding System (FACS) developed by Ekman & Friesen (1978) is the most commonly used method for measuring facial expression. Based on the FACS, facial display can be decomposed into 44 facial action units (AUs), each of which is anatomically related to the contraction of a specific set of facial muscles. The FACS has been demonstrated to be a powerful means for detecting and measuring a large number of facial expressions by virtually observing a small set of facial muscular movements. Furthermore, AUs can be used as the intermediate features for various high-level understanding. For example, it has been employed for recognizing affective states such as fatigue (Gu & Ji, 2004), pain (Williams, 2002), and depression (Heller & Haynal, 1997). Therefore, a system that can recognize AUs in real-time without human intervention is desirable for various application fields, including automated tools for behavioral research, video conferencing, affective computing, perceptual human–machine interfaces, 3D face reconstruction and animation, and others.

In general, an automatic AU recognition system consists of two key stages: the facial feature extraction stage and AU classification stage. Many methods have been devoted to these two stages. In the facial feature extraction stage, previous work can be summarized into two major groups: holistic techniques (Lien, Kanade, Cohn, & Li, 2000; Donato, Bartlett, Hager, Ekman, & Sejnowski, 1999; Fasel & Luettin, 2000; Smith, Bartlett, & Movellan, 2001; Bazzo & Lamar, 2004; Bartlett, Littlewort, Frank, Lainscsek, Fasel, & Movellan, 2005), where the face is processed as a whole, and local techniques (Lien et al., 2000; Donato et al., 1999; Cohen, Sebe, Garg, Chen, & Huang, 2003; Cohn, Reed, Ambadar, Xiao, & Moriyama, 2004; Tian, Kanade, & Cohn, 2001, 2002; Valstar, Patras, & Pantic, 2005; Zhang & Ji, 2005; Gu & Ji, 2004; Kapoor, Qi, & Picard, 2003), in which only a set of specific facial features or facial regions are considered. And the approaches on AU classification could be grouped into spatial approaches (El Kaliouby & Robinson, 2004; Lien et al., 2000; Donato et al., 1999; Cohn et al., 2004; Bazzo & Lamar, 2004; Fasel & Luettin, 2000; Smith et al., 2001; Tian et al., 2001, 2002; Kapoor et al., 2003; Bartlett et al., 2005; Valstar et al., 2005; Pantic & Rothkrantz, 2004), where AUs are analyzed frame by frame, and spatial-temporal approaches (Lien et al., 2000; Cohen et al., 2003; Zhang & Ji, 2005; Gu & Ji, 2004; Cohen et al., 2004), where AUs are recognized over time based on the temporal evolution of facial features. However, these methods all classify each AU or certain AU combinations independently and statically (although some of them analyze the temporal properties of facial features), ignoring the semantic relationships among AUs and the dynamics of AUs. Hence, these approaches cannot always recognize AUs reliably, robustly, and consistently due to the richness, ambiguity, and the dynamic nature of facial actions, as well as the uncertainties with feature extraction. Therefore, it is important to exploit the relationships among the AUs as well as the temporal development of each AU in order to improve AU recognition.

Specifically, a single AU rarely occurs alone in spontaneous facial behavior. Some patterns of AU combinations appear frequently to express natural human emotions. On the other hand, it is nearly impossible to perform some AUs simultaneously as described in the alternative rules defined in FACS (Ekman, Friesen, & Hager, 2002). Furthermore, in addition to the dynamic development of each AU, the relationships among AUs also undergo a temporal evolution. Such dynamic and semantic co-occurrence/co-absence relationships can be well modeled with a dynamic Bayesian network (DBN). The DBN is capable of representing the relationships among different AUs in a coherent and unified hierarchical structure, accounting for uncertainties in the AU recognition process with conditional dependence links, modeling the dynamics in facial behavior development with temporal links, and providing principled inference and learning techniques to systematically combine domain information and statistical information extracted from the data.

Figure 10.1 gives the flowchart of the proposed automatic AU recognition system, which consists of an offline training phase (Figure 10.1a) and an online AU recognition phase (Figure 10.1b). The system training includes training an AdaBoost classifier for each AU and learning DBN in order to correctly model the AU relationships. Advanced learning techniques are applied to learn both the structure and parameters of the DBN based on both training data and domain knowledge. The online AU recognition consists of AU measurement extraction and DBN inference. First, the face and eyes are detected in live video automatically. Then the face region is convolved with a set of multiscale and multiorientation Gabor filters, respectively, to produce wavelet features for each pixel. After that, the AdaBoost classifier combines the wavelet features to produce a measurement score for each AU. These scores are then used as evidence by a DBN for AU inference. Under

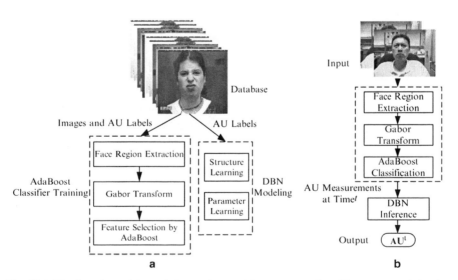

Fig. 10.1 The flowchart of the real-time AU recognition system: **a** the offline system training for AdaBoost classifiers and DBN, and **b** the online AU recognition.

such a framework, the erroneous AU measurements from the underlying computer vision techniques could be compensated by the relationships among AUs embedded in the DBN, and some AUs that are difficult to be directly recognized can be inferred indirectly from other AUs.

10.2 Related Work

A number of approaches in computer vision have been developed to recognize action units and their combinations from the video sequences or from the static images by observing the representative facial appearance changes as described in FACS. Generally, a two-stage procedure is utilized: first the features related to the corresponding AUs are extracted; then the AUs are recognized by different recognition engines based on the extracted features.

10.2.1 Facial Feature Extraction

In general, the facial feature extraction techniques could be grouped into two classes: holistic approaches, where the face is processed as a whole, and local approaches, in which only a set of specific facial features or facial regions are taken into account according to the target AU.

Among the holistic facial feature extraction methods, there are three major variations: motion extraction by dense flow estimation (Lien et al., 2000; Donato et al., 1999), motion extraction based on difference images (Donato et al., 1999; Fasel & Luettin, 2000; Smith et al., 2001; Bazzo & Lamar, 2004), and single image-based methods (Lanitis, Taylor, & Cootes, 1997; Bartlett et al., 2005). These holistic approaches include more information from the large face region, and thus have the generalization ability to recognize a full range of facial behaviors; however, its computational complexity is considerable.

Facial muscular activities would also produce the changes in the appearance and positions of permanent facial features, and in the presence of transient facial features. The motion information extracted from the eyebrows, eyes, and mouth is especially important for recognizing many action units (Cohn & Zlochower, 1995). The local methods (Donato et al., 1999; Cohen et al., 2003; Cohn et al., 2004; Lien et al., 2000; Tian et al., 2001, 2002; Valstar et al., 2005; Zhang & Ji, 2005; Gu & Ji, 2004; Kapoor et al., 2003) focus on the facial features locally. These approaches are sensitive to subtle changes in small areas, and more computationally efficient than the holistic approaches, but special-purpose features should be deliberately designed for each AU, respectively. Because the accuracy of the AU recognition fully depends on how reliably and accurately the facial features are extracted, human intervention is usually required in the initial frame to ensure a reliable reference for the subsequent frames in most of the existing facial feature extraction techniques.

10.2.2 Action Unit Classification

Given the extracted facial features, the action units are identified by recognition engines. In general, they can be divided into spatial classification approaches and spatial–temporal classification approaches.

The simplest classification method is identifying AUs based on some parametric rules of AUs (El Kaliouby & Robinson, 2004) or by template matching (Donato et al., 1999). Cohn et al. (2004) and Lien et al. (2000) employ discriminant analysis for AU recognition. Given the measurement of the facial features, the discrimination between AUs is performed by comparing posterior probabilities of AUs. Neural networks are widely used in AU classification (Donato et al., 1999; Fasel & Luettin, 2000; Smith et al., 2001; Bazzo & Lamar, 2004; Tian et al., 2001, 2002). They differ mainly in the input facial features, which could be PCA coefficients (Donato et al., 1999; Fasel & Luettin, 2000; Bazzo & Lamar, 2004), facial feature motions and transient facial features (Donato et al., 1999; Tian et al., 2001), and Gabor wavelet coefficients (Smith et al., 2001; Tian et al., 2002). Support Vector Machines (SVM) have been used for identifying AUs in Kapoor et al. (2003), Bartlett et al. (2005), and Valstar et al. (2005).

However, the major limitation of the spatial classification methods is that they don't model the temporal dynamics of a facial behavior, although the temporal evolution often reveals more information about the underlying human emotional states (Zhang & Ji, 2005). Another common limitation of such methods is that they only attempt to classify each AU independently, ignoring the semantic relationships among AUs. Recently, Pantic & Rothkrantz (2004) utilized a rule-based method with a fast-direct chaining inference procedure for AU recognition based on the description of each AU in the FACS system. However, some of the rules are not correct for more general cases. Moreover, it is not clear how these rules handle the uncertainty associated with AU measurements. Therefore, probabilistically modeling the relationships among AUs would be more desirable than enumerating some simple deterministic rules.

There have been several attempts to recognize AUs over time. Lien et al. (2000) recognized AUs based on a set of hidden markov models (HMMs). Each AU or AU combination is assigned a HMM. The classification is performed by choosing the AU or AU combination that maximizes the likelihood of the extracted facial features generated by the associated HMM. However, the huge number of HMMs required to identify a great number of potential AU combinations prevents it from real-time applications.

In addition to the above approaches, there are a few groups using Bayesian networks for facial expression classification. The research group by Cohen et al. (2003) uses Gaussian tree-augmented naive Bayes (TAN) to learn the dependencies among different facial motion features in order to classify facial expressions. However, due to TAN's structure limitations, it cannot handle complex relationships between facial features as well as temporal changes. Zhang and Ji (2005) exploit a BN to classify six basic facial expressions with a dynamic fusion strategy. Gu and Ji (2004) use a similar idea for facial event classification such as fatigue. Cohen et al. (2004)

further propose a classification-driven stochastic structure search (SSS) algorithm for learning a BN classifier to recognize facial expressions from both labeled and unlabeled data. However, in the previous BN-based facial expression recognition, AUs are modeled as hidden nodes connecting facial features and facial expressions, and are not recognized explicitly in their models. Again, they don't consider the semantic relationships among AUs as well as the dynamics of each AU.

Overall, the previous work on facial AU analysis may have the following limitations.

- The previous work based on static images could not model the temporal dynamics of an observed facial behavior. However, the psychological experiment (Bassili, 1979) suggests that facial behavior is more accurately recognized from image sequence than from a still image.
- Human intervention in the initial frame is required for most of the existing work to ensure a reliable reference image for the subsequent frames.
- Each AU combination is often treated as a new AU. However, it is nearly impossible to deal with the potential thousands of AU combinations.
- The missing features caused by occlusions, measurement errors, and low AU intensity have not been addressed effectively by the existing work.
- The existing methods only attempt to classify each AU independently, ignoring the semantic relationships among AUs.

The proposed system differs from the cited ones in that it explicitly models probabilistic relationships among different AUs and accounts for the temporal changes in facial action development with a DBN. Advanced learning techniques are used to learn both the structure and parameters of the DBN from the training database.

10.3 AU Measurement Extraction

As described above, the accuracy of face alignment would affect the performance of AU recognition. Because the position, size, and orientation of the face region are usually estimated using the knowledge of eye centers, an accurate and robust eye detector is desirable. In this work, a boosted eye detection algorithm is employed based on recursive nonparametric discriminant analysis (RNDA) features proposed in Wang et al. (2005). The eye localization follows a hierarchical principle: first a face is detected, then the eyes are located inside the detected face. An overall 94.5% eye detection rate is achieved with 2.67% average normalized error (the pixel error normalized by the distance between two eyes) (Wang et al., 2005) on a FRGC 1.0 database (Phillips et al., 2005). Given the knowledge of eye centers, the face region is divided into upper and lower face parts, each of which is normalized and scaled into a 64×64 image.

Given the normalized upper/lower face image, a measurement is extracted for each AU based on Gabor feature representation and AdaBoost classification similar to the work by Bartlett et al. (2005). Table 10.1 summarizes a list of commonly

Table 10.1 A List of AUs and Their Interpretations

AU1	AU2	AU4	AU5	AU6
Inner brow raiser	Outer brow raiser	Brow Lowerer	Upper lid raiser	Cheek raiser
AU7	AU9	AU12	AU15	AU17
Lid tightener	Nose wrinkler	Lip corner puller	Lip corner depressor	Chin raiser
AU23	AU24	AU25	AU27	
Lip tightener	Lip presser	Lips part	Mouth stretch	

Source: Adapted from (Zhang & Ji, 2005)

occurring AUs and their interpretations. Instead of extracting the Gabor wavelet features at specific feature points, the whole normalized upper/lower face region is convolved pixel by pixel by a set of Gabor filters at 5 spatial frequencies and 8 orientations. Overall, $8 \times 5 \times 64 \times 64 = 163,840$ individual Gabor wavelet features are produced as the input of each AdaBoost classifier. This feature extraction method has the advantage that it captures not only the changes in geometrical positions of permanent facial components, but also the changes in facial appearance (i.e., wrinkles, bulges) encoded by the Gabor wavelet coefficients.

The AdaBoost classifier is then employed to obtain the measurement for each AU. At first, each training sample is initialized with an equal weight. Then, weak classifiers are constructed using the individual Gabor features during AdaBoost training. In each iteration, the single weak classifier with the minimum weighted AU classification error w.r.t. the current boosting distribution is selected. Then it is linearly combined with the previously selected weak classifiers to form the final "strong" classifier with a weight that is proportional to the minimum error. The training samples are then reweighted based upon the performance of the selected weak classifier, and the process is repeated. To increase the speed of the actual algorithm, the final classifier is broken up into a series of cascaded AdaBoost classifiers. Compared with AU classification by SVM, the AdaBoost classifier significantly improves recognition efficiency (Bartlett et al., 2005).

However, this image appearance-based approach treats each AU and each frame individually, and heavily relies on the accuracy of face region alignment. In order to model the dynamics of AUs as well as their semantic relationships, and to deal with the image uncertainty, a DBN is utilized for AU inference. Consequently, the continuous output of the AdaBoost classifier is discretized into binary values and used as evidence for the subsequent AU inference via the DBN.

10.4 AU Inference with a Dynamic Bayesian Network

10.4.1 AU Relationship Analysis

As discussed before, current computer vision methods cannot perform feature extraction reliably, which limits AU recognition accuracy. Moreover, when AUs occur in a combination, they may be nonadditive; that is, the appearance of an AU in a combination is different from its appearance of occurring alone. The nonadditive effect increases the difficulty of recognizing AUs individually. Fortunately, there are some inherent relationships among AUs as described in the FACS manual (Ekman et al., 2002). For example, the alternative rules provided in the FACS manual describe the mutual exclusive relationship among AUs. Furthermore, the FACS also includes the co-occurrence rules in their old version (Ekman & Friesen, 1978), which were "designed to make scoring more deterministic and conservative, and more reliable" (Ekman et al., 2002).

In a spontaneous facial behavior, groups of AUs usually appear together to show meaningful facial expressions. For example, the happiness expression may involve AU6 (cheek raiser) + AU12 (lip corner puller) + AU25 (lips part) as in Figure 10.2a; the surprise expression may involve AU1 (inner brow raiser) + AU2 (outer brow raiser) + AU5 (upper lid raiser) + AU25 (lips part) + AU27 (mouth stretch) as in Figure 10.2(b); and the sadness may involve AU1 (inner brow raiser) + AU4 (brow lowerer) + AU15 (lip corner depressor) + AU17 (chin raiser) as in Figure 10.2c (Zhang & Ji, 2005). Furthermore, some of the AUs would appear simultaneously most of the time. For example, it is difficult to do AU2 (outer brow raiser) without performing AU1 (inner brow raiser) because the activation of AU2 tends to raise the inner portion of the eyebrow as well (Pantic & Rothkrantz, 2004). On the other hand, it is nearly impossible for some AUs to appear together. For example, the lips cannot be parted as AU25 (lips part) and pressed as AU24 (lip presser) simultaneously. In addition to the dynamic development of each AU, the relationships among AUs also undergo a temporal evolution, which can realistically reflect the evolution from a neutral state to a weak emotion, then to the apex, and finally to a releasing state. Therefore, a unified framework, which can model and learn the relationships

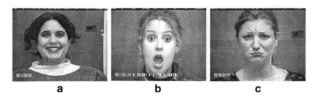

a   b   c

Fig. 10.2 Some examples of AU combinations show meaningful expressions: **a** AU6 + AU12 + AU25 represents the happiness facial expression; **b** AU1 + AU2 + AU5 + AU25 + AU27 represents the surprise facial expression; and **c** AU1 + AU4 + AU15 + AU17 represents the sadness facial expression (adapted from Kanade et al. (2000)).

among AUs as well as employ the relationships in AU recognition, will compensate the disadvantages of computer vision techniques, and thus improve the recognition accuracy.

10.4.2 AU Relationship Modeling

Due to the errors from feature extraction and the variability among individuals, the relationships among AUs and their dynamics are stochastic. A BN can be employed to model and learn such relationships described above. A BN is a directed acyclic graph (DAG) that represents a joint probability distribution among a set of variables. In a BN, nodes denote variables, and the links among nodes denote the conditional dependency among variables. The dependency is characterized by a conditional probability table (CPT) for each node.

The AU relationships are partly learned from the co-occurrence table of Table 10.2a and co-absence table of Table 10.2b. Both tables are constructed from two FACS-coded facial expression databases: Cohn and Kanade's *DFAT–504* database (Kanade et al., 2000) and the ISL database (Tong et al., 2007). For Table 10.2a, each entry $a_{i,j}$ represents the probability $P(AU_i = 1|AU_j = 1)$, and the pairwise co-occurrence dependency between two AUs is computed as below:

$$P(AU_i = 1|AU_j = 1) = \frac{N_{AU_i+AU_j}}{N_{AU_j}},$$ (10.1)

Table 10.2 (a) The Co-Occurrence Table (each entry $a_{i,j}$ represents $P(AU_i = 1|AU_j = 1)$), (b)The Co-Absence Table (each entry $a_{i,j}$ represents $P(AU_i = 0|AU_j = 0)$).

	IAU1=1	IAU2=1	IAU4=1	IAU5=1	IAU6=1	IAU7=1	IAU9=1	IAU12=1	IAU15=1	IAU17=1	IAU23=1	IAU24=1	IAU25=1	IAU27=1
AU1=1	1.000	0.988	0.190	0.907	0.047	0.072	0.028	0.118	0.187	0.155	0.052	0.058	0.352	0.777
AU2=1	0.831	1.000	0.076	0.888	0.024	0.028	0.028	0.101	0.081	0.072	0.022	0.026	0.304	0.777
AU4=1	0.239	0.115	1.000	0.098	0.328	0.834	0.910	0.123	0.507	0.591	0.504	0.497	0.151	0.021
AU5=1	0.610	0.719	0.052	1.000	0.019	0.025	0.003	0.085	0.048	0.043	0.022	0.017	0.254	0.648
AU6=1	0.032	0.019	0.176	0.019	1.000	0.301	0.303	0.570	0.117	0.131	0.118	0.163	0.269	0.001
AU7=1	0.074	0.034	0.671	0.037	0.453	1.000	0.928	0.180	0.341	0.426	0.410	0.431	0.136	0.002
AU9=1	0.010	0.013	0.267	0.002	0.167	0.338	1.000	0.017	0.228	0.263	0.077	0.054	0.032	0.001
AU12=1	0.094	0.097	0.078	0.100	0.674	0.142	0.038	1.000	0.029	0.039	0.129	0.168	0.295	0.076
AU15=1	0.123	0.064	0.264	0.046	0.114	0.220	0.404	0.024	1.000	0.661	0.424	0.479	0.005	0.007
AU17=1	0.152	0.085	0.460	0.062	0.190	0.412	0.697	0.048	0.990	1.000	0.812	0.826	0.018	0.001
AU23=1	0.020	0.010	0.154	0.013	0.067	0.156	0.080	0.063	0.249	0.319	1.000	0.766	0.009	0.002
AU24=1	0.027	0.014	0.180	0.011	0.111	0.194	0.066	0.097	0.334	0.385	0.910	1.000	0.006	0.001
AU25=1	0.533	0.554	0.181	0.570	0.602	0.202	0.131	0.560	0.013	0.027	0.034	0.021	1.000	0.998
AU27=1	0.298	0.358	0.006	0.369	0.001	0.001	0.001	0.036	0.004	0.001	0.002	0.001	0.253	1.000

(a)

	IAU1=0	IAU2=0	IAU4=0	IAU5=0	IAU6=0	IAU7=0	IAU9=0	IAU12=0	IAU15=0	IAU17=0	IAU23=0	IAU24=0	IAU25=0	IAU27=0
AU1=0	1.000	0.952	0.756	0.895	0.738	0.724	0.753	0.747	0.764	0.750	0.755	0.752	0.837	0.824
AU2=0	0.992	1.000	0.764	0.937	0.761	0.761	0.795	0.790	0.791	0.776	0.794	0.791	0.871	0.866
AU4=0	0.697	0.671	1.000	0.677	0.719	0.877	0.769	0.675	0.750	0.799	0.733	0.736	0.639	0.686
AU5=0	0.981	0.979	0.805	1.000	0.822	0.807	0.832	0.831	0.828	0.814	0.834	0.830	0.899	0.894
AU6=0	0.810	0.814	0.855	0.821	1.000	0.890	0.860	0.939	0.839	0.839	0.842	0.847	0.906	0.831
AU7=0	0.721	0.721	0.946	0.733	0.808	1.000	0.832	0.756	0.787	0.824	0.785	0.791	0.717	0.746
AU9=0	0.893	0.898	0.989	0.900	0.930	0.992	1.000	0.900	0.941	0.967	0.915	0.912	0.843	0.907
AU12=0	0.792	0.798	0.776	0.803	0.907	0.806	0.804	1.000	0.791	0.776	0.813	0.816	0.878	0.808
AU15=0	0.842	0.830	0.896	0.831	0.843	0.871	0.874	0.822	1.000	0.998	0.877	0.888	0.774	0.836
AU17=0	0.754	0.743	0.871	0.746	0.769	0.832	0.819	0.736	0.910	1.000	0.832	0.846	0.666	0.754
AU23=0	0.892	0.894	0.939	0.898	0.908	0.932	0.911	0.906	0.940	0.979	1.000	0.991	0.870	0.904
AU24=0	0.872	0.874	0.926	0.878	0.896	0.922	0.892	0.894	0.936	0.977	0.973	1.000	0.843	0.885
AU25=0	0.710	0.703	0.588	0.695	0.701	0.611	0.635	0.702	0.596	0.562	0.624	0.617	1.000	0.717
AU27=0	0.975	0.976	0.879	0.964	0.896	0.886	0.904	0.901	0.898	0.887	0.904	0.902	1.000	1.000

(b)

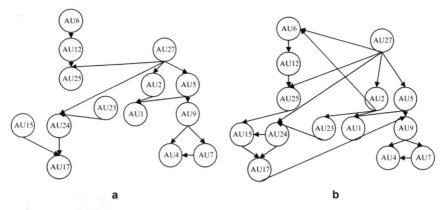

a   b

Fig. 10.3 a The prior BN for AU modeling before learning; **b** the learned BN from the training data.

where $N_{AU_i+AU_j}$ is the total number of the positive examples of the AU combination $(AU_i + AU_j)$ regardless of the presence of other AUs in the databases, and N_{AU_j} is the total number of the positive examples of AU_j in the databases.

Similarly, for Table 10.2b, each entry $a_{i,j}$ represents the probability $P(AU_i = 0|AU_j = 0)$ and the pairwise co-absence dependency between two AUs.

If the probability is higher than T_{up} or lower than T_{bottom} (T_{up} and T_{bottom} are the predefined thresholds), the two AUs are assumed to be strongly dependent, which could be modeled with a link between them in the BN. Furthermore, the dependency between two AUs is not symmetric as shown in Table 10.2; for example $P(AU_i = 1|AU_j = 1) \neq P(AU_j = 1|AU_i = 1)$. This asymmetry indicates that one AU plays the dominant role (the cause), and the other AU follows (i.e., the effect). This kind of relationship justifies the use of a directed edge instead of an undirected edge to represent the causal dependency between two AUs. In this way, an initial BN structure is manually constructed as Figure 10.3a to model the relationships among the 14 target AUs.

10.4.3 Learning BN Structure

After analyzing the AU relationships, an initial BN structure is obtained. However, it may not be correct enough to reflect the true relationships. Therefore, it is necessary to use a large amount of training data to "correct" the "guess" with a structure learning algorithm.

The structure learning algorithm first defines a score that describes the fitness of each possible structure B_s to the observed data, then a network structure is identified with the highest score. Let a domain of discrete variables be $\mathbf{X} = \{X_1, \ldots, X_N\}$, and a database of sampling data be $D = \{D_1, \ldots, D_K\}$. A score used for model selection can be defined as

$$Score(B_s) = \log p(D, B_s) = \log p(D|B_s) + \log p(B_s). \quad (10.2)$$

The two terms in Eq. (10.2) are actually the log likelihood and the log prior probability of the structure B_s, respectively. For a large database, the Bayesian information criterion (BIC) introduced by Schwarz (1978) has been used to compute the log likelihood $\log p(D|B_s)$ approximately:

$$\log p(D|B_s) \approx \log p(D|\hat{\theta}_{B_s}, B_s) - \frac{d}{2}\log(K), \qquad (10.3)$$

where θ_{B_s} is a set of network parameters, $\hat{\theta}_{B_s}$ is the maximum likelihood estimate of θ_{B_s}, d is the number of free parameters in B_s, and K is the number of sampling data in D. Thus in Eq. (10.3), the first term is used to measure how well the model fits the data, and the second term is a penalty term that punishes the structure complexity.

Instead of giving an equal prior $p(B_s)$ to all possible structures, a high probability is assigned to the prior structure P_s, which is chosen as the manually constructed model illustrated in Figure 10.3a. Let $\Pi_i(B_s)$ be a set of parent nodes of X_i in B_s. Assume δ_i is the number of nodes in the symmetric difference of $\Pi_i(B_s)$ and $\Pi_i(P_s)$, which is defined as

$$\delta_i = |(\Pi_i(B_s) \cup \Pi_i(P_s)) \setminus (\Pi_i(B_s) \cap \Pi_i(P_s))|, \qquad (10.4)$$

where $\Pi_i(B_s) \cup \Pi_i(P_s)$ represents the union of sets $\Pi_i(B_s)$ and $\Pi_i(P_s)$, $\Pi_i(B_s) \cap \Pi_i(P_s)$ is the intersection of sets $\Pi_i(B_s)$ and $\Pi_i(P_s)$, and "\" means set difference.

Then the prior of any other network $(B_s \neq P_s)$ is decreased depending on the deviation between this network structure and the provided prior network structure (Heckerman, Geiger, & Chickering, 1995) as below,

$$p(B_s) = c\kappa^{\delta}, \qquad (10.5)$$

where c is a normalization constant to make $\Sigma_m^M p(B_{sm}) = 1$, given M possible network structures; $0 < \kappa \leq 1$ is a predefined constant factor; $\delta = \Sigma_{i=1}^N \delta_i$; and N is the number of nodes in the network.

Having defined a score as Eq. (10.2), a network structure with the highest score needs to be identified by a searching algorithm. To reduce the searching space, a constraint is imposed that each node has at most two parents for model simplicity. Thus, structure learning becomes an optimization problem: find the structure that maximizes the score. In order to avoid getting stuck at a local maximum, an iterated hill-climbing is applied in this work.

1. Initialize the starting network structure.
   First, a random network structure (B_s) or the prior structure (P_s) is used as the starting network structure B_0.
2. Find a local maximum.
   A local search is performed until a local maximum is reached.

   - Starting from B_0, compute the score of each nearest neighbor of B_0, which is generated from B_0 by adding, deleting, or reversing a single arc, subject to the acyclicity constraint and the upper bound of parent nodes.

- Update B_0 with the BN that has the maximum score among all of the nearest neighbors, and go back to the previous step until no neighbors have a higher score than the current structure.

3. Randomly perturb the current network structure, and go back to step 2 until it converges.

The learned structure is shown in Figure 10.3b. Basically, the learned structure keeps all of the links in the initial structure, and adds several links, such as AU27 to AU6, AU2 to AU6, AU25 to AU15, and AU2 to AU23, which are reasonable to reflect facial expressions. For example, AU27 (mouth stretch) would mostly be contracted in the surprise facial expression, whereas AU6 (cheek raiser) would mostly happen in the happiness facial expression. The two action units are seldom present together, which agrees with the co-occurrence table of Table 10.2a, where $P(AU6 = 1|AU27 = 1)$ is very small. Overall, the learned structure reflects the data pattern in the training dataset better.

10.4.4 A Dynamic Bayesian Network

The structure learning above only focuses on learning the static BN. However, it lacks the ability to express temporal dependencies between the consecutive occurrences of certain AUs in image sequences, whereas AU is an event that develops over time. Furthermore, in addition to the dynamic development of each AU, the relationships among AUs also undergo a temporal evolution. AUs can therefore be better recognized from a sequence of observations over time instead of from a snapshot. Thus a DBN is used to model the dynamic aspect of AUs.

In general, a DBN is made up of interconnected time slices of static BNs, and the relationships between two neighboring time slices are modeled by a hidden Markov model, such that random variables at time t are influenced by other variables at time t, as well as by the corresponding random variables at time $t - 1$ only. Each time slice is used to represent the snapshot of an evolving temporal process at a time instant. Each slice of the DBN is a static BN as described in Figure 10.3b with a measurement node associated with each AU, and the neighboring time slices are interconnected by the arcs joining certain temporal variables from two consecutive slices.

Specifically, in the proposed framework, two types of conditional dependency for variables are considered at two adjacent time slices. The link of the first type connects each AU_i node at time $t - 1$ to that at time t which depicts how a single AU_i develops over time. On the other hand, the multiple AUs involved in a spontaneous facial behavior may not undergo the same development simultaneously; instead they often proceed in sequence as the intensity of facial expression varies. For example, Figure 10.4 shows how a smile is developed in an image sequence: first AU12 (lip corner puller) is contracted to express a slight smile, then AU6 (cheek raiser) and AU25 (lips part) are triggered to enhance the happiness. As the intensity

Fig. 10.4 An example image sequence displays the unsynchronized AUs' evolutions in a smile (adapted from Kanade et al. (2000)).

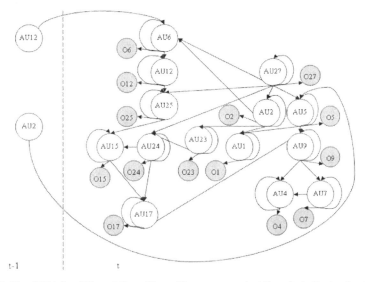

Fig. 10.5 The DBN for AU modeling. The self-arrow at each AU node indicates the temporal relationship of a single AU from the previous time step to the current time step. The arrow from AU_i at time $t-1$ to AU_j ($j \neq i$) at time t indicates the temporal relationship between different AUs. The shaded circle indicates the measurement for each AU.

of happiness increases, AU12 first reaches its highest intensity level, then AU6 and AU25 reach their apexes, respectively. Hence, the link of the second type connects AU_i node at time $t-1$ to AU_j at time t and depicts how AU_i at the previous time step affects AU_j ($j \neq i$) at the current time step.

Figure 10.5 gives the whole picture of the DBN including the shaded visual measurement nodes. For presentation clarity, the self-arrows are used to indicate the first type of temporal links. The arrow from time $t-1$ to time t indicates the second type of temporal link, which is determined manually based on the data analysis.

Furthermore, each AU node is associated with a measurement node, which is represented with a shaded circle in Figure 10.5. The links between them model the measurement uncertainty resulting from the computer vision techniques in Section 10.3. The measurement nodes provide evidence obtained through some AU recognition techniques in the inference procedure. The AU nodes are hidden nodes, whose states need to be inferred from the DBN given the evidence.

Therefore, such a DBN is capable of accounting for uncertainties in the AU recognition process, representing probabilistic relationships among AUs, modeling the dynamics in AU development, and providing principled inference solutions. In addition, with the conditional dependency coded in the graphical model, it can handle situations where several data entries for certain AUs are missing. For example, even if several AU measurements are not available with the computer vision techniques, it is still possible to infer the states of the corresponding AUs using other available measurements.

10.4.5 Learning DBN Parameters

Given the DBN structure shown in Figure 10.5, the parameters should be learned in order to infer each AU. Learning the parameters in a DBN is actually similar to learning parameters for a static BN. During DBN learning, the DBN is treated as an expanded BN consisting of two-slice static BNs connected through the temporal variables as shown in Figure 10.5. Besides learning the conditional probability tables (CPTs) for each slice, it is also necessary to learn the transition probabilities between slices. For DBN learning, the training data need to be divided into sets of time sequences of three dimensions representing the sequence index, node index, and time slice, respectively.

Let θ_{ijk} indicate a probability parameter for a DBN with the structure B_s as

$$\theta_{ijk} = p(x_i^k | pa^j(X_i), B_s), \tag{10.6}$$

where x_i^k represents the kth state of variable X_i, and $pa^j(X_i)$ is the jth configuration of the parent nodes of X_i.

Thus, the goal of learning parameters is to maximize the posterior distribution $p(\theta | D, B_s)$ (MAP) given a database D and the structure B_s (Heckerman, 1995). Assuming θ_{ij} [1] are mutually independent (Spiegelhalter & Lauritzen, 1990),

$$p(\theta | D, B_s) = \prod_{i=1}^{n} \prod_{j=1}^{q_i} p(\theta_{ij} | D, B_s), \tag{10.7}$$

where n is the number of variables in the B_s, and q_i is the number of the parent instantiations for X_i. Assuming a Bayesian Dirichlet prior probability (Heckerman, 1995), the posterior distribution $p(\theta_{ij} | D, B_s)$ can be approximated by Dirichlet distributions:

$$p(\theta_{ij} | D, B_s) = Dir(\alpha_{ij1} + N_{ij1}, \dots, \alpha_{ijr_i} + N_{ijr_i}), \tag{10.8}$$

---

[1] $\theta = (\theta_1, \cdots, \theta_n)$ is the vector of parameters, where $\theta_i = ((\theta_{ijk})_{k=2}^{r_i})_{j=1}^{q_i}$ are the parameters, and $\theta_{ij} = (\theta_{ij2}, \cdots, \theta_{ijr_i})$.

where α_{ijk} reflects the prior belief about how often the case $X_i = k$ and $pa(X_i) = j$. N_{ijk} reflects the number of cases in D for which $X_i = k$ and $pa(X_i) = j$, and r_i is the number of all instantiations of X_i.

This learning process considers both prior probability and likelihood, so that the posterior probability is maximized. Because the training data are complete, it can be actually explained as a counting process, which results in the following formula of the probability distribution parameters,

$$\theta_{ijk} = \frac{\alpha_{ijk} + N_{ijk}}{\alpha_{ij} + N_{ij}}, \qquad (10.9)$$

where $N_{ij} = \sum_{k=1}^{r_i} N_{ijk}$, and $\alpha_{ij} = \sum_{k=1}^{r_i} \alpha_{ijk}$.

10.4.6 AU Recognition Through DBN Inference

Given the AU measurements obtained through the AdaBoost technique, the probabilities of different AUs can be inferred through the DBN. Let AU_i^t indicate the node of AU i at time step t, and $\mathbf{e}^t = \{e_1^t, e_2^t, \ldots, e_{27}^t\}$ be the measurements for the 14 AUs at time step t. Thus, the probability of AU_i^t, given the available evidence $\mathbf{e}^{1:t}$, can be inferred by performing the DBN updating process as below (Korb & Nicholson, 2004).

- **Prediction:** Given the estimated probability distribution $p(AU_i^{t-1}|\mathbf{e}^{1:t-1})$, which is already inferred at time step $t-1$, the predicted probabilities $p(AU_i^t|\mathbf{e}^{1:t-1})$ can be calculated by using the standard BN inference algorithm such as a version of the junction tree algorithm (Kjaerulff, 1995).
- **Rollup:** Remove time slice $t-1$, and use the predictions $p(AU_i^t|\mathbf{e}^{1:t-1})$ for the t slice as the new prior.
- **Estimation:** Add new observations $\mathbf{e}^t$, and calculate the probability distribution over the current state $p(AU_i^t|\mathbf{e}^{1:t})$. Finally, add the slice for $t+1$.

In this way, the posterior probability of each AU is obtained given the observed measurements.

10.5 Experimental Results

10.5.1 Facial Action Unit Databases

The automatic facial AU recognition system is trained on two FACS labeled databases. The first database is the Cohn and Kanade's *DFAT*–504 database (Kanade et al., 2000), which consists of more than 100 subjects covering different races, ages, and genders. This database is collected under controlled illumination and background, and has been widely used for evaluating the facial AU recognition system. Using this database has several advantages: this database demonstrates diversity over the subjects, and it involves multiple-AU expressions. The results on the Cohn–Kanade database are used to compare with other published methods.

However, the image sequences in this database only reflect the evolution of the expression starting from neutral state and ending at the apex, but without the relaxing period, which is a necessary component for natural facial behavior. Furthermore, this database consists of only 23 expressions, which are only a small part of the many facial expressions. So the relationships among AUs extracted only from this database are not sufficient. Thus, the ISL database (Tong et al., 2007) is created to overcome the shortcomings of the Cohn–Kanade database.

The ISL database consists of 42 image sequences from ten subjects displaying facial expressions undergoing a neutral-apex-neutral evolution. The subjects are instructed to perform the single AUs and AU combinations as well as the six basic expressions. The database is collected under real-world conditions with uncontrolled illumination and background as well as moderate head motion. The results on the ISL database are intended to demonstrate the robustness in real-world applications. Overall, the combined database consists of over 14,000 images from 111 subjects. In order to extract the temporal relationships, the two databases are coded into AU labels frame by frame manually in this work.

10.5.2 Evaluation on Cohn–Kanade Database

The proposed system is first evaluated on the Cohn–Kanade database using leave-one-subject-out cross-validation for the 14 target AUs. The AdaBoost classifiers and the DBN parameters are trained on all of the data but one subject that is left out for testing. The positive samples are chosen as the training images containing the target AU at different intensity levels, and the negative samples are selected as those images without the target AU regardless the presence of other AUs.

Figure 10.6 shows the performance for generalization to novel subjects in the Cohn–Kanade database using the AdaBoost classifiers alone, using the DBN, and Bartlett et al. method (Bartlett et al., 2005),[2] respectively. With only the Adaboost classifiers, the proposed system achieves an average recognition rate of 91.2% with a positive rate of 80.7% and a false alarm rate of 7.7% for the 14 AUs, where the average recognition rate is defined as the percentage of examples recognized correctly. With the use of the DBN, the system achieves an average recognition rate of 93.33% with a significant improvement in positive rate of 86.3% and reduced false alarm rate of 5.5%.

As shown in Figure 10.6, for AUs that can be well recognized by the AdaBoost classifier, the improvement by using DBN is not that significant. However, for the

---

[2] The experiment result reported on the Website Bartlett et al. (2007) is employed for comparison. It was also trained and tested on the Cohn–Kanade database using leave-one-subject-out cross-validation and represents the state-of-the-art AU recognition techniques.

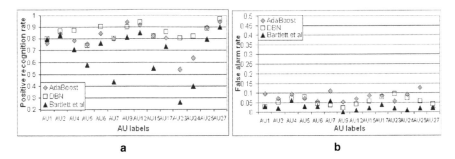

Fig. 10.6 Comparison of AU recognition results on novel subjects in the Cohn–Kanade database using the AdaBoost classifier, DBN, and the results of Bartlett et al., respectively: **a** average positive rates; **b** average false alarm rates.

AUs that are difficult to be recognized by the AdaBoost classifier, the improvements are impressive, which exactly demonstrates the benefit of using the DBN. For example, recognizing AU23 (lip tightener) and AU24 (lip presser) is difficult, because the two actions occur rarely and the appearance changes caused by these actions are relatively subtle. Fortunately, the probability of these two actions' co-occurrence is very high, because they are contracted by the same set of facial muscles. By employing such a relationship in DBN, the positive recognition rate of AU23 increases from 54% to 80.6% and that of AU24 increases from 63.4% to 82.3%. Similarly, by employing the co-absence relationship between AU25 (lips part) and AU15 (lip corner depressor), the false alarm rate of AU25 reduces from 13.3% to 5.7%.

Compared with the system performance reported by Bartlett et al. (2007) (overall average recognition rate 93.6%), the proposed system achieves a similar average recognition rate (93.33%). With a marginal increase in false alarm rate about 3%, the proposed system significantly increases the positive rate from 70.4% in Bartlett et al. (2007) to 86.3%. More important, for some specific AUs, which are difficult to be recognized, the improvements are impressive. For example, an 80.6% positive recognition rate of AU23 is obtained compared with 26.3% by Bartlett et al., and an 82.3% positive recognition rate for AU24 compared with 40% in their method.

Tian et al. (2001) achieved a similar performance by training and testing the upper-face AUs on the Ekman–Hager database, and the lower-face AUs on the Cohn–Kanade database, respectively. However, manual intervention is required in the initial frame with neutral expression in their method. Valstar et al. (2005) reported an 84% average recognition rate on the Cohn–Kanade database while training on MMI facial expression database (Pantic et al., 2005). Kapoor et al. (2003) obtained an 81.2% of recognition rate on 5 upper AUs using only 25 subjects in the Cohn–Kanade database with hand-marked pupil positions. In summary, the average performance of the proposed system is equal to or better than the previously reported systems. But the proposed system achieved much better performance on some difficult AUs.

One significant advantage worth mentioning about the proposed framework is that the use of DBN always tends to compensate the errors with the measurements from the underlying computer vision techniques. Therefore, if the proposed DBN were built on any of the AU recognition techniques mentioned in the related work, their results could be improved with low extra cost given the fact that BN inference is quite efficient in the simple network structure.

10.5.3 Experiment Results Under Real-World Conditions

In the second set of experiments, the system is trained on all of the training images from the Cohn–Kanade database and 38 image sequences with six subjects from the ISL database. The remaining four image sequences with four different subjects from the ISL database are used for testing. This experiment intends to demonstrate the system robustness for real-world environments. The system performance is reported in Figure 10.7. The average recognition rate of DBN inference is 93.27% with an average positive rate of 80.8% and a false alarm rate of 4.47%. Compared with the AU recognition results by the frame-by-frame AdaBoost classification, the AU recognition is improved significantly. The overall correct recognition rate is improved by 5.1% with an 11% increase in positive recognition rate, and a 4.4% decrease in false alarm. Especially for the AUs that are difficult to recognize, the system performance is greatly improved. For example, the recognition rate of AU7 (lid tightener) is increased from 84% to 94.8%, the recognition rate of AU15 (lip corner depressor) is improved from 71.5% to 82.9%, and that of AU23 (lip tightener) is increased from 82.3% to 94.4%.

The system enhancement comes mainly from two aspects. First, the erroneous AU measurement could be compensated by the relationships among AUs in the BN model. As mentioned above, the AU measurement extracted by the AdaBoost classification is sensitive to inaccurate image alignment. Moreover, some AUs are inherently difficult to identify. For example, the recognition of AU7 (lid tightener) is difficult, because the contraction of AU7 would narrow the eye aperture, which,

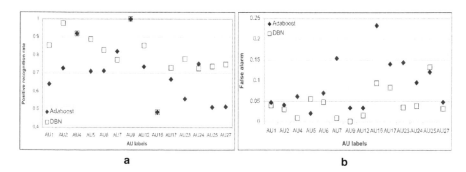

Fig. 10.7 Comparison of AU recognition results on novel subjects under real-world circumstances using the AdaBoost classifier and DBN respectively: **a** average positive rates and **b** average false alarm rates.

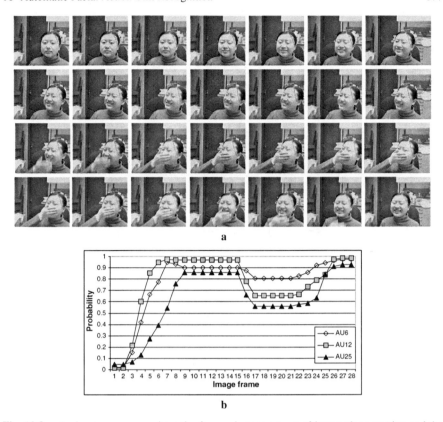

Fig. 10.8 a An image sequence where the face undergoes an out-of-image plane rotation and the mouth is occluded by the hand in some frames; **b** the *x*-axis represents the image frame number, and the *y*-axis represents the probabilities of the involved action units in the corresponding frames. The edges between the points depict the temporal evolution of each AU. Occlusion occurs from frame 15 to frame 25.

however, could also be caused by AU6 (cheek raiser) or by a relaxed eyelid. Fortunately, AU7 occurs often with AU4 (brow lowerer), which can be easily recognized. By embedding such a relationship in the DBN, the false alarm rate of AU7 is reduced greatly (from 15.4% to 1%).

Second and more important, the proposed approach could recognize an individual AU, even if there is no direct measurement for that AU due to face pose variation or occlusion. Figure 10.8a gives an image sequence, where the face pose varies in some frames. Figure 10.8b depicts the probabilities of the involved action units by the proposed approach for the image sequence. Because the AdaBoost classifiers are trained on nearly frontal view faces, some of the AU measurements obtained by the AdaBoost classifiers may not be accurate under large out-of-image-plane head rotation. The inaccurate AU measurements could be compensated by their relationships with other AUs through the DBN inference as shown in Figure 10.8b.

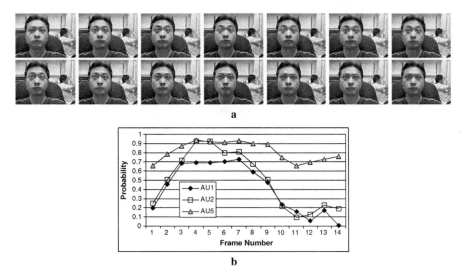

Fig. 10.9 Automatic AU recognition on an image sequence under real-world circumstances: **a** shows a subject with eyebrow rising and eyelid rising in an image sequence; **b** shows the probabilities of the involved AUs in the corresponding frames, where each curve represents the temporal evolution of a specific AU, respectively.

Figure 10.8a also shows the mouth is occluded in some frames due to occlusion by hand. The AdaBoost classifier could not recognize the action units correctly in the lower face region due to the occlusion. Figure 10.8b shows that AU12 (lip corner puller) and AU25 (lips part) could still be correctly estimated through their semantic relationships with the other AUs as well as the temporal evolution of themselves, because AU6 + AU12 + AU25 imply a happiness expression.

Figure 10.9 shows the probabilities of AUs for an image sequence. It can be seen that the probabilities change smoothly following the temporal evolution of the facial actions over time. Because there are individual differences w.r.t. the magnitudes of action units, it is difficult to determine the absolute intensity of a given subject. The dynamic modeling of facial action units can more realistically reflect the evolution of a spontaneous facial emotion, and thus can extract the relative intensity changes of the action units.

10.6 Conclusion

A fully automatic system is proposed for real-time recognition of action units in a real-world environment. Instead of recognizing each AU or AU combination individually or statically, a DBN is employed to model both the semantic and temporal relationships among various AUs. Such a model is capable of representing the relationships among different AUs in a coherent and unified hierarchical structure, accounting for nonuniqueness and uncertainties in the AU recognition process, modeling the dynamics in facial behavior development, and providing principled inference. Especially, both the structure and parameters are learned with advanced machine-learning techniques to systematically combine the domain information and statistical information extracted from the data. Therefore, the erroneous AU measurement from the underlying computer vision techniques could be compensated by exploiting the relationships among AUs; some AUs that are difficult to be directly recognized can be inferred indirectly from other AUs; and the low-intensity AUs could be recognized more reliably by using the information from other high-intensity AUs. As shown in the experiments, the DBN framework integrated with the underlying feature extraction techniques yields significant improvement of AU recognition over using computer vision techniques alone. The improvement is even more obvious in a real-world environment such as illumination variation, face pose variation, and occlusion.

References

Bartlett, M. S., Littlewort, G., Frank, M. G., Lainscsek, C., Fasel, I., & Movellan, J. R. (2005). Recognizing facial expression: Machine learning and application to spontaneous behavior. *Proceedings of CVPR05* 2, pp. 568–573

Bartlett, M. S., Littlewort, G., Movellan, J. R., Frank, M. G. (2007). Auto facs coding URL http://mplab.ucsd.edu/grants/project1/research/Fully-Auto-FACS-Coding.html.

Bassili, J. N. (1979). Emotion recognition: The role of facial movement and the relative importance of upper and lower areas of the face. *Journal of Personality and Social Psychology 37*(11), 2049–2058.

Bazzo, J. J., Lamar, M. V. (2004). Recognizing facial actions using gabor wavelets with neutral face average difference. *Proceedings of FGR04*, pp. 505–510.

Cohen, I., Cozman, F. G., Sebe, N., Cirelo, M. C., & Huang, T. S. (2004). Semisupervised learning of classifiers: Theory, algorithms, and their application to human-computer interaction. *IEEE Transactions on PAMI* 26(12), 1553–1567.

Cohen, I., Sebe, N., Garg, A., Chen, L., & Huang, T. (2003). Facial expression recognition from video sequences: Temporal and static modeling. *Computer Vision and Image Understanding 91*(1–2), 160–187.

Cohn, J. F., Reed, L. I., Ambadar, Z., Xiao, J., & Moriyama, T. (2004) Automatic analysis and recognition of brow actions and head motion in spontaneous facial behavior. *In Proceedings of IEEE Int'l Conf on Systems, Man, and Cybernetics* 1, pp. 610–616

Cohn, J. F., & Zlochower, A. (1995). A computerized analysis of facial expression: Feasibility of automated discrimination. *American Psychological Society*, New York, New York.

Donato, G., Bartlett, M. S., Hager, J. C., Ekman, P., & Sejnowski, T. J. (1999). Classifying facial actions. *IEEE Transactions, on PAMI 21*(10), 974–989.

Ekman, P., & Friesen, W. V. (1978). Facial action coding system: A technique for the measurement of facial movement. Palo Alto, CA: Consulting Psychologists Press.

Ekman, P., Friesen, W. V., & Hager, J. C. (2002). Facial action coding system: The manual. Research Nexus, Div. Salt Lake City, UT: Network Information Research Corp.

El Kaliouby, R., & Robinson, P. K. (2004). Real-time inference of complex mental states from facial expressions and head gestures. *CVPRW'04 10*, 154.

Fasel, B., & Luettin, J. (2000) Recognition of asymmetric facial action unit activities and intensities. *Proceedings of ICPR00 1*, pp. 1100–1103.

Gu, H., & Ji, Q. (2004). Facial event classification with task oriented dynamic bayesian network. *Proceedings of CVPR04* 2, pp. 870–875.

Heckerman, D. (1995). A tutorial on learning with Bayesian networks. Tech Report MSR-TR-95-06, Microsoft Research.

Heckerman, D., Geiger, D., Chickering, D. M. (1995). Learning Bayesian networks: The combination of knowledge and statistical data. *Machine Learning 20*(3), 197–243.

Heller, M., & Haynal, V. (1997). Depression and suicide faces. In: P., Ekman Rosenberg & E (Eds.) *What the face reveals*, (pp. 339–407). Oxford University Press. New York.

Kanade, T., Cohn, J. F., Tian, Y. (2000). Comprehensive database for facial expression analysis. *Proceedings of FGR00*, pp. 46–53.

Kapoor, A., Qi, Y., & Picard, R. W. (2003). Fully automatic upper facial action recognition. *IEEE Int'l Workshop on Analysis and Modeling of Faces and Gestures*, pp. 195–202.

Kjaerulff, U. (1995) dhugin: A computational system for dynamic time-sliced bayesian networks. *International Journal of Forecasting*, Special issue on Probability Forecasting, *11*, 89–111.

Korb, K. B., & Nicholson, A. E. (2004). *Bayesian artificial intelligence*. London; Chapman and Hall/CRC.

Lanitis, A., Taylor, C. J., Cootes, T. F. (1997). Automatic interpretation and coding of face images using flexible models. *IEEE Transactions on PAMI 19*(7), 743–756.

Lien, J. J., Kanade, T., Cohn, J. F., & Li, C. (2000). Detection, tracking, and classification of action units in facial expression. *Journal of Robotics and Autonomous Systems 31*, 131–146.

Pantic M, Bartlett, M (2007). Machine analysis of facial expressions. In K. Delac, Grgic M. (Eds.) *Face recognition*, (pp. 377–416), Vienna: I-Tech Education.

Pantic, M., & Rothkrantz, L. J. M. (2004). Facial action recognition for facial expression analysis from static face images. *IEEE Transactions on Systems, Man, and Cybernetics-Part B: Cybernetics 34*(3),1449–1461.

Pantic, M., Valstar, M., Rademaker, R., Maat, L. (2005). Web-based database for facial expression analysis. *Proceedings of IEEE Int'l Conf on Multmedia and Expo (ICME05)* pp. 317–321.

Phillips, P. J., Flynn, P. J., Scruggs, T, Bowyer, K. W., Chang, J., Hoffman, K., Marques, J., Min, J., & Worek, W. (2005). Overview of the face recognition grand challenge. *Proceedings of CVPR05* 1, pp. 947–954

Schwarz, G. (1978). Estimating the dimension of a model. *The Annals of Statistics 6*, 461–464.

Smith, E., Bartlett, M. S., & Movellan, J. R. (2001). Computer recognition of facial actions: A study of co-articulation effects. *Proceedings of the 8th Annual Joint Symposium on Neural Computation.*

Spiegelhalter, D., & Lauritzen, S. (1990). Sequential updating of conditional probabilities on directed graphical structures. *Networks 20*, 579–605.

Tian, Y., Kanade, T., & Cohn, J. F. (2001). Recognizing action units for facial expression analysis. *IEEE Transact. on PAMI 23*(2), 97–115.

Tian, Y., Kanade, T., & Cohn, J. F. (2002). Evaluation of Gabor-wavelet-based facial action unit recognition in image sequences of increasing complexity. *Proceedings of FGR02* (pp. 218–223).

Tong, Y., Liao, W., & Ji, Q. (2007). Intelligent systems lab (isl) database URL http://www.ecse.rpi.edu/homepages/cvrl/database/database.html.

Valstar, M. F., Patras, I., & Pantic, M. (2005). Facial action unit detection using probabilistic actively learned support vector machines on tracked facial point data. *Proceedings of CVPRW'05 on Vision for Human-Computer Interaction* pp. 76.

Wang, P., Green, M. B., Ji, Q., & Wayman, J. (2005). Automatic eye detection and its validation. *IEEE Workshop on Face Recognition Grand Challenge Experiments (with CVPR)* 3.

Williams, A. C. (2002). Facial expression of pain: An evolutionary account. *Behavioral & Brain Sciences 25*(4), 439–488.

Zhang, Y., & Ji, Q. (2005). Active and dynamic information fusion for facial expression understanding from image sequences. *IEEE Transactions on PAMI 27*(5), 699–714.

Chapter 11
Face Animation Based on Large Audiovisual Database

Jianhua Tao, Panrong Yin, and Le Xin

Abstract In this chapter, we present two methods (fused HMM inversion method and unit selection method) for the speech-driven facial animation system. It systematically addresses audiovisual data acquisition, expressive trajectory analysis, and audiovisual mapping. Based on this framework, we learn the correlation between neutral facial deformation and expressive facial deformation with the Gaussian Mixture Model (GMM). A hierarchical structure is proposed to map the acoustic parameters to lip FAPs. Then the synthesized neutral FAP streams are extended with expressive variations according to the prosody of the input speech. The quantitative evaluation of the experimental result is encouraging and the synthesized face shows a realistic quality.

11.1 Introduction

Speech-driven face animation aims to convert an incoming audio stream into a sequence of corresponding face movements. A number of its possible applications could be seen in multimodal human–computer interfaces, visual reality, and videophones. Traditionally, the rule-based method (Ezzat & Poggio, 1998) and vector quantization method (Yamamoto, Nakamura, & Shikano, 1998) are two direct and easily realized ways. But the results from them are usually inaccurate and discontinuous due to limited rules and codebooks. Neural networks are also an effective means of audiovisual mapping. For instance, Massaro, Beskow, Cohen, Fry, and Rodriguez (1999) trained a neural network model to learn the mapping from LPCs to face animation parameters; they used the current frame and five backward and five forward time steps as the input to model the context. Although the neural network

J.H. Tao (✉), P.R. Yin, and L. Xin
National Laboratory of Pattern Recognition, Institute of Automation, Chinese Academy of Sciences, Beijing
e-mail: jhtao@nlpr.ia.ac.cn

J.H. Tao, T.N. Tan (eds.), *Affective Information Processing*,
© Springer Science+Business Media LLC 2009

has the merits of a moderate amount of samples and a smooth synthesized result, it is deeply influenced by the initial parameter setting, and it is easier to be bogged down into local minima.

It is believed that Hidden Markov Models (HMMs) could achieve a high level of success in this research field. Since Yamamoto et al. (1998), much attention has been paid in this direction for the purpose of dynamic audiovisual mapping in subphonemic acoustic feature level. Brand et al. (1999) have proposed a remapping HMM to train audiovisual conversion HMMs. As with other approaches, such as mixture-based HMM (Chen & Rao, 1998) and the Hidden Markov Model Inversion method (Choi & Hwang, 1999), vocal input will directly play a key role in the process of synthesizing its visual counterpart. And it has been shown by Fu, Gutierrez-Osuna, Esposito, Kakumanu, and Garcia (2005) that the HMMI method outperformed the other two in all these representative methods.

Although the improved prediction performance can be obtained from these newly proposed HMM-based methods, some improvement can be achieved. All these methods made the assumption that it is enough to model both acoustic and visual components with the same structure, not considering the individually specific structure. Furthermore, the two tightly coupled audio speech and visual speech streams also have the intrinsic nature of loose synchronization, which resulted in a complex training process, such as in the remapping HMM.

Some hidden Markov model extensions have recently received increasing attention for speech animation. Li and Shum (2006) proposed a method of achieving dynamic audiovisual mapping by learning an Input–Output HMM (IOHMM). In that method, they train IOHMMs by explicitly modeling the output and transition probabilities conditioned on the input sequence. Xie and Liu (2006) presented an approach for speech animation using coupled HMM, which allows for explicitly modeling the characteristics of the two modalities.

In this chapter, we present a speech-driven facial animation approach using a fused HMM inversion for dynamic audiovisual mapping. The fused HMM (Pan, Levinson, Huang, & Liang, 2004) constructs a novel structure linking two tightly coupled streams according to the maximum entropy principle and the maximum information criterion. It is just suitable here for representing the relation between the audio and visual sequences explicitly. In the synthesis stage, visual counterparts are synthesized from the partial inputs (audio input) by the Baum–Welch HMM inversion, maximizing the joint probabilistic distribution in the fused HMM. When it is implemented in the predefined subsets, a relatively short time delay and realistic synthesized facial animation are obtained.

Recently, some researchers have also applied a unit selection method by reordering or concatenating existing audiovisual units to form a new visual sequence. For instance, Bregler, Covell, and Slaney (1997) reordered existing mouth frames based on recognized phonemes. Cosatto, Potamianos, and Graf (2000) selected corresponding visual frames according to the distance between a new audio track and a stored audio track, and concatenated the candidates to form the smoothest sequence. These works have proved that unit selection methods can give very high realistic facial animation results.

With this idea, in this chapter, we also introduce an unit selection method which combines the VQ method and frame-based concatenation model to facilitate audio-visual mapping. This method keeps the result as realistic as possible. Considering search efficiency and automatic performance of the system, we introduce a hierarchical structure and regard every three frames as a unit (Yin & Tao, 2005). In this work, every three frames of the input speech are not directly compared with existing frames in the corpus, because the frame-based corpus would be too large to search.

Although lip shapes are closely related to speech content (linguistic), facial expression is a primary way of passing nonverbal information (paralinguistic) which contains a set of messages related to the speaker's emotional state. Thus, it would be more natural and vivid for the talking head to show expressions when communicating with the human. In Hong's work (Hong, Wen, & Huang, 2002), he not only applied several MLPs to map LPC cepstral parameters to face motion units, but also used different MLPs to map the estimated motion units to expressive motion units. Verma, Subramaniam, Rajput, Neti, and Faruquie (2004) used optical flow between visemes to generate face animations with different facial expressions. Li, Yu, Xu, Chang, and Shum (2001) adopted three sets of cartoon templates with five levels of intensity to show expression synchronized with face animation.

Although some work has been done for expressive facial animation from speech, the naturalness of synthesized results is still an open question. In this chapter, we use a Gaussian Mixture Model (GMM) for the first time to model the correlation between neutral facial deformation and expressive facial deformation, so as to investigate the forming process of facial expression.

The rest of the chapter is organized as follows. Section 11.2 introduces the fused HMM inversion method for audiovisual mapping, Section 11.3 focuses on the unit selection method based visual synthesis, Section 11.4 analyzes the trajectories of expressive facial deformation and the GMM modeling process, Section 11.5 gives the experimental results, and Section 11.6 is the conclusion and future work description.

11.2 Fused HMM Inversion Method

11.2.1 Fused HMM

As a technique of aiming at information fusion in the feature level under the HMM framework, the fused HMM was proposed in Pan et al. (2004) and had a successful performance in bimodal feature processing (Pan et al., 2004; Zeng et al., 2005). It devises a new structure linking the two component HMMs which is optimal according to the maximum entropy principle and a Maximum Mutual Information (MMI) criterion. It has the advantage of reaching a better balance between model complexity and performance than other existing model fusion methods, such as the coupled HMM (Brand et al., 1997) and mixed-memory HMM (Saul & Jordan, 1999). It is just chosen here for representing the relation between the audio and visual sequence explicitly.

After the processing of facial and vocal data, the two tightly coupled visual feature streams $O^v = \{o_1^v, o_2^v, \cdots, o_m^v\}$ and audio feature streams $O^a = \{o_1^a, o_2^a, \cdots, o_n^a\}$ are computed from the audiovisual corpus. Because of the difference in sampling rate of the video and audio frames, n may be unequal to m. After the synchronizing segmentation of the bimodal training data, there exists an index set $I = \{i_1, i_2, \cdots, i_m\}$ for i_j indicating the index of audio frame for the jth visual frame.

Given O^v, O^a, and their corresponding HMM, the fused HMM was proposed to devise a structure linking the component HMMs by giving an optimal estimation of the joint probability $p(O^a, O^v)$. Taking advantage of the fact that the data from a single sensor can be individually modeled by a HMM, and according to the maximum entropy principle and a maximum mutual information criterion, the fusion model yields the following two structures, as shown by Pan et al. (2004).

$$p^{(1)}(O^a; O^v) = p(O^a)p(O^v|\hat{U}^a) \tag{11.1}$$

$$p^{(2)}(O^a; O^v) = p(O^v)p(O^a|\hat{U}^v), \tag{11.2}$$

where $\hat{U}^a$ and $\hat{U}^v$ are the most possible hidden state sequences, estimated by the Viterbi algorithm.

The structures shown by (11.1) and (11.2) are different. In (11.1), it is required that $\hat{U}^a$ be reliably estimated, and in (11.2) that $\hat{U}^v$ be reliably estimated. In Pan et al. (2004) and Zeng et al. (2005), the first structure is preferred, because it is believed that the hidden states of the speech HMM can be estimated more reliably for the bimodal speech processing of speaker authorization.

The training process of the fused HMM is very simple, including the following main steps. (a) Two individual HMMs, consisting of visual component HMM and audio component HMM, are trained independently by the EM algorithm. (b) The best hidden state sequences of the HMMs are found using the Viterbi algorithm. (c) The coupling parameters are determined.

Here, the first structure (11.1) is preferred, in which the coupling parameter represents the conditional probability distribution of visual observation in the visual component HMM, given states in the audio component HMM. Surely, the discrete coupling parameters in Pan et al. (2004) can be easily extended to the continuous observation as follows.

$$b_j(o^v) = \sum_{k=1}^{K} c_{jk} N(o^v|\mu_{jk}, \sum_{jk}), 1 \le j \le N., \tag{11.3}$$

where o^v is the visual feature being modeled in the visual component HMM, and this Gaussian mixture is the visual observation in audio state j.

11.2.2 Inversion of Fused HMM

The HMM inversion algorithm was proposed in Moon and Hwang's (1997) work, and applied to robust speech recognition. Then Choi and Hwang (1999) used HMM inversion in dynamic audiovisual mapping, whose usefulness has been demonstrated in Fu, Gutierrez-Osuna, Esposito, Kakumanu, and Garcia (2005). Xie and Liu (2006) also derived their audiovisual conversion algorithms for the CHMMs based on Moon's work (Moon et al., 1997). Here the Baum–Welch HMM inversion method based on the fused HMM model is derived.

As shown by Xie and Liu (2006), Choi and Hwang (1999), and Moon and Hwang (1997), the optimal visual counterpart $\hat{O}^v$ can be formulated as the optimization of the following object function, $L(O^v) = \log P(O^a, O^v | \lambda^{av})$, given a novel audio input, where O^a is the novel input audio features, and λ^{av} are the parameters of the fused HMM model. The optimization can be found by iteratively maximizing the auxiliary function $Q(\lambda^{av}, \lambda^{av}; O^a, O^v, \bar{O}^v)$ based on the Baum–Welch method,

$$\hat{O}^v = \arg\max_{\bar{O}^v} Q(\lambda^{av}, \lambda^{av}; O^a, O^v, \bar{O}^v), \tag{11.4}$$

where O^v and $\bar{O}^v$ denote the old and new visual vector sequence, respectively.

In our work, the fused model can be presented as

$$P(O^a, O^v | \lambda^{av}) = \kappa_1 P(O^a) P(O^v | \hat{U}^a) + \kappa_2 P(O^v) P(O^a | \hat{U}^v), \tag{11.5}$$

where for constants $\kappa_1 \geq 0, \kappa_2 \geq 0$ with $\kappa_1 + \kappa_2 = 1$, $\kappa_1 > \kappa_2$. It is obvious that the two HMMs will all affect the synthesis result, but have different reliabilities. It is an easy extension of the presentation in Fu et al. (2005).

The object function can be expressed as

$$\begin{aligned}
&\arg\max_{O^v} L(O^v) \\
&= \arg\max_{O^v} [\kappa_1 \log P(O^v | \hat{U}^a) + \kappa_2 \log P(O^v)] \\
&= \arg\max_{O^v} [\kappa_1 \log \sum_{m^{av}} P(O^v, m^{av} | \hat{U}^a, \lambda^{av}) + \\
&\quad \kappa_2 \log \sum_{U^v} \sum_{m^v} \log P(O^v, U^v, m^v | \lambda^{av})]
\end{aligned} \tag{11.6}$$

where m^{av} is the vector $m^{av} = \{m^{av}_{\hat{u}^a_1 1}, m^{av}_{\hat{u}^a_2 2}, \cdots, m^{av}_{\hat{u}^a_T T}\}$, and m^v is the vector $m^v = \{m^v_{u^v_1 1}, m^v_{u^v_2 2}, \cdots, m^v_{u^v_T T}\}$ that indicates the mixture component for each state at each time.

The auxiliary function can be derived as

$$\Delta l = L(\bar{O}^v) - L(O^v) \geq Q(\lambda^{av}, \lambda^{av}; O^a, O^v, \bar{O}^v) + const. \tag{11.7}$$

So

$$Q(\lambda^{av}, \lambda^{av}; O^a, O^v, \bar{O}^v)$$

$$= \kappa_1 \sum_{l=1}^{M^{av}} h_l \sum_{t=1}^{T} \log c_{\hat{u}_t^a l} + \kappa_1 \sum_{l=1}^{M^{av}} h_l \sum_{t=1}^{T} \log b_{\hat{u}_t^a l}(\bar{o}_t^v)$$

$$+ \kappa_2 \sum_{i=1}^{N} \sum_{l=1}^{M^v} \sum_{t=1}^{T} \log c_{il} \cdot H_{ilt} + \kappa_2 \sum_{i=1}^{N} \sum_{l=1}^{M^v} \sum_{t=1}^{T} \log b_{il}(\bar{o}_t^v) \cdot H_{ilt} \qquad (11.8)$$

where

$$h_l = \frac{\prod_{t=1}^{T} P(o_t^v, m_{\hat{u}_t^a t}^{av} = l | \hat{u}_t^a, \lambda^{av})}{\sum_{n=1}^{M^{av}} \prod_{t=1}^{T} P(o_t^v, m_{\hat{u}_t^a t}^{av} = l | \hat{u}_t^a, \lambda^{av})} \qquad (11.9)$$

$$H_{ilt} = \frac{P(O^v, u_t^v = i, m_{u_t^v t}^v = l | \lambda^{av})}{\sum_{i=1}^{N} \sum_{l=1}^{M^v} \sum_{t=1}^{T} P(O^v, u_t^v = i, m_{u_t^v t}^v = l | \lambda^{av})} \qquad (11.10)$$

$$P(O^v, u_t^v = i, m_{u_t^v t}^v = l | \lambda^{av}) = \sum_{j=1}^{N} \alpha_j^v(t-1) a_{ji} c_{il} b_{il}(o_t^v) \beta_i^v(t). \qquad (11.11)$$

By setting

$$\frac{\partial Q(\lambda^{av}, \lambda^{av}; O^a, O^v, \bar{O}^v)}{\partial \bar{o}_t^v} = 0,$$

we can find the re-estimated inputs $\bar{o}_t^v$ as follows.

$$\bar{o}_t^v = \frac{\kappa_1 \sum_{l=1}^{M^{av}} h_l \cdot \Sigma_l^{-1} \cdot \mu_l + \kappa_2 \sum_{i=1}^{N} \sum_{l=1}^{M} H_{ilt} \cdot \Sigma_{il}^{-1} \cdot \mu_{il}}{\kappa_1 \sum_{l=1}^{M^{av}} h_l \cdot \Sigma_l^{-1} + \kappa_2 \sum_{i=1}^{N} \sum_{l=1}^{M} H_{ilt} \cdot \Sigma_{il}^{-1}}. \qquad (11.12)$$

11.2.3 Fused HMM Inversion-Based Audiovisual Mapping

In this section, we apply T fused HMM inversion to synthesize continuous visual output with as little time delay as possible given the highly continuous audio input.

After the time synchronization in the audiovisual corpus, the same numbers of audio and visual frames are found by a series preprocessing, including upsampling. Similar to other works, we also account for coarticulation by using those several backward and forward frames as the context of the current frame. After the segmentation of bimodal information in time, the audiovisual dynamic pairs are formed by means of a tapped-delay line. And both audio and visual feature vectors are taken at 13 consecutive time frames (7 backward, current, 7 forward). Here 13 frames, considering for the 130 ms audio block, is a tradeoff between the optimization of the contextual information and the requirement of uninfected delay.

In Hong, Wen, and Huang's (2002) work, subsets are found by the divide of the audio feature space in the training corpus. Here this idea is carried a step further. In our work, those subsets are found by a two-layer clustering framework. In the first layer, the visual configuration is divided into 80 classes. In the second layer, the audio observations in same visual class are classified into different submodels, with which the very existing different audio observation in the same visual class is concerned. In this way, the audiovisual joint space is clustered based on its different observation in turn. This framework accounts for the many-to-many mapping between audio and visual features.

The 80 visual classes found in the first layer clustering will account for not only the natural deformation in the predefined number of specific visual representations, but also the intercluster variation between these visual specifications. It is achieved by using the cluster method twice.

11.2.4 Clustering Twice in Visual

It has been believed that the number of the static visual configurations relative to audio speech is limited, just as the work on static visemes shows. So we focus on discovering enough static visual representations in the first clustering time. The visual features from one single frame are imported in the k-means (40 clusters). The cluster found in this way can represent the repertoire of facial specification.

However, it is far more than enough to get a realistic facial synthesis result in this way, because of the continuous process of the facial real deformation. So the intraclass natural facial deformation is modeled here. In this way, an index sequence will accompany the visual observation sequences. Each of the indexes indicates to which cluster the current visual frame belongs. This accompanying index sequence will give us the basic variant in each visual class, which discloses the continuous essence of video. For the stability of video variation in each cluster, only the visual shapes that have enough duration in one cluster are selected for the training of a fused HMM model in that cluster.

Gaps may exist in the accompanying index sequence. Thus, only a part of the whole training data is used. As demonstrated empirically in a low-dimensional space (two-dimensional), the synthesized video output may not be continuous enough in Figure 11.1a. Furthermore, the transformation between different clusters of visual specification should also be considered. So a second clustering (40 clusters) is needed. All the frames that are not chosen in the first clustering are used. This time, these facial subsequences, including 13 consecutive time frames prepared in the same manner as the tapped-delay line, are used as the clustering input. The synthesized video output may be more continuous, as shown in Figure 11.1b, compared with Figure 11.1a.

Fig. 11.1 a The synthesized
video output may not be continuous enough, only including the intracluster variation
of the visual specification in
the whole training database.
b Considering the transformation of the intercluster visual
specification, the synthesized
video output may be more
continuous.

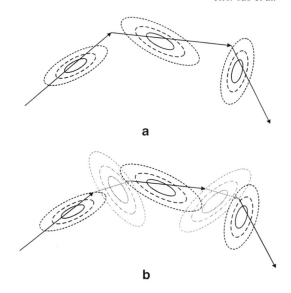

Based on the 80 clusters built in the first layer of clustering, audio observations
in same visual class are further classified in the second layer of clustering. Here, 13
consecutive time audio frames are used as input. Thus, both audio and visual pairing
observations are in the nature of continuing high-dimensional random variables. In
each cluster, a three-state right–left HMM model is trained for the visual component, a four-state right–left HMM model for the audio data, and the coupling GMM
is fitted after the best hidden state sequences of the audio component HMMs are
estimated.

In the synthesis stage, the best corresponding cluster series is selected using the
Viterbi algorithm, given audio features including its contextual information, in the
continued speech input. The cluster that has the most probability in the audio component HMM will be selected. Then we keep the synthesis processing by using the
following steps until the output of the visual parameters are lower than predefined
values in the cluster.

1. *Initialization:* Initialize the visual output based on the visual component HMM.
2. *E-step:* Compute middle variants given the equations (Equations (11.1) and
   (11.2)).
3. *M-step:* Compute updates of visual output given middle variants (Equation
   (11.3)).

11.3 Unit Selection Method

In the unit selection method, we have built a large audiovisual corpus and cluster
the audio data into a codebook according to the corresponding phoneme categories.
Each code word denotes a phoneme class. The number of phonemes in the database

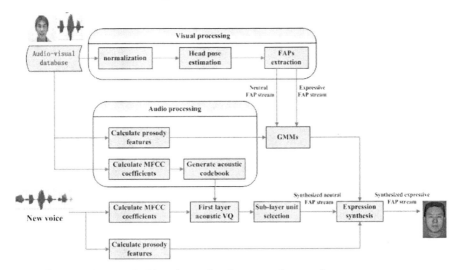

Fig. 11.2 Expressive speech-driven face animation system framework.

determines the size of the codebook. In the synthesis stage, we apply a hierarchical structure by the following steps.

1. Each frame of the input speech is compared to the codebook, giving us three different candidate codes.
2. For each candidate code, there are several audio sequences. We then use input audio data to make further comparison and get the most matched subsequences (with frames).
3. The visual distance between two adjacent candidate units is computed to ensure that the concatenated sequence is smooth.

Figure 11.2 shows a block diagram the unit selection system. We break the mapping process (see Figure 11.3) into two steps: finding the approximate candidate codes in codebooks and finding the best subsequence by calculating cost with context information. The details are presented as following.

11.3.1 Find Code Candidates

In Mandarin, we are using 48 codes including the silience part of the corpus. When beginning the synthesizing process, the distance between each frame of the input speech and the codebook is calculated. The three most approximate phoneme categories represented by candidate codes will be listed. The first layer cost $COST^1$ can be obtained by using Equation (11.13):

$$COST^1 = \left\{ dist(k); \quad k = \arg\min_n \left\| \vec{a}^t - codebook(n) \right\| \right\}. \tag{11.13}$$

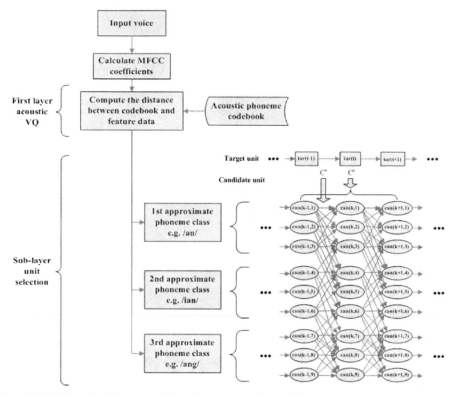

Fig. 11.3 Hierarchical structure of dynamic concatenation model.

11.3.2 Cost Computation

For each candidate code, there are several audio sequences. The sublayer cost computation is based on two cost functions:

$$COST^2 = \alpha C^a + (1 - \alpha)C^v, \qquad (11.14)$$

where C^a is the voice spectrum distance, C^v is the visual concatenation cost, and the weight "α" balances the effect of the two cost functions.

The voice spectrum distance can be defined by Equation (11.15):

$$C^a = \sum_{t=curr-p}^{p} \sum_{m=-6}^{6} w_{t,m} \left| a_{t,m}^{tar} - a_{t,m}^{can} \right| \qquad (11.15)$$

The weights w_m are determined by the method used in Wang, Wong, Pheng, Meng, and Wong (2004): we compute the linear blending weights in terms of the

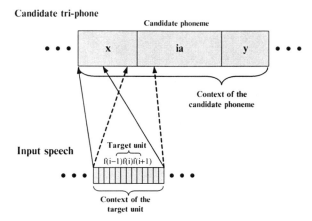

Fig. 11.4 Voice spectrum cost.

target unit's duration. The Eucilidian distance of the acoustic parameter of two frames is

$$\left| a_{t,m}^{tar} - a_{t,m}^{can} \right|.$$

The visual concatenation cost is defined by (Equation (11.16)).

$$C^v = v(can_{r-1}, can_r) \quad , \tag{11.16}$$

where $v(can_{r-1}, can_r)$ is the Euclidian distance of the adjacent visual features of two candidate sequences.

Once the two costs $COST^1$ and $COST^2$ are computed, a matrix for unit concatenation is constructed. We can finally find the best path in this graph that generates minimum COST (Equation (11.17)); Viterbi is a valid search method for this application.

$$COST = \sum_{r}^{n/3} COST^1(r)^* COST^2(r), \tag{11.17}$$

where n indicates the total number of frames in the input speech, and r means the number of target units contained in the input speech.

11.4 Neutral–Expressive Facial Deformation Mapping

The facial parameters within different emotional expressions are extremely different. Figure 11.5 shows the vertical deformation trajectory of FAP #33 for "jiu4 shi4 xia4 yu3 ye3 qu4" in neutral and surprise conditions and the vertical deformation trajectory of FAP #51 and FAP #60 in neutral and happy conditions. It is evident from Figure 11.5a that facial deformations are strongly affected by emotion. Although the trajectory of vertical movement of the right eyebrow in the surprise

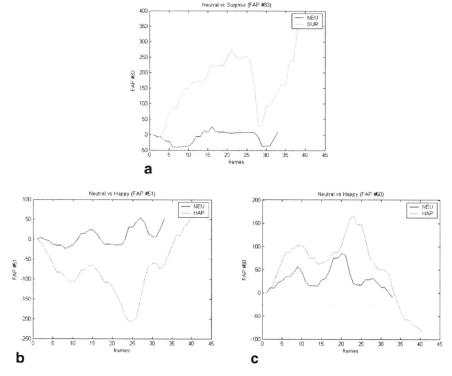

Fig. 11.5 Vertical deformation trajectories of: **a** FAP #33, **b** FAP #51, and **c** FAP #60 under different emotional states.

condition follows the trend of that in the neutral condition, the intensity is much stronger and the time duration tends to be longer.

On the other hand, the lip movement is not only influenced by the speech content, but is also affected by the speech emotional rhythm. The action of showing expressions will deform the original mouth shape. From Figures 11.5b and c, we can see that Face Animation Parameter, FAP #51, which is defined on the upper lip, moves up more under the happy condition, and FAP #51 and FAP #60 have similar vertical trajectories because of their interrelationship on the lip.

For estimating natural expressive facial deformation from neutral face movements, some GMMs are used to model the probability distribution of the neutral–expressive deformations. Each emotion category corresponds to a GMM.

$$P(Z) = \sum_{q=1}^{Q} w_q N(Z; \mu_q; \Sigma_q), \quad \sum_{q=1}^{Q} w_q = 1, \qquad (11.18)$$

where $N(Z; \mu_q; \Sigma_q)$ is the Gaussian distributed density component, μ_q and Σ_q are the qth mean vector and qth covariance matrix, w_q is the mixture weight, and Q is the number of Gaussian functions in the GMM. GMMs' parameters: (w, μ, Σ)

(Equation (11.19)) can be obtained by training with the Expectation-Maximization (EM) algorithm.

$$\mu_q = \begin{bmatrix} \mu_q^X \\ \mu_q^Y \end{bmatrix}, \quad \Sigma_q = \begin{bmatrix} \Sigma_q^{XX} & \Sigma_q^{XY} \\ \Sigma_q^{YX} & \Sigma_q^{YY} \end{bmatrix}, \quad q = 1,...,Q \quad . \tag{11.19}$$

After the GMMs are trained with the training data, the optimal estimate of expressive facial deformation (Y_{ik}) given neutral facial deformation (X_k) can be obtained according to the transform function of conditional expectation (Equation (11.20)).

$$\overline{Y_{ik}} = E\{Y_{ik}/X_k\} = \sum_{q=1}^{Q} p_q(X_k)[\mu_q^Y + \Sigma_q^{YX}(\Sigma_q^{XX})^{-1}(X_k - \mu_q^X)], \tag{11.20}$$

where $p_q(X_k)$ is the probability that the given neutral observation belongs to the mixture component (Equation (11.21)).

$$p_q(X_k) = \frac{w_q N(X_k; \mu_q; \Sigma_q)}{\sum\limits_{p=1}^{Q} w_p N(X_k; \mu_p; \Sigma_p)} \quad . \tag{11.21}$$

11.5 Experiments

11.5.1 Database Preparation

To test the models presented above, a phoneme-balanced corpus that covers all Chinese phonemes and most of the frequently used di-phones was designed. It includes a collection of 129 sentences. Based on the designed sentences. the audiovisual database were finally acquired by a commercially available motion capture system with eight cameras and a 60 Hz sampling rate. The facial motion data of a subject articulating the predesigned corpus with 3D markers on the face were acquired in real-time. The 3D trajectories of the markers and the accompanying time-aligned audio were recorded simultaneously. During the recording, each sentence is asked to be repeated five times, four of which are used as training data and once as validation data. Another nine different sentences are used as test data.

50 markers compatible with Face Definition Parameters (FDPs) were selected to encode the face shape, as shown by Figure 11.6. They were finally changed to 17 face animation parameters (FAPs) shown in Table 11.1.

For each frame of the audio-visual data, we use twelve-dimensional Mel-Frequency Cepstrum Coefficients (MFCC) coefficients as the audio feature. Some prosody parameters (F0 range, the maximum of F0s, the minimum of F0s, the

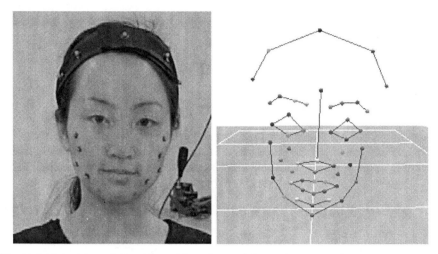

Fig. 11.6 Neutral face of the subject with markers and the motion capture data.

Table 11.1 FAPs for Visual Representation

Group	No.	FAP Name	Group	No.	FAP Name
2	#3	Open_jaw	8	#53	Stretch_l_cornerlip_o
4	#31	Raise_l_i_eyebrow	8	#54	Stretch_r_cornerlip_o
4	#32	Raise_r_i_eyebrow	8	#55	Lower_t_lip_lm_o
4	#33	Raise_l_m_eyebrow	8	#56	Lower_t_lip_rm_o
4	#34	Raise_r_m_eyebrow	8	#57	Raise_b_lip_lm_o
4	#35	Raise_l_o_eyebrow	8	#58	Raise_b_lip_rm_o
4	#36	Raise_r_i_eyebrow	8	#59	Raise_l_cornerlip_o
8	#51	Lower_t_midlip_o	8	#60	Raise_r_cornerlip_o
8	#52	Raise_b_midlip_o			

mean of F0s, and the mean of energy), which have been confirmed to be useful for emotional speech classification, were also selected for each sample.

11.5.2 Experiments with the Fused HMM Inversion Method

Figure 11.7 shows comparisons with synthesized FAP stream results with the corresponding ground-truth data frame by frame.

The comparisons between the synthesized results and targets are measured by using the normalized Mean Square Error (MSE) and average correlation coefficient (ACC) among the testing database.

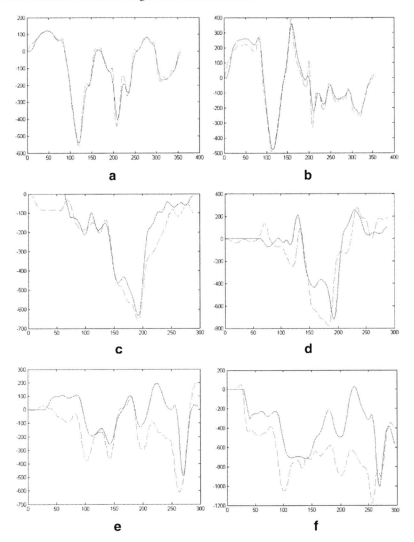

Fig. 11.7 Comparisons with synthesized FAP stream results with the corresponding ground-truth data frame by frame. The dashed red line denotes the ground FAP stream and the blue denotes the synthesized FAP stream. **a,b** validation sentence 1; **c,d** validation sentence 2; **e,f** test sentence. **a,c,e** FAP #51. **b,d,f** FAP #52.

$$\varepsilon = \frac{1}{T \cdot \sigma_v^2} \sum_{t=1}^{T} (\hat{v}_t - v_t)^2 \qquad (11.22)$$

$$\rho = \frac{1}{T} \sum_{t=1}^{T} \frac{(\hat{v}_t - \mu_{\hat{v}})(v_t - \mu_v)}{\sigma_{\hat{v}} \sigma_v}, \qquad (11.23)$$

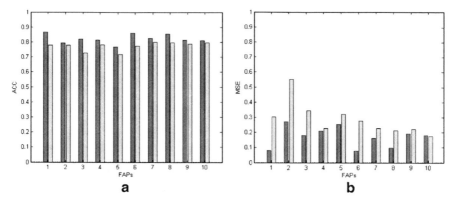

Fig. 11.8 The **a** ACC and **b** MSE for each FAP on the whole database with validation set (in green) and test set (in yellow).

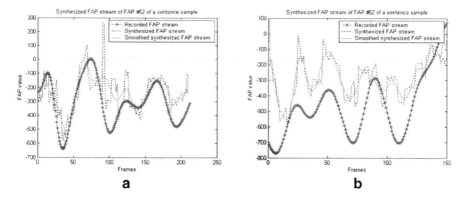

Fig. 11.9 Selected synthesized FAP #52 streams from **a** validation sentence and **b** test sentence.

where v_t and $\hat{v}_t$ denote the recorded and the predicted FAP stream individually. T is the total number of frames in the database, and μ_v, $\mu_{\hat{v}}$, σ_v and $\sigma_{\hat{v}}$ are the corresponding mean and standard deviation.

As Figure 11.8 shows, this method exhibits a good performance of visual synthesis. Although the test sentences show smaller correlation coefficients, most FAPs are still synthesized.

11.5.3 Experiments with the Unit Selection Method

In Figures 11.9a and b, we use the unit selection method and compare the synthesized FAP #52 stream with the recorded FAP stream from the validation and test sets, respectively. In Figure 11.9a, the two curves (smoothed synthesized sequence and recorded sequence) are very close, because the validation speech input is more likely to find the complete sequence of the same sentence from the corpus. In Figure 11.9b, the input speech is much different from that used in the training process. Although the two curves are not very close, their slopes are similar in most cases. To reduce the magnitude of discontinuities, the final synthesized result is smoothed by curve fitting.

11.5.4 Experiments with the Expressive generating

By using the neutral to expressive expression mapping model, we get the results in Figure 11.10. From Figure 11.10, the synthesized expressive trajectories appear to show good performance of following the trend of the recorded ones. It is noticed that the ends of the synthesized trajectories do not estimate the facial deformation well; this is mainly because the longer part of the expressive training data is a tone

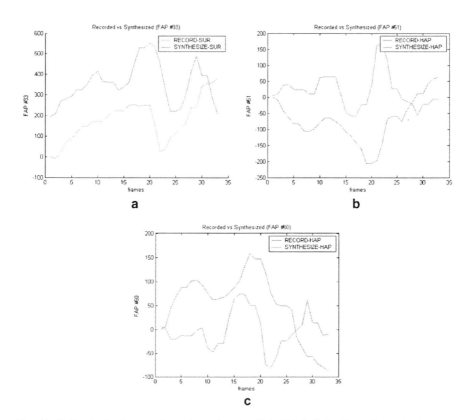

Fig. 11.10 Synthesized expressive trajectories of **a** FAP #33, **b** FAP #51, and **c** FAP #60 under different emotional states.

Table 11.2 Average Correlation Coefficients for Different Expressions

ACC	FAP #33	FAP #51	FAP #60
Hierarchical unit selection method (Neutral)	0.782	0.723	0.754
GMM for Surprise	0.737	0.656	0.688
GMM for Happy	0.729	0.725	0.701

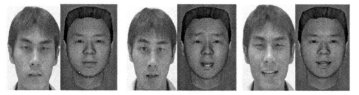

Fig. 11.11 Some frames of synthesized talking heads.

extension, so the features of the end part of two aligned sequences do not strictly correspond.

From Table 11.2, we can see that estimates for FAP #33 are generally better than those of other points on the lips. The eyebrow movements are observed to be mainly affected by expressions, whereas lip movements are not only influenced by the speech content, but also extended with emotional exhibition. The trajectories of FAP #51 and FAP #60 are determined by both content and expression, thus they have smaller correlation coefficients.

Finally, a MPEG-4 facial animation engine is used to access our synthesized FAP streams qualitatively. The animation model displays at a frame rate of 30 fps. Figure 11.11 shows some frames of synthesized talking heads compared with recorded images.

We have tried different voices on the system. The synthesized result is well matched to their voices, and the face animation seems very natural. Although the Chinese voice of a man is used in the training process, our system can adapt to other languages as well.

11.6 Conclusion

In this chapter, we have introduced two novel methods for visual speech synthesis. One is based on the fused HMM inversion, and the other one is based on unit selection.

For the fused HMM inversion method, by modeling the two coupling streams explicitly in the fused HMM, the inversion technique is used to get the visual counterpart given novel audio input. When implemented in different clusters found by two-time k-means clustering, a relatively short time delay and realistic synthesized facial animation are obtained.

For the unit selection method, a hierarchical structure is employed, so as to break the audiovisual mapping process into two steps. The first-layer acoustic codebook gives a general classification for the input speech frames. Sublayer frame-based cost computation ensures that the most approximate candidate sequence is selected. Through this method, the unit searching speed is largely enhanced, the artificial operation in the animation process is avoided, and the synthesized result stays natural and realistic.

In this chapter, we also analyzed the correlation between neutral facial deformation and expressive facial deformation and used GMM to model the joint probability distribution.

More and more researchers devote their efforts to developing realistic and real-time visual speech synthesis techniques, and many improvements have been made, but there still exist more open problems for researchers in this field. For example, expressive synthesis is presently limited to some typical emotions. The affective information represented by a speaker in a natural spiritual state is still a challenging work. In the future, more work should be done to investigate how dynamic expressive movement is related to prosody features. FAP sequences also need to be aligned with better strategy and more appropriate parameters found to smooth the synthesized trajectories.

References

Arun, K. S., Huang, T. S., & Blostein, S. D. (1987). Least-square fitting of two 3-D point sets. *IEEE Transactions on Pattern Analysis and Machine Intelligence, 9*(5), 698–700.

Brand, M. (1999). Voice puppetry. In*Proceedings of SIGGRAPH'99*, 21–28.

Brand, M., Oliver, N. & Pentland, A. (1997). Coupled hidden Markov models for complex action recognition. In *Proceedings of Computer Vision and Pattern Recognition*, 994–997.

Bregler, C., Covell, M., & Slaney, M. (1997). Video rewrite: Driving visual speech with audio, In *Proceedings of the 24th annual conference on Computer graphics and interactive techniques*, 353–360

Chen, T. & Rao, R.R. (1998), Audio-Visual Integration in Multimodal Communication, In *Proceedings of the IEEE*, Vol 86, (pp. :837–851).

Choi, K., & Hwang, J. N. (1999). Baum–Welch HMM inversion for reliable audio-to-visual conversion. In *Proceedings of the IEEE International Workshop Multimedia Signal Processing* (pp. 175–180).

Cosatto, E., Potamianos, G., & Graf, H. P. (2000). Audiovisual unit selection for the synthesis of photo-realistic talking-heads. In *IEEE International Conference on Multimedia and Expo*, 619–622

Ezzat, T., & Poggio, T. (1998). MikeTalk: A talking facial display based on morphing visemes. In *Proceedings of Computer Animation Conference*, Philadelphia, 96–102.

Fu, S. L., Gutierrez-Osuna, R., Esposito, A., Kakumanu, P. K., and Garcia, O. N. (2005). Audio/visual mapping with cross-modal hidden Markov models. *IEEE Transaction on Multimedia*, Vol 7, Issue 2, 243–252

Gutierrez-Osuna, R. et al. (2005). Speech-driven facial animation with realistic dynamics. *IEEE Transactions on Multimedia*, Vol 7, Issue 1, 33–42.

Hong, P. Y., Wen, Z., & Huang, T. S. (2002). Real-time speech-driven face animation with expressions using neural networks. *IEEE Transactions on Neural Networks,* Vol 13, Issue 4, 916–927.

Li, Y., & Shum, H. Y. (2006). Learning dynamic audio-visual mapping with input-output hidden Markov models, *IEEE Transactions on Multimedia, 8*(3), 542–549

Li, Y., Yu, F., Xu, Y. Q., Chang, E., & Shum, H. Y. (2001). Speech-driven cartoon animation with emotions. In *Proceedings of the Ninth ACM International Conference on Multimedia,* 365–371.

Liu, W. T., Yin, B. C., Jia, X. B., & Kong, D. H. (2004). Audio to visual signal mappings with HMM. In *ICASSP 2004.* 885–888.

Massaro, D. W., Beskow, J., Cohen, M. M., Fry, C. L., and Rodriguez, T. (1999). Picture my voice: Audio to visual speech synthesis using artificial neural networks. In *Proceedings of AVSP'99,* Santa Cruz, CA (pp. 133–138).

Moon, S. Y., & Hwang, J. N. (1997). Robust speech recognition based on joint model and feature space optimization of hidden Markov model. *IEEE Transactions on Neural Networks, 8*(2): 194–204.

Pan, H., Levinson, S., Huang, T. S., & Liang, Z. P. (2004). A fused hidden Markov model with application to bimodal speech processing. *IEEE Transactions on Signal Processing, 52*(3), 573–581.

Rao, R. R., & Chen, T. (1998). Audio-to-visual conversion for multimedia communication. *IEEE Transactions on Industrial Electronics, 45*(1), 15–22.

Saul, L. K., & Jordan, M. I. (1999). Mixed memory Markov model: Decomposing complex stochastic process as mixture of simpler ones, *Machine Learning, 37,* 75–88.

Tekalp, A. M., & Ostermann, J. (2000). Face and 2-D mesh animation in MPEG-4. *Signal Processing: Image Communication, 15,* 387–421.

Verma, A., Subramaniam, L. V., Rajput, N., Neti, C., & Faruquie, T. A. (2004). Animating expressive faces across languages. *IEEE Transactions on Multimedia,* Vol 6, 791–800.

Wang, J. Q., Wong, K. H. , Pheng, P. A , Meng, H. M., & Wong, T. T. (2004). A real-time Cantonese text-to-audiovisual speech synthesizer. *ICASSP04,* Vol 1, 1–653–6

Xie, L., & Liu, Z. Q. (2006). Speech animation using coupled hidden Markov models. In *The 18th International Conference on Pattern Recognition, ICPR 2006,* 1128–1131.

Xin, L., Tao, J. H., & Tan, T. N. (2007). Visual speech synthesis based on fused hidden Markov model inversion. In *Proceedings of ICIP2007,* Vol 3, 293–296.

Yamamoto, E., Nakamura, S., & Shikano, K. (1998). Lip movement synthesis from speech based on hidden Markov models. *Speech Communication,* Vol 26, 105–115.

Yin, P. R., & Tao, J. H. (2005). Dynamic mapping method based speech driven face animation system. In *The First International Conference on Affective Computing and Intelligent Interaction (ACII),* 755–763.

Zeng, Z. H., Tu, J. L., Pianfetti, B., Liu, M., Zhang, T., Zhang, Z. Q., Huang, T. S., & Levinson, S. (2005). Audio-visual affect recognition through multi-stream fused HMM for HCI. In *CVPR 2005,* Vol 2, 967–972.

Part IV
Affect in Multimodal Interaction

Chapter 12
Affect in Multimodal Information

Anna Esposito

Abstract In face-to-face communication, the emotional state of the speaker is transmitted to the listener through a synthetic process that involves both the verbal and the
nonverbal modalities of communication. From this point of view, the transmission
of the information content is redundant, because the same information is transferred
through several channels as well. How much information about the speaker's emotional state is transmitted by each channel and which channel plays the major role
in transferring such information? The present study tries to answer these questions
through a perceptual experiment that evaluates the subjective perception of emotional states through the single (either visual or auditory channel) and the combined
channels (visual and auditory). Results seem to show that, taken separately, the semantic content of the message and the visual content of the message carry the same
amount of information as the combined channels, suggesting that each channel performs a robust encoding of the emotional features that is very helpful in recovering
the perception of the emotional state when one of the channels is degraded by noise.

12.1 Introduction

The emotional information conveyed by speech as well as by facial expressions,
gestures, and gaze constitutes the main form of nonverbal information that can be
captured and analyzed in a multisensory environment, providing the motivation to
integrate information from various sources that have tended to be kept separate until
now. To understand nonverbal information, advanced signal processing and analysis
techniques have to be applied, but also more in-depth psychological and linguistic
analyses must be performed. Moreover, understanding the relationship between the

A. Esposito
Dipartimento di Psicologia, Seconda Universit di Napoli Via Vivaldi 43, 81100 Caserta, Italy
IIASS, Via Pellegrino 19, 84019, Vietri sul Mare, SA, Italy
e-mail: iiass.annaesp@tin.it, anna.esposito@unina2.it

J.H. Tao, T.N. Tan (eds.), *Affective Information Processing,*
© Springer Science+Business Media LLC 2009

verbal and nonverbal communication modes, and the progresses toward their modeling, is crucial for implementing a friendly human–computer interaction that exploits synthetic agents and sophisticated humanlike interfaces and will simplify user access to future telecommunication services.

Emotions are considered as adaptive reactions to relevant changes in the environment which are communicated through a nonverbal code from one organism to another (Plutchik, 1966). This perspective is based on several assumptions, among which, the most important is that a small set of universally shared discrete emotional categories exists from which other emotions can be derived (Ekman, 1984, 1992a; Izard, 1992, 1994; Izard, Dougherty & Hembree, 1983, Plutchik, 1993).

This small set of emotional categories includes happiness, anger, sadness, and fear, which can be reliably associated with basic survival problems such as nurturing offspring, earning food, competing for resources, and avoiding and/or facing dangers. In this context, basic emotions are brief, intense, and adapted reactions to urgent and demanding survival issues. These reactions to goal-relevant changes in the environment require "readiness to act" and "prompting of plans" in order to appropriately handle (under conditions of limited time) the incoming event producing suitable mental states, physiological changes, feelings, and expressions (Frijda, 1986, 1993).

The categorization of emotions is, however, debated among researchers and different theories have been proposed for its conceptualization, among these dimensional models (Schlosberg, 1953; Russell, 1980). Such models envisage a finite set of primary features (dimensions) in which emotions can be decomposed and suggest that different combinations of such features can arouse different affective states. Bringing the dimensional concept to an extreme, such theories suggest that, if the number of primary features extends along a continuum, it would be possible to generate an infinite number of affective states.

This idea, intriguing as it is, undermines the principle of economy that seems to rule the dynamic of natural systems, inasmuch as in this case, the evaluation of affective states may require an infinite computational time. Moreover, humans tend to categorize, because it allows us to make associations, rapidly recover information, and facilitate handling of unexpected events, and therefore, categories may be favored in order to avoid excessive processing time. Furthermore, this discrete evolutionary perspective of basic emotions has been supported through several sources of evidence, such as the findings of (1) an emotion-specific Autonomic Nervous System's (ANS) activity[1] (Bradley, Cuthbert, & Lang, 1990; Levenson, 1990, 1994); (2) distinct regions of the brain tuned to handle basic emotions (MacLean, 2000; Damasio et al., 2000; Panksepp, 2000); (3) presence of basic emotional expressions in other mammalian species (such as the attachment of infant mammals to their mothers) (Panksepp, 2003; Oatley et al., 2006); (4) universal exhibition of

---

[1] It should be noticed that not all these findings proved to be strong enough, as, for example, Caccioppo et al. (Cacioppo, Bush, & Tassinary, 1992, Cacioppo, Klein, Bernston, & Hatfield, 1993) and Bermond et al. (Bermond, Nieuwenhuyse, Fasotti, & Schuerman, 1991) disconfirmed the existence of an autonomic specificity and distinctive ANS's activity patterns for each basic emotion.

emotional expressions (such as smiling, amusement, and irritability) by infants, adults, blind and sighted (Oatley et al. 2006); (5) universal accuracy in recognizing facial and vocal expressions of basic emotions by all human beings independently of race and culture (Ekman, 1984, 1989, 1992b, Izard, 1992, 1993, 1994; Scherer & Oshinsky, 1977; Scherer, 1982).

In order to understand emotional features and develop appropriate mathematical models, it would be worthwhile to identify the meta-entities describing mental processes more complex than those devoted to the simple peripheral preprocessing of received signals. To understand how human communication exploits information from several channels which potentially contribute, act on, and support the speaker's emotional communicative goal, requires the definition and constitution of a cross-modal and cross-cultural database comprising verbal and nonverbal (gaze, facial expressions, and gestures) data and the definition of psychological experiments aimed to portray the underlying metastructure of the affective communication. Up to now, two procedures have been employed to study emotional states:

- The coding procedure that investigates emotional features eliciting emotional states through actor portrayals, induction, or clandestine recordings of naturally occurring emotions
- The decoding procedure that evaluates the listeners' ability to recognize emotional states from speech, gestures, and gaze expressions

Whatever was the exploited procedure to infer them emotions and the related perceptual cues have always been investigated, to our knowledge, considering three expressive domains separately: facial expressions, voice, and body movements, even though some studies have suggested that one of them could be preferential with respect to the others. In particular, some studies sustain that facial expressions are more informative than gestures and vocal expressions (Ekman, 1984, 1992a; Izard, 1994; Izard, Dougherty, & Hembree, 1993), whereas others suggest that vocal expressions are more faithful than facial expressions in expressing emotional states inasmuch as physiological processes, such as respiration and muscle tension, are naturally influenced by emotional responses (Burns & Beier, 1973; Pittam & Scherer, 1993; Banse et al., 1996; Scherer, Banse, Wallbott, & Goldbeck, 1991, Scherer, Banse, & Wallbott, 2001, Scherer, 2003).

It should also be noted that although the power of the vocal expressions in expressing emotional states has been tested dynamically along the time dimension because speech is intrinsically a dynamic process, for facial expressions, a long-established tradition attempts to define the facial expression of emotion in terms of qualitative targets, that is, static positions capable of being displayed in a still photograph. The still image usually captures the apex of the expression, that is, the instant at which the indicators of emotion are most marked. However, in daily experience, emotional states are also intrinsically dynamic processes and associated facial expressions vary with time. Is dynamic visual information still emotionally richer than auditory information? To our knowledge, to date, there are no data in literature that attempt to answer this question.

To answer the above questions a series of perceptual experiments are discussed, aimed at evaluating the subjective perception of emotional states in the single (either visual or auditory channel) and the combined channels (visual and auditory). Video clips extracted from Italian movies were exploited. This choice allowed us to overcome two critiques generally made to perceptual studies of the kind proposed: namely, stillness and lack of genuinity. The use of video clips avoided the stillness of the pictures in the evaluation of the emotional visual information. Moreover, even though the emotions expressed in the video clips were still simulations under studio conditions (and may not have reproduced a genuine emotion but an idealization of it), they were able to catch and engage the emotional feeling of the spectators and therefore their perceptual emotional content can be assessed quite confidently.

12.2 Multimodal Information: Collection and Annotation

The present chapter focuses on the expressions of emotions and on the perceptual features exploited to recognize them from facial expressions, voice, and body movements, and on trying to establish if there is a preferential channel for perceiving an emotional state. In this context, the term "expressions" is used to indicate what is perceived of the emotional states in face-to-face interaction. In this sense, the investigation is restricted to the perceptual appearance of emotional states, that is, the facial and vocal expressions of emotions that have received a lot of attention by many authors, whereas gestures have been, to this date, partially neglected. A summary of the main findings about the expressions of emotions in these three domains can be found in Esposito (2007a). In the following, perceptual data on the emotional information conveyed by the visual and auditory channels are reported.

12.2.1 Recognition of Emotional Facial Expressions by Children and Adults

In order to asses the differences between facial and vocal expressions of emotion, in the following are reported the results of a perceptual experiment aimed to test the recognition of static emotional facial expressions both in adults and children. To this aim, 30 stylized facial emotional expressions of five basic emotions (happiness, anger, fear, sadness, and surprise) in the form of stylized images (6 for each of the five emotions considered) were collected, under the supervision of the author, by two students (Davide De Caro and Carmine Verde) registered in the third year of their Master in Psychology, at the Second University of Naples. The stylized expressions were preferred to photos of human faces, generally used in other similar experiments, to facilitate the following recognition of emotional expressions by children, because it is the author's opinion that human faces, being richer in detail, are more difficult to be emotionally interpreted by children (and maybe also by adults).

The 30 stylized emotional images were first proposed to 43 Italian adults aged from 20 to 50 years (average age 35±6 years). The adults were asked to assign a label to the images according to the feeling expressed by the image character. It is worthwhile to mention that the stimuli were scanned at high resolution, and printed on high quality, 13 × 18 cm photo paper. As a result of this procedure, 10 images from the original group of 30 (two for each of the five emotional states under examination and those that obtained the highest emotional recognition rate) were selected to be proposed to two groups of 40 Italian children from the first (18 males and 22 females aged from six to seven) and (23 males and 17 females aged from ten to eleven) the sixth grade of primary school, respectively. The children, as were the adults, were asked to label the 10 images according to the feeling expressed by the image character. No mention was made and no label was given on the emotional state represented in the images. The percentage of correct identification of the feeling associated with each image by the adults and by both groups of children is reported in Figure 12.1.

Notice that the identification rate for surprise was 63% for first-grade children and was significantly different from both the adults and the sixth-grade children (97.5% and 93% of correct identification rate, respectively). For the remaining emotions no differences were found among the three groups of subjects. The displayed results suggest that both children and adults are able to recognize facial emotional expressions in static stylized images at a high identification rate.

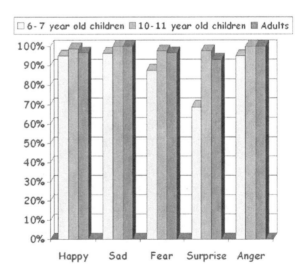

Fig. 12.1 Percentage of correct identification of the feeling associated with each image by the adults and both the groups of children.

208   A. Esposito

12.2.2 Recognition of Emotional Vocal Expressions by Children and Adults

A similar experimental setup as described above was set to test the ability of adults
and children to identify five basic emotions (as above, happiness, anger, fear, sadness, and surprise) in vocal expressions. The stimuli consisted of four emotionally
colored sentences for each emotion produced by four actors (two males and two
females). The sentences were extracted from video clips of Italian movies and were
largely recognized as being emotionally rich.

The differences from previous experiments reported in literature on the recognition of vocal emotional expressions consisted in the fact that the actors were not
asked to produce an emotional vocal expression by the experimenter. Rather, they
were acting according to the movie script and their performance was judged by the
movie director (who was supposed to be an expert) as appropriate to the required
emotional context.

The participants in the experiment were 30 adults (13 females and 17 males aged
from 20 to 50) and 30 children (16 females and 14 males aged from 7 to 8). Both
groups were asked to listen to the sentences and label them using either one of the
five emotional labels reported above or the label "other" (a total of 120 sentences
emotionally rich but without semantic emotional content).

The percentage of correct identifications for both children and adults is reported
in Figure 12.2. As can be noticed observing Figure 12.2, both adults and children
were able to recognize vocal emotional expressions and the differences were not significant, except for surprise, identified correctly by only 55% of the children against
84% of the adults. Children aged from seven to eight generally confused expressions
of surprise (both in faces or in voice) with anger, or sadness, or fear.

Figure 12.3 displays emotion recognition rates averaged over adults and children
obtained by displaying static images and by listing emotional audio.

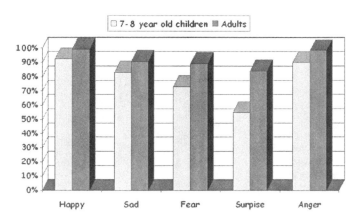

Fig. 12.2 Percentage of correct identification of the feeling associated with each vocal emotional
expression by the adults and children.

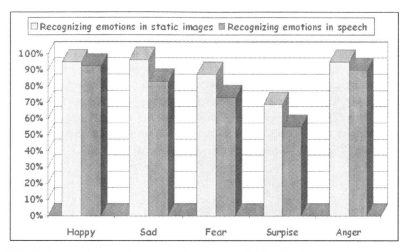

Fig. 12.3 Differences (averaged over adults' and children's identification rates) in the percentage of correct identification of the feeling associated with facial (white bars) and vocal (black bars) emotional expressions.

Compared with static stylized images, the subjects' performance in the recognition of vocal emotional expressions is less straightforward and immediate. The subjects seemed to be more discriminative through face than through voice. However, also through voice, the displayed results suggest that both children and adults are able to identify emotions at a high identification rate.

12.3 Audiovisual Mapping for Affective Expressions

As previously stated, emotions and the related perceptual cues to infer them have always been investigated considering separately either the visual information contained in the facial expressions or the auditory information contained in the vocal expressions. The debate among researchers is on which of them could be preferential with respect to the other.

Several authors sustain that facial expressions are more informative than vocal expressions (Graham, Ricci-Bitti, & Argyle, 1975; Schwartz, Fair, Salt, Mandel, & Klerman, 1976; Schwartz, Ahern & Brown, 1979; Schwartz, Weinberger, & Singer, 1981; Ekman 1989, 1992a; Caccioppo et al., 1992, 1993; Izard 1992, 1993, 1994) whereas others suggest that vocal expressions are more faithful than facial expressions because physiological processes, such as respiration and muscle tension, are naturally influenced by emotional responses (Burns & Beier, 1973; Pittam & Scherer, 1993; Banse & Scherer, 1996; Scherer et al., 1991, 2001; Scherer, 2003).

The results reported above, even though without a test for significance, seem to support the predominance of the visual channel in transferring a greater amount of emotional information as opposed to the audio. However, this conclusion is questioned here because in the above reported experiments, the nature of the stimuli used for comparing the emotional information conveyed by the audio and the visual channel is considered not appropriate. In fact, emotional facial expressions were evaluated in terms of static positions in still photographs whereas vocal expressions were evaluated along the time dimension because speech is intrinsically a dynamic process. Therefore, vocal and visual results are not comparable due to the different nature of the stimuli exploited in the analysis. A first attempt to implement a fair comparison was made by the author and the details of the experiment are described in Esposito (2007a) and discussed below for the sake of clarity.

12.3.1 Some Data on the Italian Culture

The author collected data based on extracts from Italian movies whose protagonists were carefully chosen among actors and actresses who are largely acknowledged by critics and considered capable of giving some very real and careful interpretations. The final database consisted of audio and video stimuli representing six basic emotional states: *happiness, sarcasm/irony, fear, anger, surprise*, and *sadness*. The sarcasm/irony emotional state was used to substitute that of disgust, because after one year of movie analysis only one video clip was identified for this emotion.

For each of the above-listed emotional states, 10 stimuli were identified, 5 expressed by an actor and 5 expressed by an actress, for a total of 60 audio and video stimuli. The actors and actresses were different for each of the 5 stimuli to avoid bias in their ability to portray emotional states. The stimuli were selected to be short in duration (the average stimulus' length was 3.5 s, SD = ± 1 s) first because longer stimuli may produce overlapping of emotional states and confuse the subject's perception; and second because emotional states for definition cannot last more than a few seconds becoming otherwise moods or more complex emotions (Oatley & Jenkins, 2006).

Care was taken in choosing video clips where the protagonist's face and the upper part of the body were clearly visible and where the semantic meaning of the expressed sentences was not related to the portrayed emotional state and furthermore, where the intensity level of the emotional state was moderate. As an example, sad stimuli where the actresses/actors were clearly crying or happiness stimuli where the protagonist was strongly laughing were discarded. The aim was to allow the subjects to exploit emotional signs less obvious but employed in every natural and not extreme emotional interaction. The audio and the video alone were then extracted from each video clip, resulting in a total of 180 stimuli (60 stimuli only audio, 60 only video, and 60 audio and video).

The emotional labels assigned to the stimuli were given first by two expert judges and then by three naïve judges independently. The expert judges made a decision on the stimuli, carefully exploiting emotional information on facial and vocal expressions described in the literature (Ekman, 1978; Izard, 1979, 1993) and also knowing the contextual situation the protagonist was interpreting. The naïve judges made their decision after watching the stimuli several times. There were no opinion exchanges between the experts and naïve judges even though the final agreement on the labeling between the two groups was 100%. The stimuli in each set were then randomized and proposed to the subjects participating in the experiments.

A total of 90 subjects participated in the perceptual experiments: 30 were involved in the evaluation of the audio stimuli, 30 in the evaluation of the video stimuli, and 30 in the evaluation of the video and audio stimuli. The assignment of the subjects to the task was random. Subjects were required to carefully listen and/or watch the experimental stimuli via headphones in a quiet room. They were instructed to pay attention to each presentation and decide as quickly as possible at the end, which of the six emotional states was expressed in it.

Responses were recorded on a matrix paper form (60×8) where the rows listed the stimuli numbers and the columns the six possible emotional states plus an option for any other emotion not listed in the form, plus the option that they recognized a neutral state in the presentation. Each emotional label given by the participants as an alternative to one of the six listed emotions was included in the emotional classes listed above only if criteria of synonymity and/or analogy were satisfied; otherwise it was included in a class labeled "others". For each emotional stimulus both the frequency response distribution and the percentage of correct recognition among the eight emotional classes under examination (happiness, sarcasm/irony, fear, anger, surprise, sadness, others, and neutral) were computed.

12.3.2 Results

The confusion matrices for the three different conditions (audio and video, video, and audio condition) are reported in Tables 12.1, 12.2, 12.3, respectively. The numbers are percentages computed over the number of the subject's correct answers to each stimulus and averaged over the number of the expected correct answers for each emotional state.

Table 12.1 Confusion Matrix for the Audio–Video Condition on the Italian Language

Audio and Video	Sad	Ironic	Happy	Fear	Anger	Surprise	Others	Neutral
Sad	**75**	14	0	2	2	0	4	3
Ironic	2	**64**	5	3	7	12	3	4
Happy	1	29	**50**	3	0	11	0	6
Fear	19	2	2	**48**	4	15	7	3
Anger	5	10	1	11	**60**	0	8	5
Surprise	0	8	5	14	2	**59**	0	12

Note: The numbers are percentages computed considering the number of subject's correct answers over the total number of expected correct answers (300) for each emotional state.

Table 12.2 Confusion Matrix for the Video Condition on the Italian Language

Video	Sad	Ironic	Happy	Fear	Anger	Surprise	Others	Neutral
Sad	**49**	9	6	9	3	4	7	13
Ironic	8	**49**	10	2	5	4	8	14
Happy	1	24	**61**	3	1	4	2	4
Fear	5	2	3	**59**	14	8	6	3
Anger	3	6	1	9	**68**	4	3	6
Surprise	4	7	6	11	13	**37**	4	18

Note: The numbers are percentages computed considering the number of subject's correct answers over the total number of expected correct answers (300) for each emotional state.

Table 12.3 Confusion Matrix for the Audio Condition on the Italian Language

Audio	Sad	Ironic	Happy	Fear	Anger	Surprise	Others	Neutral
Sad	**67**	7	0	7	1	1	4	13
Ironic	9	**75**	7	2	2	4	0	1
Happy	5	25	**48**	8	1	5	1	7
Fear	12	3	6	**63**	6	5	2	3
Anger	2	9	0	10	**77**	0	1	1
Surprise	5	21	3	19	4	**37**	2	9

Note: The numbers are percentages computed considering the number of subject's correct answers over the total number of expected correct answers (300) for each emotional state.

A comparative display of the data reported in Tables 12.1 through and 12.3 is depicted in Figure 12.4, which shows the number of correct answers for sadness (12.3a), irony (12.3b), happiness (12.3c), fear (12.3d), anger (12.3e), and surprise (12.3f) in the audio (grey bars), video (white bars), and audio–video (black bars) conditions. The emotional labels are reported on the x-axis and on the y-axis are the number of correct answers obtained for each emotional state.

In order to evaluate if the observed differences were significant, an ANOVA analysis was performed on the above data considering the condition (audio alone, video alone, and audio–video) as a between-subject variable and the emotional state as a six-level (a level for each emotional state) within-subject variable.

A detailed discussion of the results provided in Table 12.1 through 12.3 and in Figure 12.4, as well as on the ANOVA can be found in Esposito (2007a). In summary it was shown that the emotional information on five of the six basic emotions considered utilizes the audio as a preferential channel, except for happiness, which is better identified through the visual channel.

The audio was significantly preferential and the amount of emotional information conveyed was comparable to the audio–video condition. Moreover, the female stimuli were more affected by condition than the male stimuli, even though gender was not significant and no interaction was found between condition and gender.

There was not a significant difference in the perception of the emotional states for the audio and the audio–video condition, whereas the amount of emotional information transmitted by the video was significantly lower than that transmitted either by the audio alone or by the audio–video.

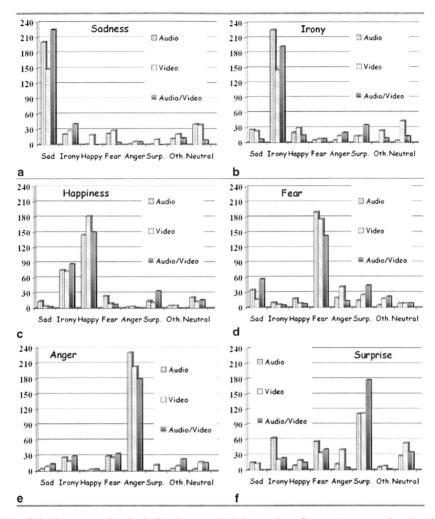

Fig. 12.4 Histograms (for the Italian language) of the number of correct answers given by the subjects participating in the perceptual experiments for the six emotional states under examination and the three different perceptual conditions (gray for audio, white for video, and black for audio–video. Colors would be different in a color version of the chapter).

12.4 An Explanation in Terms of Processing Load and Language Specificity

The data described above show a really unexpected trend and posit the basis for new interpretations of the amount of perceptual information that are found in the three different conditions. According to common sense it should be expected that subjects can better identify emotional states in the audio–video condition, because it can be assumed that the combined channels contain more or otherwise redundant information than the audio or video alone. However, the subjects perform similarly, either when the emotional information is transmitted by the audio alone or by audio–video together, whereas the video alone is less emotionally informative.

Therefore, it can be assumed that taken separately the visual and the auditory channels convey a different amount of emotional information and that, at least for Italian, the auditory channel can be considered preferential because it conveys the same amount of emotional information as audio–video channels combined. This suggests a strongly nonlinear processing of emotional cues because an assumed increase of the amount of emotional cues does not supply a comparable increase in the ability to identify them. The author suggested (Esposito, 2007a) that reduced ability is caused by an increase of the cognitive processing load and by language-specific mechanisms.

The exploitation of emotional information from a single channel in the bimodal presentation is due to the fact that the subject's cognitive load increases. She should concurrently elaborate gestures, facial and vocal expressions, dynamic temporal evolving information, and the semantics of the message. These concurrent elaborations deviate the subject's attention from the perceived emotion. Therefore, in an attempt to reduce the cognitive load, the subject exploits her language expertise, if the auditory signal is in her native language, otherwise she will rely on the ability to process visual stimuli if the audio input is in a foreign language.

The significant differences in the recognition rate between the audio and video alone reported above seem to support this hypothesis in the case of audio stimuli produced in the native language of the participating subjects. In such a condition therefore, it could be stated that when dynamic is involved, audio is better than visual because audio is intrinsically dynamic and native speakers are more accustomed to processing native vocal emotional cues dynamically, because natives rely on paralinguistic and suprasegmental information that is strictly related and unique to their own language.

They learned this information by themselves when they were emotionally involved and observed the changes in their vocal expressions. They may have learned how a given word is produced in a particular emotional state, even though the word is not semantically related to the emotional state. Consequently, they may be able to capture very small suprasegmental and paralinguistic cues not noticeable to nonnative speakers. Subtle changes in intonation, accent, stress, and other prosodic information deriving from slight changes in vocal motor control may have been learned in parallel with the language. Hence, native speakers are able to uncover more emotional information in the audio than in the video when the vocal expressions of emotions are expressed in their own language.

Nonetheless, they may rely more on visual rather than vocal information when they are requested to identify emotional states in a foreign language. This is because visual cues may share more commonalities than vocal cues being the visual processing of inputs from the outside world common to all humans, whereas the vocal processing requires both training and a specific expertise of a native language.

In light of the above considerations, it is the author's opinion that the ability of Italian subjects to correctly identify emotional information from the audio alone will vary considerably when the emotions are expressed in a foreign language and that in such a case significant differences could be observed between the audio alone and the audio–video channels combined.

12.5 A Mathematical Model

The above results can be modeled in terms of how well signals encode meaningful information and how well humans process them. In this context, several information measures have been defined (such as joint entropy, and mutual information) among variables describing both the information sent by the source and that received (Shannon & Weaver, 1949). In seeking the mathematical modeling of the above experimental data, however, both of these measures must be disregarded because of their mathematical properties. In fact, it can be proved that the joint entropy of two different sources is greater than that of a single source, and therefore, it can be expected that by increasing the number of sources, the amount of information transmitted over a communication channel will consequently increase (Shannon & Weaver, 1949).

This property does not take into account the meaning the signal can convey and what the receiver assumes to be informative about the received signal. Consequently, cases where the source can be only noise, and/or cases where extraneous information can be exploited by the receiver are not considered. Moreover, even mutual information (Shannon & Weaver, 1949) that expresses the dependence between the source and/or the receiver, cannot explain why by combining the audio and video channels the information about the emotional states does not increase and cannot explain our hypothesized differences between native and nonnative speakers and between close and distant cultural backgrounds in the perception of emotional states.

The information transfer ratio proposed by Sinanovi and Johnson (2007) seems to be a more appropriate and adequate model. Such a measure quantifies, in fact, how the receiver affects the received information by measuring the distance between the actions performed by the receiver for given received inputs and the received inputs. Assuming that the emotional information encoded through the audio and the video represents the input to a processing system, the information transfer ratio value is the ratio of the distances between the information transmitted by the sources and the distances between the outputs (for those sources) of the processing system. The information transfer ratio is described by the following equation.

$$\gamma_{XY,Z}(\alpha_0, \alpha_1) \equiv \frac{d_Z(\alpha_0, \alpha_1)}{d_X(\alpha_0, \alpha_1)} + \frac{d_Z(\alpha_0, \alpha_1)}{d_Y(\alpha_0, \alpha_1)} \quad , \tag{12.1}$$

where $\alpha 1$ indicates the changes in the emotional content of the sources with respect to a reference point α_0, which depends not on the signals themselves but on their probability functions $p_X(x; \alpha_0)$, $p_X(x; \alpha_1)$, $p_Y(y; \alpha_0)$, $p_Y(y; \alpha_1)$, and $p_Z(z; \alpha_0)$, $p_Z(z; \alpha_1)$. X and Y are the sources (audio and video), Z the processing systems, and $d(\ldots)$ indicates the Kullback–Leibler distance (Ali & Silvey, 1996) or any information-theoretic distance.

However, any information-theoretic distance generally obeys the data processing theorem (Gallager, 1968), which roughly states that the output of any processing system cannot contain more information than the processed signal. This may not be true if the receiver is a human being because the filtering actions of humans are generally arbitrary and the corresponding transfer function is unknown. Due to these difficulties, a more appropriate distance measure is suggested here based on fuzzy membership functions (Zadeh, 1988; Massaro, 1998). Fuzzy membership functions are more appropriate to model human categorization processes and allow inferring the emotional information exploiting the number of the subject's correct answers.

12.6 Automatic Approach to the Multimodal Processing of Emotions

Emotion is a topic that has received much attention during the last few years, in the context of the Human–Computer Interaction (HCI) field which involves research themes related to speech synthesis, as well as automatic speech recognition, interactive dialogue systems, wearable computers, embodied conversational agent systems, and intelligent avatars that are capable of performing believable actions and naturally reacting to human users (Bartneck, 2000; Cassell et al., 2001a; Stocky & Cassell, 2002). Along with these application requirements, research on emotions plays a fundamental role.

It is evident that the same words, the same facial expression, and/or the same gestures may be used as a joke, or as a genuine question seeking an answer, or as an aggressive challenge. Knowing what is an appropriate continuation of the interaction depends on detecting the register that the addresser is using, and a machine communicator that is unable to acknowledge the difference will have difficulty managing a naturalistic interaction.

In the HCI field, therefore, the research objectives are to identify methods and procedures capable of automatically identifying human emotional states exploiting the multimodal nature of emotions. This requires the consideration of several key aspects, such as the development and integration of algorithms and procedures for applications in communication, and for the recognition of emotional states from gestures, speech, gaze, and facial expressions, in anticipation of the implementation of intelligent avatars and interactive dialogue systems that could be exploited to improve the learning and understanding of emotional behavior and facilitate the user's access to future communication services.

Given the complexity of the problem, there has been a branching of the engineering approach toward the improvement and the development of video–audio techniques, such as video and image processing, video and image recognition, synthesis and speech recognition, object and feature extraction from audio and video, with the goal of developing new cutting-edge methodologies for synthesizing, analyzing, and recognizing emotional states from faces, speech, and/or body movements.

Concerning speech, the commonly applied approach in developing automatic systems for emotional speech recognition, analysis, and synthesis, is to start with a database of emotional speech that has been annotated with emotional tags by a panel of listeners. The next step is to perform an acoustic analysis of these data and to correlate statistics of certain acoustic features, mainly related to pitch, with the emotion tags. In the last step, the obtained parameter estimates are verified and adapted by checking the performance of an automatic dialogue system in tests through human interaction (Apple & Hecht, 1982; Cosmides, 1983; Frick, 1985; Fulcher, 1991; Banse & Scherer, 1996; Friend, 2000; Apolloni, Aversano, & Esposito, 2000; Apolloni, Esposito, Malchiodi, Orovas, Palmas, & Taylor, 2004; Hozjan & Kacic, 2003, 2006; Kakumanu, Esposito, Garcia, & Gutierrez-Osuna, 2006).

The search for acoustic features that describe emotional states in speech is performed through long-term or suprasegmental measurements because emotions are expected to last more than single speech segments and therefore, sophisticated acoustic measurements have been proposed to detect vocal expressions of emotions. Apart from F0 frequency (Bachorowski, 1999; Breitenstein, Van Lancker, & Daum, 2001; Hozjan & Kacic, 2003, 2006; Navas, Hernáez, & Luengo, 2006), these measurements include the spectral tilting, the vocal envelope—defined as the time interval for a signal to reach the maximum amplitude and decay to zero amplitude— the Long Term Average Spectrum (LTAS), the energy in different frequency bands, some inverse filtering measurements (Klasmeyer & Sendlmeier, 1995; Nushikyan, 1995), the F0 contour, the F0 maximum and minimum excursion, and the F0 jitter, random fluctuations on F0 values (Cosmides, 1983; Frick, 1985; Pittam & Scherer, 1993; Banse & Scherer, 1996). Exploiting this research line, the cited authors identified some acoustic correlates of vocal expressions for the small set of emotional states that are referred to in the literature as basic emotions (e.g., Russell, 1980; Scherer, 1989, 2003).

Yet, so far, there is little systematic knowledge about the details of the decoding process, that is, the precise acoustic cues the listeners use in inferring the speaker emotional state. The acoustic attributes that seem to play a role in signaling emotions are the same acoustic attributes that are modified by the phonetic context, by the inter- and intraspeaker variability, as well as by environmental noise. Therefore, it has been difficult to identify reliable algorithms able to detect speech differences in emotional states. Neither has a computational architecture, able to integrate emotional (prosodic) cues in speech understanding systems, yet been developed.

Moreover, because of the difficulties in collecting samples of emotions, most of the studies published in this field have been based on a few recordings of subjects simulating various emotions through readings of emotionally rich texts. These recordings can be considered satisfactory to the extent that the intended emotions can be correctly identified by listeners afterwards. By reading the same sentence with different simulated emotional states it should be possible to allow principled analysis of the speech waves and comparison of the changing acoustic features.

However, it is not obvious whether actors reproduce the genuine emotion or generate a stylized idealization of it in which some features of everyday reality are intensified, and others are disregarded. Because such emotions are acted, it is questionable whether they authentically represent the characteristics of speech used by ordinary people when they spontaneously experience similar emotions. The risk in using such kinds of artificial data is that we may be able to produce synthetic speech where it is possible to recognize the intended emotion, but we may also be aware at the same time that such an emotion is not felt or sincere (Esposito 2000, 2002).

The salient issues in emotion recognition from faces are parallel in some respects to the issues associated with voices, but divergent in others (Fasel & Luettin, 2003). As in speech, a long-established tradition attempts to define the facial expression of emotion in terms of qualitative subjects, that is, static positions capable of being displayed in a still photograph. The still image usually captures the apex of the expression, that is, the instant at which the indicators of emotion are mostly marked, whereas the natural recognition of emotions is based on continuous variations of the signals. The problem of automatic emotion recognition from faces, being a hard one, has attracted more attention during the last few years.

The analysis of a human face's emotional expression requires a number of pre-processing steps that attempt to detect or track the face, to locate characteristic facial regions such as eyes, mouth, and forehead on it, to extract and follow the movement of facial features, such as characteristic points in these regions, or model facial gestures using anatomic information about the face.

Most of the above techniques are based on a system for describing visually distinguishable facial movements, called the Facial Action Coding System (FACS) or Maximally Discriminative Facial Movement Coding System (MAX) (Ekman & Friesen, 1978, 2002; Izard, 1979, 1993). The FACS model has inspired the definition and derivation of facial animation parameters in the framework of the ISO MPEG-4 standard (Ostermann, 1998; Tekalp & Ostermann, 2000). In particular, the Facial Definition Parameters (FDPs) and the Facial Animation Parameters (FAPs) in the MPEG-4 standard have made possible the animation of synthetic faces reproducing emotional expressions through speech and faces (Elliott, 1992; Doyle, 1999; Koda, 1996; Huang & Huang, 1997; Kähler, Haber, & Seidel, 2001; Kakumanu, 2001; Morishima, 2001; Esposito, 2002; Ezzat, Geiger & Poggio, 2002; Fu, Gutierrez-Osuna, Esposito, Kakumanu, & Garcia, 2005; Gutierrez-Osuna et al., 2005).

Most of the implemented automatic systems devoted to recognize emotional facial expressions attempt to recognize only expressions corresponding to the six basic emotional states of happiness, sadness, surprise, disgust, fear, and anger (Kanade, Cohn, & Tian, 2000; Pantic & Rothkrantz, 2000, Pantic, Patras, & Rothkrantz, 2002; Kakumanu, 2006) or to recognize the so-called Action Units (AUs), that is, visible movements of a single or a small group of facial muscles that are the basic units of the FACS (Ekman & Friesen, 1978, Ekman, Friesen, & Hager, 2002; Huang & Huang, 1997) and that can be combined to define a mapping between changes in facial musculature and visible facial emotional expressions. There are 46 independent AUs that can be combined and 7000 distinct combinations of them have been observed in spontaneous interactions. In general, emotional facial expressions are recognized by tracking AUs and by measuring the intensity of their changes.

Approaches to the classification of facial expressions can be divided into spatial and spatiotemporal. In spatial approaches, facial features obtained from still images are utilized for classifying emotional facial expressions and Artificial Neural Networks (ANNs), Support Vector Machines (SVMs), and linear discriminant analysis are the mathematical models exploited (Huang & Huang, 1997; Edwards, Cootes, & Taylor, 1998; Pantic et al., 2000; Pantic, Patras, & Rothkrantz, 2002; Littlewort, Bartlett, Fasel, Susskind, & Movellan, 2004). In spatiotemporal approaches also dynamic features extracted by video sequences are taken into account and therefore the mathematical tools most exploited are the Hidden Markov Models (HMMs) and other stochastic approaches that can also take into account temporal variations (Roth, Yang, & Ahuja, 2000; Zhao, Chellappa, Phillips, & Rosenfeld, 2003; Viola and Jones, 2004; Petkov & Wieling, 2004; Phillips, Flynn, Scruggs, & Bowyer, 2005).

Concerning the role of gestures in emotional expressions, several theories have been advanced. There is an agreement among researchers having Darwin as initiator, that body movements may convey a certain amount of emotional information. However, there are no consolidated corpora that allow us to identify the role of gestures in the transmission of emotional information and if their function with respect to speech and facial expressions is primary or secondary (Butterworth & Beattie, 1978; Beattie, 1981; Feyereisen, 1983; Butterworth & Hadar, 1989; Krauss, Morrel-Samuels, & Colasante, 1991; Krauss, Chen, & Gottesman, 2000; Kendon, 2004; McNeill, 2005; Esposito, 2007b).

Studies exploiting gesture with the aim to improve the naturalness and effectiveness of interactive dialogue systems are in their seminal stage, even though some prototypes and some results that prove their efficacy have been published for the American English language (Bryll, Quek, & Esposito, 2001; Cassell et al., 2001; Esposito, 2001, 2002; Stocky & Cassell, 2002). However, these studies were often concerned with gestures (in particular, hand gestures) used jointly with verbal communication and therefore showing intimate relationships between the speaker's speech, actions, and the listener's nonverbal behaviors (Goldin-Meadow, 2003; Kendon, 2004; McNeill, 2005; Esposito & Marinaro, 2007; Esposito, 2007b).

These gestures may have nothing to do with emotions because according to Ekman and Friesen (1967, 1978) affective displays are independent of language. However, there is subjective evidence that variations in body movements (e.g., gait, body posture) and gestures (e.g., hand position) convey important information about people's emotions and there are some pioneer studies that underlined the existence of relationships among body posture, head movements, and hand gestures (in particular those named adapters by Ekman (Ekman & Friesen, 1967) and emotions (Corraze, 1980; Rosenberg & Langer, 1965; Argyle, 1988). At this date, relationships between bodily activity and emotional communicative functions remain a research field to be investigated both for a theoretical and a technological approach to their understanding and implementation.

Current research on emotions is addressing studies on the cross-modal analysis of multimodal signals through the development of a digital video–audio database of spontaneous, cross-cultural emotional transactions attempting to clarify the basic mechanisms of emotional processes both in typical and impaired conditions (Bourbakis, Esposito, & Kavraki, 2006; Bourbakis, Esposito, & Kavraki, 2007; Esposito, 2007; Esposito, Esposito, Refice, Savino, & Shattuck-Hufnagel, 2007).

Such a database would be of great interest both for the identification of the relationships and the shared information conveyed by the audio and visual communication channels and as a benchmark for comparing and evaluating the several research approaches, as well as for identifying cross-cultural differences among emotional expressions. Moreover, the database should allow the cross-modal analysis of audio and video recordings for defining distinctive, multimodal, and culturally specific emotional features and identifying emotional states from multimodal signals as well as for the definition of new methodologies and mathematical models for the automatic modeling and implementation of naturally humanlike communication interfaces.

12.7 Conclusions

The data discussed above essentially suggest that Italians did extract the same amount of emotional information either from the audio or the audio and video channels combined, whereas the video alone was less emotionally informative. An explanation was offered of this behavior that takes into account both the cognitive processing load and the language-specific mechanisms that can account for why video and audio combined transmit the same amount of emotional information of the audio alone when the native language is used. Nonetheless, humans may rely more on visual rather than vocal information when they are requested to identify emotional states in a foreign language.

The discussion on language expertise, however, raises a more fundamental question of how many of the dynamic features of emotional faces are universal. In fact, if the above results suggest that the perception of emotional vocal expressions is strictly related to language expertise nothing can be said on dynamic visual stimuli. The perceptual results reported in the literature for visual stimuli are still those obtained on static images and nothing is said on dynamic visual emotional stimuli that can also be culture-specific. This means that it could be expected that subjects perform better on culturally close visual emotional cues than on culturally distant ones. Further research is necessary to evaluate this possibility, and to determine whether the present results generalize to other geographically and socially homogeneous groups of subjects. Further experiments are also needed in order to quantify how much of such dynamical emotional information is universally shared and how much is culture-specific.

The present chapter reports perceptual data showing that native speakers do extract emotional information from both auditory and visual channels. However, in the bimodal presentations, they exploit auditory (or language-specific prosodic and paralinguistic information) cues when the audio signal is in their native language and visual cues only when the audio is in a foreign language. An attempt is made to explain this phenomenon in terms of the subject's cognitive load and language expertise. A mathematical model is suggested, based on the information transfer ratio and a fuzzy measure of distance among the source signals.

Acknowledgments This work has been funded by COST 2102 "*Cross Modal Analysis of Verbal and Nonverbal Communication*," www.cost2102.edu, and by Regione Campania, L.R. N.5 del 28.03.2002, Project ID N. BRC1293, Bando Feb. 2006. Acknowledgment goes to Tina Marcella Nappi for her editorial help.

References

Ali, S. M., & Silvey, S. D. (1996). A general class of coefficients of divergence of one distribution from another. *Journal of Royal Statistic Society, 28*,131–142.

Apolloni, B., Aversano, G., & Esposito, A. (2000). Preprocessing and classification of emotional features in speech sentences. In Y. Kosarev (Ed.), *Proceedings. IEEE Workshop on Speech and Computer* (pp. 49–52).

Apolloni, B., Esposito, A., Malchiodi, D., Orovas, C., Palmas, G., & Taylor, J. G. (2004). A general framework for learning rules from data. *IEEE Transactions on Neural Networks,* 15(6), 1333–1350.

Apple, W., & Hecht, K. (1982). Speaking emotionally: The relation between verbal and vocal communication of affect. *Journal of Personality and Social Psychology, 42*, 864–875.

Argyle, M. (1988). *Bodily communication*. New York: Methuen.

Bachorowski, J. A. (1999). Vocal expression and perception of emotion. *Current Directions in Psychological Science, 8*, 53–57.

Banse, R., & Scherer, K. (1996). Acoustic profiles in vocal emotion expression. *Journal of Personality & Social Psychology 70*(3), 614–636.

Bartneck, C. (2000). *Affective expressions of machines*. Eindhoven: Stan Ackerman Institute.

Beattie G. W. (1981). Language and non-verbal communication: The essential synthesis. *Linguistics, 19*, 1165–1183.

Bermond, B., Nieuwenhuyse, B., Fasotti, L., & Schuerman, J. (1991). Spinal cord lesions, peripheral feedback, and intensities of emotional feelings. *Cognition and Emotion 5*, 201–220.

Bourbakis, N. G., Esposito, A., & Kavraki, D. (2006). Analysis of invariant meta-features for learning and understanding disable people's emotional behavior related to their health conditions: A case study. In *Proceedings of Sixth International IEEE Symposium BioInformatics and BioEngineering*, IEEE Computer Society (pp. 357–369).

Bourbakis, N. G., Esposito, A., & Kavraki, D. (2007). Multi-modal interfaces for interaction-communication between hearing and visually impaired individuals: Problems & issues. In *Proceedings of the International Conference on Tool for Artificial Intelligence*, Patras, Greece, Oct. 29–31 (pp. 1–10).

Bradley, M. M., Cuthbert, B. N., & Lang, P. J. (1990). Startle reflex modification: Emotion or attention? *Psychophysiology, 27*, 513–523.

Breitenstein, C., Van Lancker, D., & Daum, I. (2001). The contribution of speech rate and pitch variation to the perception of vocal emotions in a German and an American sample. *Cognition & Emotion, 15*(1), 57–79.

Bryll, R., Quek, F., & Esposito, A. (2001). Automatic hand hold detection in natural conversation. In *Proceedings of IEEE Workshop on Cues in Communication*, Hawai, December 9.

Burns, K. L., & Beier, E. G. (1973). Significance of vocal and visual channels in the decoding of emotional meaning. *Journal of Communication, 23*, 118–130.

Butterworth, B. L., & Beattie, G. W. (1978). Gestures and silence as indicator of planning in speech. In R. N. Campbell & P. T. Smith (Eds.), *Recent Advances in the Psychology of Language* (pp. 347–360). New York: Olenum Press.

Butterworth, B. L., & Hadar, U. (1989). Gesture, speech, and computational stages: a reply to McNeill. *Psychological Review, 96*, 168–174.

Caccioppo, J. T., Bush, L. K., & Tassinary, L. G. (1992). Microexpressive facial actions as functions of affective stimuli: Replication and extension. *Personality and Social Psychology Bulletin, 18*, 515–526.

Caccioppo, J. T., Klein, D. J., Bernston, G. C., & Hatfield, E. (1993). The psychophysiology of emotion. In J. M. Lewis & M. Haviland-Jones (Eds.), *Handbook of Emotion* (pp. 119–142). New York: Guilford Press.

Cañamero, D. (1997). Modelling motivations and emotions as a basis for intelligent behavior. In *Proceedings of International Conference on Autonomous Agents,* Marina del Rey, CA (pp. 148–155).

Cassell, J., Nakano, Y., Bickmore, T., Sidner, C., & Rich, C. (2001a). Non-verbal cues for discourse structure. *Association for Computational Linguistics Joint EACL – ACL Conference* (pp. 106–115).

Cassell, J., Vilhjalmsson, H., & Bickmore, T. (2001b). BEAT: The behavior expression animation toolkit. In *Proceedings of SIGGRAPH* (pp. 477–486).

Corraze, G. (1980). *Les communications nonverbales*. Paris: Presses Universitaires de France.

Cosmides, L. (1983). Invariances in the acoustic expressions of emotions during speech. *Journal of Experimental Psychology, Human Perception Performance, 9*, 864–881

Damasio, A. R., Grabowski, T. J., Bechara, A., Damasio, H., Ponto, L. B., Parvizi, J., & Hichwa, R. D. (2000). Subcortical and cortical brain activity during the feeling of self-generated emotions. *Nature Neuroscience, 3*, 1049–1056.

Doyle, P. (1999). When is a communicative agent a good idea? In *Proceedings of International Workshop on Communicative and Autonomous Agents,* Seattle (pp. 1–2).

Edwards, G. J., Cootes, T. F., & Taylor, C. J. (1998). Face recognition using active appearance models. In *Proceedings of the European Conference on Computer Vision, 2*, 581–695.

Ekman, P. (1984). Expression and the nature of emotion. In K. Scherer & P. Ekman (Eds.), *Approaches to emotion* (pp. 319–343). Hillsdale, NJ: Lawrence Erlbaum.

Ekman, P. (1989). The argument and evidence about universals in facial expressions of emotion. In H. Wagner & A. Manstead (Eds.), *Handbook of social psychophysiology* (pp. 143–164). Chichester: Wiley.

Ekman, P. (1992a). Facial expression of emotion: New findings, new questions. *Psychological Science, 3*, 34–38.

Ekman, P. (1992b). An argument for basic emotions. *Cognition and Emotion, 6*, 169–200.

Ekman, P., & Friesen, W. V. (1967). Head and body cues in the judgement of emotion: A reformulation. *Perceptual Motor Skills 24*, 711–724.

Ekman, P., & Friesen, W. V. (1977). *Manual for the facial action coding system*. Palo Alto: Consulting Psychologists Press.

Ekman, P., & Friesen, W. V. (1978). *Facial action coding system: A technique for the measurement of facial movement*. Palo Alto, CA: Consulting Psychologists Press.

Ekman, P., Friesen, W. V., & Hager, J. C. (2002). *The facial action coding system* (2nd ed.). Salt Lake City: Weidenfeld & Nicolson.

Elliott, C. D. (1992). The affective reasoner: A process model of emotions in a multi-agent system. Ph.D. Thesis, Institute for the Learning Sciences, Northwestern University, Evanston, Illinois

Esposito, A. (2000). Approaching speech signal problems: An unifying viewpoint for the speech recognition process. In S. Suarez Garcia & R. Baron Fernandez (Eds.), *Memoria of Taller Internacional de Tratamiento del Habla, Procesamiento de Vos y el Language*. CIC–IPN Obra Compleata, Mexico.

Esposito, A. (2002). The importance of data for training intelligent devices. In B. Apolloni & C. Kurfess (Eds.), *From synapses to rules: Discovering symbolic knowledge from neural processed data* (pp. 229–250). Dordrecht: Kluwer Academic Press.

Esposito, A. (2007a). The amount of information on emotional states conveyed by the verbal and nonverbal channels: Some perceptual data. In Y. Stilianou et al. (Eds.), *Progress in nonlinear speech processing* (LNCS 4392, pp. 245–264), New York: Springer-Verlag.

Esposito, A. (2007b). COST 2102: Cross-modal analysis of verbal and nonverbal communication (CAVeNC). In A. Esposito et al. (Eds.), *Verbal and nonverbal communication behaviours* (LNCS, 4775, pp. 1–10). New York: Springer-Verlag.

Esposito, A., Duncan S., & Quek F. (2002): Holds as gestural correlated to empty and filled pauses. In *Proceedings of ICSLP, 1* (pp. 541–544).

Esposito, A., Esposito, D., Refice, M., Savino, M., & Shattuck-Hufnagel, S. (2007). A preliminary investigation of the relationships between gestures and prosody in Italian. In A. Esposito et al. (Eds.), *Fundamentals of verbal and nonverbal communication and the biometric issue.* NATO Publishing Series, Human and Societal Dynamics (18, pp. 4164–4174). The Netherlands: IOS Press.

Esposito, A., Esposito, D., & Trojano, L. (2007). Gestures, pauses, and aphasia: Four study cases. In *Proceedings of the IEEE International Symposium on Research on Assistive Technologies*, Dayton, OH, April 16 (pp. 59–63).

Esposito, A., Gutierrez-Osuna, R., Kakumanu, P., Garcia, O.N. (2002). Optimal data encoding for speech driven facial animation. Wright State University Tech. Rep. N. CS-WSU-04-02, Dayton, OH.

Esposito, A., & Marinaro, M. (2007). What pauses can tell us about speech and gesture partnership. In A. Esposito et al. (Eds.), *Fundamentals of verbal and nonverbal communication and the biometric issue*, NATO Publishing Series, Human and Societal Dynamics (18, pp. 45–57). The Netherlands: IOS Press.

Esposito, A., McCullough K. E., Quek F. (2001). Disfluencies in gesture: Gestural correlates to filled and unfilled speech pauses. In *Proceedings of IEEE Workshop on Cues in Communication*, Hawai, December 9 (pp. 1–6).

Ezzat T., Geiger G., & Poggio, T. (2002). Trainable videorealistic speech animation. In *Proceedings of SIGGRAPH*, San Antonio, TX, July (pp. 388–397).

Fasel, B., & Luettin, J. (2003). Automatic facial expression analysis: A survey. *Pattern Recognition, 36*, 259–275.

Feyereisen, P. (1983). Manual activity during speaking in aphasic subjects. *International Journal of Psychology, 18*, 545–556.

Frick, R. (1985). Communicating emotions: The role of prosodic features. *Psychological Bulletin, 93*, 412–429.

Friend, M. (2000). Developmental changes in sensitivity to vocal paralanguage. *Developmental Science, 3*, 148–162.

Frijda, N. H. (1986). *The emotions.* Cambridge, UK: Cambridge University Press.

Frijda, N. H. (1993). Moods, emotion episodes, and emotions. In J. M. Lewis & M. Haviland-Jones (Eds.), *Handbook of emotion* (pp. 381–402). New York: Guilford Press.

Fu, S., Gutierrez-Osuna, R., Esposito, A., Kakumanu, P., & Garcia, O. N. (2005). Audio/visual mapping with cross-modal hidden Markov models. *IEEE Transactions on Multimedia, 7*(2), 243–252.

Fulcher, J. A. (1991). Vocal affect expression as an indicator of affective response. *Behavior Research Methods, Instruments, & Computers, 23*, 306–313.

Gallager, R. G. (1968). *Information theory and reliable communication.* New York: John Wiley & Sons.

Goldin-Meadow, S. (2003). *Hearing gesture: How our hands help us think.* Cambridge, MA: Belknap Press at Harvard University Press.

Graham, J., Ricci-Bitti, P. E., & Argyle, M. (1975). A cross-cultural study of the communication of emotion by facial and gestural cues. *Journal of Human Movement Studies, 1*, 68–77.

Gutierrez-Osuna, R., Kakumanu, P., Esposito, A., Garcia, O.N., Bojorquez, A., Castello, J., & Rudomin I. (2005). Speech-driven facial animation with realistic dynamic. *IEEE Transactions on Multimedia, 7*(1), 33–42.

Hozjan, V., & Kacic, Z. (2003). Context-independent multilingual emotion recognition from speech signals. *International Journal of Speech Technology, 6*, 311–320.

Hozjan, V., & Kacic, Z. (2006). A rule-based emotion-dependent feature extraction method for emotion analysis from speech. *Journal of the Acoustical Society of America, 119*(5), 3109–3120.

Huang, C. L., & Huang, Y. M. (1997). Facial expression recognition using model-based feature extraction and action parameters classification. *Journal of Visual Commumication and Image Representation, 8*(3), 278–290.

Izard, C. E. (1979). The maximally discriminative facial movement coding system (MAX). Unpublished manuscript. Available from Instructional Resource Center, University of Delaware.

Izard, C. E. (1992). Basic emotions, relations among emotions, and emotion–cognition relations. *Psychological Review, 99*, 561–565.

Izard, C. E. (1993). Organizational and motivational functions of discrete emotions. In J. M. Lewis & M. Haviland-Jones (Eds.), *Handbook of emotions* (pp. 631–641). New York: Guilford Press.

Izard, C. E. (1994). Innate and universal facial expressions: Evidence from developmental and cross-cultural research. *Psychological Bulletin, 115*, 288–299.

Izard, C. E., Dougherty, L. M., & Hembree, E. A. (1983). A system for identifying affect expressions by holistic judgments. Unpublished manuscript. Available from Instructional Resource Center, University of Delaware.

Kähler K., Haber, J., & Seidel, H. (2001). Geometry-based muscle modeling for facial animation. In *Proceedings of the International Conference on Graphics Interface* (pp. 27–36).

Kakumanu, P. (2006). Detecting faces and recognizing facial expressions. PhD thesis. Wright State University, CSE Department, Dayton, OH.

Kakumanu, P., Esposito, A., Garcia, O. N., & Gutierrez-Osuna, R. (2006). A comparison of acoustic coding models for speech-driven facial animation. *Speech Commumication, 48*, 598–615.

Kakumanu, P., Gutierrez-Osuna R., Esposito, A., Bryll, R., Goshtasby A., & Garcia, O. N. (2001). Speech driven facial animation. In *Proceedings of ACM Workshop on Perceptive User Interfaces*, Orlando, 15–16 November (pp. 1–4).

Kanade, T., Cohn, J., & Tian, Y. (2000). Comprehensive database for facial expression analysis. In *Proceedings of the 4th IEEE International Conference on Automatic Face and Gesture Recognition* (pp. 46–53).

Kendon, A. (2004). *Gesture: Visible action as utterance.* Cambridge, UK: Cambridge University Press.

Klasmeyer, G., & Sendlmeier W. F. (1995). Objective voice parameters to characterize the emotional content in speech. In K. Elenius & P. Branderudf (Eds.), *Proceedings of ICPhS 1995*, (1, pp. 182–185). Arne Strömbergs Grafiska, Stockholm.

Koda, T. (1996). Agents with faces: A study on the effect of personification of software agents. Masters thesis, MIT Media Lab, Cambridge, MA, Stockholm.

Krauss, R., Chen, Y., & Gottesman, R. F. (2000). Lexical gestures and lexical access: A process model. In D. McNeill (Ed.), *Language and gesture* (pp. 261–283). UK: Cambridge University Press.

Krauss, R., Morrel-Samuels, P., & Colasante, C. (1991). Do conversational hand gestures communicate? *Journal of Personality and Social Psychology, 61*(5), 743–754.

Levenson, R. W. (1992). Autonomic nervous system differences among emotions. *Psychological Science, 3*, 23–27.

Levenson, R. W. (1994). Human emotion: A functional view. In P. Ekman & R. J. Davidson (Eds.), *The nature of emotion: Fundamental questions* (pp. 123–126). New York: Oxford University Press.

Littlewort, G., Bartlett, M. S., Fasel, I., Susskind, J., & Movellan, J. R. (2004). Dynamics of facial expression extracted automatically from video. In *IEEE Conference on Computer Vision and Pattern Recognition*, http://citeseer.ist.psu.edu/711804.html.

MacLean, P. (2000). Cerebral evolution of emotion. In J. M. Lewis & M. Haviland-Jones (Eds.), *Handbook of emotions* (pp. 67–83). New York: Guilford Press.

Massaro, D. W. (1998). *Perceiving talking faces*. Cambridge, MA: MIT Press.

McNeill, D. (2005). *Gesture and thought*. Chicago: University of Chicago Press.

Morishima, S. (2001). Face analysis and synthesis. *IEEE Signal Processing Magazine, 18*(3), 26–34.

Navas, E., Hernáez, I., & Luengo, I. (2006). An objective and subjective study of the role of semantics and prosodic features in building corpora for emotional TTS. *IEEE Transactions on Audio, Speech, and Language Processing, 14* (4), 1117–1127.

Nushikyan, E. A. (1995). Intonational universals in texual context. In K. Elenius & P. Branderudf (Eds.), *Proceedings of ICPhS 1995* (1, pp. 258–261). Arne Strömbergs Grafiska, Stockholm.

Oatley, K., Jenkins, J. M. (2006). *Understanding emotions* (2nd ed.). Oxford, England: Blackwell.

Ostermann, J. (1998). Animation of synthetic face in MPEG-4. In *Proceedings of Computer Animation* (pp. 49–51). Philadelphia, June 8–10.

Overview of the MPEG-4 Standard (1999). ISO/IEC JTC1/SC29/WG11 M2725, Seoul, South Korea.

Panksepp, J. (2000). Emotions as natural kinds within the mammalian brain. In J. M. Lewis and M. Haviland-Jones (Eds.), *Handbook of emotions* (2nd ed., pp. 137–156). New York: Guilford Press.

Panksepp, J. (2003). At the interface of the affective, behavioral, and cognitive neurosciences: Decoding the emotional feelings of the brain. *Brain and Cognition 52*, 4–14.

Pantic, M., Patras, I., & Rothkrantz, J. M. (2002). Facial action recognition in face profile image sequences. In *Proceedings IEEE International Conference Multimedia and Expo* (pp. 37–40).

Pantic, M., & Rothkrantz, J. M. (2000). Expert system for automatic analysis of facial expression. *Image and Vision Computing Journal, 18*(11), 881–905.

Petkov, N., & Wieling, M. B. (2004). Gabor filtering augmented with surround inhibition for improved contour detection by texture suppression. *Perception, 33*, 68c.

Phillips, P. J., Flynn, P. J., Scruggs, T., & Bowyer, K. W. (2005) Overview of the face recognition grand challenge. In *Proceedings of IEEE Conference on Computer Vision and Pattern Recognition*.

Pittam J., & Scherer K. R. (1993). Vocal expression and communication of emotion. In J. M. Lewis & M. Haviland-Jones (Eds.), *Handbook of emotion* (pp. 185–197). New York: Guilford Press.

Plutchik, R. (1966). Emotions as adaptive reactions: Implications for therapy. *Psychoanalytic Review, LIII*, 2: 105–110.

Plutchik, R. (1993). Emotion and their vicissitudes: Emotions and psychopathology. In J. M. Lewis & M. Haviland-Jones (Eds.), *Handbook of Emotion* (pp. 53–66). New York: Guilford Press.

Rosenberg, B. G., & Langer, J. (1965). A study of postural gestural communication. *Journal of Personality and Social Psychology 2*(4), 593–597.

Roth, D., Yang, M., & Ahuja, N. (2000). A snow-based face detector. *Advances in Neural Information Processing Systems, 12*, 855–861.

Russell, J. A. (1980). A circumplex model of affect. *Journal of Personality and Social Psychology, 39*, 1161–1178.

Scherer, K. (2003). Vocal communication of emotion: A review of research paradigms. *Speech Communication 40*, 227–256.

Scherer, K. R. (1982). *Experiencing emotion: A cross-cultural study*, Cambridge: Cambridge University Press.

Scherer, K. R. (1989). Vocal correlates of emotional arousal and affective disturbance. In H. Wagner, & A. Manstead (Eds.) *Handbook of social psychophysiology* (pp. 165–197). New York: Wiley UK.

Scherer, K. R., Banse, R., & Wallbott, H. G. (2001). Emotion inferences from vocal expression correlate across languages and cultures. *Journal of Cross-Cultural Psychology, 32*, 76–92.

Scherer, K. R., Banse, R., Wallbott, H. G., & Goldbeck, T. (1991). Vocal cues in emotion encoding and decoding. *Motivation and Emotion, 15*, 123–148.

Scherer, K. R., & Oshinsky, J. S. (1977). Cue utilization in emotion attribution from auditory stimuli. *Motivation and Emotion, 1*, 331–346.

Schlosberg, H. (1953). Three dimensions of emotion. *Psychological Review, 61*(2), 81–88.

Schwartz, G. E., Ahern, G. L., & Brown, S. (1979). Lateralized facial muscle response to positive and negative emotional stimuli. *Psychophysiology, 16*, 561–571.

Schwartz, G. E., Fair, P. L., Salt, P., Mandel, M. R., & Klerman, G. L. (1976). Facial muscle patterning to affective imagery in depressed and non-depressed subjects. *Science, 192*, 489–491.

Schwartz, G. E., Weinberger, D. A., & Singer, J. A. (1981). Cardiovascular differentiation of happiness, sadness, anger, and fear following imagery and exercise. *Psychosomatic Medicine, 43*, 343–364.

Shannon, C. E., & Weaver, W. (1949). *Mathematical theory of communication*. Chicago, USA: University of Illinois Press.

Sinanovic, S., & Johnson, D. H. (2007). Toward a theory of information processing. *Signal Processing, 87*, 1326–1344, http://www-ece.rice.edu/~dhj/cv.html#publications.

Stocky, T., & Cassell, J. (2002). Shared reality: Spatial intelligence in intuitive user interfaces. In *Proceedings of Intelligent User Interfaces* (pp. 224–225), San Francisco.

Tekalp. M., & Ostermann J. (2000). Face and 2-D mesh animation in MPEG-4. *Signal Processing and Image Communication, 15*, 387–421.

Viola A, P., & Jones, M. J. (2004). Robust real-time face detection. *International Journal of Computer Vision 57*(2), 137–154.

Zadeh, L. A. (1988). Fuzzy logic. *IEEE Computer, 21*(4), 83–93.

Zhao, W., Chellappa, R., Phillips, P. J., & Rosenfeld, A. (2003). Face recognition: A literature survey. *ACM Computing Surveys, 35*(4), 399–458.

Chapter 13
Nonverbal Feedback in Interactions

Kristiina Jokinen

13.1 Introduction

Understanding how nonverbal aspects of communication support, complement, and in some cases, override verbal communication is necessary for human interactions. It is also crucial for designing and implementing interactive systems that aim at supporting flexible interaction management using natural language with users. In particular, the need for more comprehensive communication has become obvious in the ubiquitous computing context where context-aware applications and automatic services require sophisticated knowledge management and adaptation to various user needs. Interactions with smart objects, services, and environments need to address challenges concerning natural, intuitive, easy, and friendly interaction. For instance, the *Roadmap for Smart Human Environments* (Plomp et al., 2002) envisages that smart environments will be populated by several context-aware devices which communicate with each other and with the users. The systems will identify their current context of use, adapt their behaviour accordingly, and also allow natural interaction.

In this chapter, I discuss verbal and nonverbal communication especially for the purposes of designing and developing interactive systems. I report on machine-learning experiments conducted on annotated gesture and facial expression data, and focus on the feedback and turn-taking processes that are important in building shared understanding of the semantics and flow of interaction.

The chapter is structured as follows. Challenges for natural interaction in the technological context are introduced in Section 13.2, whereas issues related to interaction management and conversational strategies are presented in Section 13.3. Section 13.4 discusses gestures, face expressions, and their communicative functions as annotated in the data, and Section 13.5 reports on the data analysis and results from the machine-learning classification and clustering experiments. Finally, Section 13.6 draws conclusions and discusses the results in a wider context for future research.

K. Jokinen
University of Helsinki and University of Tampere, Finland
e-mail: Kristiina.Jokinen@helsinki.fi

J.H. Tao, T.N. Tan (eds.), *Affective Information Processing,*
© Springer Science+Business Media LLC 2009

13.2 Interaction Challenges in Ubiquitous Context

The ubiquitous computing paradigm (Weiser, 1991) envisages that in the future, pervasive technologies and the opportunities by mobile communication will be deployed through a digital environment that is sensitive, adaptive, and responsive to the users' needs, habits, and emotions; is aware of the presence of mobile and wireless appliances; and finally, is ubiquitously accessible via natural interaction. The ubicom paradigm aims at "invisible intelligence" in embedded computer systems, that is, integration of electronic functions in ordinary devices such as cars, home appliances, factory automation, mobile phones, and so on. We are already familiar with smart home appliances such as sensor-based lights and water taps, or wristwatches and clothing monitoring one's physiological state, as well as geoinformatic navigation and location services via GPS, GPRS, and Bluetooth.

The ubicom paradigm also includes new interaction techniques as alternatives for complementing and compensating graphical and speech user interfaces: eye-gaze and tactile interfaces (touchscreens, pens) as well as interfaces using movement and kinetics. They point towards richer, more natural interaction between the user and the application, and various research projects investigate how to incorporate natural interfaces into the emerging technology and make everyday communication with the technology reality. For instance, Norros, Kaasinen, Plomp and Rämä (2003) consider multimodal user interface techniques among the main research challenges for enabling technologies, and they list speech, hearing, gesturing, and gaze as serious modality candidates that can enhance future human–technology interfaces, especially because these are extensively used in human–human interaction.

Unfortunately, current interface technology is still largely based on written styles of interaction that are closer to the use of command language than conversational interactions. Applications, such as spoken dialogue systems, navigation systems, and various Web-based applications, tend to suffer from rather rigid modes of interaction, and the users are forced to adapt their human communication strategies to the needs of the technology. However, natural (spoken) language as a primary interaction mode seems to bring in tacit assumptions of humanlike communication, and expectations of the systems being able to respond using similar communication capabilities become high. For instance, Jokinen and Hurtig (2006) showed that users evaluated the same system differently depending on what they thought was the primary mode of interaction: the users who were told that the system had a graphical–tactile interface with a possibility to input spoken language commands, evaluated the speech interface significantly better than those users who thought they were mainly interacting with a speech-based system which also happened to have multimodal facilities.

The challenge that ubiquitous technology faces in the present information society is thus not so much in producing systems that enable interaction in the first place, but to design and build systems that support human–technology interaction in a natural and intuitive way. Jokinen (2000) already listed three challenges for building intelligent systems: cooperation and collaboration, learning and knowledge acquisition, and social interaction. In other words, as an increasing number of interactive applications will appear, the users will expect these systems to have interfaces that support their normal modes of everyday interaction: smart environments should not only enable user-controlled command interfaces but equip applications with a capability to have easy and friendly interactions with the user.

Moreover, new algorithms will be required for the detection and recognition of speech information along with gestural and facial expressions, and existing technologies will need to be adapted to accommodate these models. For instance, various speaker states can be estimated from the small changes across time in the prosodic characteristics of frequent nonverbal speech sounds, and by mimicking these small dynamic changes, the equivalent affective states can be signaled in speech synthesis (Campbell, 2007). In a similar manner, gestures and face expressions can be extracted from the data, and their form features be automatically linked to appropriate communicative functions. Because emerging technology allows recognition of gestures and faces via cameras and sensors, the incorporation of human communication models into smart applications in the future does not seem totally impossible. Simulations based on manual analysis of corpora on gestures and face expressions are already incorporated in the development of embodied conversational agents (see, e.g., André and Pelachaud, forthcoming).

However, it is necessary to say a few words about what it actually means to communicate in a natural way. First, we need to be careful when assigning qualities such as "naturalness" to various means and modes through which the users can interact with ubiquitous applications. Although the keyboard and mouse seem the most "natural" means to interact with computers at the moment, it is not impossible that less common ways such as gesturing, gazing, and spoken conversational interfaces will be the natural and most common techniques tomorrow. In fact, given that the most natural communication medium for humans is language, it is likely that technology will advance towards the direction where speech-based interaction complements different multimodal and graphical interfaces.

The main question in the design and development of more natural interaction systems, however, is what it actually means to communicate in a natural way in different situations. For instance, gesturing is natural when pointing and giving spatial information, whereas face and eye-gazing express emotions and focus of attention best. Speech, on the other hand, is not suitable if one is concerned about disturbing others or privacy issues, or if the enablements for speech communication are not fulfilled at all. Consequently, in the context of interactive systems, the adjective "natural" should not only refer to the system's ability to use natural language and verbal communication, but to support functionality that the user finds intuitive and easy. We can say that the interactive systems should *afford* natural interaction.

The concept of affordance was originally introduced by Gibson (1979) in the visual perception field to denote the properties of the world upon which the actors can act. We can distinguish real and perceived affordances depending on whether we talk about the uncountable number of actionable relationships between the actor and the world, or about the action possibilities that are perceived by the user, respectively. The concept was brought to product design and human–computer interaction by Norman (1988). In HCI, the (perceived) affordance is related to the properties of the object that readily suggest to the user what are the appropriate ways to use the artifact. The smart technology environment should thus afford various natural interaction techniques; that is, interfaces should lend themselves to natural use without the users needing to think and reason how the interaction should take place in order to get the task completed.

Considering natural interaction in different environments, we should also mention intercultural aspects of communication. Interaction strategies that are natural in one context need not be natural in another one, and their straightforward implementation in applications can lead to embarrassing misunderstandings, unsatisfactory interactions, and bad service. Hence, it is important to investigate natural interaction techniques in different cultural contexts, and study what are relevant differences in verbal and nonverbal communication and how the meaningful content is perceived in different linguistic contexts (cf. Campbell & Jokinen (2008)).

13.3 Challenges in Interaction Management

Human–human interaction is based on cooperation which emerges from the speaker's communicative capability to act in a relevant and rational manner. Cooperation depends on the speakers' shared goal, cognitive and ethical consideration of each other, and on the mutual trust that the partner follows the same communicative principles (the so called "ideal cooperation;" Allwood, (2001)).

In human–computer interaction, the new design paradigm does not regard the computer only as a tool, but as an agent with which the user interacts with (Jokinen, 2008). The agent metaphor has also been applied in the autonomous agent systems (see e.g. Maes 1990), and the introduction of chat-bots and conversational avatars has brought interface agents in as future web surfing and interaction means. Especially interactions with spoken dialogue systems tend to elicit agent-like interactions as the users apply the principles of Ideal Cooperation in their interaction with the speech applications even though they know that the partner is a computer: system responses are perceived as rational contributions and evaluated with respect to their intelligibility and helpfulness from the human point of view. The agent metaphor has been applied in the autonomous agent systems (see, e.g., Maes (1990)), and the introduction of chat-bots and conversational avatars has brought interface agents in as future Web surfing and interaction means.

In the Constructive Dialogue Model (CDM, Jokinen (2008)), interaction management is regarded as coordinated action by rational agents. Cooperation manifests itself in the system properties that allow users to interact in a natural manner, that is, in the ways in which the system affords cooperative interaction.

The agents are engaged in the activity whereby they exchange new information on a shared goal, and their communicative behaviour is based on their observations about the world as well as on their reasoning, within the dialogue context, about the effect of the exchanged new information to the underlying goals. The agents' goals can range from rather vague "keep the channel open"-type social goals to more specific, task-oriented goals such as planning a trip, providing information, or giving instructions.

To ensure maximal impact, the agents must make new information as clearly available for the partner as possible, by using suitable lexical items, prosody (pitch, stress, volume, speed), and nonverbal means (gestures, gazing, face expressions), and the partner must be aware of these means in order to integrate the intended meaning in the shared context. An important topic in interaction management is thus related to information presentation: planning and generation of appropriate responses, giving feedback, and managing topic shifts.

Another important topic deals with verbal and nonverbal signals that regulate the flow of information. Such aspects as looking at the conversational partner or looking away provide indirect cues of the partner's willingness to continue interaction, whereas gazing at particular elements in the vision field tells us what the partner's focus of attention is, and thus they give guidance for appropriate presentation of information as well as suitable analysis and response to the partner's contribution. For instance, in our data (see below), turn-taking by interruption or after a silence is usually accompanied by looking down whereas acceptance after being designated as the next speaker is accompanied by gazing the previous speaker. When the speakers end their turns, they rapidly gaze the other participants as if looking for feedback or turn-acceptance from them.

Communication also requires that the basic enablements, or Contact, Perception, and Understanding (CPU) are fulfilled (Allwood, Traum, & Jokinen, 2000; Allwood, Cerrato, Jokinen, Navarretta, & Paggio, 2007). The agents must constantly monitor each other and the communicative situation and, if some of the enablements are not fulfilled, react to the problems. For instance, if the agent has lost contact, is not interested, or does not understand the partner's contribution, he is obliged to make these CPU problems known to the partner, who, consequently, must adapt her communication strategies to the level that is appropriate in the situation. The feedback on CPU enablements is important in smooth communication, and as it is often expressed nonverbally, the agents must be sensitive to the relevant nonverbal signals that are used, either intentionally or unintentionally, to indicate the state of communicative activity.

The main challenge for the Constructive Dialogue Model lies in the grounding of language: updating one's knowledge of what the conversation is about and constructing shared knowledge accordingly. In AI, grounding mainly concerns the agents' understanding of the relation between language and the physical environment, and is regarded as one of the main research problems (Harnard, 1990). In dialogue management, grounding has been modelled via a presentation–acceptance cycle that the speakers are involved in (Clark & Wilkes-Gibbs, 1986), and as a particular dialogue act that the agents perform as part of the dialogue plan (Traum, 1999). It can also be seen as the speakers' conformation to the general requirements of cooperative and coordinated interaction (Allwood, 2001; Allwood et al. 2000), which is the approach adopted also in the Constructive Dialogue Model (CDM).

Grounding takes place as a side effect of the process where the agents construct shared understanding of the underlying goals by exchanging and evaluating new information. Obliged by the communicative obligations to give feedback about the CPU enablements, the agents must check their understanding of the exchanged concepts and propositional facts with respect to their knowledge of the world, and by doing so they also ground the concepts in the given situation.

It must be emphasized that grounding, as defined above, does not presuppose that the agents automatically share the representation or the real-world referent of the grounded concepts with each other, let alone the same agent their earlier representations in different situations. In fact, it may be that the reason why concepts and propositions seem universal and shared among the agents is due to the agents' repeated exposure to same kind of communicative situations, and their cognitive convergence towards a similar conceptual model of the world. In other words, the shared knowledge that is learnt in the interactions and induced from the environment is the result of the agents' cooperation in fairly similar situations rather than something intrinsic to the agents or the environment as such.

Following this line of thought, we will approach the notion of the embodiment of linguistic knowledge via action and interaction. This is much discussed in experimental psychology and neuroscience, and interesting research is being conducted concerning how linguistic representations are constituted by sensorimotor activity and experience, and how language use is based on motor representations as well as certain brain regions (see more, e.g., Tomasello (1992), Barsalou (1999), Thompson (2001), Arbib (2003), and Mandler (2004)). Of course, neurocognitive processing is rather distant to our definition of grounding, i.e. building a shared conceptual understanding of the interactive situation through cooperation, and the relation between high-level communication and the processing of sensory information is far from clear, there is a link through the speaker's experience and learning to their conceptualization of the world. We will not go further into this kind of discussion in this article, although acknowledge its relatedness to the grounding in general.

13.4 Nonverbal Feedback

Nonverbal communication concerns gestures, face expressions, gazing, and posture, as well as speech sounds which do not convey propositional content (usually called backchannelling or feedback particles such as *uhuh, hmm, yeah, ooh*, etc.). It functions as an important part of smooth and successful interaction by conveying information about the partner's cognitive state, emotions, and attitudes (Feldman & Rim, 1991). As argued above, it is also important in constructing the shared context of communication.

The construction of the shared context is an interactive grounding process whereby the agents evaluate and give feedback to each other on the current state of communication. In the widest sense, feedback thus refers to the agent's response to the partner's utterance in general; that is, it is a conscious or unconscious reaction to the changes that take place in the agent's communicative environment. In this chapter, feedback is used in a more restricted sense: it refers to the agent's evaluation of the basic CPU enablements for interaction (see above). It is thus an expression of the agent's monitoring of the interaction, signalling to the partner how the agent finds the overall state of their interaction.

Feedback is commonly divided into different types depending on how explicit and languagelike the expression is. We can talk about utterances such as *That's fine*, *What a mess*, *ok*, *yeah*, *well*, as feedback-giving dialogue acts, or speech sounds and grunts such as *hmm*, *huh*, *uhuh* as backchannelling; the difference is that the latter do not make up a turn but signal the agent's acceptance and acknowledgement in the background. Nonverbal means often accompany verbal utterances, and can be rather effective means to express one's viewpoint.

The relation between verbal and nonverbal communication, especially the role of nonverbal communication in giving feedback, is still insufficiently understood, although active research is going on in the related areas such as nonverbal speech interaction (Campbell, 2007; Campbell & Ohara, 2005), emotional speech (Douglas, Campbell, Cowie & Roach, 2003), alignment (Pickering & Garrod, 2004; Katagiri, 2005), audiovisual gestures and speech (Swerts & Krahmer, 2005), and types and communicative functions of gestures and face expressions (Allwood et al. 2007; Jokinen & Ragni, 2007; Jokinen, Paggio, & Navarretta (2008)): Face and gesture communication has of course been widely studied as such (Kendon, 2004; Duncan & Fiske, 1977), and also in the context of embodied conversational agents (Cassel, Sullivan, Prevost & Churchill, 2003; André & Pelachaud, forthcoming), affective computing (Tao, forthcoming), and robotics (Steels, 2003; Mavridis & Roy, 2006; Beira et al., 2006).

Pertinent research topics deal with the relation of symbolic meaning to nonverbal actions such as gestures, and if nonverbal actions help the listeners to better distinguish communicative functions of spoken utterances and "noise" from meaningful words in speech. It is also important to understand how nonverbal aspects of communication support the presentation of information and how the different knowledge sources are coordinated in interactions. In the next section, I elaborate some aspects of cooperative interaction in relation to the speakers' gestures and face expressions, and discuss how these nonverbal signs are used to convey meaning. The main question in this respect concerns what exactly is the relation between the communicative functions of gestures and face on one hand, and the attributes that describe their shape and dynamics.

13.5 Corpus Analysis and Experiments

In the context of the Nordic Multimodal Interaction Network MUMIN, we have conducted preliminary quantitative studies on the communicative function of gestures and face expressions, focusing especially on the use of nonverbal signs in turn-taking and feedback-giving processes, as well as on the interpretation of the semiotic content of the communicative signs. We developed the MUMIN coding scheme and applied it to the analysis of short video clips in Swedish, Finnish, and Danish (Allwood et al., 2007). A slightly modified scheme was applied to Estonian data (Jokinen & Ragni 2007), and to comparing Estonian and Danish data (Jokinen et al., 2008).

The MUMIN scheme assumes that gestures and face expressions are closely related to the communicative intentions of the speakers. The attributes concerning shape and dynamics are not very detailed, because the aim was to capture significant features for interpersonal communication rather than describing gestures or facial expressions as such. It consists of a number of hierarchically organised attributes, and quite unlike other annotation schemes, it uses the semiotic classification of signs as the basis of pragmatic and semantic analysis.

The communicative signs are analysed into iconic, indexical, and symbolic ones, following the definitions of J. S. Peirce. The iconic gestures describe the properties of the referent, and correspond to descriptive gestures in McNeill (1992). The indexical gestures have two subcategories, indexical-deictic and indexical-beat, both of which are indices to the context. The former refers to pointing gestures which pick up an object in the physical context, whereas the latter refers to gestures which emphasise the important part of the utterance or, as the name suggests, give rhythm to the speech. Table 13.1 shows the annotation categories for gestures, and Table 13.2 those for face and head. A more detailed analysis is in Allwood et al. (2007).

The Estonian dialogues that are used as the basis of the experiments reported below are two videotaped meeting dialogues, each lasting about half an hour. The first meeting concerned the design of a new school building and the second one was the school building inspection meeting. The participants were three students who were given specific roles in the scenarios. Although the dialogues were based on controlled scenarios, the participants behaved naturally, and their nonverbal activity (hand gestures, feedback, face expressions) can be considered unconscious and

Table 13.1 Gesture Annotation

Shape and Dynamics Features	Values
Handedness	Both-Hands, Single-H
Trajectory	Up, Down, Sideways, Complex,
Emotion-attitude	Neutral, Happy, Sad, Surprised, Disgusted, Angry, Frightened
Semantic-pragmatic Features	Values
Semiotic type	Indexical-Deictic
	Indexical-Beat
	Feedback-give-CPU
	Feedback-give-CP
	Feedback-accept
Communicative function	Feedback-nonaccept
	Feedback-elicit
	Turn (Take, Accept, Yield, End, Hold)

Table 13.2 Face and Head Annotations

Shape and Dynamics Features	Values
Gaze	Up, Down, Side, Interlocutor,
Head	Nod (single/repeated), Jerk, Forward, Backward, Tilt (single/repeated), Side-turn, Shake, Waggle, Other
Emotion-attitude	Neutral, Happy, Sad, Surprised, Disgusted, Angry, Frightened,
Semantic-pragmatic Features	**Values**
Semiotic type	Indexical Deictic
	Indexical Beat
Communicative function	Feedback give CPU
	Feedback give CP
	Feedback accept
	Feedback nonaccept
	Feedback-elicit
	Turn (Take, Accept, Yield, End, Hold)

representative for the current purposes. Two video clips were selected for our studies. They were transcribed by native speakers and annotated by two annotators using the Anvil annotation tool (Kipp, 2001).

The machine-learning experiments were set up to investigate how well the selected attributes can distinguish communicative functions of face and gesture categories. We used the Weka software package (Witten & Frank, 2005), and performed various experiments on the attribute classes' feedback, turn management, and semiotic type. The Face data consisted of 89 objects with seven attributes, and the Gesture data consisted of 34 objects with six attributes (communicative function was divided into two separate attributes, feedback and turn-management, inasmuch as these functions are not exclusive of each other, but can occur simultaneously on an element). It should be noted that the numbers of meaningful face and gesture objects differ significantly: face expressions seem to have a more prominent role in interaction management than gesticulation (the same tendency is also found in other language annotations; see Jokinen et al. (2008)).

We first experimented with various classification algorithms in Weka, trying to establish reliability of the attribute sets in predicting communicative functions and semiotic types of the data objects. The best classification accuracy (percentage of correctly classified objects in tenfold cross-classification) was achieved by Support Vector Machine (the SMO version) with the given Weka parameter values. The results are shown in Table 13.3. On the significance level 0.01, the results for Face are better than the baseline classification (ZeroR, or the most frequent category), but not for Gestures. The reason may be the small dataset or, as already pointed out, the coarseness of gesture annotation that does not pick up the most distinguishing features. In particular, verbal dialogue acts and prosodic prominence were not marked, and it is assumed that communicative gesticulation is especially related

Table 13.3 Classification Accuracy with Support Vector Machine (SMO) and ZeroR

	Face		Gesture	
	SMO	ZeroR	SMO	ZeroR
Feedback	69.9 + / − 16.4	46.1 + / − 3.8	54.2 + / − 22.0	55.0 + / − 17.2
Turn management	73.1 + / − 14.9	70.8 + / − 5.4	92.5 + / − 16.9	95.0 + / − 10.5
Semiotic type	82.2 + / − 19.7	56.3 + / − 2.2	76.7 + / − 12.9	73.3 + / − 10.2

to emphasising or complementing verbal expressions in one's own communication management, rather than coordinating interpersonal communication with turns and feedback.

Concerning meaningful clustering of the communicative gestures and face expressions with the given attributes, we also conducted EM-clustering in Weka. The algorithm tries to maximize the overall likelihood of the data given the clusters, and the clustering was evaluated with clusters-to-classes evaluation. The purpose of the study was to detect meaningful correspondences among the data elements in the same cluster, and also to determine which specific attributes are important in the different clusters.

Due to the small number of data objects, the results may not allow generalisation although some interesting preliminary results can be drawn. If we cluster the face data according to possible feedback values, two clusters can be found with the log likelihood of −5.1523. The first cluster, with prior probability of 0.42, corresponds to the value Accept, and the second cluster, with prior probability of 0.58, corresponds to the value CPU. The fact that these clusters are discovered from the data corroborates the hypothesis that the most prominent feedback function of face data is to signal to the partner the state of communication and whether the information is accepted as a relevant piece of information in the shared knowledge.

The clustering of face data with respect to turn management also produces two clusters, with the log likelihood of −5.4766. The first cluster with prior probability of 0.26, corresponds to the value Take, and the the second cluster with prior probability of 0.74, corresponds to the value Hold. These clusters seem reasonable, because turn management usually deals with taking turns or holding one's turn.

Finally, the clustering of face data into semiotic types produces two clusters, with the log likelihood of −5.6706. The first cluster corresponds to the value Indexical-deictic, with prior probability of 0.76, and the second cluster to Indexical-beat, with prior probability of 0.24. These clusters are also reasonable because Iconic and Symbolic gestures have rather specific definitions.

As for the clustering of gesture data, only single clusters were produced. This is clearly due to the small dataset: the exploratory cluster analysis simply cannot discover structures that would allow sorting of the objects into groups that exhibit maximal similarity among the group members, and minimal with those not in the group.

Table 13.4 Attribute Selection for Face Attributes

	Average Merit	Average Rank	Attribute
Feedback	$90.9 +/- 11.1$	$1.0 +/- 0$	Head
	$58.2 +/- 6.3$	$2.1 +/- 0.3$	Turn management
	$42.4 +/- 7.2$	$3.2 +/- 0.6$	Emotion-Attitude
	$39.9 +/- 2.6$	$3.7 +/- 0.5$	Gaze
	$22.1 +/- 1.7$	$5.0 +/- 0$	Semiotic-Type
	$9.3 +/- 1.8$	$6.0 +/- 0$	General-Face
Turn management	$58.1 +/- 5.8$	$1.0 +/- 0$	Feedback
	$35.2 +/- 4.7$	$2.2 +/- 0.4$	Head
	$32.3 +/- 5.4$	$2.8 +/- 0.4$	Gaze
	$12.8 +/- 1.5$	$4.3 +/- 0.5$	Semiotic-Type
	$10.0 +/- 2.2$	$4.7 +/- 0.5$	Emotion-Attitude
	$1.5 +/- 0.1$	$6.0 +/- 0$	General-Face
Semiotic-Type	$44.4 +/- 18.0$	$1.5 +/- 1.5$	Emotion-Attitude
	$35.1 +/- 3.7$	$2.0 +/- 0.5$	Head
	$27.3 +/- 4.5$	$3.0 +/- 0.5$	General-Face
	$22.1 +/- 1.5$	$3.7 +/- 0.6$	Feedback
	$13.2 +/- 1.8$	$4.9 +/- 0.3$	Turn
	$10.6 +/- 1.8$	$5.9 +/- 0.3$	Gaze

Table 13.5 Attribute Selection for Gesture Attributes

	Average Merit	Average Rank	Attribute
Feedback	$35.7 +/- 2.6$	$1.0 +/- 0$	Emotion-Attitude
	$19.1 +/- 2.0$	$2.0 +/- 0$	Trajectory
	$9.4 +/- 1.7$	$3.3 +/- 0.5$	Semiotic-Type
	$8.9 +/- 2.1$	$3.7 +/- 0.5$	Turn
	$5.0 +/- 1.1$	$5.0 +/- 0$	Handedness
Turn management	$20.3 +/- 2.3$ $1.0 +/- 0$	Emotion-Attitude	
	$14.3 +/- 2.9$	$2.0 +/- 0$	Feedback
	$9.3 +/- 1.8$	$3.0 +/- 0$	Trajectory
	$2.5 +/- 0.6$	$4.5 +/- 0.5$	Semiotic-Type
	$2.4 +/- 1.2$	$4.5 +/- 0.5$	Handedness
Semiotic-Type	$24.0 +/- 3.0$	$1.0 +/- 0$	Trajectory
	$8.1 +/- 1.1$	$2.1 +/- 0.3$	Emotion-Attitude
	$3.5 +/- 0.8$	$3.2 +/- 0.4$	Feedback
	$2.5 +/- 1.6$	$3.9 +/- 0.7$	Handedness
	$0.7 +/- 0.6$	$4.8 +/- 0.6$	Turn

The final exploration with the data concerns the importance of the attributes in the clustering and classification. The attribute selection was performed via chi-squared attribute evaluation with Weka's Ranker as the ranking algorithm and tenfold cross-classification as the evaluation mode. The selected attributes with the Face data are given in Table 13.4, and the attributes for the Gesture data in Table 13.5.

13.6 Conclusions and Future Work

The article has focused on an important aspect of communication fluency, that of using verbal and nonverbal feedback. It has argued that in order to develop ubiquitous systems and services that address challenges for flexible human–technology interaction, a better understanding of human–human communication is needed. Because interactions do not only consist of verbal requests and exchanges of propositional facts, but also of a large repertoire of multimodal and nonverbal signs, the challenge requires language understanding in a wide sense, that is, study on both verbal and nonverbal communication.

The overall approach for interaction management can be found in the framework of the Constructive Dialogue Model which integrates feedback, information flow, and the construction of shared knowledge into the same general framework of the communicating agents. The agents aim at fulfilling their intentions by planning their actions under the constraints of their individual knowledge and general communicative obligations, and they are obliged to monitor the CPU enablements of communication and give feedback of the current state of communicative activities.

On the basis of empirical data analysis, communicative functions of gestures and face expressions as well as their semiotic interpretations were discussed. As the dataset is small, it is not possible to draw firm generalisations about how nonverbal signs are used in the construction of a shared context, but the analysis gives us positive encouragement to investigate the relation and interdependence of gestures, face expressions, and communicative functions further. We will continue the research with a larger annotated corpus.

The experimental models sketched in the chapter can be used as a starting point for designing and developing dialogue systems that afford natural and intuitive interactions with human users. Their integration in interactive models is backed up with the emerging technology which can recognize the shape and trajectory features that were used in the analysis. Future research should focus on identifying the types of sequences that constitute communicative actions on the basis of the observations of the partner's feedback behaviour, and thus contribute to the design and development of intuitive interactive systems.

Acknowledgements The author wishes to thank Mare Koit for supportive discussions, and all the students who took part in the author's course, Multimodal Corpus Collection and Analysis, at the University of Tartu, Estonia, for their contributions in the annotation of the Estonian data.

References

Allwood, J. (2001). The structure of dialog. In M. Taylor, D. Bouwhuis, & F. Nel (Eds.), *The structure of multimodal dialogue II* (pp. 3–24). Amsterdam: Benjamins.

Allwood, J, Cerrato, L., Jokinen, K., Navarretta, K., & Paggio, P. (2007). The MUMIN coding scheme for the annotation of feedback, turn management and sequencing phenomena. In J.C.

Martin, P. Paggio, P. Kuenlein, R. Stiefelhagen, & F. Pianesi (Eds), Multimodal corpora for modelling human multimodal behaviour. Special issue of the *International Journal of Language Resources and Evaluation*, *41*(3–4), 273–287. http://www.springer.com/journal/10579/.

Allwood, J., Traum, D., & Jokinen, K. (2000). Cooperation, dialogue and ethics. Special issue on collaboration, cooperation and conflict in dialogue systems, *International Journal of Human–Computer Studies*, *53*(6), 871–914.

André, E., & Pelachaud, C. (forthcoming). Interacting with embodied conversational agents. In K. Jokinen & F. Cheng (Eds.), *New trends in speech-based interactive systems*. New York: Springer.

Arbib, M. (2003). The evolving mirror system: A neural basis for language readiness. In M. Christiansen and S. Kirby (Eds.), *Language evolution* (pp. 182–200).Oxford: Oxford University Press, Barsalou, L. W. (1999) Perceptual symbol systems. *Behavioral and Brain Sciences, 22,* 577–660.

Beira, R., Lopes, M., Praca, M., Santos-Victor, J., Bernardino, A., Mettay, G., Becchiz, F., & Saltar, R. (2006). Design of the robot-cub (iCub) head. In *Proceedings of the IEEE International Conference on Robotics and Automation*, Orlando, FL (pp. 94–100).

Campbell, N. (2007). On the use of nonverbal speech sounds in human communication. In N. Campbell (Ed.), *Verbal and Nonverbal Communication Behaviors* (LNAI 4775, pp.117–128). New York: Springer.

Campbell, N., & Jokinen, K. (2008). Non-verbal information resources for constructive dialogue management. Tutorial at the *LREC 2008*. Marrakech, Marocco.

Campbell, N., & Ohara, R. (2005). How far can non-verbal information help us follow a conversation? Preliminary experiments with speech-style and gesture tracking. In *Proceedings of the ATR Symposium on the Cross-Modal Processing of Faces & Voices. No laughing matter.*

Cassell, J., Sullivan J., Prevost, S., & Churchill, E. (Eds.)(2000). *Embodied conversational agents.* Cambridge, MA: MIT Press.

Clark, H., & Wilkes-Gibbs, D. (1986). Referring as a collaborative process. *Cognition 22,* 1–39.

Douglas, C. E., Campbell, N., Cowie, R., & Roach, P. (2003). Emotional speech: Towards a new generation of databases. *Speech Communication, 40,* 33–60.

Duncan, S., Jr., & Fiske, D.W. (1977). *Face-to-face interaction: Research, methods and theory.* Hillsdale, NJ: Lawrence Erlbaum. Distributed by John Wiley & Sons.

Garrod, S., & Doherty, G. (1994). Conversation, co-ordination and Convention: An empirical investigation of how groups establish linguistic conventions. *Cognition, 53,*181–215.

Gibson, J. J. (1979). *The ecological approach to visual perception.* Boston: Houghton Mifflin.

Harnard, S. (1990). The symbol grounding problem. *Physica D, 42,* 335–346.

Jokinen, K. (2000). Learning dialogue systems. In *Proceedings of the LREC Workshop from Spoken Dialogue to Full Natural Interactive Dialogue.* Athens (pp. 13–17).

Jokinen, K. (2007). Interaction and mobile route navigation application. In L. Meng, A. Zipf, & S. Winter (Eds.), *Map-based mobile services - Usage context, interaction and application.* New York: Springer Series on Geoinformatics.

Jokinen, K. (2008). *Constructive Dialogue Management – Speech interaction and rational agents.* Hoboken, NJ: John Wiley & Sons.

Jokinen, K., & Hurtig, T. (2006). User expectations and real experience on a multimodal interactive system. In *Proceedings of the Interspeech 2006*, Pittsburgh, PA.

Jokinen, K., Paggio, P., & Navarretta, C. (2008). Distinguishing the communicative functions of gestures – An experiment with annotated gesture data. In *Proceedings of the Conference on Machine-Learning in Multimodal Interaction.*

Jokinen, K., & Ragni, A. (2007). On the annotation and analysis of multimodal corpus. In *Proceedings of the 3rd Baltic Conference on Human Technology.* Kaunas, Lithuania.

Katagiri, Y. (2005). Interactional alignment in collaborative problem solving dialogues, In *Proceedings of the 9th International Pragmatics Conference*, Riva del Garda Italy.

Kendon, A. (2004). *Gesture: Visible action as utterance.* Cambridge: Cambridge University Press.

Kipp, M. (2001). Anvil – A generic annotation tool for multimodal dialogue. In *Proceedings of the Seventh European Conference on Speech Communication and Technology* (pp. 1367–1370).

Maes, P. (Ed.) (1990). *Designing autonomous agents: Theory and practice from biology to engineering and back.* Cambridge, MA: MIT Press.

Mandler, J. (2004). *The foundations of mind: Origins of conceptual thought.* Oxford: Oxford University Press.

Mavridis, N., & Roy, D. (2006). Grounded situation models for robots: where words and percepts meet. In *IEEE/RSJ International Conference on Intelligent Robots and Systems (IROS).*

McNeill, D. (1992). *Hand and mind: What gestures reveal about thought.* Chicago: University of Chicago Press.

Norman, D. A. (1988). *The psychology of everyday things.* New York: Basic Books.

Norros, L., Kaasinen, E., Plomp, J., & Rämä, P. (2003) Human–technology interaction research and design. VTT roadmaps. VTT Research Notes 2220. Espoo: VTT Industrial Systems,

Peirce, C. S. (1931). *Elements of logic. Collected papers of Charles Sanders Peirce.* C. Hartshorne and P. Weiss (Eds.) (vol. 2). Cambridge, MA: Harvard University Press.

Pickering, M. & Garrod, S. (2004). Towards a mechanistic psychology of dialogue, *Behavioral and Brain Sciences 27,* 169–226.

Plomp, J., Ahola, J., Alahuhta, P., Kaasinen, E., Korhonen, I., Laikari, A., Lappalainen, V., Pakanen, J., Rentto, K., & Virtanen, A. (2002). Smart human environments. In: Sipilä, M. (Ed.). *Communications Technologies. The VTT Roadmaps.* Espoo: Technical Research Centre of Finland, VTT Research Notes 2146, pp. 61–81.

Steels, L. (2003). Evolving grounded communication for robots. *Trends in Cognitive Science, 7*(7), 308–312.

Swerts, M., & Krahmer, E. (2005). Audiovisual prosody and feeling of knowing. *Journal of Memory and Language, 53,* 81–94.

Tao, J. (forthcoming). Multimodal information processing for affective computing. In K. Jokinen and F. Cheng (Eds.), *New trends in speech-based interactive systems.* New York: Springer.

Thompson, E. (2001). Empathy and consciousness. *Journal of Consciousness Studies, 8,* 1–32.

Tomasello, M. (1992). *First verbs: A case study of early grammatical development.* Cambridge: Cambridge University Press.

Traum, D. (1999). Computational models of grounding in collaborative systems. In *Working Papers of the AAAI}Fall Symposium on Psychological Models of Communication in Collaborative Systems, AAAI,* Menlo Park, CA (pp. 124–131).

Weiser, M. (1991). The computer for the twenty-first century. *Scientific American, 265*(3): 94–10.

Witten, I. H., & Frank, E. (2005). *Data mining: Practical machine learning tools and techniques* (2nd ed.). San Francisco: Morgan Kaufmann.

Chapter 14
Emotion Recognition Based on Multimodal Information

Zhihong Zeng, Maja Pantic, and Thomas S. Huang

14.1 Introduction

Here is a conversation between an interviewer and a subject occurring in an Adult Attachment Interview (Roisman, Tsai, & Chiang, 2004). AUs are facial action units defined in Ekman, Friesen, and Hager (2002).

The interviewer asked: "Now, let you choose five adjective words to describe your childhood relationship with your mother when you were about five years old, or as far back as you remember."

The subject kept smiling (lip corner raiser AU12) when listening. After the interviewer finished the question, the subject looked around and lowered down her head (AU 54) and eyes (AU 64). Then she lowered and drew together the eyebrows (AU4) so that severe vertical wrinkles and skin bunching between the eyebrows appeared. Then her left lip raise[d] (Left AU10), and finger scratched chin.

After about 50 second silence, the subject raise her head (AU53) and brow (AU1+AU2), and asked with a smile (AU12): "Should I . . . give what I have now?"

The interviewer response with smiling (AU12): "I guess, those will be when you were five years old. Can you remember?"

The subject answered with finger touching chin: "Yeap. Ok. Happy (smile, AU 6+AU12), content, dependent, (silence, then lower her voice) what is next (silent, AU4+left AU 10), honest, (silent, AU 4), innocent."

Z. Zeng (✉)
University of Illinois at Urbana-Champaign, Imperial College London
e-mail: zhzeng@ifp.uiuc.edu

M. Pantic
Imperial College London / University of Twente, Netherlands
e-mail: m.pantic@imperial.ac.uk

T.S. Huang
University of Illinois at Urbana-Champaign, Imperial College London
e-mail: huang@ifp.uiuc.edu

J.H. Tao, T.N. Tan (eds.), *Affective Information Processing*,
© Springer Science+Business Media LLC 2009

This is an exemplar interaction occurring in a natural human interaction setting where the verbal and nonverbal behavior involves the coordination of multiple modalities (facial expression, speech (linguistic and paralinguistic information), gesture, gaze, head movement, and context). Generally, humans consciously or unconsciously use these modalities to express and interpret emotional behavior in such a way that the interaction can go smoothly. Each of these modalities has a unique contribution in the exchange of information of human behavior, as described in the other chapters. However, unimodal analysis is not sensitive enough to capture all the emotion content of the interactions, nor reliable enough to understand the meaning of the emotion behavior.

Take the above conversation as an instance. If we just listen to what the participants said, we will miss much behavior during the silence. On the other hand, if we just watch the facial actions without the audio channel, we may not reliably interpret the smiles (AU12, AU6+AU12), frowns (AU4), head raise (AU53), brow raise (AU2), and unilateral upper lip raise (left AU10). The subject's complex behavior (e.g., greeting, thinking, uncertainty, and induced emotion) must be understood by integrating physical features from multiple modalities (facial expression, speech, gesture, gaze, and head movement) with context. For example, the first smile of the subject may just mean that she was following what the interviewer was saying whereas the last smile of the subject may mean joy induced by her childhood experience recall.

Many psychological studies have theoretically and empirically demonstrated the importance of integration of information from multiple modalities to yield a coherent representation and inference of emotions (e.g., Ambady & Rosenthal, 1992; Scherer, 1999; Russell, Bachorowski, & Fernandez-Dols, 2003; Yoshimoto, Shapiro, O'Brian, & Gottman, 2005). Emotion research requires the study of the configuration of these emotion-related modalities, and multimodal integration is a key to understanding how humans efficiently and reliably express and perceive human emotional behavior.

With the development of science and technology, more and more researchers from the engineering and psychological communities have explored the possibility of using computers to automatically analyze human emotion displays. We have witnessed significant progress in the field of machine analysis of human emotion behavior, especially facial expression and vocal expression (Picard, 1997; Cowie et al.., 2001; Pantic & Rothkrantz, 2003; Pentland, 2005; Cohn, 2006).

It has also been shown by several studies that integrating the information from multiple modalities leads to improvement of machine recognition performance of emotion over unimodal approaches (Song, Bu, Chen, & Li, 2004; Fragopanagos & Taylor, 2005; Caridakis, Malatesta, Kessous, Amir, Paouzaiou, & Karpouzis, 2006; Zeng et al., 2007b; Zeng, Tu, Pianfetti, & Huang, 2008b).

The improved reliability of multimodal approaches can be explained from an engineering perspective. Current techniques for different modalities have different limitations; for instance, detection and tracking of facial expressions are sensitive to head pose, clutter, and variations in lighting conditions, speech processing is sensitive to auditory noise, and detection of physiological responses is influenced by intrusion of wearable devices. Multimodal fusion provides a possibility to make use of complementary information from multiple modalities and reduce the current technical limitations in automatic emotion analysis.

Based on the fact that change in emotion plays an essential role in our daily life, especially in social interaction, some researchers have explored the possibility of enabling the computer to recognize human emotion behavior, with the goal of building a natural and friendly human–computer interaction (HCI) environment. Examples of affect-sensitive, multimodal HCI systems include the system of Lisetti and Nasoz (2002), which combines facial expression and physiological signals to recognize the user's emotion such as fear and anger and then to adapt an animated interface agent to mirror the user's emotion; the multimodal system of Duric et al., (2002), which applies a model of embodied cognition that can be seen as a detailed mapping between the user's emotional states and the types of interface adaptations; the proactive HCI tool of Maat and Pantic (2006) capable of learning and analyzing the user's context-dependent behavioral patterns from multisensory data and of adapting the interaction accordingly, the automated Learning Companion of Kapoor, Burleson, and Picard (2007) that combines information from cameras, a sensing chair and mouse, wireless skin sensor, and task state to detect frustration in order to predict when the user needs help; and the multimodal computer-aided learning system at Beckman Institute UIUC [1] illustrated in Figure 14.1 where the computer avatar offers an appropriate tutoring strategy based on the information of user's

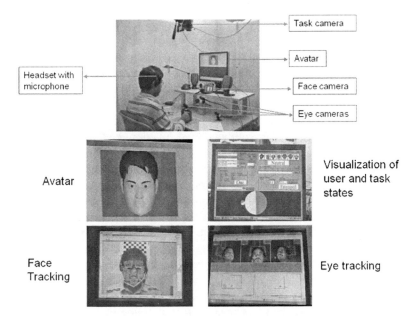

Fig. 14.1 A prototype of multimodal computer-aided learning system.

[1] http://itr.beckman.uiuc.edu.

facial expression, eye movement, keywords, eye movement, and task state. These systems represent initial efforts towards the future socially aware, multimodal HCI.

This chapter is intended to provide an overview of the research on automatic human emotion recognition based on the information from multiple modalities (audio, visual, and physiological responses). Multimodal fusion includes audio-visual fusion, visual-physiological fusion, multi-audio-cue fusion (linguistic and paralinguistic information), multi-visual-cue fusion (facial expression, gaze, head movement, and body movement), and audio-visual-physiological fusion. Although the combination of all modalities (i.e., audio-visual-physiological fusion) is expected to be the best choice for emotion analysis (Yoshimoto, Shapiro, O'Brian, & Gottman, 2005), there is no reported effort toward inclusion of all the modalities into an automatic emotion-sensitive computing system.

The chapter is organized as follows. Section 14.2 provides a brief description of emotion, emotion expression, and perception, from a psychological perspective. Section 14.3 provides a detailed review of the related studies, including multimedia emotion databases, existing automatic multimodal emotion recognition methods, and recent authors' efforts toward this research direction. Section 14.4 discusses some of the challenges that researchers face in this field. Finally we draw conclusions from this chapter.

14.2 Human Emotion Expression and Perception

Although the researchers in the emotion-related research communities (psychology, linguistics, neuroscience, anthropology, and other related disciplines) have not reached consensus on the answer to the question, "What is emotion," a widespread accepted description of emotion consists of multiple components (cognitive appraisal, action tendencies, motor expression, physiological symptoms, subjective feeling) that represent the different aspects of emotion (Scherer, 1999; Cohn, 2006). All of these components concurrently work and function relative to each other during an emotion episode.

Unfortunately, the states of cognitive appraisal, action tendencies, and subjective feeling are not observable, so the emotional states can only be inferred through observed emotion expression, detected physiological symptoms, and self-report if possible. Human judgment of emotion is mainly based on emotion expression (facial expression, speech, gesture, body movement, and gaze). If two individuals are close enough or touch each other, they may perceive some physiological symptoms, such as heartbeat and sweat on the skin, which provide an additional perspective to infer emotion reaction.

The emotion inference from observable behavior and physiological symptoms is definitely an ill-posed problem, so the context of emotion induction acts as a constraint to reduce the ambiguity of emotion judgment. The context can be any information to characterize the situation in which an emotion behavior occurs, including who the emotion expresser and receiver are, what the expresser is doing, when and

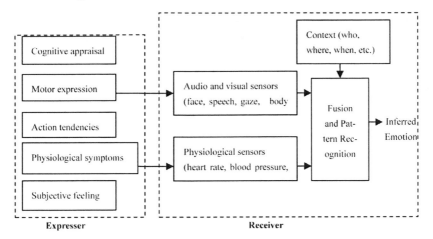

Fig. 14.2 A emotion emission diagram from expresser to receiver.

where the emotion behavior occurs, and so on. Figure 14.2 illustrates a diagram of multimodal emotion expression and perception in which the audio and visual sensors of the receiver (i.e., human eyes and ears) capture the emotion expressions (facial expression, speech, body movement, and gaze), and physiological sensors (i.e., skin) track the physiological responses, and a fusion and pattern recognition module (brain) integrates all related information of audio and visual expressions and physiological responses with the context and makes the judgment of emotion.

In the last three decades, we have witnessed significant progress toward the understanding of emotion behavior and psychological responses, especially based on single modalities of nonverbal behaviors (facial and vocal expressions; Ekman & Friesen, 1975, Ekman, 1982, Ekman & Rosenberg, 2005; Russell, Bachorowski, & Fernandez-Dols, 2003; Harrigan, Rosenthal, & Scherer, 2005). Some promising manual coding systems have been proposed, such as the Facial Action Unit System (Ekman, Friesen, & Hager, 2002) for facial expression and the Feeltrace system (Cowie, Douglas-Cowie, Savvidou, McMahon, Sawey, & Schröder, 2000) for audiovisual expression.

Psychologists have various opinions about the importance of different nonverbal cues in human emotion judgment. Ekman (1982) found that the relative contributions of facial expression, speech, and body gesture to emotion judgment depend both on the emotional state and the environment where the emotional behavior occurs whereas some studies (e.g., Ambady & Rosenthal, 1992) indicated that a facial expression in the visual channel is the most important emotion cue. Many studies have theoretically and empirically demonstrated the advantage of integration of multiple modalities in human emotion perception over single modalities (Ambady & Rosenthal, 1992; Scherer, 1999; Russell et al., 2003; Yoshimoto et al., 2005).

A large number of studies in psychology, linguistics, and neuroscience confirm the correlation between some emotional displays (especially prototypical emotions) and specific audio and visual signals (e.g., Ambady & Rosenthal, 1992;

Cowie et al., 2001; Russell et al., 2003; Ekman & Rosenberg, 2005) and psychological responses (Picard, Vyzas, & Healey, 2001; Stemmler, 2003). Human judgment agreement is typically higher for facial expression modality than it is for vocal expression modality. However, the amount of the agreement drops considerably when the stimuli are spontaneously displayed expressions of emotional behavior rather than posed exaggerated displays.

Recent research results indicated that body movement and gaze significantly facilitate the expression and perception of emotion. Specifically, body movement (i.e., head, limbs, and torso) can provide information of the emotion intensity together with facial and vocal expression, and gaze changes (direct versus averted gaze (Adams & Kleck, 2003), widened eyes, tensed lower lids (Ekman & Friesen, 1975)) are relevant to feeling and attitudes.

Detection of physiological change provides a window into the inner world of human emotion experience (Picard et al., 2001; Stemmler, 2003). But current technology of physiological sensors limits its application in emotion analysis: the available wearable physiological sensors imply wiring the subjects, which make it difficult to elicit emotional displays without influencing results; it can be tricky to gather accurate physiological data because the physiological sensing systems are influenced by other nonemotional factors, including skin–sensor interface influence (positioning of the sensors, application of amounts of gel), human activity, and hormones.

Thus, the progress of physiological research of emotion has been overshadowed by that of audio and visual expression research. Recently, some new physiological sensors have been applied for automatic emotion analysis, such as a sensor mouse in the study (Liao, Zhang, Zhu, Ji, & Gray, 2006), sensor chair in the study (Kapoor & Picard, 2005, Kapoor, Burleson, & Picard, 2007), and wireless noninvasive armband in the study (Lisetti & Nasoz, 2004).

These emotion-related modalities (audio and visual expression, physiological responses) are often studied separately. This precludes finding evidence of the correlation between them. Relatively few studies (Yoshimoto et al., 2005) proposed some pragmatic scheme to integrate all of these modalities to analyze emotion in the interaction setting (such as the conversation between committed couples). However, translating this scheme into one engineering framework for the purposes of automatic emotion recognition remains challenging.

On the other hand, a growing body of research in cognitive sciences argues that the dynamics of human behavior are crucial for its interpretation (Scherer, 1999; Russell et al., 2003; Ekman & Rosenberg, 2005). For example, it has been shown that temporal dynamics of facial behavior represents a critical factor for distinction between spontaneous and posed facial behavior (e.g., Cohn et al., 2004; Ekman & Rosenberg, 2005; Valstar, Pantic, Ambadar, & Cohn, 2006) as well as for categorization of complex behaviors like shame, and amusement (e.g., Ekman & Rosenberg, 2005). Based on these findings, we may expect that temporal dynamics of each modality separately and their temporal correlations play an important role in the recognition of human naturalistic emotion behavior. However, these are virtually unexplored areas of research.

Another largely unexplored area of research is the relationship between emotion and context. The interpretation of human behavioral signals is context-dependent. For example, a smile can be a display of politeness, irony, joy, or greeting. To interpret a behavioral signal, it is important to know the context in which this signal has been displayed: where the expresser is (e.g., inside, on the street, in the car), what his or her current task is, who the receiver is, and who the expresser is (Russell et al., 2003).

14.3 Multimodal Emotion Recognition

With the advance of technology, an increased number of studies on machine analysis of multimodal human emotion displays have emerged in recent years. It has been shown by several experimental studies that integrating the information from multiple modalities leads to an improved performance of emotion behavior recognition. The study of Chen, Huang, Miyasato, and Nakatsu in 1998 represents an early attempt toward multimodal emotion recognition, focusing on audiovisual fusion. In this section we first offer a brief overview of the existing databases of multimedia recordings of human emotion displays, which provide the basis of automatic emotion analysis. Next we examine available multimodal computing methods for emotion recognition. We focus here on the efforts recently proposed in the literature that represent multimodal approaches to the problem of multimodal human affect recognition. For exhaustive surveys of the past work in machine analysis of multimodal emotion expressions, readers are referred to the survey papers by Cowie et al.(2001), Pantic and Rothrantz (2003, 2006), Sebe, Cohen, and Huang (2005), and Zeng, Pantic, Roisman, and Huang, (2008a).

14.3.1 Multimodal Databases

Authentic emotion expressions are difficult to collect because they are relatively rare and short-lived, and filled with subtle context-based changes that make it difficult to elicit emotion displays without influencing results. In addition, manual labeling of spontaneous emotional expressions for ground truth is very time consuming, error prone, and expensive. This state of affairs makes automatic analysis of spontaneous emotional expression a very difficult task. Due to these difficulties, most of the existing studies on automatic analysis of human emotion displays were based on the "artificial" material of deliberately expressed emotions, especially six basic emotions (i.e., happiness, sadness, anger, disgust, anger, surprise), elicited by asking the subjects to perform a series of emotional expressions in front of a camera and/or microphone. As a result, the majority of the existing systems for human emotion recognition aim at classifying the input expression as the basic emotion category (Cowie et al., 2001; Pantic & Rothkrantz, 2003; Sebe et al., 2005).

However, increasing evidence suggests that deliberate behavior differs in visual appearance, audio profile, and timing from spontaneously occurring behavior. For example, Whissell shows that the posed nature of emotions in spoken language may differ in the choice of words and timing from corresponding performances in natural settings (Whissell, 1989). When it comes to facial behavior, there is a large body of research in psychology and neuroscience demonstrating that spontaneous and deliberately displayed facial behavior has differences both in utilized facial muscles and their dynamics (Ekman & Rosenberg, 2005).

For instance, many types of spontaneous smiles (e.g., polite) are smaller in amplitude, longer in total duration, and slower in onset and offset time than posed smiles (Cohn, Reed, Ambadar, Xiao, & Moriyama, 2004; Ekman & Rosenberg, 2005). Similarly, it has been shown that spontaneous brow actions (AU1, AU2, and AU4 in the FACS system) have different morphological and temporal characteristics (intensity, duration, and occurrence order) than posed brow actions (Valstar et al., 2006). It is not surprising, therefore, that methods of automated human emotion analysis that have been trained on deliberate and often exaggerated behaviors usually fail to generalize to the subtlety and complexity of spontaneous emotion behavior.

These findings and the general lack of a comprehensive reference set of audio and/or visual recordings of human emotion displays motivated several efforts aimed at the development of datasets that could be used for training and testing of automatic systems for human emotion analysis. Table 14.1 lists some noteworthy audiovisual data resources that were reported in the literature. For each database, we provide the following information: emotion elicitation method (i.e., whether the elicited emotion displays are posed or spontaneous), size (the number of subjects and available data samples), modality (audio and/or visual), emotion description (category or dimension), and labeling scheme. For other surveys of existing databases of human emotion behavior, the readers are referred to Cowie et al. (2005), Pantic et al. (2005), and Zeng, Hu, Liu, Fu, and Huang, (2006).

As far as the databases of deliberate emotion behavior are concerned, the following databases need to be mentioned. The Chen–Huang audiovisual database (Chen, 2000) is to our knowledge the largest multimedia database containing facial and vocal deliberate displays of basic emotions and four cognitive states. The FABO database of Gunes and Piccardi (2006) contains videos of facial expressions and body gestures portraying posed displays of basic and nonbasic emotional states (six prototypical emotions, uncertainty, anxiety, boredom, and neutral).

The existing datasets of spontaneous emotion behavior were collected in one of the following scenarios: human–human conversation (Bartlett et al., 2005; Douglas-Cowie et al., 2003; Roisman et al., 2004), human–computer interaction (SAL), and clips from television (Douglas-Cowie et al., 2003). In most of the existing databases discrete emotion categories are used as the emotion descriptors. The labels of prototypical emotions are often used, especially in the databases of deliberate emotion behavior. In databases of spontaneous emotion behavior, dimensional descriptions in the evaluation-activation space (SAL[2]; Douglas-Cowie et al., 2003), and some

---

[2] http://emotion-research.net/toolbox/toolboxdatabase.2006-09-26.5667892524.

Table 14.1 Multimedia Databases of Human Emotion Behavior

References	Elicitation Method	Size	Emotion Description	Labeling
FABO face and body gesture (Gunes and Piccardi, 2006)	Posed: two cameras to record facial expressions and body gestures, respectively	23 adults Mixed races Available: 210 videos	Category: 6 basic emotions, neutral, uncertainty, anxiety, boredom	N/A
Chen-Huang '00 (Chen, 2000)	Posed	100 adults, 9900 visual and AV expressions	Category: 6 basic emotions, and 4 cognitive states (interest, puzzle, bore, frustration)	N/A
Adult Attachment Interview '04 (Roisman et al., 2004)	Natural: subjects were interviewed to describe the childhood experience	60 adults Each interview last 30–60min	Category: 6 basic emotions, embarrassment, contempt, shame, general positive and negative.	FACS
RU-FACS '05 (Bartlett et al., 2005)	Natural: subjects were tried to convince the interviewers they were telling the truth	100 adults	Category: 33 AUs	FACS
SAL '05[2]	Induced: subjects interacted with artificial listener with different personalities	24 adults 10 h	Dimensional labeling/categorical labeling	FEEL-TRACE
Belfast database '03 (Douglas-Cowie et al., 2003)	Natural: clips taken from television and realistic interviews with research team	125 subjects. 209 sequences from TV, 30 from interview	Dimensional labeling/categorical labeling	FEEL-TRACE

application-dependent emotional states are usually used as the data labels. Interest, boredom, confusion, frustration, uncertainty, anxiety, embarrassment, contempt, and shame are some examples of the used application-dependent emotion-interpretative labels.

Facial Action Units (AUs) (Ekman et al., 2002) are very suitable to describe the richness of spontaneous facial behavior, as the thousands of anatomically possible facial expressions can be represented as the combination of a few dozens of AUs. Hence, the labeling schemes used to code data include FACS AUs (Roisman et al., 2004; Bartlett et al., 2005) and the Feeltrace system for evaluation-activation dimensional description ((Douglas-Cowie et al., 2003; SAL[2]).

Worthy of mention are the FABO face and body gesture database, SAL database, and Belfast database which are publicly accessible, representing efforts toward enhancing communication and establishing reliable evaluation procedures in this field.

14.3.2 Audiovisual Computing

Influenced by basic emotion theory, most of the existing audiovisual emotion recognition studies investigated recognition of the basic emotions from deliberate displays. Relatively few efforts have been reported toward detection of nonbasic emotional states from deliberate displays. Those include the work of Zeng and his colleagues (Zeng et al., 2004, 2006, 2007b, 2008b), and that of Sebe et al. (2006), who added four cognitive states (interest, puzzlement, frustration, and boredom) considering the importance of these cognitive states in human–computer interaction. A related study conducted on naturalistic data is that of Pal, Iyer, and Yantorno (2006), who designed a system to detect hunger and pain as well as sadness, anger, and fear from infant facial expressions and cries.

Most of the existing methods for audiovisual emotion analysis are based on deliberately posed emotion displays (Go, Kwak, Lee, & Chun, 2003; Busso et al., 2004; Song et al., 2004; Zeng et al., 2004, 2006, 2007b; Wang & Guan, 2005; Hoch, Althoff, McGlaun, & Rigoll, 2005; Sebe et al., 2006). Recently a few exceptional studies have been reported toward audiovisual emotion analysis in spontaneous emotion displays. For example, Fragopanagos et al. (2005), Pal et al. (2006), Caridakis et al. (2006), Karpouzis et al. (2007), and Zeng et al. (2007a) used the data collected in psychological research interviews (Adult Attachment Interview), Pal et al. (2006) used recordings of infant affective displays, whereas Fragopanagos and Taylor (2005), Caridakis et al. (2006), and Karpouzis et al. (2007), used the data collected in *Wizard of Oz* scenarios.

Because the available data were usually insufficient to build a robust machine-learning system for recognition of fine-grained emotional states (e.g., basic emotions), recognition of coarse emotional states was attempted in most of the aforementioned studies. The study of Zeng et al. (2007) focuses on audiovisual recognition of positive and negative emotion, whereas other studies report on classification of audiovisual input data into the quadrants in evaluation-activation space (Fragopanagos et al., 2005; Caridakis et al., 2006; Karpouzis et al., 2007).

The studies reported in Fragopanagos et al., (2005), Caridakis et al. (2006), and Karpouzis et al. (2007) applied the FeelTrace system that enables raters to continuously label changes in emotion expressions. However, note that the study discussed in Fragopanagos et al. (2005) reported on a considerable labeling variation among four human raters due to the subjectivity of audiovisual emotion judgment. More specifically, one of the raters mainly relied on audio information when making judgments whereas another rater mainly relied on visual information. This experiment actually also reflects the asynchronization of audio and visual expression. In order to reduce this variation of human labels, the study of Zeng et al. (2007) made the assumption that facial expression and vocal expression have the same coarse emotional states (positive and negative), and they then directly used FACS-based labels of facial expressions as audiovisual expression labels.

The data fusion strategies utilized in the current studies on audiovisual emotion recognition are feature-level, decision-level, or model-level fusion. An example of feature-level fusion is the study in Busso et al. (2004) that concatenated the prosodic features and facial features to construct joint feature vectors which are then used to build an emotion recognizer. However, the different time scales and metric levels of features coming from different modalities, as well as increasing feature-vector dimensions influence the performance of a emotion recognizer based on a feature-level fusion.

The vast majority of studies on bimodal emotion recognition reported on decision-level data fusion (Go et al., 2003; Zeng et al., 2004, 2007b; Busso et al., 2004; Hoch et al., 2005; Wang & Guan, 2005; Pal et al., 2006).

In decision-level data fusion, the input coming from each modality is modeled independently and these single-modal recognition results are combined at the end. Because humans display audio and visual expressions in a complementary and redundant manner, the assumption of conditional independence between audio and visual data streams in decision-level fusion is incorrect and results in the loss of information of mutual correlation between the two modalities.

To address this problem, some model-level fusion methods have been proposed that aim at making use of the correlation between audio and visual data streams (e.g., Song et al., 2004; Fragopanagos et al., 2005; Caridakis et al., 2006; Sebe et al., 2006; Zeng et al., 2006, 2008b; Karpouzis et al., 2007). Zeng et al., (2008b) presented multistream fused HMM to build an optimal connection among multiple streams from audio and visual channels according to maximum entropy and the maximum mutual information criterion. Zeng et al. (2006) extended this fusion framework by introducing a middle-level training strategy under which a variety of learning schemes can be used to combine multiple component HMMs. Song et al. (2004) presented tripled HMM to model correlation properties of three component HMMs that are based individually on upper face, lower face, and prosodic dynamic behaviors. Fragopanagos and Taylor (2005) proposed an artificial neural network with a feedback loop called ANNA to integrate the information from face, prosody and lexical content. Caridakis et al. (2006) and Karpouzis et al. (2007) investigated combining the visual and audio data streams by using relevant neural networks. Sebe et al. (2006) used a Bayesian network to fuse the facial expression and prosody expression.

14.3.3 Other Multimodal Computing

In addition to the above-mentioned audiovisual emotion recognition studies mainly based on facial expression and prosody expression, a few studies were constructed to investigate the multi-visual-cue fusion, including fusion of facial expressions and head movements (Cohn et al., 2004; Zhang & Ji, 2005; Ji, Lan, & Looney, 2006), fusion of facial expression and body gesture (Balomenos, Raouzaiou, Ioannou, Drosopoulos, Karpouzis, & Kollias, 2005; Gunes & Piccardi, 2005), fusion of facial expression and gaze (Ji et al., 2006), and fusion of facial expression and head and shoulder movement (Valstar et al., 2007), based on the supplemental contribution of gaze and head and body movement to emotion recognition.

Relatively few reports of automatic emotion recognition are found regarding integration of facial expressions and postures from a sensor chair (Kapoor et al., 2005, 2007), and the integration of facial expression and physiological signals (temperature, heart rate, and skin conductivity) from a sensor mouse (Liao et al., 2006), with the aim of improvement of emotion recognition performance.

With the research shift toward analysis of spontaneous human behavior, analysis of only acoustic information will not suffice for identifying subtle changes in vocal emotion expression. Several audio-based studies investigated the combination of acoustic features and linguistic features (language and discourse) to improve vocal emotion recognition performance. Typical examples of linguistic-paralinguistic-fusion methods are those of Litman & Forbes-Riley (2004) and Schuller, Villar, Rigoll, and Lang (2005), who used spoken words and acoustic features; of Lee and Narayanan, (2005), who used prosodic features, spoken words and information of repetition; of Graciarena, Shriberg, Stolcke, Enos, & Kajarekar (2006), who combined prosodic, lexical, and cepstral features; and of Batliner et al. (2003), who used prosodic features, Part-Of-Speech (POS), Dialogue Act (DA), repetitions, corrections, and syntactic-prosodic boundary to infer the emotion.

Finally, virtually all present approaches to automatic emotion analysis are context-insensitive. Exceptions from this overall state of the art in the field include just a few studies. Pantic & Rothkrantz (2004) investigated interpretation of facial expressions in terms of user-defined interpretation labels. Ji et al. (2006) investigated the influence of context (work condition, sleeping quality, circadian rhythm, and environment, physical condition) on fatigue detection, and Kapoor and Picard (2005) investigated the influence of the task states (difficulty level and game state) on interest detection. Litman et al. (2004) also investigated the role of context information (e.g., subject, gender, and turn-level features representing local and global aspects of the dialogue) on audio emotion recognition.

14.3.4 Exemplar Methods

We introduce in this section our efforts toward machine understanding of multimodal affective behavior, which were published in related conferences and journals.

14.3.4.1 Audiovisual Posed Affective Expression Recognition

The team of Zeng and Huang made efforts (Zeng et al., 2004, 2006, 2007, 2008) toward audiovisual posed affective expression recognition, based on the data of 20 subjects (10 females and 10 males) from the database Chen–Huang (Chen, 2000). Although the subjects displayed affect expressions on request, the subjects chose how to express each state. They were simply asked to display facial expressions and speak appropriate sentences. Each subject was required to repeat each state with speech three times. Therefore, for every affective state, there are $3 * 20 = 60$ video sequences. And there are a total of $60 * 11 = 660$ sequences for 11 affective states. The time of every sequence ranged from 2–6 seconds.

A tracking algorithm called Piecewise Bezier Volume Deformation (PBVD) tracking (Tao & Huang, 1999) was applied to extract facial features in our experiment. This face tracker uses a 3D facial mesh model embedded in multiple Bezier volumes. The tracker can track head motion and local deformations of the facial features. The local deformations of facial features in terms of 12 predefined motions shown in Figure 14.3 are used for affect recognition.

For audio feature extraction, the entropic signal processing system named get_f0, was used to output the pitch F0 for the fundamental frequency estimate, RMS energy for the local root mean squared measurements, prob_voice for the probability of voicing, and the peak normalized cross-correlation value that was used to determine the output F0. The feature selection experimental results in Zeng et al. (2007) showed pitch and energy are the most important audio factors in affect classification. Therefore, in our experiment, we only used these two audio features for affect recognition. Some prosody features, such as frequency and duration of silence, could have implications in the HMM structure of energy and pitch.

For integrating coupled audio and visual features, we present a model-level fusion, called multistream fused HMM (MFHMM) (Zeng et al., 2008b) which devises a new structure linking the multiple component HMMs which is optimal according to the maximum entropy principle and maximum mutual information (MMI) criterion. In the MFHMM framework, the different streams are modeled by different fused HMM components which connect the hidden states of one HMM to the

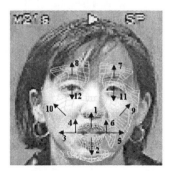

Fig. 14.3 Facial motion units.

Fig. 14.4 Accuracies of different methods under various audio SNR conditions.

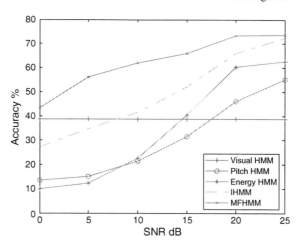

observation of other HMMs. The details of MFHMM, including its learning and inference algorithms, can be found in Zeng et al. (2008b).

We applied leave-one-person-out cross-validation to test our person-independent affect recognition algorithm. In our experiment, the composite facial feature from video, energy, and pitch features from audio are treated as three coupled streams, and modeled by three component HMMs. We used five methods to make decisions: face-only HMM, audio-only HMM, independent HMM fusion (IHMM), and MFHMM. IHMM is multistream HMM that assumes the independence among different stream.

The experimental results under varying levels of audio SNR are shown in Figure 14.4. They demonstrate that audiovisual fusion outperforms unistream methods in most cases; that is, both IHMM and MFHMM are better than visual HMM, pitch HMM, and energy HMM. The exceptions are that the accuracies of IHMM in 0 and 5 dB audio SNR are lower than visual HMM. That shows that the IHMM combination scheme cannot achieve better performance than individual modality when the performance of certain individual streams is very bad. On the other hand, the performance of MFHMM is still a little higher than the visual-only HMM in 0 dB audio SNR. Thus, MFHMM is more robust for processing noisy data than IHMM.

14.3.4.2 Audiovisual Spontaneous Affective Expression Recognition

The team of Zeng and Huang also explored recognition of audiovisual spontaneous affective expressions occurring in a psychological interview named the Adult Attachment Interview (AAI) that is used to characterize individuals' current states of mind with respect to past parent–child experiences. We present the Adaboost multistream hidden Markov model (Adaboost MHMM; Zeng et al., 2007) to integrate audio and visual affective information.

In order to capture the richness of facial expression, we used a 3D face tracker (Tao & Huang, 1999) to extract facial texture images that were then transformed into low-dimensional subspace by locality preserving projection (LPP). We used pitch and energy in the audio channel to build audio HMM in which some prosody features, such as frequency and duration of silence, could have implications. In the audiovisual fusion stage, we treated the component HMM combination as a multi-class classification problem in which the input is the probabilities of HMM components and the output is the target classes, based on the training combination strategy (Zeng et al., 2006). We used the Adaboost learning scheme to build fusion of the component HMMs from audio and visual channels.

Based on the Adaboost learning scheme, these estimated likelihoods of component HMMs were used to construct a strong classifier which is a weighted linear combination of a set of weak classifiers. A set of weaker hypotheses was estimated, each using likelihood of positive or negative emotion of a single-component HMM. The final hypothesis was obtained by weighted linear combination of these hypotheses where the weights were inversely proportional to the corresponding training errors.

The personal-dependent recognition was evaluated on the two subjects (one female and one male). The emotion recognition results of unimodal (audio-only or visual-only) methods and audiovisual fusion are shown in Figure 14.5. Two combination schemes (weighting and training) were used to fuse the component HMMs from the audio and visual channels. Acc MHMM means MHMM with the weighting combination scheme in which the weights are proportional to stream normalized recognition accuracies. Adaboost MHMM means MHMM with the Adaboost learning schemes as described in Section 14.6.

Because we treated the multistream fusion as a multiclass classification problem, there was a variety of methods that could be used to build the fusion. In addition to Adaboost MHMM, we used LDC and KNN approaches to build this audiovisual fusion, which are Ldc MHMM and Knn MHMM in Figure 14.5.

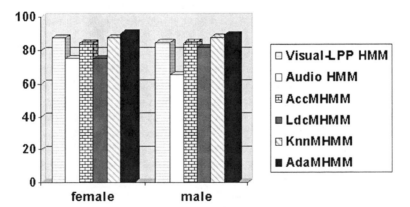

Fig. 14.5 Performance comparison among different modalities and different fusions.

The performance comparison of these fusion methods is as follows: Adaboost MHMM > Knn MHMM > Acc MHMM > Ldc MHMM. The results demonstrate that the training combination outperforms the weighting combination, except Ldc MHMM which is a linear fusion. Adaboost MHMM is the best among these four fusion methods. Results show that Adaboost MHMM and Knn MHMM are better than unimodal HMM (i.e., visual-only HMM and audio-only HMM). That suggests that multiple modalities (audio and visual modalities) can provide more affective information and have the potential to obtain better recognition performance than a single modality.

In Figure 14.5, the accuracy of Acc MHMM equals the visual-only HMM for male data but is worse than visual-only HMM for female data. Ldc MHMM is worse than visual-only HMM in female and male cases. Both Acc MHMM and Ldc MHMM are linear bimodal fusion. That suggests that the fusion method plays an important role in audiovisual emotion recognition. Although the linear bimodal combination is reasonable and intuitive, it is not guaranteed to obtain the optimal combination in a realistic application. It is even possible that this combination is worse than individual component performance, as shown in our experiments.

14.3.4.3 Multi-Visual-Cue Analysis of Posed Versus Spontaneous Expressions

Pantic's team proposed a system of automatic discrimination between posed and spontaneous smiles based on multiple visual cues including facial expression (described in terms of AUs that produce it) and head and shoulder movements (Valstar et al., 2007). Although few systems have been recently reported on automatic discrimination between spontaneous and posed facial behavior (i.e., Valstar et al., 2006; Littlewort et al., 2007), this is the only reported effort so far to automatically discern spontaneous from deliberately displayed behavior based on multiple visual cues.

Conforming with the research findings in psychology, the method relies on characteristics of temporal dynamics of facial, head, and shoulder actions and employs parameters such as speed, intensity, duration, and occurrence order of visual behavioral cues to classify smiles present in an input video as either deliberate or genuine smiles.

A cylindrical head tracker, proposed by Xiao et al. (2003), was used to track head motion; auxiliary particle filtering tracking method, proposed by Pitt and Shephard (1999), was used to track the tip points of the shoulders; and particle filtering with factorized likelihood, proposed by Patras and Pantic (2004), was used to track 20 facial characteristic points such as the corners of the mouth and the eyes (see Figure 14.6). Using the tracking data, the presence (i.e., activation) of AU6 (raised cheeks), AU12 (lip corners pulled up), AU13 (lip corners pulled up sharply), head movement (moved off the frontal view), and shoulder movement (moved off the relaxed state), were detected first. For each of these behavioral cues, the temporal segments (neutral, onset, apex, and offset) were also determined.

Fig. 14.6 Illustration of the tracking procedure used by Valstar et al. (2007).

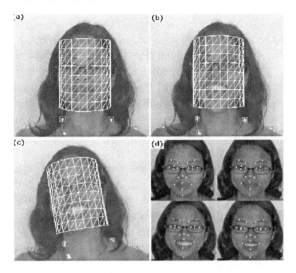

To detect the activated AUs and their temporal segments, the AU detector proposed by Valstar and Pantic (2006), which combines Gentle Boost ensemble learning and Support Vector Machines, was used. To detect head and shoulder actions and their temporal segments a rather simple rule-based expert system was used. Then a set of midlevel feature parameters was computed for every temporal segment of each present behavioral cue. These parameters included the segment duration, the mean and the maximum displacements of the relevant points in x- and y-directions, the maximum velocity in x- and y-directions, and the asymmetry in the displacements.

In addition, the second-order polynomial functional representation of the displacements of the relevant points, and the order in which the behavioral cues have been displayed, were computed as well. Gentle Boost has been used to learn the most informative parameters for distinguishing between spontaneous and volitional smiles and these parameters have been used further to train a separate Support Vector Machine for each temporal segment of each of the five behavioral cues (i.e., in total 15 GentleSVMs). The outcomes of these 15 GentleSVMSs are then combined and a probabilistic decision function determines the class (spontaneous or posed) for the entire smile episode. When trained and tested on a set containing 100 samples of volitional smiles and 102 spontaneous smiles from the MMI Facial Expression database (Pantic et al., 2005, Pantic & Bartlett, 2007), the proposed method attained a 94% correct recognition rate (0.964 recall with 0.933 precision) when determining the class (spontaneous or posed) of an input facial expression of smile.

14.3.4.4 Audiovisual Laughter Detection

Research in cognitive sciences provided some promising hints that vocal outbursts and nonlinguistic vocalizations such as yelling, laughing, and sobbing may be very important cues for decoding someone's affect/attitude (Russell et al., 2003), eported (Zeng et al., 2008a). Most of these efforts are based only on audio signals such as the method for automatic laughter detection proposed by Truong and van Leeuwen, (2007).

However, because it has been shown by several experimental studies in either psychology or signal processing that integrating the information from audio and video leads to an improved performance of human behavior recognition (e.g., Petridis and Pantic (2008)), few pioneering efforts toward audiovisual recognition of nonlinguistic vocal outbursts have been recently reported including audiovisual analysis of infants' cries proposed by Pal et al. (2006) and audiovisual laughter recognition proposed by Petridis and Pantic (2008). The latter is the only effort reported so far aimed at automatic discrimination between laughter and speech in naturalistic data based on both facial and vocal expression.

The method uses particle filtering with factorized likelihood, proposed by Patras and Pantic 2004), to track 20 facial characteristic points such as the corners of the mouth and the eyes in an input video. Then it uses principal component analysis (PCA) to distinguish changes in the location of facial points caused by changes in facial expression from those caused by rigid head movements. The changes in facial expression are used in further processing. To detect laughter from the audio signal, spectral features, namely perceptual linear prediction coding features and their temporal derivatives, have been used.

Both feature-level fusion and decision-level fusion have been investigated. To achieve decision-level fusion, the input coming from each modality (audio and video) was modeled independently by a neural network preceded by Ada Boost, which learns the most informative features for distinguishing between laughter and speech as shown by the relevant modality. Then, these single-modal recognition results were combined at the end using the SUM function. To achieve feature-level fusion, audio and video features were concatenated into a single feature vector (by up-sampling so that the video frame rate equaled the audio frame rate of 50 frames per second).

The resulting feature vector was then used to train the target Ada neural network. When trained and tested on a set of 40 audiovisual laughter segments and 56 audiovisual speech segments from the AMI corpus (http://corpus.amiproject.org/), the proposed method attained an average 86% correct recognition rate (feature-level fusion: 0.869 recall with 0.767 precision; decision-level fusion: 0.817 recall with 0.823 precision) when determining the class (speech or laughter) of an input audiovisual episode.

14.4 Challenges

There are two new trends in the research on automatic human emotion recognition: analysis of spontaneous emotion behavior and multimodal analysis of human emotion behavior including audiovisual analysis, combined audio-based linguistic and nonlinguistic analysis, and multicue visual analysis based on facial expressions, gaze, head movements, and/or body gestures. Several previously recognized problems have been addressed including the development of more comprehensive datasets of training and testing material. At the same time, several new challenging issues have been recognized, including the necessity of studying the temporal correlations between the different modalities (audio and visual) as well as between various behavioral cues (e.g., face, gaze, head, and body gestures, and linguistic and paralinguistic information). This section discusses these issues.

14.4.1 Databases

Acquiring valuable spontaneous emotion behavior data and the related ground truth is far from being solved. To our knowledge, there is still no database of emotion behavior that records data of all emotion-related modalities (facial and vocal expression, physiological responses, body movement, and gaze). In addition, although much effort has been made toward collection of audiovisual databases of spontaneous human emotion behavior, most of the data contained in the available databases currently lack labels. In other words, no metadata are available that could identify the emotional state displayed in a video sample and the context in which this emotional state was displayed.

Although some promising coding systems have been proposed to label the facial action (e.g., FACS (Ekman et al., (2002)), and audiovisual expression (e.g., Feeltrace (Cowie et al. 2000)), how to reliably code all emotion-related modalities for automatic emotion systems remains an open issue. Much work is needed to understand the correlation of the dynamic structure of these modalities. The metadata about the context in which the recordings were made such as the utilized stimuli, the environment, and the presence of other people, are needed because these contextual variables may influence masking of the emotional reactions. In addition, human labeling of emotion behavior is very time consuming and full of ambiguity due to human subjective perception. Improving the efficiency and reliability of labeling multimodal emotion databases is critical in the recognition of spontaneous emotion.

Readers are referred to Pantic and Rothkrantz (2003), Pantic et al. (2005), Cowie et al. (2005), and Zeng et al., (2006), which discussed a number of specific research and development efforts needed to build a comprehensive, readily accessible reference set of emotion displays that could provide a basis for benchmarks for all different efforts in the research on machine analysis of human emotion behavior.

14.4.2 Multimodal Computing

Although all agree that multisensory fusion including audiovisual data fusion, linguistic and paralinguistic data fusion, multi-visual-cue data fusion would be highly beneficial for machine analysis of human emotion, it remains unclear how this should be accomplished. Studies in neurology on fusion of sensory neurons (Stein & Meredith, (1993) are supportive of early data fusion (i.e., feature-level data fusion) rather than of late data fusion (i.e., decision-level fusion). However, it is an open issue how to construct suitable joint feature vectors composed of features from different modalities with different time scales, different metric levels, and different temporal structures. Simply concatenating audio and video features into a single feature vector, as done in the current human emotion analyzers that use feature-level data fusion, is obviously not the solution to the problem.

Due to these difficulties, most researchers choose decision-level fusion in which the input coming from each modality is modeled independently and these single-modal recognition results are combined at the end. Decision-level fusion, also called classifier fusion, is now an active area in the fields of machine learning and pattern recognition. Many studies have demonstrated the advantage of classifier fusion over the individual classifiers due to the uncorrelated errors from different classifiers (e.g., Kuncheva, 2004). Various classifier fusion methods (fixed rules and trained combiners) have been proposed in the literature, but optimal design methods for classifier fusion are still not available. In addition, because humans simultaneously employ tightly coupled audio and visual modalities, multimodal signals cannot be considered mutually independent and should not be combined only at the end as is the case in decision-level fusion.

Model-level fusion or hybrid fusion that aims at combining the benefits of both feature-level and decision-level fusion methods may be a good choice for this fusion problem. However, based on existing knowledge and methods, how to model multimodal fusion for spontaneous emotion displays is largely unexplored. A number of issues relevant to fusion require further investigation, such as the optimal level of integrating these different streams, the optimal function for the integration, as well as inclusion of suitable estimations of the reliability of each stream. In addition, how to build context-dependent multimodal fusion is an open and highly relevant issue.

Here we want to stress that temporal structures of the modalities (facial and vocal) and their temporal correlations play an extremely important role in the interpretation of human naturalistic, multimodal emotion behavior. Yet these are virtually unexplored areas of research, due to the fact that facial expression and vocal expression of emotion are usually studied separately.

An important related issue that should be addressed in multimodal emotion recognition is how to make use of information about the context (environment, observed subject, his or her current task) in which the observed emotion behavior was displayed. Emotions are intimately related to a situation being experienced or imagined by a human. Without context, a human may misunderstand the observed person's emotion expressions. Yet, with the exception of a few studies investigating the influence of context on emotion recognition (e.g., Litman & Forbes-Riley, 2004; Pantic & Rothkrantz, 2004; Kapoor & Picard, 2005; Kapoor et al., 2007; Ji et al., 2006), virtually all existing approaches to machine analysis of human emotion are context-insensitive.

Building a context model that includes person ID, gender, age, conversation topic, and workload needs help from other research fields such as face recognition, gender recognition, age recognition, topic detection, and task tracking. Because the problem of context sensing is very difficult to solve, pragmatic approaches (e.g., activity- and/ or subject-profiled approaches) should be taken.

14.5 Conclusion

Multimodal information fusion is a process that enables human ability to assess emotional states robustly and flexibly. In order to understand the richness and subtlety of human emotion behavior, the computer should be able to integrate all emotion-related modalities (facial expression, speech, body movement, gaze, and physiological response). Multimodal emotion recognition has received rather less research attention than single modality, due to the complexity of multimodal processing and the availability of relevant training and test material. As this chapter describes, we have witnessed increasing efforts toward machine analysis of multimodal emotion recognition in the last decade. Specifically, some databases of acted and spontaneous emotion displays have been collected by researchers in the field, and a number of promising methods for multimodal analysis of human spontaneous behavior have been proposed.

In the meantime, several new challenging issues have been identified. Let us reconsider the interview scenario described in the introduction where the subject expressed her emotion by using facial expression, speech (linguistic content and paralinguistic behavior), head movement, and gaze in an efficient way. The complexity of the occurring emotion behavior challenges our current knowledge and approaches in machine analysis of emotion behavior.

In order to enable the computer to reliably perceive human emotion displays as humans do, much effort across multiple research disciplines is needed to address the following important issues: build a comprehensive, readily accessible reference set of emotion displays that could provide a basis for benchmarks for all different efforts in the field; develop methods for spontaneous emotion behavior analysis that are robust to the observed person's arbitrary movement, occlusion, complex and noisy background; devise models and methods for human emotion analysis that take into consideration temporal structures of the modalities and temporal correlations between the modalities (and/or multiple cues), and context (subject, his or her task, environment); and develop better methods for multimodal fusion.

The progress of research on automatic emotion recognition based on multimodal behavior and physiological components will greatly contribute to developing a comprehensive understanding of the mechanisms involved in human behavior, and enhancing human–computer interaction through emotion-sensitive and socially intelligent interfaces.

Acknowledgment We would like to thank Professor Glenn I. Roisman for providing the valuable videos and FACS codes of the Adult Attachment Interview. This work of Zhihong Zeng and Thomas Huang was supported in part by the Beckman Postdoctoral Fellowship and NSF CCF 04-26627. The work of Maja Pantic has been funded in part by EU IST Program Project FP6-0027787 (AMIDA) and EC's 7th Framework Program [FP7/2007-2013] under grant agreement no. 211486 (SEMAINE).

References

Adams, R. B & Kleck, R.E(2003). Perceived gaze direction and the processing of facial displays of emotion. *Psychological Science, 14,* 644–647.

Ambady, N., & Rosenthal, R. (1992). Thin slices of expressive behavior as predictors of interpersonal consequences: A meta-analysis. *Psychological Bulletin, 111*(2), 256–274.

Balomenos, T., Raouzaiou, A., Ioannou, S., Drosopoulos, A., Karpouzis, K., & Kollias, S. (2005). *Emotion analysis in man-machine interaction systems* (LNCS 3361; pp. 318–328). New York: Springer.

Bartlett, M. S., Littlewort, G., Frank, M., Lainscsek, C., Fasel, I., & Movellan, J. (2005), Recognizing facial expression: machine learning and application to spontaneous behavior. In *IEEE International Conference on Computer Vision and Pattern Recognition* (pp. 568–573).

Batliner, A., Fischer, K., Hubera, R., Spilkera, J., & Noth, E. (2003). How to find trouble in communication. *Speech Communication, 40,* 117–143.

Busso, C., Deng, Z., Yildirim, S., Bulut, M., Lee, C. M., et al. (2004), Analysis of emotion recognition using facial expressions, speech and multimodal information. In *Proceedings of the International Conference on Multimodal Interfaces* (pp. 205–211).

Caridakis, G., Malatesta, L., Kessous, L., Amir, N., Paouzaiou, A. & Karpouzis, K. (2006). Modeling naturalistic affective states via facial and vocal expression recognition. In *Proceedings of the International Conference on Multimodal Interfaces* (pp. 146–154).

Chen, L., Huang, T. S., Miyasato, T., & Nakatsu, R. (1998). Multimodal human emotion/expression recognition. In *Proceedings of the International Conference on Automatic Face and Gesture Recognition* (pp. 396–401).

Chen, L. S. (2000), Joint processing of audio-visual information for the recognition of emotional expressions in human-computer interaction, PhD thesis, University of Illinois at Urbana-Champaign, USA.

Cohn, J. F. (2006). Foundations of human computing: Facial expression and emotion. In *Proceedings of the International Conference on Multimodal Interfaces* (pp. 233–238).

Cohn, J. F., Reed, L. I., Ambadar, Z., Xiao, J., & Moriyama, T. (2004). Automatic analysis and recognition of brow actions and head motion in spontaneous facial behavior. In *Proceedings of the International Conference on Systems, Man & Cybernetics, 1* (pp. 610–616).

Cohn, J. F., & Schmidt, K. L.(2004). The timing of facial motion in posed and spontaneous smiles. *International Journal of Wavelets, Multiresolution and Information Processing, 2,* 1–12.

Cowie, R., Douglas-Cowie, E., & Cox, C. (2005). Beyond emotion archetypes: Databases for emotion modeling using neural networks. *Neural Networks, 18,* 371–388.

Cowie, R., Douglas-Cowie, E., Savvidou, S., McMahon, E., Sawey, M., & Schröder, M. (2000). 'Feeltrace': An instrument for recording perceived emotion in real time. In *Proceedings of the ISCA Workshop on Speech and Emotion* (pp. 19–24).

Cowie, R., Douglas-Cowie, E., Tsapatsoulis, N., Votsis, G., Kollias, S., Fellenz, W., & Taylor, J. G. (2001), Emotion recognition in human-computer interaction, *IEEE Signal Processing Magazine,* January (pp. 32–80).

Douglas-Cowie, E., Campbell, N., Cowie, R., & Roach, P. (2003). Emotional speech: Towards a new generation of database. *Speech Communication, 40*(1–2), 33–60.

Duric, Z., Gray, WD., Heishman, R., Li, F., Rosenfeld, A., Schoelles, M. J., Schunn, C., & Wechsler, H. (2002). Integrating perceptual and cognitive modeling for adaptive and intelligent human–computer interaction. *Proceedings of the IEEE, 90*(7), 1272–1289.

Ekman, P. (Ed.) (1982). *Emotion in the human face* (2nd ed.). New York: Cambridge University Press.

Ekman, P., & Friesen, W. V. (1975). *Unmasking the face*. Englewood Cliffs, NJ: Prentice-Hall.

Ekman, P., Friesen, W. V., & Hager, J. C. (2002). *Facial Action Coding System*. Salt Lake City, UT: A Human Face.

Ekman P., & Rosenberg, E. L. (2005). What the face reveals: Basic and applied studies of spontaneous expression using the facial action coding system (2nd ed.). Oxford University Press, University of Illinois at Urbana-Champaign, USA.

Fragopanagos, F., & Taylor, J. G. (2005), Emotion recognition in human–computer interaction. *Neural Networks, 18*, 389–405.

Go, H. J., Kwak, K. C., Lee, D. J., & Chun, M.G. (2003). Emotion recognition from facial image and speech signal. In *Proceedings of the International Conference of the Society of Instrument and Control Engineers* (pp. 2890–2895).

Graciarena, M., Shriberg, E., Stolcke, A., Enos, J. H. F., & Kajarekar, S. (2006). Combining prosodic, lexical and cepstral systems for deceptive speech detection. In *Proceedings of the International Conference on Acoustics, Speech and Signal Processing, 1*, 1033–1036.

Gunes, H., & Piccardi, M. (2005). Affect recognition from face and body: early fusion vs. late fusion. In *Proceedings of the International Conference on Systems, Man and Cybernetics* (pp. 3437–3443).

Gunes, H., & Piccardi, M. (2006). A bimodal face and body gesture database for automatic analysis of human nonverbal affective behavior. *International Conference on Pattern Recognition, 1*, 1148–1153.

Harrigan, J. A., Rosenthal, R., & Scherer, K. R. (2005). *The new handbook of methods in nonverbal behavior research* (pp. 369–397). Oxford University Press, USA.

Hoch, S., Althoff, F., McGlaun, G., & Rigoll, G. (2005), Bimodal fusion of emotional data in an automotive environment. In *ICASSP, II* (pp. 1085–1088).

Ji, Q., Lan, P., & Looney, C. (2006). A probabilistic framework for modeling and real-time monitoring human fatigue. *IEEE SMC-Part A, 36*(5), 862–875.

Kapoor, A., Burleson, W., & Picard, R. W. (2007). Automatic prediction of frustration. *International Journal of Human–Computer Studies, 65*(8), 724–736.

Kapoor, A., & Picard, R. W. (2005). Multimodal affect recognition in learning environment. In *ACM International Conference on Multimedia* (pp. 677–682).

Karpouzis, K., Caridakis, G., Kessous, L., Amir, N., Raouzaiou, A., Malatesta, L., & Kollias, S. (2007). Modeling naturalistic affective states via facial, vocal, and bodily expression recognition (LNAI 4451; pp. 91–112). New York: Springer.

Kuncheva, L. I. (2004). *Combining pattern classifier: Methods and algorithms*. Hoboken, NJ: John Wiley and Sons.

Lee, C. M., & Narayanan, S. S. (2005). Toward detecting emotions in spoken dialogs. *IEEE Transactions on Speech and Audio Processing, 13*(2), 293–303.

Liao, W., Zhang, W., Zhu, Z., Ji, Q., & Gray, W. (2006), Toward a decision-theoretic framework for affect recognition and user assistance. *International Journal of Human-Computer Studies, 64*(9), 847–873.

Lisetti, C. L., & Nasoz, F. (2002). MAUI: A multimodal affective user interface. In *Proceedings of the International Conference on Multimedia* (pp. 161–170).

Lisetti, C. L., & Nasoz, F. (2004). Using noninvasive wearable computers to recognize human emotions from physiological signals. *EURASIP Journal on Applied Signal Processing, 11*, 1672–1687.

Litman, D. J., & Forbes-Riley, K. (2004), Predicting student emotions in computer-human tutoring dialogues. In *Proceedings of the 42nd Annual Meeting of the Association for Computational Linguistics (ACL)*, July (pp. 352–359).

Littlewort, G. C., Bartlett, M. S., & Lee, K. (2007). Faces of pain: Automated measurement of spontaneous facial expressions of genuine and posed pain. In *Proceedings of the ACM International Conference on Multimodal Interfaces* (pp. 15–21).

Maat, L., & Pantic, M. (2006). Gaze-X: Adaptive affective multimodal interface for single-user office scenarios, In *Proceedings of the ACM International Conference on Multimodal Interfaces* (pp. 171–178).

Pal, P., Iyer, A. N., & Yantorno, R. E. (2006). Emotion detection from infant facial expressions and cries. In *Proceedings of the International Conference on Acoustics, Speech & Signal Processing, 2* (pp. 721–724).

Pantic, M., & Bartlett, M. S. (2007). Machine analysis of facial expressions. In K. Delac and M. Grgic, (Eds.), *Face recognition* (pp. 377–416). Vienna, Austria: I-Tech Education.

Pantic, M., Pentland, A., Nijholt, A., & Huang, T. S. (2006). Human computing and machine understanding of human behavior: A survey. In *International Conference on Multimodal Interfaces* (pp. 239–248).

Pantic M., & Rothkrantz, L. J. M. (2003), Toward an affect-sensitive multimodal human-computer interaction, *Proceedings of the IEEE, 91*(9, Sept.), 1370–1390.

Pantic, M., & Rothkrantz, L. J. M. (2004). Case-based reasoning for user-profiled recognition of emotions from face images. In *International Conference on Multimedia and Expo* (pp. 391–394).

Pantic, M., Valstar, M. F, Rademaker, R., & Maat, L. (2005). Web-based database for facial expression analysis. In *International Conference on Multimedia and Expo* (pp. 317–321).

Patras, I., & Pantic, M. (2004). Particle filtering with factorized likelihoods for tracking facial features, In *Proceedings of the IEEE International Conference on Face and Gesture Recognition* (pp. 97–102).

Pentland, A. (2005). Socially aware, computation and communication, *IEEE Computer, 38*, 33–40.

Petridis, S., & Pantic, M. (2008). Audiovisual discrimination between laughter and speech, In *IEEE Int'l Conf. Acoustics, Speech, and Signal Processing* (pp. 5117–5120).

Picard, R. W. (1997). *Affective computing*. Cambridge, MA: MIT Press.

Picard, R. W., Vyzas, E., & Healey, J. (2001). Toward machine emotional intelligence: Analysis of affective physiological state. *IEEE Transactions on Pattern Analysis and Machine Intelligence, 23*(10), 1175–1191.

Pitt, M. K., & Shephard, N. (1999). Filtering via simulation: auxiliary particle filtering. *Journal of the American Statistical Association, 94*, 590–599.

Roisman, G. I., Tsai, J. L., & Chiang, K. S. (2004). The emotional integration of childhood experience: Physiological, facial expressive, and self-reported emotional response during the adult attachment interview. *Developmental Psychology, 40*(5), 776–789.

Russell, J. A., Bachorowski, J., & Fernandez-Dols, J. (2003). Facial and vocal expressions of emotion. *Ann. Rev. Psychol. 54*, 329–349.

Scherer K. R. (1999). Appraisal theory. In T. Dalgleish & M. J. Power (Eds.), *Handbook of cognition and emotion*, New York: Wiley, 637–663.

Schuller, B., Villar, R. J., Rigoll, G., & Lang, M. (2005). Meta-classifiers in acoustic and linguistic feature fusion-based affect recognition. In *International Conference on Acoustics, Speech, and Signal Processing* (pp. 325–328).

Sebe, N., Cohen, I., Gevers, T., & Huang, T. S. (2006). Emotion recognition based on joint visual and audio cues. In *International Conference on Pattern Recognition* (pp. 1136–1139).

Sebe, N., Cohen, I., & Huang, T. S. (2005). Multimodal emotion recognition. In *Handbook of Pattern Recognition and Computer Vision*. Singapore: World Scientific.

Song, M., Bu, J., Chen, C., & Li, N. (2004), Audio-visual based emotion recognition—A new approach. In *International Conference on Computer Vision and Pattern Recognition* (pp. 1020–1025).

Stein, B., & Meredith, M. A. (1993). *The merging of senses*. Cambridge, MA: MIT Press.

Stemmler, G. (2003). Methodological considerations in the psychophysiological study of emotion. In R. J. Davidson, K. R. Scherer, & H. H. Goldsmith (Eds.), *Handbook of affective sciences* (pp. 225–255). Oxford University Press, USA.

Tao, H., & Huang, T. S. (1999), Explanation-based facial motion tracking using a piecewise Bezier volume deformation mode. In *CVPR'99, 1* (pp. 611–617).

Truong, K. P., & van Leeuwen, D. A. (2007) Automatic discrimination between laughter and speech, *Speech Communication, 49*, 144–158.

Valstar, M. F., Gunes, H., & Pantic, M. (2007). How to distinguish posed from spontaneous smiles using geometric features. *In ACM Int'l Conf. Multimodal Interfaces* (pp. 38–45).

Valstar, M., Pantic, M., Ambadar, Z., & Cohn, J. F. (2006). Spontaneous vs. posed facial behavior: Automatic analysis of brow actions. In *International Conference on Multimedia Interfaces* (pp. 162–170).

Valstar, M. F., & Pantic, M. (2006). Fully automatic facial action unit detection and temporal analysis. *Proceedings of IEEE International Conference on Computer Vision and Pattern Recognition, 3*,149.

Wang, Y., & Guan, L. (2005), Recognizing human emotion from audiovisual information. In *ICASSP, II* (pp. 1125–1128).

Whissell, C. M. (1989). The dictionary of affect in language. In R. Plutchik & H. Kellerman (Eds.). *Emotion: Theory, research and experience. The measurement of emotions* (vol. 4; pp. 113–131). New York: Academic Press.

Xiao, J., Moriyama, T., Kanade, T., & Cohn, J. F. (2003). Robust full-motion recovery of head by dynamic templates and re-registration techniques. *International Journal of Imaging Systems and Technology, 13*(1), 85–94.

Yoshimoto, D., Shapiro, A., O'Brian, K., & Gottman, J. M. (2005). Nonverbal communication coding systems of committed couples. In *New handbook of methods in nonverbal behavior research*, J.A. Harrigan, R. Rosenthal, and K. R. Scherer (Eds.) (pp. 369–397), USA.

Zeng, Z., Hu, Y., Liu, M., Fu, Y., & Huang, T. S.(2006), Training combination strategy of multi-stream fused hidden markov model for audio-visual affect recognition. In *Proceedings of the ACM International Conference on Multimedia* (pp. 65–68).

Zeng, Z., Hu, Y., Roisman, G. I., Wen, Z., Fu, Y., & Huang, T. S. (2007a), Audio-visual spontaneous emotion recognition. In T. S. Huang, A. Nijholt, M. Pantic, & A. Pentland (Eds.) *Artificial Intelligence for Human Computing* (LNAI 4451, pp. 72–90). New York, Springer.

Zeng, Z., Pantic, M., Roisman, G. I., & Huang, T. S. (2008a). A survey of affect recognition methods: Audio, visual and spontaneous expressions. *IEEE Transactions on Pattern Analysis and Machine Intelligence* (in press).

Zeng, Z., Tu, J., Liu, M., Zhang, T., Rizzolo, N., Zhang, Z., Huang, T. S., Roth, D., & Levinson, S. (2004), Bimodal HCI-related Emotion Recognition, In *International Conference on Multimodal Interfaces* (pp. 137–143).

Zeng, Z., Tu, J., Pianfetti, B., & Huang, T. S. (2008b). Audio-visual affective expression recognition through multi-stream fused HMM. *IEEE Transactions on Multimedia*, June 2008, *10*(4), 570–577.

Zeng, Z., Tu, J., Liu, M., Huang, T. S., Pianfetti, B., Roth, D., & Levinson, S. (2007b). Audio-visual affect recognition. *IEEE Transactions on Multimedia, 9*(2), 424–428.

Zhang, Y., & Ji, Q. (2005). Active and dynamic information fusion for facial expression understanding from image sequences. *IEEE Transactions on Pattern Analysis and Machine Intelligence, 27*(5), 699–714.

Chapter 15
A Multimodal Corpus Approach for the Study of Spontaneous Emotions

Jean-Claude Martin and Laurence Devillers

Abstract The design of future interactive affective computing systems requires the representation of spontaneous emotions and their associated multimodal signs. Current prototypes are often limited to the detection and synthesis of a few primary emotions and are most of the time grounded on acted data collected in-lab. In order to model the sophisticated relations between spontaneous emotions and their expressions in different modalities, an exploratory approach was defined. We collected and annotated a TV corpus of interviews. The collected data displayed emotions that are more complex than the six basic emotions (anger, fear, joy, sadness, surprise, disgust). We observed superpositions, masking, and conflicts between positive and negative emotions. We report several experiments that enabled us to provide some answers to questions such as how to reliably annotate and represent the multimodal signs of spontaneous complex emotions and at which level of abstraction and temporality.

We also defined a copy-synthesis approach in which these behaviors were annotated, represented, and replayed by an expressive agent, enabling a validation and refinement of our annotations. We also studied individual differences in the perception of these blends of emotions. These experiments enabled the identification and definition of several levels of representation of emotions and their associated expressions that are relevant for spontaneous complex emotions.

15.1 Introduction

Studies of nonverbal behaviors in the social sciences have been numerous for the last 40 years. Theoretical frameworks, methodologies, and conceptual coding schemes have been defined for the study of gestures, facial expressions, their relations to speech, and their relations to communicative meanings and emotions. Emotions

J.-C. Martin (✉) and L. Devillers
LIMSI-CNRS, France
e-mail: MARTIN@LIMSI.FR; DEVIL@LIMSI.FR

J.H. Tao, T.N. Tan (eds.), *Affective Information Processing*,
© Springer Science+Business Media LLC 2009

have been studied mostly in individual modalities (speech, facial expressions, and movement) and often via instructed acting of single labeled emotions, although the existence of emotional blends has been demonstrated by several researchers. Several elicitation protocols use controlled in-lab recording, inducing limitations with respect to the spontaneity of the behaviors and the emotional and interaction context (e.g., narrative monologues).

Studying the roots of multimodal behaviors in several modalities is a long-term task that requires the collective effort of several disciplines. Designing multimodal human–computer interfaces requires computational models of human multimodal behaviors. During the last ten years, an increasing number of pluridisciplinary studies have concentrated on digital collection, annotation, and analysis of multimodal communicative and emotional behaviors. They produced digital resources, coding schemes, annotation software, and statistical measures computed in the specific context of the videotaped situations. The high cost of manual annotation leads to a continuum between two extreme approaches: exploratory approaches using detailed annotation of short video sequences (e.g., TV spots), and statistical approaches using a more limited set of higher-level annotations but in longer video sequences (e.g., meetings). This high cost of manual annotation also calls for a better integration of automatic image and audio preprocessing in the manual annotation process.

Such computer-based approaches produce quantitative information that can be processed by software for producing computational models of multimodal communication. They enable incremental annotations and iterative testing of different hypotheses. These pluridisciplinary studies involving computer science researchers are usually driven by results from the literature in the social sciences obtained for similar research questions but in different situations. These digital corpus-based studies produce detailed and contextual annotations of situated interaction behaviors (Goodwin, 2000). Instead of taking as granted results from the nonverbal literature in social sciences when considered out of the interaction context, corpus-based approaches enable us to assess how these results stand in other interaction situations (Martin, 2006).

Yet there is still a gap between the numerous nonverbal studies from social sciences and the relatively few multimodal corpora. In order to produce computational models of multimodal behaviors, more corpora are needed (e.g., spontaneous emotions, multiparty interactive behaviors, and interpersonal relations). Current corpus-based approaches often display several limitations. Few corpora have jointly collected and analyzed speech, gestures, and facial expression. Few corpora have studied multimodal behaviors during noninstructed acted emotions. Nonverbal perceptive tests are often limited to real data (e.g., videotaped behaviors) although they could benefit from controlled replay by virtual characters. Finally, although several corpus-based approaches have been defined for the study of multimodal human communication, there is still a lack of a federative methodological and software framework. Few studies tackled the whole range of processes and iterative steps that are required in such an approach: manual and automatic annotations, validation of manual annotations, computation of representations, generation, and perceptual evaluation.

Current human–computer interfaces are limited compared to the everyday multimodal communication we use when engaging with other people in normal day-to-day interactions or in emotionally loaded interactions. In our human–human interactions, we combine several communication modalities such as speech and gestures in a spontaneous and subtle way. Whereas current human–computer interfaces make an extensive use of graphical user interfaces combining keyboard, mouse, and screen, multimodal human–computer interfaces aim at an intuitive interaction using several humanlike modalities such as speech and gestures which require no training to use.

An Embodied Conversational Agent (ECA) is a human–computer interface endowed with conversational capacities inspired by human communication such as the management of turn-taking and feedback in several modalities (Cassell et al., 1994; Cassell, Bickmore, Campbell, Vilhjálmsson, & Yan, 2000). Surveys of ECA can be found in Rist et al. (2003), Kipp (2004), Pelachaud et al. (2004), and Buisine (2005) with a recent one focusing on expressiveness (Vinayagamoorthy et al., 2006). Using an ECA is expected to lead to an intuitive and friendly interaction, for example, via the display of emotional expressions that can be useful for applications in education, for example, as a means of motivating students.

During the last ten years, researchers have developed prototypes covering several areas of ECAs: reasoning, communicative and expressive behavior generation, and 2D and 3D animation. More recently, a focus was put on the design of expressive agents, representation languages, evaluation of ECAs, and individual behaviors and personalities in ECAs. A few studies have started to tackle bidirectional communication, systematic evaluation with relevant user groups (children), differences of production and perception of multimodal behavior with respect to users' profile (gender, age, cognitive profile, personality traits), and display and perception of blended emotions in both gestures and facial expressions. Most systems rely on the literature in social sciences. Few systems are experimentally grounded on the collection of situated behaviors.

This chapter provides an overview of a multimodal corpus-based approach that we have defined over the last years for studying expression and perception of spontaneous emotions. Section 15.2 describes some related work. Section 15.3 describes the multimodal corpus. Section 15.4 describes the manual and automatic annotations that have been done. Section 15.5 summarizes how we replayed some annotated behaviors with an expressive agent. Section 15.6 explains how this multimodal corpus and the replayed behaviors helped us to find individual differences in the perception of multimodal expression of spontaneous emotions.

15.2 Related Work

Human communicative modalities include speech, hand gestures (and other bodily movements), facial expressions, gaze (and pupil dilation), posture, spatial behavior, bodily contact, clothes (and other aspects of appearance), nonverbal vocalizations, and smell (Argyle, 2004). There is a wide literature on nonverbal communication (Siegman & Feldstein, 1985; Feldman & Rim, 1991; Argyle, 2004; Knapp & Hall, 2006).

15.2.1 Affect and Their Multimodal Expression

Charles Darwin wrote that facial expressions of emotions are universal, not learned differently in each culture; that they are biologically determined, the product of man's evolution (Darwin 1872). Since then, several researchers have experimentally observed that this was true for some emotions (happiness, sadness, surprise, fear, anger, disgust), although there are cultural differences in when these expressions are shown (elicitation and display rules).

Three approaches to emotion representation and annotation are generally used (Scherer, 2000): verbal discrete categories, continuous abstract dimensions, and appraisal dimensions. The *discrete verbal categories* approach consists in selecting a set of labels for representing emotions using words. Several studies use a list of "primary" emotions showed as being universal in their display: surprise, fear, disgust, anger, happiness, sadness (Ekman & Friesen, 1975).

Ekman defined basic emotions not as a single affective state but rather as a family of related states, each sharing nine characteristics such as "distinctive universal signals" (Ekman & Friesen, 1975). For example, anger is described by 60 facial expressions. The selection of the proper set of emotional labels is thus a question of research per se.

The Humaine NoE proposed a list of 48 emotion categories. Plutchik (1980) combined such primary emotion labels to produce other labels for "secondary" emotions. For example, love is a combination of joy and acceptance, whereas submission is a combination of acceptance and fear. The *continuous dimension approach* consists in defining a multidimensional space in which emotions are represented by points such as valence-evaluation (from negative to positive emotions) or intensity (Douglas-Cowie, Campbell, Cowie, & Roach, 2003; Craggs & Wood, 2004).

Finally, *appraisal dimensions* are used for describing the emotional processes and the related emotional events. The central contribution of appraisal theories is to specify a set of criteria, dimensions, or checks that are presumed to underlie the emotion-constituent appraisal process. In other words, as an event unfolds, the individual concerned would evaluate its significance on a number of criteria such as pertinence of the consequences to one's well-being, conduciveness or obstructiveness for one's plans and goals, and the ability to cope with such consequences.

In Scherer's component process model, these criteria are called stimulus evaluation checks (SECs; Sander, Grandjean, & Scherer, 2005). Gratch and Marsella (2004) defined a computational appraisal model of emotion. The Ortony, Clore, and Collins (1988; OCC) model is also often used in affective computing for representing the different categories of emotional events and situations.

Emotions are expressed in several modalities (Collier, 1985). Ekman (2003a) described in detail the distinctive clues of the face to each basic emotion but also depending on the intensity of the emotion and its meaning how many areas can/must be involved and how their signals are modified according to intensity. For example, surprise can be shown in just two areas of the face, with the third area uninvolved. Each of these two-area surprise faces has a slightly different meaning: eyes + brows = questioning surprise; eyes + mouth = astonished surprise; brows + mouth = dazed or less interested surprise.

Ekman also described in a systematic manner the *blending* of facial expressions for all the possible pairs of six acted basic emotions (happiness, sadness, surprise, fear, anger, disgust) (Ekman & Friesen, 1975). Ekman photographed models who were instructed to move particular facial muscles. He photographed three areas that are capable of independent movement: the brow/forehead; the eyes/lids and the root of the nose; the lower face including the cheeks, mouth, and most of the nose and chin. He artificially composed the three areas of the collected static images. He also illustrated the context that can lead to each of these blends (e.g., a woman being both angry and sad after a driver has run over her dog).

He explains the complexity of these blended behaviors with regard to the timing and subtleties of individual emotions (the families of facial expressions). A blend does not require that different facial areas show different emotions. It can also be achieved by blending the appearance of the two emotions within each area of the face. For example, the blend anger/disgust is described by: lips are pressed (anger) and upper lip is raised (disgust), and nose wrinkled (disgust). Sequences of facial expressions have also been studied as indicators of appraisal processes such as the sequential evaluation checks (Kaiser & Wehrle, 2001, 2004).

Several researchers also experimentally studied expression of emotion in movement. Wallbott (1998) conducted a study in which actors were asked to elicit the following emotions: elated joy, happiness, sadness, despair, fear, terror, cold anger, hot anger, disgust, contempt, shame, guilt, pride, and boredom. The actors had to utter meaningless sentences. Twelve drama students were asked to code body movements and postures performed by these actors. Only categories with more than 75% intercoder agreement between two coders were kept: position of upper body (away from camera, collapsed), position of shoulders (up, backward, forward), position of head (downward, backward, turned sideways, bent sideways), position of arms (lateralized hand/arm movements, stretched out frontal, stretched out sideways, crossed in front of chest, crossed in front of belly, before belly, stemmed hips), position of hands (fist, opening/closing, back of hand sideways, self-manipulator, illustrator, emblem, pointing), and movement quality (movement activity, spatial expansion, movement dynamics, energy, and power). Body movements included jerky or active; body postures included closeness, openness, and symmetry or asymmetry of the different body limbs.

Wallbott observed distinctive patterns of movement and postural behavior associated with some of the emotions studied. Some of these distinctive features seem to be typical of certain emotions, such as "arms crossed in front of chest" for the emotion of pride, or the number of "self-manipulators" for shame. A number of

Table 15.1 Discriminative Features of Movement Quality

Emotion	Movement Quality
Hot anger	High movement activity, expansive movements, high movement dynamics
Elated joy	High movement activity, expansive movement, high movement dynamics
Happiness	Low movement dynamics
Disgust	Inexpensive movements
Contempt	Low movement activity, low movement dynamics
Sadness	Low movement activity, low movement dynamics
Despair	Expansive movements
Terror	High movement activity
Boredom	Low movement activity, inexpensive movements, low movement dynamics

Source: Wallbott (1998).
Note: Features of body parts and posture not shown.

movement and posture categories merely distinguish between "active" emotions (such as hot anger or elated joy), and more "passive" emotions. His results indicate that movement and postural behavior are indicative of the intensity of different emotions. Movement and postural behavior when encoding different emotions (at least as captured with the categories used here) are to some degree specific to at least some emotions.

However, actors and actresses differ to a large degree in their ability to encode the emotions in movement and posture, as well as in their idiosyncrasies of encoding style. Although some actors seem to be very good in producing different movement and posture patterns for the different emotions, other actors seem to use rather stereotyped movements and postures even when encoding different emotions. This finding highlights the fact that the differences between emotions as reported above seem to be rather stable phenomena, which reach significant results irrespective of the large differences between the actors and actresses employed in the study.

On the other hand, this finding highlights that studies using only one or very few actors or very few indicators of emotion in terms of movement behaviors may be misleading in that some variance of the findings is due to the different actors, whereas for some other indicators (movement or posture categories) the variance due to actors may be higher than the variance due to emotion, such as for the categories of "head turns sideways" or "arms hanging down" or "arms before belly." This indicates that the actors' idiosyncrasies in encoding different emotions via body movements and postures cannot be neglected. Similar studies were conducted on expressive body movements during acted data (DeMeijer, 1989; Newlove, 1993; Boone & Cunningham, 1998).

15.2.2 Multimodal and Emotional Corpora

Analog video has been used for a long time for observing and manually annotating nonverbal behaviors. For the last ten years, several studies using digital video and computer-based annotations have been conducted in a variety of contexts and data (laboratory, meeting, TV material, field studies). Compared to the social sciences experiments described in the above sections, the digital corpus-based studies we summarize in this section aim at producing computational models of multimodal behavior including details of individual behaviors that are required for the design of human–computer interfaces. Surveys of multimodal corpora can be found in Maybury and Martin (2002), Wegener Knudsen et al. (2002a,b), Martin, den Os, Kuhnlein, Boves, Paggio, and Catizone, R. (2004), and Martin et al. (2006a).

Several digital corpora have been recently dedicated to the study of emotions (Devillers et al., 2006). As we mentioned above, there has been much psychological research on emotional behavior in individual modalities such as speech (Banse & Scherer, 1996; Cowie, 2000; Schröder 2003), facial expressions (Ekman, 1999), and body movements (DeMeijer, 1989; Newlove, 1993; Boone & Cunningham, 1998; Wallbott, 1998).

Most of these studies about emotion use "acting" in a restricted sense. Most of them consist in recording, in a laboratory environment, actors who are expressing emotions instructed via single labels of emotions (e.g., anger), sometimes using scripts (Wallbott, 1998). Recent studies in the affective computing area also use a similar restricted acting protocol: use of markers on the body to recognize four acted basic emotions (Kapur, Virji-Babul, Tzanetakis, & Driessen, 2005), use of motion capture of static postures during acting of two nuances of four basic emotions (e.g., sad and depressed; De Silva, Kleinsmith, & Bianchi-Berthouze, 2005), use of video processing of facial expressions and upper body gestures during six acted emotional behaviors (Gunes & Piccardi, 2005).

Digital multimodal emotional corpora have recently been collected enabling the high resolution and controlled collection of a wide variety of directed and scripted acted gestures, facial expressions, and speech emotional behaviors. This is the case of the GEMEP corpus (Bänziger, Pirker, & Scherer, 2006).

Enos and Hirschberg (2006) analyze objections and arguments for emotion portrayals. They have collected a corpus of emotional behaviors by adding context to emotion portrayals. They suggest two approaches for eliciting emotional speech via acting. The scenario approach uses a description of the character, the situation, the actor's goals, and the goals of other characters. The script approach makes direct use of the actor's training and skills via the acting of original scenes taken from theatre plays. Another means of involving acting in the study of emotional expression is to have actors replay videotaped behaviors and compare the perceived naturalness of both. In Frigo (2006), naturalistic behaviors collected from TV interviews are replayed by actors. The genuinness and validity of acting is evaluated by naive subjects in order to study the differences in speech between naturalistic versus acted conditions.

These different corpora enable us to study several dimensions of emotional corpora that have an impact on the observed behaviors:

- Location of recording (laboratory/TV on stage/TV in street/natural environment (e.g., at home))
- Instructions staging/spontaneous/portrayed/posed
- Timescale (minutes (TV clip)/hours (meeting)/days)
- Awareness of being filmed; awareness of emotion study
- Subjects (actors/experts on emotion/ordinary people)
- Interactivity; monologue/multiparty/social constraints on interactivity
- Human–human or human–computer or mixed
- Number of recorded modalities, resolution, and quality of collected data; intrusiveness of recording media

15.2.3 Expressive Virtual Agents

Designing expressive virtual agents is a long-term challenge raising several research questions about: the architecture of such systems, the computation and selection of verbal and nonverbal behaviors, their synchronization, their representation, and finally the evaluation at multiple levels of the usefulness, efficiency, and friendliness of such interfaces. One main issue is to find lifelike combinations of modalities during emotional behaviors.

One makes a distinction between two parts in an ECA: its body and its mind. The body is in charge of the display of the behaviors. The mind is in charge of the reasoning, planning, and management of the interaction with the user or the surrounding environment (Pelachaud et al., 2004). Several models have been proposed for the selection and animation of behaviors in an ECA (Cassell, Bickmore, Campbell, Vilhjálmsson, & Yan, 2000; Prendinger & Ishizuka, 2004). André, Rist, van Mulken, Klesen, and Baldes (2000) describe the design of dialogue for agents. One approach consists in inserting gesture tags in the text to be spoken by the agent (Cassell, Vilhjàlmsson, & Bickmore, 2001). Automatic learning of these manual rules for gesture selection and timing from manual specifications is proposed in Kipp (2006). With respect to the temporal synchronization of the modalities, the gestures are often timed so that the stroke coincides with the stressed syllable of the co-occurring concept in speech (Cassell et al., 1994). For a deep generation approach a modality-free representation language would become necessary where abstract messages and functions are encoded that have not yet been assigned a modality or surface form; the shallow approach omits this modality-free representation (Kipp, 2004).

Greta incorporates conversational and emotional qualities (Pelachaud, 2005; Poggi, Pelachaud, de Rosis, Carofiglio, & De Carolis, 2005). To determine speech accompanying nonverbal behaviors, the system relies on the taxonomy of communicative functions proposed by Poggi (2003). A behavior is defined as a list of communicative functions, meaning, signal, expressivity, and context. For example, looking away from the interlocutor (signal) conveys a take-turn meaning, within the communicative function "turn allocation."

Conflicts between incompatible signals are managed by a dedicated module (Pelachaud & Poggi, 2002). It also includes a model of gesture manner, called gesture expressivity, that acts on the production of communicative gestures. The model of expressivity is based on studies of nonverbal behavior (Wallbott & Scherer, 1986; Gallaher, 1992; Wallbott, 1998). Expressivity is described as a set of six dimensions (Hartmann, Mancini, & Pelachaud, 2005). Each dimension acts on a characteristic of communicative gestures. Spatial extent describes how large the gesture is in space. Temporal extent describes how fast the gesture is executed. Power describes how strong the performance of the gesture is. Fluidity describes how two consecutive gestures are co-articulated, one merging with the other. Repetition describes how often a gesture is repeated. Overall activity describes how many behavior activities there are over a time span.

For the face, the expressivity dimensions act mainly on the intensity of the muscular contraction and its temporal course. In order to consider individual agents, an individual expressive profile can be assigned to the agent specifying in which modalities the agent is the most expressive. The expressivity attributes can act over a whole animation, on gestures, phases, or on every frame.

As we explain above, real-life emotions are often complex and involve several simultaneous emotions (Ekman & Friesen, 1975; Scherer, 1998; Ekman, 2003b). They may occur either as the quick succession of different emotions, the superposition of emotions, the masking of one emotion by another one, the suppression of an emotion or the overacting of an emotion. We refer to a blend of emotions to denote these phenomena. These blends produce "multiple simultaneous facial expressions" (Richmond & Croskey, 1999).

Depending on the type of blending, the resulting facial expressions are not identical. A masked emotion may leak over the displayed emotion (Ekman & Friesen, 1975); whereas superposition of two emotions will be shown by different facial features (one emotion being shown on the upper face and another one on the lower face; Ekman & Friesen, 1975).

Distinguishing these various types of blends of emotions in ECA systems is relevant as perceptual studies have shown that people are able to recognize facial expression of felt emotion (Ekman, 1982; Wiggers, 1982) as well as fake emotion (Ekman & Friesen, 1982) from real life as well as on ECAs (Pandzic & Forchheimer, 2002). Moreover, in a study on a deceiving agent, Rehm & André (2005) found that the users were able to differentiate when the agent was displaying expressions of felt emotion or expression of fake emotion.

Aiming at understanding if facial features or regions play identical roles in emotion recognition, researchers performed various perceptual tasks or studied psychological facial activity (Bassili, 1979; Cacioppo, Petty, Losch, & Kim, 1986; Gouta & Miyamoto, 2000; Constantini, Pianesi, & Prete, 2005). They found that positive emotions are mainly perceived from the expression of the lower face (e.g., smile) and negative emotion from the upper face (e.g., frown). One can conclude that reliable features for positive emotion, that is, features that convey the strongest

276 J.-C. Martin and L. Devillers

characteristics of a positive emotion, are in the lower face. On the other hand, the most reliable features for negative emotion are in the upper face. Based on these findings a computational model for facial expressions of blend of emotions was defined in Ochs, Niewiadomski, Pelachaud, and Sadek (2005). It composes facial expressions from those of single emotions using fuzzy logic based rules.

Other researchers study how to generate such mixed emotions in ECAs (Karunaratne & Yan, 2006; Lee, Kao, & Soo, 2006; Carofiglio, de Rosis, & Grassano, in press). Arfib (2006) uses time-warping to align video of one emotion and vocal tempo of another emotion using a time-warping algorithm, hence artificially creating multimodal blends of emotions

Some studies rely on computer-based annotation of videotaped human behaviors. Such an approach has two advantages: it is experimentally grounded and thus can be more relevant for the task at hand than general rules provided by the literature. The second advantage is that it enables us to model individual use of nonverbal behaviors, which can be a means to achieve animated agents with a personality (Kipp, 2004). Videos of users interacting with the SAL system were manually annotated and used for the definition of a list of nonverbal behavior generation rules (Lee & Marsella, 2006). The multimodal behavior of a human storyteller was annotated in de Melo and Paiva 2006) and used for the design of an ECA in a narrative application. A parametric model for iconic gesture generation is defined by Tepper, Kopp, and Cassell (2004) following the analysis of a video corpus. Cartoons have been used as a video material for studying the role of irregularities and discontinuities modulations in expressivity (Ech Chafai, Pelachaud, Pelé, & Breton, 2006).

André (2006) addresses several issues related to the use of corpus-based approaches to behavior modeling for virtual humans via observation, modeling, generation, and perception. She reviews different approaches such as "understanding via learning to generate" (e.g., Wachsmuth), "analysis by observation and synthesis" (e.g., Krahmer), and "study, model, build, test cycle" (e.g., Cassell). The author also recommends starting from a model when collecting data.

Video corpora of TV interviews (Douglas-Cowie et al., 2005) enable us to explore how people behave during spontaneous emotions not only by their facial expression but also by their gestures or their speech (Douglas-Cowie et al., 2005). Yet, these corpora call for means of validating subjective manual annotations of emotion. Few researchers have used ECAs for validating such manual annotations by testing how people perceive the replay of annotated behaviors by an agent. These issues are raised in the next sections.

15.3 Collecting Spontaneous Multimodal Expressions of Affects: The EmoTV Corpus

The design of affective interfaces such as credible expressive characters in storytelling applications requires the understanding and the modeling of relations between realistic emotions and behaviors in different modalities such as facial expressions, speech, body movements, and hand gestures. Until now, most experimental studies of multimodal behaviors related to emotions have considered only basic and acted emotions and their relation with monomodal behaviors such as facial expressions (Ekman, 2003) or body movements (Wallbott, 1998).

We were seeking answers to the following questions. How can we collect multimodal expressions of spontaneous emotions? How should we represent multimodal behaviors occurring during emotions? What are the relevant behavioral dimensions to annotate? What are the differences between basic acted emotions and nonacted emotions regarding multimodal expression? How do we validate these manual annotations? Can they be used to specify the behaviors of an Embodied Conversational Agent? What are the respective contributions of the audio and visual channels in the perception of such complex emotions?

Several studies on multimodal behavior involve TV material but seldom with a focus on emotion. The Belfast naturalistic database which was collected before we started our work on EmoTV contains similar emotional interviews annotated with a continuous approach (Douglas-Cowie, Campbell, Cowie, & Roach, 2003).

We collected EmoTV, an audiovisual corpus featuring 89 video clips of emotionally rich monologues from TV interviews (with various topics such as politics, law, sports, etc.; Devillers, Abrilian, & Martin, 2005; Martin, Abrilian, & Devillers, 2005). EmoTV does not aim at computing statistical models of multimodal emotional behaviors that can be used to detect a user's emotional state. Instead, it is an exploratory corpus aiming at (1) exploring emotions other than in-lab recorded, (2) identifying the relevant levels enabling the annotation of emotional phenomena, (3) illustrating the computation of relations between the different levels of representation such as emotions and multimodal behaviors, (4) investigating the use for the specification of behavior to be displayed by an animated character, and (5) defining ways for validating the subjective annotation of emotional phenomena.

In this perspective, we have explored several directions of annotations, each with a different subset of the EmoTV clips selected as relevant for this direction of annotation. Several experiments were conducted on the annotation of emotion in EmoTV (Devillers, Abrilian, & Martin, 2005; Devillers et al., 2006). In the next sections, we focus on the use of this corpus for the study of multimodal perception and expression.

15.4 Coding Multimodal Behaviors in the EmoTV Corpus

15.4.1 A Scheme for Coding Multimodal Expressive Behaviors

We have grounded our coding scheme on requirements collected from both the parameters described as perceptually relevant for the study of emotional behavior, and the features of the emotionally rich TV interviews that we have selected. The following measures sound relevant for the study of emotional behaviors: the expressivity of movements, the number of annotations in each modality, their temporal features (duration, alternation, repetition, and structural descriptions of gestures), the directions of movements, and the functional description of relevant gestures. We have selected some nonverbal descriptors from the existing studies listed above. We have defined the coding scheme at an abstract level and then implemented it as a XML file for use with the Anvil tool (Kipp, 2001). This section describes how each modality is annotated in order to enable subsequent computation of the relevant parameters of emotional behavior listed above. Each track is annotated one after the other (e.g., the annotator starts by annotating the first track for the whole video and then proceeds to the next track). The duration and order of annotations is available in the annotations.

For the speech transcription, we annotate verbal and nonverbal sounds[1] as hesitations, breaths, and so on. Most annotated tags are: "laugh", "cries", "b" (breath), and "pff". We do the word-by-word transcription using Praat.[2]

In the videos only the upper bodies of people are visible. Torso, head, and gestures tracks contain both a description of pose and movement. Pose and movement annotations thus alternate. The direction of movement, its type (e.g., twist vs. bend), and the angles can be computed from the annotations in the pose track. Movement quality is annotated for torso, head, shoulders, and hand gestures. The attributes of movement quality that are listed in the studies reported in the previous section and that we selected as relevant for our corpus are: the number of repetitions, the fluidity (smooth, normal, jerky), the strength (soft, normal, hard), the speed (slow, normal, fast), and the spatial expansion (contracted, normal, expanded). The annotation of fluidity is relevant for individual gestures as several of them are repetitive. The first annotation phase revealed that a set of three possible values for each expressive parameter was more appropriate than a larger set of possible values.

The head pose track contains pose attributes adapted from the FACS coding scheme (Ekman & Walla, 1978): front, turned left/right, tilt left/right, upward/downward, forward/backward. Head primary movement observed between the start and the end pose is annotated with the same set of values as the pose attribute. A secondary movement enables the combination of several simultaneous head movements that are observed in EmoTV (e.g., head nod while turning the head). Facial expressions are coded using combinations of Action Units (the low level we used for the first annotation phase was based on FAPS and was inappropriate for manual annotation of emotional videos).

As for gesture annotation, we have kept the classical attributes (McNeill, 1992; Kipp, 2004) but focused on repetitive and manipulator gestures that occur frequently in EmoTV, as we observed during the first annotation phase. Our coding scheme enables the annotation of the structural description ("phases") of gestures as their temporal patterns might be related to emotion: preparation (bringing arm and hand into stroke position), stroke (the most energetic part of the gesture), sequence of strokes (a number of successive strokes), hold (a phase of stillness just before or just after the stroke), and retract (movement back to rest position).

[1] http://www.ldc.upenn.edu/.

[2] http://www.fon.hum.uva.nl/praat/.

We have selected the following set of gesture functions ("phrases") as they were observed in our corpus: manipulator (contact with body or object, movement that serves functions of drive reduction or other noncommunicative functions, such as scratching oneself), beat (synchronized with the emphasis of the speech), deictic (arm or hand is used to point at an existing or imaginary object), illustrator (represents attributes, actions, relationships about objects and characters), and emblem(movement with a precise, culturally defined meaning). Currently, the hand shape is not annotated because it is not considered a main feature of emotional behavior in our survey of experimental studies nor in our videos.

15.4.2 Computing Measures from Annotations

With this new coding scheme, 455 multimodal annotations of behaviors in the different modalities were done by one coder on the 19 emotional segments on four videos selected for their multimodal rich content (e.g., expressive gesture) for a total duration of 77 seconds. These annotations have been validated and corrected by a second coder. The average required annotation time was evaluated to 200 seconds to annotate 1 second of such video featuring rich multimodal behaviors. This annotation time might decrease during future annotations as the coders learn how to use the scheme more efficiently. We developed software for parsing the files resulting from annotation and for computing measures. It enables the comparison of the "expressivity profile" of different videos which feature blended emotions, similarly to the work done by Hartmann, Mancini, and Pelachaud (2002) on expressive embodied agents. For example videos #3 and #36 are quite similar regarding their emotion labels, average intensity, and valence (although their durations are quite different).

Modalities involving movements in these videos are also similar (head, then torso, and then hand gestures). The relations between the extreme values of expressive parameters are also compatible in the two videos: fast movements are more often perceived than slow movements, hard movements more often than soft, jerky more often than smooth, and contracted more often than expanded. Video #30 with a similar average intensity (4) has a quite different expressive profile with a positive valence but also more head movements and no hand gestures. Even more movements are evaluated as being fast, but compared with videos #3 and #36, movements in this video are more perceived as soft and smooth. The goal of such measures is to explore the dimensions of emotional behavior in order to study how multimodal signs of emotion are combined during nonacted emotion.

15.4.3 Comparing Manual Annotations and Automatic Processing

Annotating a multimodal corpus of real-life emotions is challenging inasmuch as it involves subjective perception and requires time-consuming manual annotations of

Table 15.2 Expressivity Profiles of Three Videos Involving Blended Emotions

Video#	#3	#36	#30
Duration	37s	7s	10s
Emotion labels	Anger (55%), Despair (45%)	Anger (62%), Disappointment (25%), Sadness (13%)	Exaltation (50%), Joy (25%), Pride (25%)
Average intensity (1: min – 5: max)	5	4.6	4
Average valence (1: negative, 5: positive)	1	1.6	4.3
% Head movement	56	60	72
% Torso movement	28	20	27
% Hand movement	16	20	0
% Fast vs. Slow	47 vs. 3	33 vs. 13	83 vs. 0
% Hard vs. Soft	17 vs. 17	20 vs. 0	0 vs. 27
% Jerky vs. Smooth	19 vs. 8	6 vs. 0	5 vs. 50
% Expanded vs. Contracted	0 vs. 38	13 vs. 20	0 vs. 33

emotion at several levels. This manual annotation might benefit from image processing via the automatic detection of emotionally relevant video segments. Estimation of movement quantity by automatic image processing might validate the manual annotations of movements during the time-based annotation of the video, and also of emotional activation at the level of the whole video. Finally automatic annotation might ease the manual annotation process by providing movement segmentation and precise values of expressive parameters such as the speed, the spatial expansion, or the fluidity of a gesture. Yet, manual annotation and image processing provide information at different levels of abstraction and their integration is not straightforward. Furthermore, most of the work in image processing of emotional behavior has been done on high-quality videos recorded in laboratory situations where emotions might be less spontaneous than during nonstaged TV interviews.

In this section we illustrate the comparison of manual and automatic processing on ten videos from the EmoTV corpus (Martin et al., 2007; Figure 15.1). The goals of this work were to explore (1) the applicability of image processing techniques to low-resolution videos from TV, and (2) how image processing might be used for the validation of manual annotation of spontaneous emotional behavior. We selected ten clips that feature movements in a wide variety of contexts such as indoor versus outdoor settings.

We compared the values obtained for (1) the manual annotation of emotional activation (average of annotations by three expert coders), (2) the automatic estimation of movement quantity at the level of the whole video clip, and (3) the percentage of seconds of each video for which there is at least one manual annotation of movement (head, hand, or torso). The three measures listed above provide different estimations of the quantity of multimodal activity related to the emotion. We computed

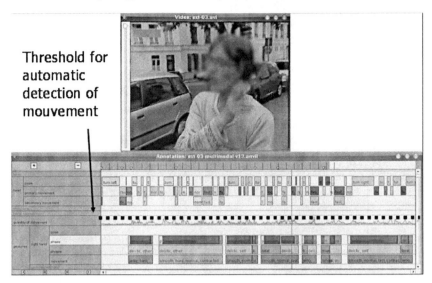

Fig. 15.1 Integration in the Anvil tool (Kipp, 2004) of manual annotations (colored blocks) of head movements (upper tracks) and hand gestures (lower tracks), and results of image processing for the estimation of movement quantity (continuous line in the middle)

correlation coefficients between these values. The correlation analysis suggests that measures (1) and (2) are significatively correlated ($r = 0,64$, $p < 0,05$). This shows that the automatic processing of our ten videos validates the manual annotation of activation at the global level of each video. The correlation analysis also suggests that (1) and (3) may be correlated ($r = 0.49$). Finally, the correlation analysis suggests that (2) and (3) may be correlated ($r = 0,42$). However, due to the small sample size, these two measures do not reach statistical significance. More data are needed to confirm these two results.

Future directions include the separate estimation of movement quantity for different body parts of the image (including tracking of these areas) in order to cope with people moving in the background, the automatic extraction of values for the expressive parameters such as the spatial extent (Caridakis et al., 2006, Eq. 2), the validation of the manual annotation of activation at the level of emotional segments of the videos and normalization over these segments, the relations between the estimation of movement quantity and the gesture phases (preparation, stroke, retraction), the use of temporal filters for improving the automatic detection of movements, and finally the inclusion of torso annotation in the union of movement annotation only if it includes a skin area. Recent advances in the automatic extraction of gesture expressivity replayed by the Greta agent can be found in Caridakis et al. (2006).

15.5 Replaying Multimodal Behaviors with an Expressive Agent

Our aim here is not only to reproduce multimodal behaviors with an ECA but also to study the coordination between modalities during emotional behaviors, in particular in the case of complex emotions and to explore individual differences.

In order to design ECAs with such humanlike qualities, one preliminary step is to identify the levels of representation of emotional behavior. For example, regarding the analysis of videos of real-life behaviors, before achieving the long-term goal of fully automatic processing of emotion from low levels (e.g., image processing, motion capture) to related behaviors in different modalities, a manual annotation phase might help to identify the representation levels that are relevant for the perception of complex emotions.

Because the externalization of nonverbal behaviors plays an important role in the perception of emotions, our approach is to model what is visible; that is, we consider the signals and how they are displayed and perceived. We do not model the processes that were made to arrive at the display of such and such signals; we simply model the externalization part. We are interested in understanding and modeling how a given emotion would be both perceived and expressed quantitatively and qualitatively.

Similarly to the copy-synthesis approaches that have been developed for speech, the replay by an ECA of these manually annotated behaviors can be useful for the validation of the model relating emotions and multimodal behaviors. We thus defined an imitation approach similar to the one proposed by Kipp (2004) for individual conversational gestures and based on observation, modeling, and generation (Martin et al., 2006b; Figure 15.2). This copy-synthesis approach produced animations of expressive behaviors that we used in a perception test that we describe below (Buisine, Abrilian, Niewiadomski, Martin, Devillers, & Pelachaud, 2006).

Affective behaviors in Embodied Conversational Agents (ECAs) can be quite useful for experimental studies on the perception of multimodal emotional behaviors as one can turn on/off a given signal or even a given modality. We designed an experimental study aiming at evaluating if people properly detect the signs of different emotions in multiple modalities (speech, facial expressions, gestures) when they appear to be superposed or masked. It compares the perception of emotional behaviors in videos of TV interviews with similar behavior replayed by an expressive agent. The facial expressions of the agent are defined using two approaches, namely the computational model of blend of emotions, and the annotation of the facial expressions from the video. We are interested in evaluating possible differences between visual only versus audiovisual perception as well as possible gender differences. We aim to test if findings reported in Feldman, Philippot, and Custrini (1991) can be replicated here, that is, if women do show a tendency to recognize better facial expressions of emotions.

The first goal of this study was to test whether subjects perceive a combination of emotions in our ECA animations. Our results showed that subjects tend to perceive one emotion as being predominant: in the superposition example, subjects ordered basic anger first; in the disappointment masked by joy, basic joy and facial blending replay were rated similarly. However, this result is partially contradicted when

Fig. 15.2 Screen-dump of the perception test : four different animations and four sliders for selecting a similarity value for each animation; the original video (nonblurred during the test) is displayed separately; the video and the animations feature the facial expressions and the hand gestures

analyzing the result from the labeling task where most subjects associated several emotion labels with the animation they considered as being the most similar to the video. The macro-classes of emotion that they selected are consistent with previous annotations of the videos with 3 expert coders (and 40 coders for the superposition example (Abrilian, Devillers, & Martin, 2006).

In the animations of single emotions that we designed for the superposition example, subjects perceived a secondary emotion, possibly through nonverbal or verbal cues brought by our method of copying the original video. In addition, our experimental protocol enabled us to compare two conditions, audio and no audio. The four animations corresponding to the superposition example were better discriminated in the no-audio condition; the addition of verbal cues had the effect of lowering the differences between the animations. Moreover, users chose a larger set of emotions to label the animations in the audio condition.

In the superposition animations, subjects better perceived the sadness/despair dimension in the audio condition. We may thus infer that, in this particular sequence, anger was primarily displayed by nonverbal behaviors whereas despair was mostly expressed by the verbal stream. In the disappointment-masked-by-joy example, subjects perceived negative emotions better in the audio condition. This suggests that the person in this video sequence controlled her nonverbal behavior (positive emotions perceived in the mute condition) better than her verbal behaviors (negative cues perceived in the audio condition). This strong effect of verbal behavior may be due to the fact that we used the original voice and not a synthesized voice.

It is compatible with previous studies on the whole corpus in which two coders annotated the videos in three conditions (audio only, video only, audio and video; Abrilian et al., 2005). We had observed a high level of quantitative agreement over the whole corpus for the three conditions for "Anger". The coders agreed on the "Pain" label for the "Audio only" and "Audio and video" conditions but not for the "Video only" condition, which could be explained by the fact that acoustic cues show this emotion well.

The second goal of this study was to evaluate our two approaches for replaying blends of emotions (multiple levels replay (Martin et al., 2006) and facial blending replay (Niewiadomski, 2007)). Our global analysis showed that neither of the two approaches was consistently preferred. We may first mention that the two replay approaches share some common features which may partly explain why it was not so easy to discriminate between them: they were elaborated on the basis of the same annotations and they both included some behaviors automatically generated by the Greta system.

However, we can notice that the facial blending replay was significantly better ranked than the multiple levels replay in the masking example. Conversely in the superposition example, the two types of replay did not differ significantly except for female subjects who gave higher similarity scores to the multiple levels replay. These results suggest that facial blending replay was more appropriate in the masking example and multiple levels replay in the superposition example. These results alone are not sufficient to understand this interaction. It could be due to the nature of complex emotions (superposition, masking), or to the particular emotions tested here (anger/despair, disappointment/joy), or to the modalities available (with or without hand gesture). For example, the size of the face is not the same in our superposition and in the masking examples.

In the superposition example, male and female subjects judged differently the animation generated by the facial blending replay. Male and female subjects also gave different confidence scores to their ranking in the superposition example: female subjects were more confident in their answers. Such a result is consistent with the classical view that female subjects have better abilities to decode nonverbal cues (Feldman et al., 1991).

15.6 Extraversion and Perception of Movement Expressivity

This section reports on a perceptive test on movement expressivity that has been set up for studying how people perceive multimodal behaviors in our TV interviews. We considered six expressivity parameters used in research on movement expressivity (Wallbott, 1998; Hartmann et al., 2005): activation, repetition, spatial extent, speed, strength, fluidity. The goals of this experiment were to (1) to collect global annotations of movements expressivity on a subset of our EmoTV corpus, (2) to compare the annotations of movement expressivity with the multimodal annotations done by two expert coders on the same videos, and (3) to compare the annotations of movement expressivity with the annotations of emotion and audio clues done on the same videos.

We selected 29 video clips from our EmoTV corpus (24 of the clips were rich in multimodal behaviors, and 5 clips contained very little). The subjects had to train on 2 video clips (the first one containing many movements and the other containing no movement) before beginning the experiment on the 27 remaining clips. The clips feature TV interviews of one single character (male or female), recorded indoor or outdoor. Twenty subjects (11 males, 9 females), age between 19 and 54 (average 32) had to annotate their perception of the expressivity of head, torso or hand movements. Eight subjects were students in computer science, eight were researchers, teachers, or engineers, and four were in laboratory administration. Subjects had to watch each clip at least three times, before marking on a line (representing both terminals of a parameter) the level of the following parameters: activation (from passive to active), repetition (from only once to several repetitions), spatial extent (from contracted to expanded), speed (from slow to fast), strength (from weak to strong), and fluidity (from jerky to fluid). The order of presentation of the 27 clips was randomized.

We have validated subjects' annotations by verifying that the five clips, containing no or few movements, were all correctly annotated with low expressivity values. We observed that high spatial extended movements mostly led to fluid movements; perception of high activity was often linked to highly repeated and strong movements. Finally, we observed that the following four dimensions of expressivity were correlated across subjects: spatial extent, activation, repetition, and strength. Low or no correlations were observed for speed and fluidity. We asked each subject to fill a personality test, Eysenck Personality Questionnaire (EPQ). We found that extrovert subjects rated all expressive parameters with lower values than introvert subjects (Martin et al., 2007).

15.7 Conclusions

We presented our contributions to the definition and computation of representations of multimodal behaviors grounded on video corpora of spontaneous emotional behaviors. We illustrated how this approach was used to contribute to research on the design of expressive agents. The results produced by these studies are: a methodological framework for the study of multimodal communication and the design of multimodal human–computer interfaces; coding schemes and representations of multimodal information at several levels of abstraction and temporality; analyses of the relations of multimodal expressivity and emotion; perception and impact of different multimodal behaviors of animated agents on different subjects (blends of emotions); consideration of different categories of users (gender, personality traits); combined manual annotation and automatic annotations (image processing of EmoTV videos); and copy-synthesis approach for replaying annotated behaviors.

To summarize, these studies provide three contributions to the design of multimodal human–computer interfaces. First, these studies revealed several individual differences between subjects with respect to gender and personality traits with regard to the perception of spontaneous emotional behaviors. Second, we iteratively defined a methodological framework for studying multimodal communication including the annotation, representation, generation, and perception of situated multimodal behaviors. Third, this framework was used to compute representations such as expressive emotional profiles for the annotation and replay of emotional behaviors.

Acknowledgments This work has been partially supported by the Network of Excellence HUMAINE (Human-Machine Interaction Network on Emotion) IST-2002-2.3.1.6/Contract no. 507422 (http://emotion-research.net/). We are very grateful to Sarkis Abrilian, Stéphanie Buisine, and the Humaine partners.

References

Abrilian, S., Devillers, L., Buisine, S., & Martin, J.-C. (2005). EmoTV1: Annotation of real-life emotions for the specification of multimodal affective interfaces. In *11th International Conference on Human-Computer Interaction (HCII'2005)*, Las Vegas, NV, Electronic proceedings, LEA.

Abrilian, S., Devillers, L., & Martin, J.-C. (2006). Annotation of emotions in real-life video interviews: Variability between coders. In *5th International Conference on Language Resources and Evaluation (LREC'2006)*, Genoa, Italy, 2004–2009.

André, E. (2006). Corpus-based approaches to behavior modeling for virtual humans: A critical review. In *Modeling Communication with Robots and Virtual Humans. Workshop of the ZiF: Research Group 2005/2006 Embodied Communication in Humans and Machines*. Scientific organization: Bielefeld: Ipke Wachsmuth, Newark: Günther Knoblich.

André, E., Rist, T., van Mulken, S., Klesen, M., & Baldes, S. (2000). The automated design of believable dialogues for animated presentation teams. In J. S. J. Cassell, S. Prevost, & E. Churchill (Eds.). *Embodied conversational agents*. Cambridge, MA: MIT Press: 220–255.

Arfib, D. (2006). Time warping of a piano (and other) video sequences following different emotions. In *Workshop on Subsystem Synchronization and Multimodal Behavioral Organization* held during Humaine Summer School, Genova.

Argyle, M. (2004). *Bodily communication* (second ed.). London and New York: Routledge. Taylor & Francis.

Banse, R. & Scherer, K. (1996). Acoustic profiles in vocal emotion expression. *Journal of Personality and Social Psychology 70*(3), 614–636.

Bänziger, T., Pirker, H., & Scherer, K. (2006). GEMEP – GEneva multimodal emotion portrayals: A corpus for the study of multimodal emotional expressions. In *Workshop: Corpora for research on emotion and affect. 5th International Conference on Language Resources and Evaluation (LREC'2006)*, Genova, Italy. http://www.limsi.fr/Individu/martin/tmp/LREC2006/WS-MM/final/proceedings-WS-MultimodalCorpora-v3.pdf. 15–19.

Bassili, J. N. (1979). Emotion recognition: The role of facial movement and the relative importance of upper and lower areas of the face. *Journal of Personality and Social Psychology 37*(11), 2049–2058.

Boone, R. T. & Cunningham, J. G. (1998). Children's decoding of emotion in expressive body movement: The development of cue attunement. *Developmental Psychology 34*(5), 1007–1016.

Buisine, S. (2005). Conception et Évaluation d'Agents Conversationnels Multimodaux Bidirectionnels. http://stephanie.buisine.free.fr/, Doctorat de Psychologie Cognitive - Ergonomie, Paris V. 8 avril 2005. Direction J.-C. Martin & J.-C. Sperandio. http://stephanie.buisine.free.fr/.

Buisine, S., Abrilian, S., Niewiadomski, R., Martin, J.-C., Devillers, L., & Pelachaud, C. (2006). Perception of blended emotions: from video corpus to expressive agent. In *6th International Conference on Intelligent Virtual Agents (IVA'2006)*. Marina del Rey, CA, 21–23 August. http://iva2006.ict.usc.edu/. USA: Springer, 93–106.

Cacioppo, J. T., Petty, R. P., Losch, M. E., & Kim, H. S. (1986). Electromyographic activity over facial muscle regions can differentiate the valence and intensity of affective reactions. *Journal of Personality and Social Psychology 50*, 260–268.

Caridakis, G., Raouzaiou, A., Karpouzis, K., & Kollias, S. (2006). Synthesizing gesture expressivity based on real sequences. In *Workshop on Multimodal Corpora. From Multimodal Behaviour Theories to Usable Models. 5th International Conference on Language Resources and Evaluation (LREC'2006)*, Genova, Italy. http://www.limsi.fr/Individu/martin/tmp/LREC2006/WS-MM/final/proceedings-WS-MultimodalCorpora-v3.pdf, 19–23.

Carofiglio, V., de Rosis, F. and Grassano, R. (in press). Dynamic models of mixed emotion activation. In L. Canamero & R. Aylett (Eds.). *Animating expressive characters for social interactions*. Amsterdam, John Benjamins.

Cassell, J., Bickmore, T., Campbell, L., Vilhjálmsson, H., & Yan, H. (2000). Human conversation as a system framework: Designing embodied conversational agents. In J. S. Cassell, Jr., S. Prevost, & E. Churchill (Eds.), *Embodied conversational agents*. Cambridge, MA: MIT Press: 29–63.

Cassell, J., Pelachaud, C., Badler, N., Steedman, M., Achorn, B., Becket, T., Douville, B., Prevost, S., & Stone, M. (1994). Animated conversation: Rule-based generation of facial expression, gesture and spoken intonation for multiple conversational agents. *ACM SIGGRAPH'94*. http://www.cs.rutgers.edu/~mdstone/pubs/siggraph94.pdf, 413–420.

Cassell, J., Vilhjàlmsson, H., & Bickmore, T. (2001). BEAT: The Behavior Expression Animation Toolkit. In *28th Annual Conference on Computer Graphics and Interactive Techniques (SIGGRAPH'01)*, Los Angeles. CA: ACM Press. http://doi.acm.org/10.1145/383259.383315, 477–486.

Collier, G. (1985). Emotional expression. Hillsdale, NJ: Lawrence Erlbaum. http://faculty.uccb.ns.ca/~gcollier/

Constantini, E., Pianesi, F., & Prete, M. (2005). Recognizing emotions in human and synthetic faces: The role of the upper and lower parts of the face. In *Intelligent User Interfaces (IUI'05)*, San Diego, CA. USA: ACM, 20–27.

Cowie, R. (2000). Emotional states expressed in speech. In *ISCA ITRW on Speech and Emotion: Developing a Conceptual Framework for Research*, Newcastle, Northern Ireland, 224–231.

Craggs, R. & Wood, M. M. (2004). A categorical annotation scheme for emotion in the linguistic content. In *Affective Dialogue Systems (ADS'2004)*, Kloster Irsee, Germany.

Darwin, C. (1872). *The expression of emotion in man and animal*. Chicago: University of Chicago Press (reprinted in 1965). http://darwin-online.org.uk/EditorialIntroductions/Freeman_TheExpressionoftheEmotions.html.

DeMeijer, M. (1989). The contribution of general features of body movement to the attribution of emotions. *Journal of Nonverbal Behavior 13*, 247–268.

de Melo, C. & Paiva, A. (2006). A story about gesticulation expression. In *6th International Conference on Intelligent Virtual Agents (IVA'06)*, Marina del Rey, CA. Springer, 270–281.

De Silva, P. R., Kleinsmith, A., & Bianchi-Berthouze, N. (2005). Towards unsupervised detection of affective body posture nuances. In *1st International Conference on Affective Computing and Intelligent Interaction (ACII'2005)*, Beijing, China: Springer, 32–40.

Devillers, L., Abrilian, S., & Martin, J.-C. (2005). Representing real life emotions in audiovisual data with non basic emotional patterns and context features. In *1st International Conference on Affective Computing and Intelligent Interaction (ACII'2005)*, Beijing, China, Berlin: Spinger-Verlag. http://www.affectivecomputing.org/2005, 519–526.

Devillers, L., Cowie, R., Martin, J.-C., Douglas-Cowie, E., Abrilian, S., & McRorie, M. (2006a). Real life emotions in French and English TV video clips: An integrated annotation protocol combining continuous and discrete approaches. In *5th international conference on Language Resources and Evaluation (LREC'2006)*, Genoa, Italy.

Devillers, L., Martin, J.-C., Cowie, R., Douglas-Cowie, E., & Batliner, A. (2006b). Workshop corpora for research on emotion and affect. In *5th International Conference on Language Resources and Evaluation (LREC'2006)*, Genova, Italy. http://www.limsi.fr/Individu/martin/tmp/LREC2006/WS-MM/final/proceedings-WS-MultimodalCorpora-v3.pdf.

Douglas-Cowie, E., Campbell, N., Cowie, R., & Roach, P. (2003). Emotional speech; Towards a new generation of databases. *Speech Communication 40*, 33–60.

Douglas-Cowie, E., Devillers, L., Martin, J.-C., Cowie, R., Savvidou, S., Abrilian, S., & Cox, C. (2005). Multimodal databases of everyday emotion: Facing up to complexity. In *9th European Conf. Speech Communication and Technology (Interspeech'2005)*, Lisbon, Portugal, 813–816.

Ech Chafai, N., Pelachaud, C., Pelé, D., & Breton, G. (2006). Gesture expressivity modulations in an ECA application. In *6th International Conference on Intelligent Virtual Agents (IVA'06)*, Marina del Rey, CA. Springer, 181–192.

Ekman, P. (1982). *Emotion in the human face*. Cambridge University Press.

Ekman, P. (1999). Basic emotions. In T. Dalgleish and M. J. Power (Eds.), *Handbook of cognition & emotion*. New York: John Wiley, 301–320.

Ekman, P. (2003a). Emotions revealed. Understanding faces and feelings. Weidenfeld & Nicolson. http://emotionsrevealed.com/index.php.

Ekman, P. (2003b). *The face revealed*. London: Weidenfeld & Nicolson.

Ekman, P. & Friesen, W. V. (1975). *Unmasking the face. A guide to recognizing emotions from facial clues*. Englewood Cliffs, NJ: Prentice-Hall Inc.

Ekman, P. & and Friesen, W. (1982). Felt, false, miserable smiles. *Journal of Nonverbal Behavior 6*(4), 238–251.

Ekman, P. & Walla, F. (1978). Facial action coding system (FACS). http://www.cs.cmu.edu/afs/cs/project/face/www/facs.htm.

Enos, F. & Hirschberg, J. (2006). A framework for eliciting emotional speech: capitalizing on the actor's process. In *Workshop on Corpora for Research on Emotion and Affect. 5th International Conference on Language Resources and Evaluation (LREC'2006)*, Genova, Italy. http://www.limsi.fr/Individu/martin/tmp/LREC2006/WS-MM/final/proceedings-WS-MultimodalCorpora-v3.pdf, 6–10.

Feldman, R. S., Philippot, P., & Custrini, R. J. (1991). Social competence and nonverbal behavior. In R. S. F. B. Rimé (Ed.), *Fundamentals of nonverbal behavior*. Cambridge University Press: 329–350.

Feldman, R. S., & Rim, B. (1991). *Fundamentals of nonverbal behavior*. Cambridge University Press.

Frigo, S. (2006). The relationship between acted and naturalistic emotional corpora. In *Workshop on Corpora for Research on Emotion and Affect. 5th International Conference on Language Resources and Evaluation (LREC'2006)*, Genova, Italy. http://www.limsi.fr/Individu/martin/tmp/LREC2006/WS-MM/final/proceedings-WS-MultimodalCorpora.v3.pdf.

Gallaher, P. (1992). Individual differences in nonverbal behavior: Dimensions of style. *Journal of Personality and Social Psychology, 63*, 133–145.

Goodwin, C. (2000). Action and embodiment within situated human interaction. *Journal of Pragmatics 32*, 1489–1522.

Gouta, K. & Miyamoto, M. (2000). Emotion recognition, facial components associated with various emotions. *Shinrigaku Kenkyu 71*(3), 211–218.

Gratch, J. & Marsella, S. (2004). A domain-independent framework for modeling emotion. *Journal of Cognitive Systems Research 5*(4), 269–306.

Gunes, H. & Piccardi, M. (2005). Fusing face and body display for bi-modal emotion recognition: Single frame analysis and multi-frame post integration. In *1st International Conference on Affective Computing and Intelligent Interaction (ACII'2005)*, Beijing, China: Springer, 102–110.

Hartmann, B., Mancini, M., & Pelachaud, C. (2002). Formational parameters and adaptive proto-type instantiation for MPEG-4 compliant gesture synthesis. In *Computer Animation (CA'2002)*, Geneva, Switzerland. IEEE Computer Society, 111–119.

Hartmann, B., Mancini, M., & Pelachaud, C. (2005). Implementing expressive gesture synthesis for embodied conversational agents. In *Gesture Workshop (GW'2005)*, Vannes, France.

Kaiser, S. & Wehrle, T. (2001). Facial expressions as indicators of appraisal processes. In K. R. Scherer, A. Schorr, & T. Johnstone (Eds.), *Appraisal theories of emotions: Theories, methods, research*. New York: Oxford University Press, 285–300.

Kaiser, S. & Wehrle, T. (2004). Facial expressions in social interactions: Beyond basic emotions. In L. Cañamero & R. Aylett (Eds.). *Advances in consciousness research. Animating expressive characters for social interactions*. Amsterdam: John Benjamins publishing company.

Kapur, A., Virji-Babul, N., Tzanetakis, G. & Driessen, P. F. (2005). Gesture-based affective com-puting on motion capture data. In *1st International Conference on Affective Computing and Intelligent Interaction (ACII'2005)*, Beijing, China: Springer, 1–8.

Karunaratne, S. & Yan, H. (2006). Modelling and combining emotions, visual speech and gestures in virtual head models. *Signal Processing: Image Communication 21*, 429–449.

Kipp, M. (2001). Anvil – A generic annotation tool for multimodal dialogue. In *7th European Conference on Speech Communication and Technology (Eurospeech'2001)*, Aalborg, Denmark. http://www.dfki.uni-sb.de/~kipp/research/index.html. 1376–1370.

Kipp, M. (2004). Gesture generation by imitation. From human behavior to computer character animation. Boca Raton, FL, Dissertation.com. http://www.dfki.de/~kipp/dissertation.html.

Kipp, M. (2006). Creativity meets automation: Combining nonverbal action authoring with rules and machine learning. In *6th International Conference on Intelligent Virtual Agents (IVA'06)*, Marina del Rey, CA. Springer, 230–242.

Knapp, M. L. & Hall, J. A. (2006). *Nonverbal communication in human interaction* (sixth ed.). Belmont, CA: Thomson Wadsworth.

Lee, B., Kao, E., & Soo, V. (2006). Feeling ambivalent: A model of mixed emotions for virtual agents. In *6th International Conference on Intelligent Virtual Agents (IVA'06)*, Marina del Rey, CA. Springer, 329–342.

Lee, J. & Marsella, S. (2006). Nonverbal behavior generator for embodied conversational agents. In *6th International Conference on Intelligent Virtual Agents (IVA'06)*, Marina del Rey, CA. Springer, 243–255.

Martin, J. C. (2006). Multimodal human-computer interfaces and individual differences. Annota-tion, perception, representation and generation of situated multimodal behaviors. Habilitation à diriger des recherches en Informatique. Université Paris XI. 6th December 2006.

Martin, J.-C., Abrilian, S., Buisine, S., & Devillers, L. (2007). Individual differences in the per-ception of spontaneous gesture expressivity. In *3rd Conference of the International Society for Gesture Studies*, Chicago, USA, 71.

Martin, J.-C., Abrilian, S., & Devillers, L. (2005). Annotating multimodal behaviors oc-curring during non basic emotions. In *1st International Conference on Affective Com-puting and Intelligent Interaction (ACII'2005)*, Beijing, China, Berlin: Springer-Verlag. http://www.affectivecomputing. org/2005, 550–557.

Martin, J.-C., Caridakis, G., Devillers, L., Karpouzis, K., & Abrilian, S. (2007). Manual anno-tation and automatic image processing of multimodal emotional behaviours: Validating the annotation of TV interviews. Special issue of the *Journal on Personal and Ubiquitous Comput-ing on Emerging Multimodal Interfaces* following the special session of the AIAI 2006 Con-ference. New York: Springer. http://www.personal-ubicomp.com/. http://www.springerlink.com/content/e760255k7068332x/

Martin, J.-C., den Os, E., Kuhnlein, P., Boves, L., Paggio, P. and Catizone, R. (2004). Workshop multimodal corpora: Models of human behaviour for the specification and eval-uation of multimodal input and output interfaces. In *Association with the 4th Interna-tional Conference on Language Resources and Evaluation LREC2004* http://www.lrec-conf.org/lrec2004/index.php, Lisbon, Portugal: Centro Cultural de Belem,. http://www.limsi.fr/Individu/martin/tmp/LREC2006/WS-MM/final/proceedings-WS-MultimodalCorpora-v3.pdf.

Martin, J.-C., Kuhnlein, P., Paggio, P., Stiefelhagen, R., & Pianesi, F. (2006a). Workshop multimodal corpora: From multimodal behaviour theories to usable models. In *Association with the 5th International Conference on Language Resources and Evaluation (LREC2006)*, Genoa, Italy. http://www.limsi.fr/Individu/martin/tmp/LREC2006/WS-MM/final/proceedings-WS-MultimodalCorpora-v3.pdf.

Martin, J.-C., Niewiadomski, R., Devillers, L., Buisine, S., & Pelachaud, C. (2006b). Multimodal complex emotions: Gesture expressivity and blended facial expressions. Special issue of the *Journal of Humanoid Robotics on Achieving Human-like Qualities in Interactive Virtual and Physical Humanoids, 3*(3). C. Pelachaud and L. Canamero (Eds.), 269–291. http://www.worldscinet.com/ijhr/ 03/0303/S0219843606000825.html.

Maybury, M. & Martin, J.-C. (2002). Workshop on multimodal resources and multimodal systems evaluation. In *Conference On Language Resources And Evaluation (LREC'2002)*, Las Palmas, Canary Islands, Spain. http://www.limsi.fr/Individu/martin/research/articles/ws14.pdf.

McNeill, D. (1992). *Hand and mind – What gestures reveal about thoughts*. Chicago: University of Chicago Press, IL.

Newlove, J. (1993). *Laban for actors and dancers*. New York: Routledge.

Niewiadomski, R. (2007). A model of complex facial expressions in interpersonal relations for animated agents, PhD. dissertation, University of Perugia. http://www.dipmat.unipg.it/~radek/tesi/niewiadomski_thesis.pdf.

Ochs, M., Niewiadomski, R., Pelachaud, C., & Sadek, D. (2005). Intelligent expressions of emotions. In *First International Conference on Affective Computing and Intelligent Interaction (ACII'2005)*, Beijing, China.

Ortony, A., Clore, G. L., & Collins, A. (1988). *The cognitive structure of emotions*. Cambridge, MA: Cambridge University Press.

Pandzic, I. S. & Forchheimer, R. (2002). *MPEG-4 facial animation. The standard, implementation and applications*. John Wiley & Sons, LTD.

Pelachaud, C. (2005). Multimodal expressive embodied conversational agent. In *ACM Multimedia, Brave New Topics session*. Singapore 6–11 November, 683–689.

Pelachaud, C., Braffort, A., Breton, G., Ech Chadai, N., Gibet, S., Martin, J.-C., Maubert, S., Ochs, M., Pelé, D., Perrin, A., Raynal, M., Réveret, L. and Sadek, D. (2004). Agents conversationels: Systèmes d'animation Modélisation des comportements multimodaux applications: Agents pédagogiques et agents signeurs. Action Spécifique du CNRS Humain Virtuel. (Eds.).

Pelachaud, C. & Poggi, I. (2002). Subtleties of facial expressions in embodied agents. *Journal of Visualization and Computer Animation*. Special Issue: Graphical Autonomous Virtual Humans. Issue Edited by Daniel Ballin, Jeff Rickel, Daniel Thalmann, *13*(5): 301–312. http://www.dis.uniroma1.it/~pelachau/JVCA02.pdf.

Plutchik, R. (1980). A general psychoevolutionary theory of emotion. Emotion: Theory, research, and experience: Vol. 1. In R. Plutchik and H. Kellerman (Eds.), *Theories of emotion*. New York, Academic Press, 3–33.

Poggi, I. (2003). *Mind markers. Gestures. meaning and use*. M. Rector, I. Poggi, and N. Trigo (Eds.). Oporto, Portugal University Fernando Pessoa Press, 119–132.

Poggi, I., Pelachaud, C., de Rosis, F., Carofiglio, V., & De Carolis, B. (2005). *GRETA. A believable embodied conversational agent. multimodal intelligent information presentation*. O. Stock and M. Zancarano (Eds.). Kluwer.

Prendinger, H. & Ishizuka, M. (2004). *Life-like characters. Tools, affective functions and applications*. New York: Springer.

Rehm, M. & André, E. (2005). Catch me if you can - Exploring lying agents in social settings. In *International Conference on Autonomous Agents and Multiagent Systems (AAMAS'2005)*, Utrecht, the Netherlands, 937–944.

Richmond, V. P. & Croskey, J. C. (1999). *Non verbal behavior in interpersonal relations*. Needham Heights, MA: Allyn & Bacon, Inc.

Rist, T., André, E., Baldes, S., Gebhard, P., Klesen, M., Kipp, M., Rist, P., & Schmitt, M. (2003). *A review of the development of embodied presentation agents and their application fields. Life-like characters: Tools, affective functions, and applications*. H. Prendinger & M. Ishizuka (Eds.). New York: Springer, 377–404.

Sander, D., Grandjean, D., & Scherer, K. (2005). A systems approach to appraisal mechanisms in emotion. *Neural Networks 18*: 317–352.

Scherer, K. R. (1998). Analyzing Emotion Blends. *Proceedings of the Xth Conference of the International Society for Research on Emotions*, Würzburg, Germany, Fischer, A.142–148.

Scherer, K. R. (2000). *Emotion. Introduction to social psychology: A European perspective*. M. H. W. Stroebe (Ed.), Oxford: Blackwell, pp. 151–191.

Schröder, M. (2003). Experimental study of affect burst. *Speech Communication*. Special issue following the ISCA Workshop on Speech and Emotion *40*(1–2): 99–116.

Siegman, A. W. & Feldstein, S. (1985). Multichannel integrations of nonverbal behavior. LEA.

Tepper, P., Kopp, S., & Cassell, J. (2004). Content in context: Generating language and iconic gesture without a gestionary. In *Workshop on Balanced Perception and Action in ECAs at Autonomous Agents and Multiagent Systems (AAMAS)*, New York, NY.

Vinayagamoorthy, V., Gillies, M., Steed, A., Tanguy, E., Pan, X., Loscos, C., & Slater, M. (2006). Building expression into virtual characters. In *Eurographics Conference State of the Art Reports* http://www.cs.ucl.ac.uk/staff/m.gillies/expressivevirtualcharacters.pdf.

Wallbott, H. G. (1998). Bodily expression of emotion. *European Journal of Social Psychology 28*: 879–896. http://www3.interscience.wiley.com/cgi-bin/abstract/1863/ABSTRACT.

Wallbott, H. G. & Scherer, K. R. (1986). Cues and channels in emotion recognition. *Journal of Personality and Social Psychology 51*(4), 690–699.

Wegener Knudsen, M., Martin, J.-C., Dybkjær, L., Berman, S., Bernsen, N. O., Choukri, K., Heid, U., Kita, S., Mapelli, V., Pelachaud, C., Poggi, I., van Elswijk, G., & Wittenburg, P. (2002a). Survey of NIMM data resources, current and future user profiles, markets and user needs for NIMM resources. In *ISLE Natural Interactivity and Multimodality. Working Group Deliverable D8.1*. http://isle.nis.sdu.dk/reports/wp8/.

Wegener Knudsen, M., Martin, J.-C., Dybkjær, L., Machuca Ayuso, M.-J., Bernsen, N. O., Carletta, J., Heid, U., Kita, S., Llisterri, J., Pelachaud, C., Poggi, I., Reithinger, N., van Elswijk, G., & Wittenburg, P. (2002b). Survey of multimodal annotation schemes and best practice. In *ISLE Natural Interactivity and Multimodality. Working Group Deliverable D9.1*. February. http://isle.nis.sdu.dk/reports/wp9/.

Wiggers, M. (1982). Judgments of facial expressions of emotion predicted from facial behavior. *Journal of Nonverbal Behavior 7*(2), 101–116.

Chapter 16
Physiological Sensing for Affective Computing

Christian Peter, Eric Ebert, and Helmut Beikirch

Abstract Sensing affective states is a challenging undertaking and a variety of approaches exist. One of the oldest but yet often neglected way is to observe physiological processes related to sympathetic activity of the autonomic nervous system. A reason for physiological measurements not being used in emotion-related HCI research or affective applications is the lack of appropriate sensing devices. Existing systems often don't live up to the high requirements of the real life in which such applications are to be used. This chapter starts with a short overview of the physiological processes affective applications rely on today, and commonly used techniques to access them. After this, requirements of affective applications for physiological sensors are worked out. A design concept meeting the requirements is drawn and exemplary implementations including evaluation results are described.

16.1 Introduction

For affective applications becoming reality, sensors providing them with information on the user are a necessity. Although solutions for speech, facial, and even gesture data are worked on steadily (Schroeder, 2004; ACII, 2005, 2007; CHI, 2005, 2006, 2007; HCII, 2007; Peter & Beale, 2008), physiological data are widely

C. Peter (✉)
Fraunhofer Institute for Computer Graphics Rostock, Joachim Jungius Str. 11, 18059 Rostock, Germany
e-mail: cpeter@igd-r.fraunhofer.de

E. Ebert
arivis Multiple Image Tools GmbH, Kröpeliner Str. 54, 18055 Rostock, Germany
e-mail: eric.ebert@arivis.com

H. Beikirch
University of Rostock, Faculty of Computer Science and Electrical Engineering,
Albert-Einstein-Str. 2, 18059 Rostock, Germany
e-mail: helmut.beikirch@uni-rostock.de

J.H. Tao, T.N. Tan (eds.), *Affective Information Processing*,
© Springer Science+Business Media LLC 2009

neglected as a reliable information source regarding a user's emotion.[1] This can mainly be attributed to no appropriate sensor systems being available that are easy to use, robust, and reliable. Physiological data, however, bear the potential for a qualitatively better and at the same time easier assessment of ongoing emotional processes in a person. As physiological reactions are usually not consciously controlled, they provide undisguised information on the user's current affective state. Having reliable access to physiological data would hence provide for an information source that might even prove to be more trustworthy than those relied on today.

This chapter starts with summarizing in a condensed form the physiological processes affective applications are based on today. Most common ways to measure related physiological parameters are briefly described with an eye on specifics of real-world HCI applications. This is expanded by working out requirements for devices to measure physiological parameters in real-world affective computing scenarios. Based on these, a concept for affective sensors is developed and exemplary implementations of it are described.

16.2 Measuring Emotion-Related Physiological Processes

16.2.1 Physiological Background

Emotions are manifested in physiological changes controlled by the autonomous nervous system (ANS). Those changes can be easily observable ones, such as facial expressions, gestures, or body movements, more subtle ones such as changes in the voice, or modifications of parameters usually not recognized by a human observer, for instance, blood pressure, heart rate, or electrodermal activity.

These changes can be attributed to three physiological processes (Cacioppo, Tassinary, & Berntson, 2000; Schwartz & Andrasik, 2003):

1. Muscle tension
2. Peripheral vasoconstriction
3. Electrodermal activity

These three processes are well recognized as being deeply involved in emotional arousal and there is increased agreement of them being associated with valence, that is, the degree of perceived pleasantness of an event.

In the following we briefly describe these processes, ways to measure them, and issues to bear in mind in the HCI context. The physiological information is mainly taken from Cacioppo et al. (2000) and Schwartz and Andrasik (2003); for more details please refer to these sources.

16.2.1.1 Muscle Tension

Muscle tension can most easily be observed in postural changes and gestures. But apart from these which mainly reflect arousal, more subtle affect-related muscle

---

[1] In this chapter, "emotion" stands as a general term for emotion-related, or affective states.

activity can be observed in the face, including indicators for valence. Ekman et al. (Ekman & Friesen, 1976; Ekman, Levenson, & Friesen, 1983; Ekman & Davidson, 1994) have distinguished specific patterns of facial muscle activity related to emotions. They define 32 "action units" which, according to them, can be used to decode certain affective states (Ekman & Friesen, 1978).[2]

However, muscle contraction itself is not measurable in sufficient resolution and accuracy for inferring ANS triggered activities. Hence, correlates of it have to be used. Most commonly used methods to infer muscle tension are electromyography and visual observation.

Electromyography

The most common way to infer muscle tension is measuring changes in the electrical potentials actuating the muscle fibers, which are accessible through surface electrodes attached to the skin above the muscle. This principle is called surface electromyography (sEMG), or just EMG. The measurand is usually provided in microvolts (mV).

EMG measurements obviously are affected by voluntary movements of the body part. Also, high and low frequencies originated by the sensing circuitry itself might affect the sensor readings. Hence, a bandwidth filter should be applied to the measurements. EMG signals usually are in the range of 10 to 1000 Hz. Note that different EMG devices use different bandwidths. Hence, measurements acquired with different devices are not directly comparable.

Visual Observation

Another way to infer muscle tension is to monitor the human with video cameras and apply sophisticated algorithms to distinguish specific body movements (gestures) or even subtle changes in the person's face. This very promising approach is described in more detail in Chapter 10 of this book.

16.2.1.2 Peripheral Vasoconstriction (Blood Flow)

Peripheral vasoconstriction refers to a decrease in the diameter of blood vessels. Because it is not yet possible to noninvasively measure the diameter of blood vessels (or the muscle activity that causes this) directly, correlates of it have to be used. Most commonly used methods for this are measurement of the peripheral (skin) temperature and photo transmission.

---

[2] FACS online. http://www.face-and-emotion.com/dataface/facs/description.jsp, accessed February 26, 2008.

Peripheral (Skin) Temperature

Changes in the diameter of blood vessels bring with them a varying volume of blood in that body part per time. This, in turn, results in the surrounding tissue getting warmer or cooler, depending on the actual diameter of the contained blood vessels. These effects can be particularly well observed in the extremities, where relatively little tissue contains relatively many blood vessels.

Measuring changes in skin temperature for inferring peripheral vasoconstriction can be done with rather simple and off-the-shelf temperature sensors. It is hence established as a quite robust and frequently used method in, for example, biofeedback applications and psychological studies. It is, however, prone to changes in environmental temperature. Room temperature and airflow around the probe or body part will affect the reading. Cool or moving air absorbs more warmth than warm or still air. Also, a high room temperature may affect the skin temperature because skin temperature cannot cool much below room temperature. Furthermore, changes of the size of the contact area of sensor and skin influence the measurements. Such changes are often caused by movements or pressure on the sensing elements. Measurands of temperature readings are usually provided in degree Celsius (°C) or Fahrenheit (F).

The following terms can often be found characterizing skin temperature devices. *Accuracy* describes how close the sensor reading is to the actual temperature. For the purpose of affect sensing, this is less important than its actual changes. *Resolution* refers to the smallest temperature change the device is able to detect. In an affect sensing context, resolutions better than 1° are necessary, for example, 0.1°. However, a higher resolution also increases the risk of artifacts being taken as changes in vasoconstriction. *Response time* refers to the time it takes for a change in the measurand resulting in a response in the device. It depends on the material used for the sensing elements, and the volume of material that needs to be heated (or cooled) to the new temperature.

Photo Transmission

Another way to indirectly infer the amount of blood flow in extremities is by light. A light source (usually a light emitting diode (LED)) transmits light into a finger, for example, and a nearby light receptor measures the amount of light reaching the other side of the finger or being reflected off the bone. The amount of light changes with the volume of blood passed by the light.

The advantage of this method is that it also allows further analysis such as of the heart rate or, when choosing the right frequencies of light, the amount of hemoglobin within the blood, a measure of oxygenation of the blood. The disadvantage of this method is that it is quite sensitive against movements. Artifacts are mostly caused by movements of either the body part, or the sensing element against the body part. Movements of the body part, for example, the hand, cause more or less blood flowing into the extremities due to centrifugal forces. Although these changes are too short to be detected by temperature sensors due to their relatively high response time, photo transmission devices are well able to observe them. These changes can be of similar amplitude and frequency as those caused by ANS activity and hence pose significant problems in non-lab settings. Movement of the sensing elements against the body part causes a change in the path of light resulting in measurement changes. It also may cause daylight entering the path of light, resulting in more photons reaching the receiving part.

16.2.1.3 Sweat Gland Activity, Electrodermal Activity (EDA)

As with the other two physiological processes associated with sympathetic activity, sweat gland activity is not directly measurable. The most common way to infer the activity of the glands is by measuring the change of the electrical conductivity of the skin. Because sweat contains a number of electrically conductive minerals, a higher activity of the glands leads to an increased conductivity.

To measure electrodermal activity, a small voltage is applied on an area with a high concentration of sweat glands (e.g., palms of the hand, or the foot). The measured electrical current between the two electrodes correlates with the sweat glands' activity. Usually, measurements are given as conductance level, because conductance increases in a linear manner with sweat gland activity.

Skin conductance is measured in μS (micro Siemens), and skin resistance in $k\Omega$ (kilo Ohms).

Terms often used to describe electrodermal activity are: GSR (Galvanic Skin Response), SCL (Skin Conductance Level), SCR (Skin Conductance Response), SRL (Skin Resistance Level), and SRR (Skin Resistance Response). The respective L and R versions refer to the (tonic) background level (L), and the time-varying (phasic) response (R).

The *tonic* level (SCL, SRL) effectively represents a baseline, or resting level. It usually changes very slowly and represents the relative level of sympathetic arousal of a person. The *phasic* changes (SCR, SRR) are short episodes of increased gland activity caused by increased sympathetic arousal, generated by a stimulus. SCR reactions on a stimulus appear about 1–2 seconds after the stimulus, stay on a certain level depending on the intensity of the stimulating event and how long it lasts, and then fall back to the tonic level.

It is important to bear in mind that a phasic change might lead to an elevated baseline if the person's sympathetic system does not completely recover from the triggering event. Conversely, when the person's sympathetic system "relaxes" over time, the tonic level might decrease over time. Consequently, for affective computing applications, not just the phasic changes are of interest, but also changes to the tonic level. However, this can only be taken into account when measurements are taken permanently at the same location. Temporarily detached electrodes or changing electrode positions may result in different absolute values, wrongly suggesting a change in the tonic skin conductance level.

Note also that baseline changes caused by sympathetic reactions are difficult to distinguish from measurement drifts caused by internal processes in the sensing electronics. If the device requires electrode gel to be used, chemical reactions within the gel over time can lead to measurement drifts as well.

Note also that measurement devices for EDA are not standardized in any way. Measurements taken with a device from one manufacturer usually are not directly comparable with measurements taken with a device from another manufacturer.

After this short overview of possible ways to infer changes in the affective state of a user, we now give a short account of the related state of research in the HCI domain.

16.2.2 HCI Related State of the Art

Although facial expressions are one of the most obvious manifestations of emotions (Ekman & Davidson, 1994), detecting them is still a challenge (see Cowie et al. (2001)) although some progress has been made in recent years (Fasel & Luettin, 2003; Aleksic & Katsaggelos, 2006; CHI 2006, 2007; ACII 2007). Problems arise especially when the observed person moves about freely, because facial features can only be observed when the person is facing a camera. Speech parameters have also been examined for correlations with emotions with increasingly acceptable results (Burkhardt & Sendlmeier 2000; Douglas-Cowie, Cowie, & Campbell, 2003; Küstner, Tato, Kemp, & Meffert, 2004; Laukka, Juslin, & Bresin, 2005; Ververidis & Constantine Kotropoulos, 2006; CHI 2006, 2007; ACII 2007). Challenges here are similar to those for facial features. As the person moves about, it is necessary to track her position to get adequate measures of the speech signal.

Gesture and body movement also contain signs of emotions (Coulson 2004; Kleinsmith, de Silva, & Bianchi-Berthouze, 2005; Kleinsmith & Bianchi-Berthouze, 2007; Castellano, Villalba, & Camurri, 2007; Crane & Gross, 2007). A large vocabulary of semantic primitives has been identified by communication researchers, anthropologists, and psychologists. Apart from symbols (e.g., thumbs up), semantics can be found based on the fact that distinct emotions are associated with distinct qualities of body movement, such as tempo or force.

Emotion-related changes of physiological parameters have also been studied in the HCI context (Palomba & Stegagno, 1993; Scheirer, Fernandez, Klein, & Picard, 2002; Ward & Marsden, 2003; Branco, Firth, Encarnacao, & Bonato, 2005; Herbon, Peter, Markert, van der Meer, & Voskamp, 2005; Mandryk, Inkpen, & Calvert, 2006; Li & Chen, 2006). Although there are different approaches and opinions on how to best ascribe physiological measurements to emotional states, there is consent that it is well possible to do so (Scheirer et al. 2002; Peter & Herbon, 2006). Scheirer et al. (2002) investigated standard signal patterns for recognizing emotions. They defined "ground truths" which are frequently referred to and against which to compare patterns in the measured signals and on which to base classifications.

As for today, emotion recognition based on physiological readings can be considered as one of the most promising approaches to measure affect in the real world, although several challenges are to be met here as well.

16.3 Requirements on Physiological Sensors in the HCI Context

A number of commercial systems are available for measuring emotion-related peripheral physiological parameters such as skin conductivity, skin temperature, or heart rate. Those systems have been developed for either recreational purposes (sports), or for medical or psychological studies, which usually take place in fixed lab environments with the subject asked to sit as motionless as possible in front of a display, occasionally hitting buttons on a keyboard or computer mouse.

For studies on affect and emotion in everyday human–computer interaction scenarios, in natural settings at home, at work, or on the move, the available systems prove to be unsuitable due to the restrictions they pose on the subject or the limited quality of data they provide. A few authors already addressed this problem (Haag, Goronzy, Schaich, & Williams, 2004; Jovanov, Milenkovic, Otto, & deGroen, 2005). They identified the following important limitations for wider acceptance of the existing biosensors and health monitoring systems for continuous monitoring.

Limitations of current systems:

- Unwieldy wires between sensors and a processing unit
- Lack of system integration of individual sensors
- Interference on a wireless communication channel shared by multiple devices
- Nonexistent support for massive data collection and knowledge discovery
- Data availability only offline or bound to lab setting

Jovanov et al. (2005) emphasize the negative effects of unwieldy wires between electrodes and the monitoring system, as these limit the subject's activity and level of comfort and thus negatively influence the measured results.

Real-life HCI applications have special requirements on physiological sensors. They differ from medical applications in that they need to be very robust, unobtrusive, and flexible in providing their data. The following list represents the main features a sensor system for use in affective computing scenarios should possess.

- *Robustness:* The device needs to be unsusceptible to movements of any kind. It is not acceptable to ask a subject of a study or a user of an affective system to not move at certain times or to pay attention to wires or cables while performing tasks. Hence, the system should be designed to avoid the occurence of movement artifacts as much as possible, and it should take care of the remaining occurrences of artifacts.
- *Unobtrusiveness:* The system should not hinder the user's movements in any way in order to avoid user distraction or frustration, and to support voluntary continuous use of the system. To achieve this, data communication from the sensing

device to a processing host should be wireless, as wires of any kind should be avoided for their usually distracting or irritating effect. For the same reason, sensing elements should not be visible to the user or subject; that is, they should be integrated within the system. A small form factor and light weight are also essential. The lighter and smaller a device is, the less it will be noticed.

- *Easy usage:* There should be no need for the user to connect different components in a predescribed fashion to get the system running, to place electrodes at specific body parts using tape or Velcro, or to configure and adjust software prior to collecting data. Also, energy consumption should be low to allow for a long operation time without the need of changing or recharging batteries.
- *Immediate access:* Data should be immediately available. For studies, the experimenter should get permanent and in-time feedback on the subject's performance. For affective applications, permanent provision of actual data is essential to allow for continuous adaptation of the system to an ever-changing user state.
- *Ease of integration:* There should always be sensible data available to speed up data processing and ease analyses. Error-handling should be done within the device, freeing the developer from caring about lost connections, transmission errors, badly fitted electrodes, and other technical side aspects. Furthermore, data should be provided in an open format.
- *Standard conformance:* Being also an aspect of ease of integration, data should be made available in engineering units. This avoids inclusion of sensor-specific conversion formulae into applications, increasing flexibility and eliminating the risk of conversion errors.

These requirements are the main features identified as necessary for a physiological sensor system to be used as an affective input device. Obviously, these requirements are of varying importance in different scenarios, and each scenario might add further specific requirements to the list.

As mentioned above, existing commercial systems being designed for medical or recreational purposes show different limitations which make them less suitable for use in real-world scenarios in the affective computing domain.

A concept for devices meeting the identified requirements is worked out in the following section.

16.4 Concept for Affective Physiological Sensors

For a system to meet the criteria identified above, a distributed architecture with wirelessly connected components seems to be most appropriate (Fig. 16.1). A small and lightweight sensor unit should be placed close to the body of the user, ideally hiding any wires and being comfortable to wear. A base unit should take care of validating, pre-processing, and storing the data, as well as making them available immediately to processing applications. The base unit should be freely positionable within a sensible range of the sensor unit to allow, for instance, the experimenter to monitor the captured data immediately and out of sight of the subject, or for the

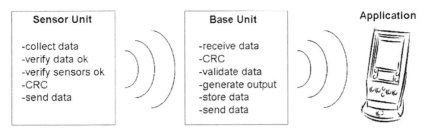

Fig. 16.1 Conceptual system overview.

office worker to go for a cup of coffee. Of course, the system should be able to cope with the base unit losing contact with the sensor unit, or multiple sensor units communicating with one or many base units at the same time.

16.4.1 Components

16.4.1.1 Sensor Unit

For acquisition of peripheral physiological data, sensor elements need direct contact to the subject's skin. To avoid long wires leading from the electrodes to the data processing electronics, the sensor unit should be close to the actual measuring points.

To allow for easy usage and hence increased acceptance of the system, all electronics and wires should be invisibly integrated in a device or clothing usually worn by people, for instance, a glove, wristband, brassiere, jewellery, or a headband. As has been shown in different studies (e.g., Picard & Scheirer, 2001; Peter, 2007), those integrated devices are quickly accepted and users soon forget about being monitored.

The main task of the sensor unit is to capture the data and to perform basic pre-evaluations on them, such as detecting measurement errors or sensor failures. If errors occur, appropriate action should be taken, such as readjustment of the sensing elements, calibration of circuitry, or notification of the base unit. Before the data can be transmitted, they have to be wrapped in an appropriate transmission protocol, and a checksum has to be generated.

16.4.1.2 Base Unit

The base unit is to receive the data from one or many sensor units. Data should get a timestamp as soon as they are received to allow for assigning the data to application events and to make it possible to correlate them with data from other sensor parts, for example, correlate skin temperature with room temperature and skin conductance measurements. After validating the checksum, data are evaluated for sensibility, based on stored information of typical values, measurement history, physical laws, and possibly under consideration of other sensor's results. For instance, when all sensors don't send sensible data, it is likely that the sensor unit is not attached properly to the user. When just one sensor reports unusual data, there might be a problem with that sensor, or a single sensing element might not be properly attached. In case of a sensor error, the sensor unit could, for instance, be reset. If, for instance, a bad attachment of the sensor unit is assumed, the user could be notified and asked for assistance.

Based on the evaluation result, output data will be prepared in a next step. Because it is desirable to provide sensible data continuously, missing or bad data have to be treated, for instance, by filling gaps with likely estimated data. Where alterations have been performed on the data, this has to be made known to the processing applications, along with other reliability information. Prepared like this, the data can be sent out continuously to a processing host. For applications with no permanent link to a processing host, the possibility to store the data locally should be provided.

16.5 Exemplary Implementation

16.5.1 First System: EREC-I

A sensor system that follows the concept described above has been developed in the frame of a master's thesis (Ebert, 2005). It has been named EREC for *E*motion *REC*ognition system. It measures skin conductivity, heart rate, skin temperature, and, as auxiliary information, ambient air temperature. The base unit features a display to visualize the current state of the system. Basic user input is possible by buttons, for example, to indicate interesting events. As a special feature for applications and mobile devices, the base unit can generate events, such as detection of certain physiological states, which can be made available to the outside world. Communication between sensor unit and base unit is done wirelessly using an ISM (Industry, Scientific, and Medical) band transmitter. With the used transmitter, the maximum range is 10–30 meters indoors and up to 300 meters outdoors. The first prototype of the system uses a glove as garment hosting the sensor unit (Figure 16.2).

16.5.1.1 EREC-I Sensor Unit

All sensing electronics and sensor elements, except for the heart rate, are integrated in a glove. This allows for short and hidden wires from the sensing elements for skin temperature and skin conductivity to the electronics. As heart rate sensor, a conventional chest belt is used. The heart rate receiver from Polar is designed to be mounted near the hand and could hence also be integrated in the glove.

Fig. 16.2 The first prototype EREC-I consists of a glove hosting the sensor elements and the processing electronics, and the base unit with display, memory card, and serial port.

The skin conductivity sensor is implemented twofold. This helps to increase the robustness of the system significantly. Data evaluation checks can be performed more reliably based on those duplicate data. The skin temperature is taken at two different positions as well but integrated in one sensor, leading to higher accuracy and higher resolution. Also in the sensor unit, the ambient air temperature near the device is measured. This is another important factor for calculating sensor status and data reliability, inasmuch as skin temperature and skin conductivity vary with changing environmental temperature.

Skin temperature as well as skin conductivity are sampled 20 times per second each. Heart rate data are sent out by the heart rate sensor immediately after a beat has been detected. The collected data are digitized instantly and assessed for sensor failure as described in the data validation section below.

Based on the evaluation results, output data are prepared in a next step. In the case of bad or temporarily no data from a sensor, previous data are used to estimate the likely current value. In this case, a flag in the transmission protocol is set accordingly. Wrapped into the protocol and fitted with a CRC checksum, the data are sent out by the integrated ISM-band transmitter.

16.5.1.2 EREC-I Base Unit

The base unit receives the data transmitted from the sensor unit. Thanks to the wireless connection, multiple sensor units, each with a unique identifier, can easily be used. Immediately after the data have been received they get a timestamp. After a positive checksum evaluation, data are validated and enhanced as described in the data validation section below. The validation results are stored along with the data and their timestamp on a local exchangeable memory card. If desired, they can also be sent out permanently to a host computer using a serial connection, in this version RS232.

Also in the base unit, the environmental temperature is taken again. This is to provide for an additional indicator on environmental changes the person might be exposed to and complements the according measurement of the sensor unit (although the sun might shine on the hands of the user, resulting in a higher local temperature near the hand, the room might still be chilly).

All data are made available in engineering units. The temperature is represented in degrees Celsius with a resolution of $0.1°C$. The skin resistance comes in kilo ohms with a resolution of 300 kilo ohms. The heart rate comes in beats per minute with a resolution of 1 bpm. Transmission speed of the validated and enhanced data to a processing host is for each of the sensors 5 validated values per second.

16.5.2 Second System: EREC-II

After first tests and evaluations (Peter et al., 2007), a number of changes to the system have been recommended by users, leading to the development of EREC-II.

EREC-II consists of two parts as well. The sensor unit still uses a glove to host the sensing elements for skin resistance and skin temperature, however, the electronics are now put in a separate wrist pocket. It also collects heart rate data from a Polar heart rate chest belt and measures the environmental air temperature. The base unit is wirelessly connected to the sensor unit, receives the prevalidated sensor data, evaluates them, stores them on local memory, and/or sends the evaluated data to a processing host. In the following, more details are given in comparison to the EREC-I system. A description of the development steps and individual evaluations is given in Peter et al. (2007).

16.5.2.1 EREC-II Sensor Unit

The sensor unit is functionally identical to that of EREC-I, with small changes to the circuit layout. The sensing elements are fixed now on a cycling glove. As shown in Figure 16.3, the processing electronics are now hidden in a wrist pocket, with the sensing elements connected to it by a short covered lead. Although this actually is against the requirement of no wires being visible, it provides various benefits which, in our experience, outweigh the disadvantage of one cable being visible. Most important, this increases the flexibility in using the system by allowing to connect various designs of sensor gloves to the electronics part (e.g., different sizes, color, or fabric). Also, it allows to use gloves of lighter and more airy material which increases comfort and fit of the glove. Furthermore, due to the electronics being placed above the wrist, the user's movements are less affected by weight and size of the electronics module. Finally, the glove can be washed in a usual manner because no delicate electronics are integrated in it. Feedback from users confirmed the appropriateness of this decision.

Fig. 16.3 In EREC-II, the sensing circuitry is accommodated by a wrist pocket, making the glove lighter and more airy. It also allows for more flexible system arrangements.

16.5.2.2 EREC-II Base Unit

The base unit has undergone a major redesign. It now has a pocket-size case, no display, and uses an SD card for storing data permanently. The data are stored on the card in the common FAT format allowing the readout of data with any standard PC. The serial connection to a computer now uses USB.

The user interface consists of light emitting diodes for communicating different sensor and system states, and pushbuttons for the user to mark special events. As with EREC-I, sensor data are received from the sensor unit, transport errors are assessed, and reliability checks are performed each time new data are received. Validated data are sent out immediately to a connected PC and stored on the memory card. We also now provide raw measurement data for detailed low-level analyses, if desired.

16.5.3 Data Validation

Data are validated throughout the system at two levels: a low-level evaluation is performed on the data in the sensor unit, and a higher-level validation is carried out in the base unit with respect to usefulness of the data. Validation is based on the SEVA (Self Validation) standard (Zhou, Archer, Bowles, Clarke, Henry, & Peter, 1999; Henry, 2001).

16.5.3.1 Low-Level Validation

The sensor unit collects data from several sensors. In the configuration described in this chapter there are two skin resistance sensors, one skin temperature sensor, one ambient air temperature sensor, and one heart rate sensor. Except for the air temperature sensor, all sensors need direct connection to the user's body. As the user moves about, sensing elements might become temporarily detached. Those cases are handled at the data level by the sensor unit. If no data are received from a sensing element, a "best estimate" is sent instead. A flag in the transmission protocol is set in this case, indicating that the data are estimates. If no data have been received from a sensor for a longer period of time (e.g., for 10 samples), a sensor status flag is set accordingly in the transmission protocol.

16.5.3.2 High-Level Validation

Based on the data and sensor status received from the base unit and on the checksum result, the status of each sensor is analyzed continuously. Validated SEVA data are generated based on these results and additional knowledge of physiology and sensor characteristics. The following data are produced (in accordance with suggestions from Henry (2001)).

- *Validated measurement value (VMV):* This corresponds to the actually measured value as long as no problem occurs and the data are in a sensible range. In case of measurement problems, further considerations of the most likely value are made. In the case where data move out of a predefined range or develop unusual values (i.e., heart rate over 200 bpm, jump of skin temperature by $2°C$ within 0.2 seconds), a VMV value will be estimated based on previously received data and stored measurand characteristics.
- *Validated uncertainty (VU):* The VU denotes the likely error of the VMV. It can be seen as an "uncertainty band" enclosing the VMV.
- *Measurement value status (MVS):* This is a discrete parameter indicating the reliability of the VMV. According to the SEVA standard, possible values are: clear (valid measurement), blurred (estimated data after known errors have occurred), dazzled (estimated data with uncertain cause of problems), and blind (estimated data of increasing uncertainty).
- *Device status (DS):* The device status indicates how operational a sensor is. The SEVA standard proposes six states: good (no problems), testing (sensor in self-test), suspect (malfunction possible but not yet verified), impaired (malfunction with low impact), bad (serious malfunction diagnosed), and critical (sensor not operational).
- *Detailed diagnostics (DD):* In case of an error, precise information on the error is provided (e.g., no data, wrong CRC, data out of range).

Those SEVA data are stored in the base unit and communicated to processing applications, along with the data.

16.6 Evaluation

EREC-II has been used by independent groups in various studies and different application fields (Peter et al., 2007; Tischler, Peter, Wimmer, & Voskamp, 2007). In a medical environment, the emotion-related physiological reactions during a treatment session were examined. Other studies investigated human performance in sports, dealt with driver assistance and driving experience issues, or included EREC in a multimodal affective sensing framework.

The results of those evaluations show that EREC's functionality as well as the chosen design meet the requirements of real-world applications. The system has been considered easy to use and proved to be robust and reliable.

EREC-II's design consisting of a lightweight glove and a wrist pocket has been rated appropriate. Particularly the meshed fabric at the top of the glove was rated very comfortable by all subjects. For the electronics being put into a separate wrist pocket, it was rated good by all test teams. The possibility to exchange gloves to suit left- and right-handed persons as well as different hand sizes has been particularly welcomed. However, integration of the module into the glove has been suggested as well to increase acceptability of the device by subjects.

The EREC-II base unit impressed with its small size, the easy USB connection, and the SD card with its common file format. Storing and accessing the data have finally been experienced as easy and convenient. For more detailed evaluation results please refer to Peter et al. (2007) and Tischler et al. (2007).

16.7 Conclusions

In this chapter we gave a short overview of common ways to access physiological data to infer changes in the affective state of a person. With a number of commercial systems being available to measure a huge variety of physiological parameters, the choices are manifold and difficult alike for affective computing researchers and developers. Furthermore, available systems are designed for other domains with different requirements and other constraints than real-world HCI applications have. We therefore worked out fundamental requirements to be met by physiological sensors for use in the affective computing domain.

Although the list is nonexclusive, it can be taken as guide for the researcher to choose the most appropriate device for the specific purpose in mind, and for sensor developers to make their devices fit for the emerging affective computing market. Based on these requirements we suggest a design concept for affective physiological sensors and report on the development of two systems implementing it.

Finally it can be said that, despite the challenges, physiological sensors have strong potential to serve as standard input devices for affective systems. Their ability to deliver permanent information on the user's current state recommends them as an auxiliary, ground-truthing information source.

References

ACII (2005). *First International Conference on Affective Computing and Intelligent Interaction,* Beijing 2005. New York: Springer-Verlag .

ACII (2007). *Second International Conference on Affective Computing and Intelligent Interaction,* Lisbon, Portugal.

Aleksic, P. S., & Katsaggelos, A. K. (2006). Automatic facial expression recognition using facial animation parameters and multi-stream HMMs. *IEEE Transactions on Information Forensics and Security, 1*(1, March), 3–11.

Branco, P., Firth, P., Encarnacao, L. M., & Bonato, P. (2005). Faces of emotion in human-computer interaction. In *Proceedings of the CHI 2005 Conference,* Extended Abstracts (pp. 1236–1239). New York: ACM Press.

BS 7986 (2004). Industrial process measurement and control – Data quality metrics. Available from BSI Customer Services email: orders@bsi-global.com.

Burkhardt, F., & Sendlmeier, W. F. (2000). Verification of acoustical correlates of emotional speech using formant-synthesis. In *ISCA Workshop on Speech and Emotion,* 151–156.

Cacioppo, J. T., Tassinary, L. G., & Berntson, G. G. (Eds.) (2000). *Handbook of psychophysiology* (2nd ed.). Cambridge University Press, Cambridge, UK.

Castellano, G., Villalba, S. D., & Camurri, A. (2007). Recognising human emotions from body movement and gesture dynamics. affective computing and intelligent interaction. In *Second International Conference, ACII 2007,* Lisbon, September 12–14, Proceedings, Series: LNCS 4738. New York: Springer-Verlag.

CHI (2005). *Proceedings of the SIGCHI conference on human factors in computing systems, CHI 2005,* Portland, OR, April. New York: ACM Press.

CHI (2006). *Proceedings of the SIGCHI conference on human factors in computing systems.* Montréal, Québec, Canada April 22–27. New York: ACM Press.

CHI (2007). *SIGCHI conference on human factors in computing systems (CHI 2007),* April 28–May 3, San Jose, CA.

Coulson, M. (2004). Attributing emotion to static body postures: Recognition accuracy, confusions, and viewpoint dependence. *Journal of Nonviolent Behavior, 28,* 117–139.

Cowie, R., Douglas-Cowie, E., Tsapatsoulis, N., Votsis, G., Kollias, S., Fellenz, W., & Taylor, J. G. (2001). Emotion recognition in human computer interfaces. *IEEE Signal Processing Magazine, 18*(1), 32–80.

Crane, E., & Gross, M. (2007). Motion capture and emotion: Affect detection in whole body movement. Affective computing and intelligent interaction. In *Second International Conference, ACII 2007,* Lisbon, September 12–14, 2007, Proceedings, Series: LNCS 4738. New York: Springer-Verlag.

Douglas-Cowie, E., Cowie, R., & Campbell, N. (2003). Speech and emotion. *Speech Communication, 40,* 1–3.

Ebert, E. (2005). Weiterentwicklung und Verifikation eines Messsystem zur Erfassung human-physiologischer Sensordaten unter Berücksichtigung des SEVA-Konzepts. Master Thesis, University of Rostock

Ekman, P., & Davidson, R. J. (Eds.) (1994). *The nature of emotion: Fundamental questions.* New York: Oxford University Press.

Ekman, P., & Friesen, W. (1976). *Pictures of facial affect.* Palo Alto, CA: Consulting Psychologists Press.

Ekman, P., & Friesen, W. (1978). *Facial action coding system: A technique for the measurement of facial movement.* Palo Alto, CA: Consulting Psychologists Press.

Ekman, P., Levenson, R. W., & Friesen, W. (1983). Autonomic nervous system activity distinguishes among emotions. In *Science 221.* The American Association for Advancement of Science, *221*(4616), 1208–1210.

Fasel B., & Luettin J. (2003). Automatic facial expression analysis: A survey. *Pattern Recognition, 36*(1), 259–275.

Haag, A., Goronzy, S., Schaich, P., & Williams, J. (2004). Emotion recognition using bio-sensors: First steps towards an automatic system. In André et al. (Eds.), *Affective dialogue systems, Proceedings of the Kloster Irsee Tutorial and Research Workshop on Affective Dialogue Systems*, LNCS 3068 (pp. 36–48). New York: Springer-Verlag.

HCII (2007). *The 12th International Conference on Human-Computer Interaction*, 22–27 July 2007, Beijing.

Henry M. (2001). Recent developments in self-validating (SEVA) sensors. Sensor Review, *21*(1), 16–22, MCB University Press. 0260–2288.

Herbon, A., Peter, C., Markert, L., van der Meer, E., & Voskamp, J. (2005). Emotion studies in HCI – a new approach. In *Proceedings of the 2005 HCI International Conference*, Las Vegas (Vol. 1), CD-ROM.

Jovanov, E., Milenkovic, A., Otto, C., & deGroen, P. C. (2005). A wireless body area network of intelligent motion sensor for computer assisted physical rehabilitation. *Journal of NeuroEngineering and Rehabilitation 2005*, 2, 6.

Kleinsmith, A., & Bianchi-Berthouze, N. (2007). Recognizing affective dimensions from body posture. In *Affective Computing and Intelligent Interaction, Second International Conference, ACII 2007*, Lisbon, September 12–14, 2007, Proceedings, Series: LNCS 4738. New York: Springer-Verlag.

Kleinsmith, A., de Silva, P., & Bianchi-Berthouze, N. (2005). Grounding affective dimensions into posture features. In *Proceedings of the First International Conference on Affective Computing and Intelligent Interaction* (pp. 263–270). Heidelberg: Springer.

Küstner, D., Tato, R., Kemp, T., & Meffert, B. (2004). Towards real life applications in emotion recognition; comparing different databases, feature sets, and reinforcement methods for recognizing emotions from speech. In André et al. (Eds.), *Affective Dialogue Systems, Proceedings of the Kloster Irsee Tutorial and Research Workshop on Affective Dialogue Systems*, LNCS 3068. New York: Springer-Verlag.

Laukka, P., Juslin, P. N., & Bresin, R. (2005). A dimensional approach to vocal expression of emotion. *Cognition and Emotion, 19*(5), 633–653.

Li L., & Chen J. (2006). Emotion recognition using physiological signals from multiple subjects. In *Proceedings of the 2006 International Conference on Intelligent Information Hiding and Multimedia Signal Processing* (pp. 355–358). Los Alamitos, CA: IEEE Computer Society.

Mandryk, R. L., Inkpen, K. M., & Calvert, T. W. (2006). Using psychophysiological techniques to measure user experience with entertainment technologies. *Behaviour and Information Technology (Special Issue on User Experience)*, 25, 141–158.

Palomba, D., & Stegagno, L. (1993). Physiology, perceived emotion and memory: Responding to film sequences. In N. Birbaumer & A. Öhman (Eds.), *The Structure of Emotion* (pp. 158–168). Toronto: Hogrefe & Huber.

Peter, C., & Beale, R. (Eds.) (2008). *Affect and Emotion in Human-Computer Interaction*, LNCS 4868. Heidelberg: Springer.

Peter, C., & Herbon, A. (2006). Emotion representation and physiology assignments in digital systems. In *Interacting With Computers, 18*(2), 139–170.

Peter C., Schultz, R., Voskamp, J., Urban, B., Nowack, N., Janik, H., Kraft, K., & Göcke, R. (2007). EREC-II in use – Studies on usability and suitability of a sensor system for affect detection and human performance monitoring. In J. Jacko (Ed.), *Human-Computer Interaction, Part III, HCII 2007*, LNCS 4552 (pp. 465–474). Heidelberg: Springer-Verlag.

Picard, R., & Scheirer, J. (2001). The galvactivator: A glove that senses and communicates skin conductivity. In *Ninth International Conference on Human-Computer Interaction*, New Orleans. LA, 1538–1542.

Scheirer, J., Fernandez, R., Klein, J., & Picard, R.W. (2002). Frustrating the user on purpose: A step toward building an affective computer. *Interacting with Computers, 14*(2): 93–118.

Schröder, M. (2004). *Proceedings of the HUMAINE Workshop From Signals to Signs of Emotion and Vice Versa*, Santorini.

Schwartz, M. S., & Andrasik, F. (2003). Biofeedback: A practitioner's guide (3rd ed.). New York: Guilford Press.

Tischler, M. A., Peter, C., Wimmer, M., & Voskamp, J. (2007). Application of emotion recognition methods in automotive research. In D. Reichardt & P. Levi (Eds), *Proceedings of the 2nd Workshop Emotion and Computing – Current Research on Future Impact* (pp. 55–60).

Ververidis, D., & Constantine Kotropoulos, C. (2006). Emotional speech recognition: Resources, features, and methods. *Speech Communication, 48*, 1162–1181.

Ward, R. D., & Marsden, P. H. (2003). Physiological responses to different web page designs. *International Journal of Human-Computer Studies, 59*(1/2): 199–212.

Zhou, F., Archer, N., Bowles, J., Clarke, D., Henry, M., & Peter, C. (1999). A general hardware platform for sensor validation. *IEE Colloquium on Intelligent and Self-Validating Sensors*, Oxford.

Chapter 17
Evolutionary Expression of Emotions in Virtual Humans Using Lights and Pixels

Celso M. de Melo and Ana Paiva

Abstract Artists express emotions through art. To accomplish this they rely on lines, shapes, textures, color, light, sounds, music, words, and the body. The field of virtual humans has been neglecting the kind of expression we see in the arts. In fact, researchers have tended to focus on gesture, face, and voice for the expression of emotions. But why limit ourselves to the body? In this context, drawing on accumulated knowledge from the arts, this chapter describes an evolutionary model for the expression of emotions in virtual humans using lights, shadows, filters, and composition. Lighting expression uses lighting techniques from the visual arts to convey emotions through the lights in the environment. Screen expression uses filters and composition to manipulate the virtual human's pixels themselves in a way akin to painting. Emotions are synthesized using the OCC model. To learn how to map affective states into lighting and screen expression, an evolutionary model that relies on genetic algorithms is used. The crossover and mutation operators generate alternatives for the expression of some affective state and a critic ensemble, composed of artificial and human critics, selects among the alternatives.

17.1 Introduction

The anger which I feel here and now ... is no doubt an instance of anger ... ; but it is much more than mere anger: it is a peculiar anger, not quite like any anger that I ever felt before.

C.M. de Melo (✉)
USC, University of Southern California
e-mail: demelo@usc.edu

A. Paiva
IST Technical University of Lisbon and INESC-ID, Avenida Prof. Cavaco Silva Taguspark, 2780-990 Porto Salvo, Portugal
e-mail: ana.paiva@inesc-id.pt

J.H. Tao, T.N. Tan (eds.), *Affective Information Processing*,
© Springer Science+Business Media LLC 2009

In this passage by Collingwood (1938), the artist is trying to express an emotion. But, this isn't just any emotion. This is a unique emotion. As he tries to make sense of it, he expresses it using lines, shapes, textures, color, light, sound, music, words, and the body. This perspective of art as the creative expression of emotions is not new and exists, at least, since the Romanticism (Oatley, 2003; Sayre, 2007). The idea is that when the artist is confronted with unexpected events, emotions are elicited and a creative response is demanded (Averill, Nunley, & Tassinary, 1995). Thus, through the creative expression of her feelings, the artist is trying to understand their peculiarity. But art is not simply an outlet for the artist's emotions. From the perspective of the receiver, through its empathic emotional response to a work of art, it is also seen as a means to learn about the human condition (Elliot, 1966; Oatley, 2003). Emotions are, therefore, intrinsically related to the value of art.

Affective computing is neglecting the kind of expression we see in the arts. The state-of-the-art in the related virtual humans field is a case in point. Virtual humans are embodied characters that inhabit virtual worlds and look, think, and act as humans (Gratch et al., 2002). Thus far, researchers focused on gesture (Cassell, 2000), face (Noh & Neumann, 1998), and voice (Schroder, 2004) for emotion expression. But, in the digital medium we need not be limited to the body.

In this context, drawing on accumulated knowledge from art theory, this work proposes to go beyond embodiment and synthesize expression of emotions in virtual humans using light, shadow, composition, and filters. This approach, therefore, focuses on two expression channels: lighting and screen. In the first case, the work is inspired by the principles of lighting, regularly explored in theatre or film production (Alton, 1949; Malkiewicz & Gryboski, 1986; Millerson, 1999; Birn, 2006), to convey the virtual human's affective state through the environment's light sources. In the second case, the work acknowledges that, at the metalevel, virtual humans are no more than pixels on the screen that can be manipulated, in a way akin to the visual arts (Birn, 2006; Gross, 2007; Zettl, 2008), to convey emotions. Now, having defined which expression channels to use, it remains to define how to map affective states into lighting and screen expression.

This work explores genetic algorithms (GAs; Mitchell, 1998) to learn mappings between affective states and the expression channels. Genetic algorithms seem appropriate for several reasons. First, there are no available datasets exemplifying what constitutes correct expression of emotions using lights or screen. Thus, standard supervised machine-learning algorithms, which rely on a teacher, seem unsuitable. Furthermore, art varies according to time, individual, culture, and what has been done before (Sayre, 2007). Therefore, the artistic space should be explored in search of creative—that is, new and aesthetic—expression.

Genetic algorithms, defining a guided search, are, thus, appropriate. Second, the virtual humans field is new and novel forms of expression are available. Here, the GAs' clear separation between generation and evaluation of alternatives is appropriate. Alternatives, in this new artistic space, can be generated using biologically inspired operators: selection, mutation, crossover, and so on. Evaluation, in turn, could rely on fitness functions drawn from art theory. Finally, it has been argued that art is adaptive as it contributes to the survival of the artist (Dissanayake, 1988). This, of course, meets the GAs' biological motivation.

The remainder of the chapter is organized as follows. Section 17.2 provides background on virtual humans and describes the digital medium's potential for expression of emotions, focusing on lighting and screen expression. Section 17.3 describes the virtual human model, detailing the lighting and screen expression channels. Section 17.4 describes the evolutionary approach that maps affective states into the expression channels. Section 17.5 applies the model to learn how to map anger into lighting expression. Finally, Section 17.6 draws some conclusions and discusses future work.

17.2 Background

17.2.1 Expression in the Arts

There are several conceptions about what expression in the arts is. First, it relates to beauty as the expression of beauty in nature (Batteux, 1969). Second, it relates to culture as the expression of the values of any given society (Geertz, 1976). Third, it relates to individuality as the expression of the artists' liberties and values (Kant & Bernard, 1951). Finally, it relates to emotions as the expression of the artist's feelings. In fact, many acknowledge the importance of emotions for appreciating and attributing value to the arts.

From the perspective of the creator, expression is seen as a way of understanding and coming to terms with what he is experiencing affectively (Collingwood, 1938). From the perspective of the receiver, through its empathetic emotional responses to a work of art, it is seen as a means to learn about the human condition (Elliot, 1966; Oatley, 2003). Finally, artistic expression is a creative endeavor (Kant & Bernard 1951; Gombrich, 1960; Batteux, 1969; Sayre, 2007) and there is no set of rules that artists use to reach a result (Collingwood, 1938). Furthermore, according to the Romanticism philosophy, art is the creative expression of latent affective states (Oatley, 2003). In fact, Gombrich (1960) argues that this idiosyncrasy in expression is inescapable and emerges when the artist's visual perceptions are confronted with his existing mental schemas, including ideas and preconceptions. This chapter tries to explore the kind of expression we see in the arts in the context of virtual humans. A simple rule-based approach is avoided and, instead, a machine-learning approach, which is more likely to be able to adapt to dynamic artistic values, is pursued to learn mappings between emotional states and light and screen expression.

17.2.2 Expression of Emotions in the Digital Medium

Digital technology is a flexible medium for the expression of emotions. In virtual worlds, inhabited by virtual humans, in addition to embodiment, at least four expression channels can be identified: camera, lights, sound, and screen. The camera defines the view into the virtual world. Expressive control, which is inspired by cinema and photography, is achieved through selection of shot, shot transitions, shot framing, and manipulation of lens properties (Arijon, 1976; Katz, 1991; Block, 2001; Malkiewicz & Mullen, 2005).

Lights define which areas of the scene are illuminated and which are in shadow. Furthermore, lights define the color in the scene. Expressive control, which is inspired by the visual arts, is achieved through manipulation of light type, placement and angle; shadow softness and falloff; and color properties such as hue, brightness, and saturation (Alton, 1949; Malkiewicz & Gryboski, 1986; Millerson, 1999; Birn, 2006).

Sound refers to literal sounds (e.g., dialogue), nonliteral sounds (e.g., effects), and music. Expressive control, which is inspired by drama and music, is achieved through selection of appropriate content for each kind of sound (Juslin & Sloboda, 2001; Zettl, 2008).

Finally, the screen is a metachannel referring to the pixel-based screen itself. Expression control, which is inspired by cinema and photography, is achieved through manipulation of pixel properties such as depth and color (Birn, 2006; Zettl, 2008).

17.2.3 Expression of Emotions in Virtual Humans

Virtual humans are embodied characters that inhabit virtual worlds (Gratch et al., 2002). First, virtual humans look like humans and, thus, research draws on computer graphics for models to control the body and face. Second, virtual humans think and act like humans and, thus, research draws on the social sciences for models to produce synchronized verbal and nonverbal communication as well as to convey emotions and personality. Emotion synthesis usually resorts to cognitive appraisal theories of emotion, being the Ortony, Clore, and Collins (OCC) theory (Ortony et al., 1988), one of the most commonly used. Emotion expression tends to focus on conveying emotions through synchronized and integrated gesture (Cassell, 2000), facial (Noh and Neumann, 1998), and vocal (Schroder 2004) expression. In contrast, this work goes beyond the body using lights, shadows, composition, and filters to express emotions.

The approach described here is also in line with research on motion modifiers which add emotive qualities to neutral expression. Amaya, Bruderlin, and Calvert (1996) use signal-processing techniques to capture the difference between neutral and emotional movement which would, then, be used to confer emotive properties to other motion data. Chi and colleagues (2000) propose a system which adds expressiveness to existent motion data based on the effort and shape parameters of a dance movement observation technique called Laban Movement Analysis. Hartmann, Mancini, and Pelachaud (2005) draw from psychology six parameters for gesture modification: overall activation, spatial extent, temporal extent, fluidity, power, and repetition. Finally, de Melo and Paiva (2005) propose a model for expression of emotions using the camera, light and sound expression channels. However, this model does not focus on virtual humans, uses a less sophisticated light channel than the one proposed here, does not explore screen expression, and uses simple rules instead of an evolutionary approach.

17.2.4 Expression of Emotions Using Light

This work explores lighting to express virtual humans' emotions. Lighting is the deliberate control of light to achieve expressive goals. Lighting can be used for the purpose of expression of emotions and aesthetics (Alton, 1949; Malkiewicz & Gryboski, 1986; Millerson, 1999; Birn, 2006). To achieve these goals, the following elements are manipulated (Millerson, 1999; Birn, 2006).

(a) Type, which defines whether the light is a point, directional, or spotlight.

(b) Direction, which defines the angle. Illumination at eye-level or above is neutral, whereas below eye-level is unnatural, bizarre, or scary.

(c) Color, which defines color properties. Color definition based on hue, saturation, and brightness (Hunt, 2004) is convenient as these are, in Western culture, regularly manipulated to convey emotions (Fraser & Banks, 2004).

(d) Intensity, which defines exposure level.

(e) Softness, which defines how hard or soft the light is. Hard light, with crisp shadows, confers a harsh mysterious environment. Soft light, with soft transparent shadows, confers a happy, smooth, untextured environment.

(f) Decay, which defines how light decays with distance.

(g) Throw pattern, which defines the shape of the light. Shadows occur in the absence of light. Although strictly related to lights, they tend to be independently controlled by artists.

Shadows can also be used to express emotions and aesthetics (Alton, 1949; Malkiewicz & Gryboski, 1986; Millerson, 1999; Birn, 2006) through manipulation of the following elements.

(a) Softness, which defines how sharp and transparent the shadow is. The denser the shadow, the more dramatic it is.

(b) Size, which defines the shadow size. Big shadows confer the impression of an ominous dramatic character. Small shadows confer the opposite impression.

Lighting transitions change the elements of light and shadow in time. Transitions can be used to express the mood of the scene (Millerson, 1999; Birn, 2006). Digital lighting provides more expressive control to the artist as, besides giving free control of all light and shadow elements, the image's pixels can now be manipulated in a way akin to painting.

17.2.5 Expression of Emotions Using Pixels

At a metalevel, virtual humans and virtual worlds can be seen as pixels on a screen. Thus, as in painting, photography, or cinema, it is possible to manipulate the image itself for expressive reasons. In this view, this chapter explores composition and filtering for the expression of emotions. Composition refers to the process of arranging different aspects of the objects in the scene into layers which are then manipulated and combined to form the final image (Birn, 2006). Here, aspects refer to the ambient, diffuse, specular, shadow, alpha, or depth object components. Composition has two main advantages: it increases efficiency as different aspects can be held fixed for several frames, and it increases expressiveness as each aspect can be controlled independently. Composition is a standard technique in film production.

Filtering is a technique where the scene is rendered into a temporary texture which is then manipulated using shaders before being presented to the user (Zettl, 2008). Shaders replace parts of the traditional rendering pipeline with programmable units (Moller & Haines, 2002). Vertex shaders modify vertex data such as position, normal, and texture coordinates. Pixel shaders modify pixel data such as color and depth. Filtering has many advantages: constant performance is independent of scene complexity, it is very expressive due to the variety of existing filters (St-Laurent, 2004), and it is scalable as several filters can be concatenated.

17.2.6 Evolutionary Approaches

We are not aware of any prior attempt to use evolutionary algorithms to express emotions in virtual humans. Nevertheless, they have been widely explored in computer graphics. Karl Sims (1991) explores a genetic programming approach using symbolic Lisp expressions to generate images, solid textures, and animations. The artist Steven Rooke (World, 1996) uses a set of low- and high-level primitives to guide his genetic programming approach to generate images within his own style. Contrasting with the previous approaches, genetic algorithms have been used to evolve shaders (Lewis, 2001), fractals (Angeline, 1996), animations (Ventrella, 1995) and complex three-dimensional objects (Todd & Latham, 1992).

In all previous systems, the user interactively guides the evolution process. However, attempts have been made to automate this process. Representative is the NEvAr system (Machado, 2006) that proposes an artificial critic which first extracts features from the images in the population and then applies a neural network, trained with appropriate examples, to select the fittest. This project explores both the interactive and artificial critic approaches. In the latter case, the critic is based on rules from art theory.

17.3 The Model

The virtual human model is summarized in Figure 17.1. The virtual human itself is structured according to a three-layer architecture (Blumberg & Galyean, 1995; Perlin & Goldberg, 1996). The *geometry layer* defines a 54-bone human-based skeleton that deforms the skin. The skin, in turn, is divided into body groups: head, torso, arms, hands, and legs. The *animation layer* defines keyframe and procedural animation mechanisms. The *behavior layer* defines speech and gesticulation expression and supports a language for multimodal expression control. Finally, several expression modalities are built on top of this layered architecture. Bodily expression manipulates face, postures, and gestures. Further details on bodily expression, which are not addressed here, can be found in de Melo and Paiva (2006a,b). Lighting expression explores the surrounding environment and manipulates light and shadow. Screen expression manipulates the virtual human pixels themselves. These expression channels are detailed next.

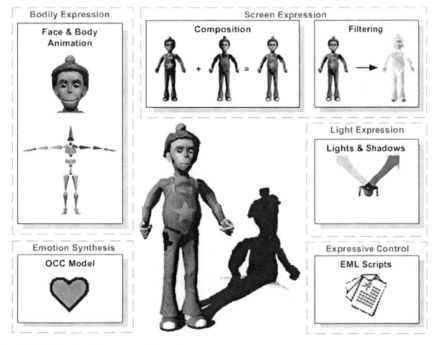

Fig. 17.1 The virtual human model.

17.3.1 Lighting Expression

Lighting expression relies on a local pixel-based lighting model. The model supports multiple sources, three light types and shadows using the shadow map technique (Moller & Haines, 2002). The detailed equations for the lighting model are described elsewhere (de Melo & Paiva, 2007). Manipulation of light and shadow elements (Section 17.2.4) is based on the following parameters.

(a) *Type*, which defines whether to use a directional, point or spotlight.

(b) *Direction* and *position*, which, according to type, control the light angle.

(c) *Ambient, diffuse*, and *specular colors*, which define the color of each of the light's components in either RGB (red, green, blue) or HSB (hue, saturation, and brightness) format.

(d) *Ambient, diffuse*, and *specular intensity*, which define the intensity of each of the components' colors. Setting intensity to 0 disables the component.

(e) *Attenuation, attnPower, attnMin, attnMax*, which simulate falloff. Falloff is defined as $attenuation^{attnPower}$ and is 0 if the distance is less than *attnMin* and 1 beyond a distance of *attnMax*.

(f) *Throw pattern*, which constrains the light to a texture using componentwise multiplication.

(g) *Shadow color*, which defines the shadow color. If set to grays, shadows become transparent; if set to white, shadows are disabled.

(h) *Shadow softness*, which defines the falloff between light and shadow areas.

Finally, sophisticated lighting transitions, such as accelerations and decelerations, are based on parametric cubic curve interpolation of parameters (Moller & Haines, 2002).

17.3.2 Screen Expression

Screen expression explores composition and filtering. Filtering consists of rendering the scene to a temporary texture, modifying it using shaders and, then, presenting it to the user. Several filters have been explored in the literature (St-Laurent, 2004) and this work explores some of them: (a) the *contrast filter*, Figure 17.2b, which controls virtual human contrast and can be used to simulate exposure effects; (b) the *motion blur filter*, Figure 17.2c, which simulates motion blur and is usually used in film to convey nervousness; (c) the *style filter*, Figure 17.2d, which manipulates the virtual human's color properties to convey a stylized look; and (d) the *HSB filter*, which controls the virtual human hue, saturation, and brightness. Filters can be concatenated to create compound effects and its parameters interpolated using parametric cubic curve interpolation (Moller & Haines, 2002).

Composition (Birn, 2006) refers to the process of arranging different aspects of the objects in the scene into layers, independently manipulating the layers for expressive reasons, and combining the layers to form the final image. A layer is characterized as follows.

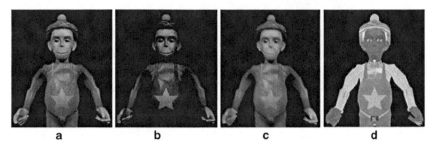

Fig. 17.2 Filtering manipulates the virtual human pixels. In **a** no filter is applied. In **b** the contrast filter is used to reduce contrast and create a more mysterious and harsh look. In **c** the motion blur is used to convey nervousness. In **d** the style filter, which is less concerned with photorealism, conveys an energetic look.

(a) It is associated with a subset of the objects that are rendered when the layer is rendered. These subsets need not be mutually exclusive.
(b) It can be rendered to a texture or the backbuffer. If rendered to a texture, filtering can be applied.
(c) It has an ordered list of filters that are successively applied to the objects. It only applies if the layer is being rendered to a texture.
(d) It is associated with a subset of the lights in the scene. Objects in the layer are only affected by these lights.
(e) It defines a lighting mask, which defines which components of the associated lights apply to the objects.
(f) It can render only a subset of the virtual human's skin body groups.
(g) The layer combination is defined by the order and blending operation. The former defines the order in which layers are rendered into the backbuffer. The latter defines how are the pixels to be combined.

17.3.3 Synthesis of Emotions

Virtual human emotion synthesis is based on the Ortony, Clore, and Collins (1988; OCC) model. All 22 emotion types and local and global variables are implemented. Furthermore, emotion decay, reinforcement, arousal, and mood are also considered. Emotion decay is, as suggested by Picard (1997), represented by an inverse exponential function. Emotion reinforcement is, so as to simulate the saturation effect (Picard 1997), represented by a logarithmic function. Arousal, which relates to the physiological manifestation of emotions, is characterized as follows. It is positive, decays linearly in time, reinforces with emotion eliciting, and increases the elicited emotion's potential. Mood, which refers to the longer-term effects of emotions, is characterized as follows. It can be negative or positive; converges to zero linearly in time; reinforces with emotion eliciting; if positive, increases the elicited emotion's potential, and if negative, decreases it. Further details about this model can be found elsewhere (de Melo & Paiva, 2005).

17.3.4 Expression of Emotions

A markup language, called *Expression Markup Language (EML)*, is used to control multimodal expression. The language supports arbitrary mappings of emotional state conditions and synchronized body, light, and screen expression. The language is structured into modules. The core module defines the main elements. The time and synchronization module defines multimodal synchronization mechanisms based on the W3C's SMIL 2.0 specification.[1] The body, gesticulation, voice, and face modules control bodily expression. The light module controls light expression, supporting modification of light parameters according to specific transition conditions. The screen module controls screen expression, supporting modification of the composition layer's filter lists. Finally, the emotion module supports emotion synthesis and emotion expression. Regarding emotion synthesis, any of the OCC emotion types can be elicited. Regarding emotion expression, the module supports the specification of rules of the form:

$$\{emotionConditions\}^* \cdot \{bodyAc \mid lightAc \mid screenAc \mid emotionAc\}^*,$$

where emotional conditions—*emotionConditions*—evaluate mood, arousal or active emotions' intensity or valence; expressive actions—*bodyAc*, *lightAc* and *screenAc*—refer to body, light, or screen actions as defined by its respective modules; and emotion actions—*emotionAc*—elicit further emotions.

Even though convenient, the definition of rules is unlikely to capture the way artistic expression works (Section 17.2.1). There are, in fact, several rules and guidelines for effective artistic expression available in the literature. However, the expression of emotions in the arts is essentially a creative endeavor and artists are known to break these rules regularly (Sayre, 2007). Thus, a better approach should rely on machine-learning theory, which would support automatic learning of new rules and more sophisticated mappings between emotional states and bodily, environment, and screen expression. In the next section an approach for learning such mappings which is based on genetic algorithms is described.

17.4 Evolutionary Expression of Emotions

In this section an evolutionary model that learns mappings between affective states and multimodal expression is presented. The model revolves around two key entities: the *virtual human* and the *critic ensemble*. The virtual human tries to evolve the best way to express some affective state. For every possible state, it begins by generating a random set of *hypotheses*, which constitute a *population*. The population evolves resorting to a genetic algorithm under the influence of feedback from the critic ensemble. The ensemble is composed of *human* and *artificial critics*.

[1] SMIL: Synchronized Multimedia Integration Language (SMIL). http://www.w3.org/Audio Video/.

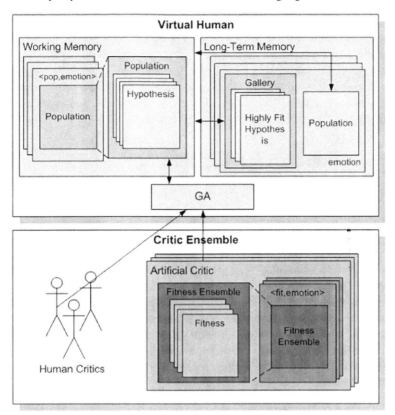

Fig. 17.3 The evolutionary model for expression of emotions in virtual humans.

The set of evolving populations (one per affective state) is kept in the working memory. The genetic algorithm only operates on populations in *working memory*. These can be saved persistently in the *long-term memory*. Furthermore, high fitness hypotheses (not necessarily from the same population) are saved in the long-term memory's *gallery*. Hypotheses from the gallery can, then, provide elements to the initial population, thus promoting high fitness hypotheses evolution. This model is summarized in Figure 17.3 and detailed in the following sections.

17.4.1 Genetic Algorithm

At the core of the model lies a standard implementation of the genetic algorithm (Mitchell, 1998). The algorithm's inputs are:

- The *critic ensemble* which ranks candidate hypotheses.
- *Stopping criteria* to end the algorithm. This can be maximum number of iterations, a fitness threshold, or both.

- The *size of the population, p,* to be maintained.
- The *selection method, SM,* to select probabilistically among the hypotheses in a population. Two methods can be used: *roulette wheel,* which selects a hypothesis according to the ratio of its fitness to the sum of all hypotheses fitness (see (1)); *tournament selection,* which selects with some probability *p.,* the most fit of two hypotheses selected according to (17.1). Tournament selection often yields a more diverse population than roulette wheel (Mitchell, 1999):

$$\Pr(h_i) = \frac{fitness(h_i)}{\sum\limits_{j=i}^{p} fitness(h_i)}. \tag{17.1}$$

- The *crossover rate, r*
- The *mutation rate, m*
- The *elitism rate, e*

The algorithm begins by setting up the initial population. This can be generated at random or loaded from long-term memory (Section 17.4.4). Thereafter, the algorithm enters a loop, evolving populations, until the stopping criterion is met. In each iteration, first, $(1-r)p$ percent of the population is selected for the next generation; second, $rp/2$ pairs of hypotheses are selected for crossover and the offspring are added to the next generation; third, *m* percent of the population are randomly mutated; fourth, *e* percent of hypotheses from the population are copied unchanged to the next generation. The rationale behind elitism is to avoid losing the best hypotheses when a new generation is evolved (Mitchell, 1998). Evaluation, throughout, is based on feedback from the critic ensemble (Section 17.4.5). The algorithm is summarized as follows.

```
GA(criticEnsemble, stoppingCriteria, p, sel, r, m, e)
// criticEnsemble: A group of fitness functions
// stoppingCriteria: Criteria to end the algorithm
// (no. of iterations or threshold)
// p: The number of hypothesis per population
// SM: The selection method (roulette wheel or
tournament selection)
// r: The crossover rate
// m: The mutation rate
// e: The elitism rate
{
  Initialize population: P := Generate p hypotheses
     at random or load from LTM
  Evaluate: For each h in P, compute fitness(h)
  while(!stop) {
    Create a new Generation, Ps
    Select prob. according to SM, (1-r)p members
of P to add to Ps
```

```
   Crossover rp/2 prob. selected pairs and add
offspring to Ps
   Mutate m percent of Ps
   Select probabilistically e percent of P and
replace in Ps
Update P := Ps
Evaluate, according to criticEnsemble, each h in P
   }
}
```

17.4.2 Hypotheses

The hypothesis encoding is structured according to expression modalities; see Figure 17.4. At the top level the virtual human hypothesis is subdivided into the lighting, screen, and body hypotheses. The lighting hypothesis refers to a *three-point lighting* configuration (Millerson, 1999; Birn, 2006). This technique is composed of the light roles: (a) *key light*, which is the main source of light; (b) *fill light*, which is a low-intensity light that fills an area that is otherwise too dark; and (c) *back light*, which is used to separate the character from the background. In this case, only the key and fill lights are used, as these define the main illumination in the scene (Millerson, 1999) and the back light can be computationally expensive (Birn, 2006).

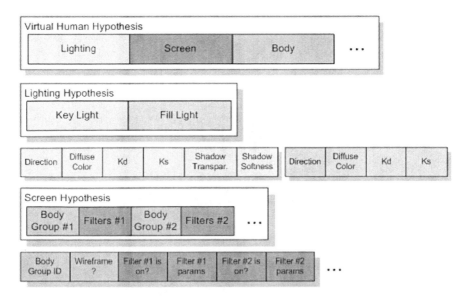

Fig. 17.4 Hypotheses encoding.

Both lights are modeled as directional lights and only the key light is set to cast shadows, according to standard lighting practice (Birn, 2006). Only a subset of the parameters, defined in Section 17.3.1, is evolved: (a) *direction*, which corresponds to a bidimensional float vector corresponding to angles about the x- and y-axis w.r.t. the camera–character direction. The angles are kept in the range $[-75.0; 75.0]$ as these correspond to good illumination angles (Millerson, 1999); (b) *diffuse color*, which corresponds to a RGB vector; (c) K_d, which defines the diffuse color intensity; (d) K_s, which defines the specular color intensity; and (e) *shadow opacity*, which defines how transparent the shadow is. Finally, the fill light parameters are similar to the key light's, except that all shadow parameters are ignored.

The screen hypothesis is structured according to the virtual human's skin body groups. For each body group, a sequence of filters is applied. Filters were defined in Section 17.3.2. For each filter, a field is defined for each of its parameters, including whether it is active. Filters are applied to the body groups in the order they appear. Notice that order can change through the crossover operation.

17.4.3 Operators

This work makes use of two genetic operators, shown in Figure 17.5: *crossover* and *mutation*. Crossover takes two parent hypotheses from the current generation and creates two offspring by recombining portions of the parents. Recombination is parameterwise. The parent hypotheses are chosen probabilistically from the current

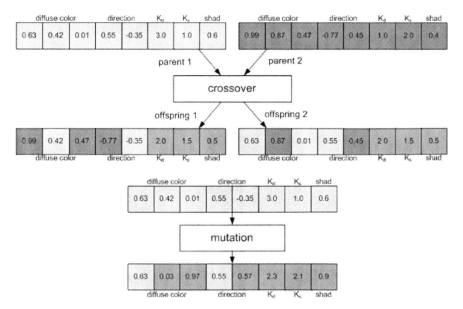

Fig. 17.5 The crossover and mutation genetic operators.

population. Thus, the idea is to combine highly fit parents to try to generate offspring with even higher fitness. The percentage of the current population that is subjected to crossover is defined by the crossover rate, r. Mutation exists to provide a continuous source of variation in the population. This operator essentially randomizes the values of a random number of the hypothesis' parameters. The operator is constrained to generate within-domain values for each parameter. The percentage of the current population that is subjected to mutation is defined by the mutation rate, m.

17.4.4 Working and Long-Term Memory

The virtual human needs to keep track of several populations, one per affective state, even though only a single one is evolving at any instant of time. The working memory keeps the current state of evolving populations. In real life, creating an artistic product may take a long time (Sayre, 2007). Therefore, to accommodate this characteristic, the whole set of evolving populations can be saved, at any time, in long-term memory. Implementationwise this corresponds to saving all information about the population in XML format. Furthermore, the interaction between working and long-term memory provides the foundation for lifelong learning.

Finally, a gallery is saved in long-term memory to accommodate the higher fitness hypotheses, independently of the population from which they originated. The gallery can then be used to feed hypotheses to the initial population, thus promoting rapid generation of highly fit hypotheses. More important, the gallery is a dataset that can be used to learn models using supervised learning. This use of the gallery is further addressed in the future work section.

17.4.5 Critic Ensemble

The critic ensemble defines several *critics* per affective state. Critics can be artificial, in which case fitness is inspired by art theory, or human, in which case fitness reflects the subjective opinion of the critic. An artificial critic consists of a set of *population fitness functions* and a set of *hypothesis fitness functions*. A population fitness function calculates the hypothesis' fitness with respect to the others in the population. A hypothesis fitness function assigns an absolute fitness to each hypothesis, independently of the others. Both kinds of fitness function are normalized to lie in the range [0.0;1.0]. As the critic may define several functions, weights are used to differentiate their relative importance. Thus, for each kind, the set fitness is the weighted average among all constituent functions, as in (17.2). Finally, the final fitness is the weighted combination of the population and hypothesis functions sets, as in (17.3). Section 17.5 exemplifies one artificial critic.

$$f^{set} = \frac{w_i * f_i}{\sum_i w_i} \qquad (17.2)$$

$$f^{final} = W_{pop} * f^{set}_{pop} + W_{hyp} * f^{set}_{hyp}. \qquad (17.3)$$

The model supports interactive evolution where humans can influence the selection process by assigning subjective fitness to the hypotheses. There are several advantages to bringing humans into the evaluation process (Sayre, 2007): (a) art literature is far from being able to fully explain what is valued in the arts; and (b) art is dynamic and values different things at different times. Furthermore, bringing humans into the evaluation process accommodates individual, social, and cultural differences in expression of emotions (Keltner et al., 2003; Mesquita, 2003). Furthermore, as discussed in future work, if the fitness functions are unknown, then the model might be made to learn from human experts. Two disadvantages are that humans may reduce variety in the population, causing convergence to a specific style, and that the evolution process becomes much slower. For these reasons, the human fitness function (as well as any other) may be selectively deactivated.

17.5 Results

In this section the evolutionary model is used to learn a mapping between the emotion "anger" and lighting expression. Having described the lighting expression hypothesis encoding (Section 17.4.2), what is needed is to define the set of critics that will guide the selection process. In this example, human critics are ignored and a single artificial critic is defined. To build an artificial critic it is necessary to define an appropriate set of population and hypothesis fitness functions that reflect the expression of anger as well as their weights (Section 17.4.5). However, to demonstrate the flexibility of the current approach, in addition to aiming at effective expression of anger, we also add fitness functions that reflect lighting aesthetics. In both cases, these fitness functions try to reflect guidelines from art theory regarding the expression of anger, effectively and aesthetically, through lighting. In some cases, these functions might be conflicting, which is perfectly acceptable in art production (Sayre, 2007). Conflicts are handled by assigning appropriate weights to the functions.

Six hypothesis fitness functions and one population fitness function are proposed. The hypotheses' set weight is set to 0.75 and the population's set weight to 0.25. The fitness functions are as follows.

- The *red color function*, with weight 4.0, assigns higher fitness the smaller the Euclidean distance between the light's diffuse color to pure red, as in (17.4). This function is applied both to the key and fill lights. Red was chosen because, in Western culture, red tends to be associated with excitation or nervousness (Fraser & Banks, 2004).

$$f = \frac{1}{dist + 1}. \tag{17.4}$$

- The *low-angle illumination function*, with weight 1.5, assigns higher fitness the closer the Euclidean distance between the key light's angle about the x-axis to $20°$. The rationale is that illumination from below is unnatural, bizarre, and frightening (Millerson, 1999).
- The *opaque shadow function*, with weight 1.0, assigns higher fitness the closer the key light's shadow opacity parameter is to 0. This favors darker shadows. The rationale is that hard crisp shadows convey a mysterious and harsh character (Millerson, 1999; Birn, 2006).
- The *low complexity function*, with weight 0.5, assigns higher fitness to less complex hypotheses. The rationale is that humans naturally value artifacts that can express many things in a simple manner (Machado, 2006). What constitutes low complexity in lighting is hard to define, but here we define a low complexity hypothesis as having diffuse color equal to a grayscale value (i.e., with equal RGB components); K_d equal to 2.0, giving a neutral diffuse component; and K_s equal to 0.0, giving a null specular component.
- The *key high-angle* function, with weight 0.5, assigns higher fitness the closer the Euclidean distance is between the key light's angle about the x-axis to $\pm 30°$. This is a standard guideline for good lighting (Millerson, 1999). Notice, first, this is an aesthetics function and, second, it contradicts the low-angle illumination function.
- The *key-fill symmetry* function, with weight 0.5, assigns higher fitness if the fill light angles are symmetrical to the key light's. This is also a standard guideline for good lighting (Millerson, 1999).
- The *novelty* function, with weight 0.5, assigns higher fitness the less similar the hypothesis is with respect to the rest of the population. This is, therefore, a population fitness function. The rationale in this case is that novelty is usually appreciated in the arts (Sayre, 2007). Notice also that this function puts some internal pressure on the population, forcing the hypotheses to keep changing to differ from each other.

17.5.1 Parameters Selection

Having defined the critics, before actually running the genetic algorithm it is necessary to configure the following parameters: p, the population size; r, the crossover rate; m, the mutation rate; e, the elitism rate; and SM, the selection method. As the value chosen for these parameters influences the speed and efficacy of the evolution, it is important to choose optimal values. In this sense, we began by running the genetic algorithm, for a small number of iterations, with typical values of these parameters (Mitchell, 1998): p in $\{25,50\}$; r in $\{0.6,0.7\}$; m in $\{0.0,0.1,0.2\}$; e in $\{0.0,0.1\}$; and SM in $\{$roulette wheel, tournament selection$\}$. This amounts to 48 different configurations. Each configuration was run for ten iterations and ranked

Table 17.1 Top 20 Parameter Configurations[a]

R	(p, r, m, e, SM)	HF	AF	V	AV
1	(50, 0.70, 0.00, 0.10, TS)	0.86	0.59	3.01	2.51
2	(25, 0.70, 0.00, 0.00, TS)	0.84	0.59	2.97	2.47
3	(50, 0.60, 0.00, 0.10, TS)	0.85	0.59	2.97	2.47
4	(50, 0.60, 0.00, 0.00, TS)	0.85	0.59	2.97	2.47
5	(25, 0.60, 0.00, 0.00, TS)	0.85	0.58	2.96	2.45
6	(50, 0.70, 0.10, 0.10, TS)	0.86	0.57	2.95	2.45
7	(50, 0.70, 0.00, 0.00, TS)	0.84	0.60	2.95	2.48
8	(25, 0.70, 0.00, 0.10, TS)	0.85	0.57	2.91	2.43
9	(25, 0.70, 0.20, 0.00, TS)	0.84	0.58	2.90	2.42
10	(25, 0.70, 0.10, 0.00, TS)	0.83	0.58	2.89	2.40
11	(50, 0.70, 0.10, 0.00, TS)	0.83	0.58	2.88	2.44
12	(50, 0.70, 0.20, 0.00, TS)	0.83	0.58	2.87	2.44
13	(50, 0.70, 0.20, 0.10, TS)	0.84	0.56	2.87	2.40
14	(50, 0.60, 0.20, 0.10, TS)	0.85	0.55	2.86	2.40
15	(50, 0.60, 0.10, 0.00, TS)	0.84	0.55	2.86	2.37
16	(25, 0.60, 0.20, 0.00, TS)	0.83	0.56	2.85	2.38
17	(25, 0.60, 0.10, 0.00, TS)	0.82	0.56	2.83	2.38
18	(25, 0.70, 0.10, 0.10, TS)	0.82	0.55	2.83	2.36
19	(50, 0.60, 0.20, 0.00, TS)	0.83	0.56	2.82	2.38
20	(50, 0.60, 0.10, 0.00, RW)	0.83	0.54	2.82	2.36

[a]R = rank; SM = selection method; TS = tournament selection; RW = roulette wheel; HF = highest fitness; AF = average fitness; V = value; AV = average value.

according to the best *population value* among all iterations. Population value is defined as

$$value = 2*HF + 2*AF - HD - G, \tag{17.5}$$

where HF is the highest fitness hypothesis, AF is the average fitness, HD is the highest hypothesis dominance, which refers to the ratio of number of occurrences of a certain hypothesis to population size, and G is the ratio between generation number and maximum number of generations. Thus, population value favors populations with highly fit hypotheses, low dominance, and from earlier generations. The top 20 parameter configurations are shown in Table 17.1. Looking at the results, it is possible to observe that the optimal configuration is $p = 50$, $r = 0.70$, $m = 0.00$, $e = 0.10$, and $SM = tournamentSelection$. Notice that, in this case, the mutation rate is 0 and the 19 best results use tournament selection.

17.5.2 Evolution Analysis

Having determined the optimal parameters for the proposed fitness functions, the genetic algorithm was run for 50 iterations. A graph showing the evolution of the population value, average fitness, and highest fitness is shown in Figure 17.6. Looking

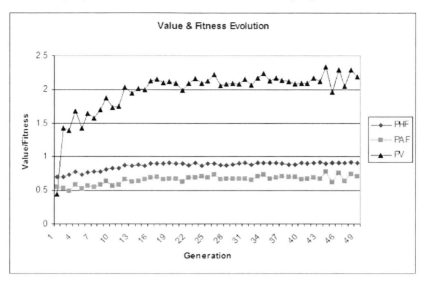

Fig. 17.6 Value and fitness evolution of a 50-iteration run with optimal parameters.

at the graph, it is possible to see that the value and fitness increase quickly up until approximately the 25th iteration. After this point, the highest fitness is already close to 1.0, however, it is still slowly improving.

The actual values for the top 20 generations, with respect to population value, are shown in Table 17.2. Looking at the results it is clear that the populations with the best value occur mostly in later iterations. In fact, the 44th generation was evaluated as having the best value of 2.3324, with its best hypothesis having a fitness of 0.9005. Table 17.3 details the top 20 hypotheses, with respect to fitness, for the 44th population.

Visual inspection of the evolving hypotheses shows that the hypotheses were accurately reflecting the fitness functions. This evolution is clearly shown in Figure 17.7, which shows five of the initial populations' hypotheses as well as five of the hypotheses in the 44th generation. The first population, which was randomly generated, has high variance and most hypotheses have relatively low fitness. Evolution, which in this case relied mostly on the crossover operation, successively combined hypotheses that best reflected the fitness functions. In the 44th generation, which had the best population value, most hypotheses illuminate the character with a red color, from below and with opaque shadows. Even so, the hypotheses still differ from each other, perhaps, reflecting the novelty function.

The highest fit hypothesis belongs to the 48th generation and had a fitness of 0.9181. Visually it is similar to the one at the bottom right in Figure 17.7. The exact hypothesis' parameters are: (a) *diffuse color* (RGB) = (0.99, 0.08, 0.234); (b) *direction* (XY) = $(-43.20°, 25.65°)$; (c) $K_d = 2.32$; (d) $K_s = 1.30$; (e) *shadow opacity* = 0.54. However, the importance of the best hypothesis should be deemphasized in favor of a set of highly fit hypotheses. This set is likely to be more useful because,

Table 17.2 Top 20 Generations of a 50-Iteration Run Using Optimal Parameters[a]

G	PHF	PAF	PV
44	0.9005	0.7857	2.3324
48	0.9181	0.7492	2.2947
46	0.9106	0.756	2.2933
34	0.9083	0.7338	2.2441
26	0.8941	0.7353	2.2188
49	0.9106	0.7136	2.1884
33	0.9061	0.7124	2.1771
36	0.9138	0.6914	2.1704
42	0.9095	0.6944	2.1677
23	0.9113	0.6921	2.1667
17	0.8958	0.7005	2.1525
31	0.9129	0.6808	2.1473
37	0.8983	0.711	2.1386
35	0.9118	0.6814	2.1263
25	0.9038	0.6886	2.1249
16	0.903	0.6884	2.1229
19	0.9114	0.6759	2.1146
38	0.8903	0.6961	2.1129
43	0.9171	0.6784	2.1112
18	0.9001	0.6704	2.101

[a]G = generation; PHF = population highest fitness; PAF = population average fitness; PV = population value.

aside from reflecting the emotion in virtue of high fitness, it allows for variety in conveying the emotion. This set could be constructed using the gallery in the long-term memory (Section 17.4.4).

Overall, the model seems to be able to evolve appropriate populations of hypotheses that reflect the fitness functions. However, the success of the mappings hinges on the quality of the critics' feedback. If it is clear that the final hypotheses in Figure 17.7 reflect the fitness functions, it is not that these functions actually reflect anger. The selection of appropriate fitness functions as well as accommodating feedback from human critics is the subject of our future work.

17.6 Conclusions

Drawing on accumulated knowledge from the arts, this work proposes a virtual human model for the expression of emotions that goes beyond the body and uses light, shadow, composition, and filters. Lighting expression relies on a pixel-based lighting model that provides many of the light and shadow parameters regularly used in the visual arts. Screen expression explores filtering and composition. Filtering consists of rendering the scene to a temporary texture, manipulating it using shaders, and then presenting it to the user. Filters can be concatenated to generate a combined

Table 17.3 Top 20 Hypotheses from the 44th Generation Population of the 50-Iteration Run Using Optimal Parameters[a]

HF	HCHD
0.90011	0.02
0.89791	0.02
0.89741	0.02
0.89741	0.02
0.89741	0.02
0.88901	0.02
0.85121	0.02
0.85121	0.02
0.85121	0.02
0.85121	0.02
0.85121	0.02
0.84852	0.04
0.84851	0.02
0.84851	0.02
0.84851	0.02
0.84601	0.02
0.84601	0.02
0.84601	0.02

[a]HF = hypotheses fitness; HC = number of times the hypothesis occurs in the population; HD = hypothesis dominance, that is, the ratio of HC over population size.

effect. In composition, aspects of the scene are separated into layers, which are independently manipulated before being combined to generate the final image. Regarding emotion synthesis, the OCC emotion model is integrated.

To learn mappings from affective states to multimodal expression, an evolutionary approach is proposed based on genetic algorithms. Hypotheses encode a three-point lighting configuration and a set of filters that are to be applied to the virtual human's skin body groups. The initial population is either created randomly or loaded from long-term memory into working memory. One population is maintained for each affective state. Generation of alternatives is achieved through the crossover and mutation operators. Selection of alternatives is supervised by a critic ensemble composed of both human and artificial critics. The latter consist of a set of fitness functions that should be inspired by art theory. Several parameters influence the genetic algorithm search: population size, crossover rate, mutation rate, elitism rate, selection method, fitness functions, and fitness function weights. Finally, a gallery is maintained with very high fitness hypotheses. These can, later, be fed into the current population to promote the generation of new highly fit offspring.

This work has demonstrated the evolutionary model for the case of learning how to express anger using lighting expression. By visual inspection it is clear that the evolution reflects the fitness functions. However, the following questions arise:

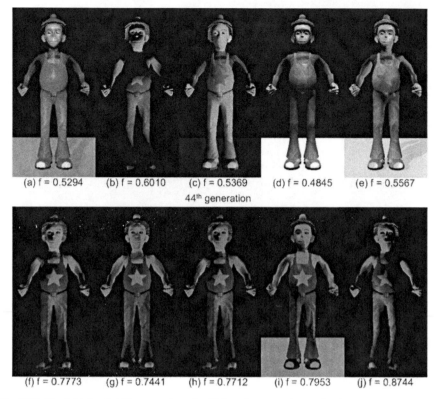

(a) f = 0.5294   (b) f = 0.6010   (c) f = 0.5369   (d) f = 0.4845   (e) f = 0.5567

44th generation

(f) f = 0.7773   (g) f = 0.7441   (h) f = 0.7712   (i) f = 0.7953   (j) f = 0.8744

Fig. 17.7 The initial and 44th generation of a 50-iteration run using optimal parameters.

Do the fitness functions reflect the intended affective states? Are the fitness functions' weights correct? These issues need to be addressed in the near future.

First, the results should be confronted with people's intuitions about the expression of emotions, perhaps in the form of inquiries. Furthermore, it seems clear that art literature is insufficient to provide a comprehensive set of fitness functions. Thus, second, human critics should be brought into the evolution loop. Both regular people and artists should be involved. In this setting, the system could be made to learn new fitness functions from human feedback and the existent fitness functions' weights could be updated, perhaps using a reinforcement learning mechanism. It would, of course, be interesting to expand the mappings to the six basic emotions (Ekman, 1999) —anger, disgust, fear, joy, sadness, and surprise—and, furthermore, to explore more complex affective states. The gallery could also be used to feed supervised learning algorithms to generate models that explain highly fit hypotheses. These models could, then, feed a self-critic which would, in tandem with the artificial and human critics, influence the selection process. Finally, an obvious extension to this work is exploring the camera and sound expression channels of which much knowledge already exists in the arts (Sayre, 2007).

References

Alton, J. (1949). *Painting with light*. New York: Macmillan.

Amaya, K., Bruderlin, A., & Calvert, T. (1996). Emotion from motion. In *Proceedings of Graphics Interface'96* (pp. 222–229).

Angeline, P. (1996). Evolving fractal movies. In *Proceedings of the First Annual Conference in Genetic Programming* (pp. 503–511).

Arijon, D. (1976). *Grammar of film language*. New York: Hastings House.

Averill, J., Nunley, E., & Tassinary, L. (1995). Voyages of the heart: Living an emotionally creative life. *Contemporary Psychology, 40*(6), 530.

Batteux, C. (1969). *Les Beaux Arts Réduits à un meme Principe*. Genève: Slatkine Reprints.

Birn, J. (2006). [digital] *Lighting and rendering* (2nd ed.). London: New Riders.

Block, B. (2001). *The visual story: Seeing the structure of film, TV, and new media*. Boston: Focal Press.

Blumberg, B., & Galyean, T. (1995). Multi-level direction of autonomous creatures for real-time virtual environments. *Proceedings of SIGGRAPH'95, 30*(3), 173–182.

Cassell, J. (2000). Nudge, nudge, wink, wink: Elements of face-to-face conversation for embodied conversational agents. In J. Cassell, J. Sullivan, and E. Churchill (Eds.), *Embodied conversational agents* (pp. 1–27). Cambridge, MA: MIT Press.

Chi, D., Costa, M., Zhao, L., et al. (2000). The EMOTE model for effort and shape. In *Proceedings of SIGGRAPH 2000* (pp. 173–182).

Collingwood, R. (1938). *The principles of art*. Oxford, UK: Clarendon Press.

de Melo, C., & Paiva, A. (2005). Environment expression: Expressing emotions through cameras, lights and music. In *Proceedings of Affective Computing Intelligent Interaction (ACII'05)* (pp. 715–722).

de Melo, C., & Paiva, A. (2006a). Multimodal expression in virtual humans. *Computer Animation and Virtual Worlds Journal, 17*(3), 215–220.

de Melo, C., & Paiva, A. (2006b) A story about gesticulation expression. In *Proceedings of Intelligent Virtual Agents (IVA'06)* (pp. 270–281).

de Melo, C., & Paiva, A. (2007). The expression of emotions in virtual humans using lights, shadows, composition and filters. In *Proceedings of Affective Computing Intelligent Interaction (ACII'07)* (pp. 546–557).

Dissanayake, E. (1988). *What is art for?* Seattle: University of Washington Press.

Ekman, P. (1999). Facial expressions. In: T. Dalgleish and M. Power (Eds.), *Handbook of cognition and emotion*. New York: John Wiley & Sons.

Elliot, R. (1966). Aesthetic theory and the experience of art paper. In *Proceedings of the Aristotelian Society, NS 67*, III–26.

Fraser, T., & Banks, A. (2004). *Designer's color manual: The complete guide to color theory and application*. San Francisco: Chronicle Books.

Geertz, C. (1976). Art as a cultural system. *Modern Language Notes, 91*(6), 1473–1499.

Gombrich, E. (1960). *Art and illusion; A study in the psychology of pictorial representation*. New York: Pantheon Books.

Gratch, J., Rickel, J., Andre, E., et al (2002). Creating interactive virtual humans: Some assembly required. *IEEE Intelligent Systems, 17*(4), 54–63.

Gross, L., & Ward, L. (2007). *Digital moviemaking* (6th ed.). Belmont, CA: Thomson/Wadsworth.

Hartmann, B., Mancini, A., & Pelachaud, C. (2005). Implementing expressive gesture synthesis for embodied conversational agents. In *Proceedings of Gesture Workshop* (pp. 173–182).

Hunt, R. (2004). *The reproduction of colour*. West Sussex, UK: John Wiley & Sons,

Juslin, P., & Sloboda, J. (2001). *Music and emotion: Theory and research*. New York: Oxford University Press.

Kant, I., & Bernard, J. (1951). *Critique of judgment*. New York: Hafner.

Katz, S. (1991). *Film directing shot by shot: Visualizing from concept to screen*. Studio City, CA: Focal Press.

Keltner, D., Ekman, P., Gonzaga, G., et al. (2003). Facial expression of emotion. In: R. Davidson, K. Scherer, & J. Goldsmith (Eds.), *Handbook of affective sciences* (pp. 415–433). New York: Oxford University Press.

Lewis, M. (2001). Aesthetic evolutionary design with data flow networks. PhD thesis, Ohio State University.

Machado, F. (2006). Inteligencia artificial e arte. PhD thesis, Universidade de Coimbra.

Malkiewicz, K., & Gryboski, B. (1986). *Film lighting: Talks with Hollywood's cinematographers and gaffers*. New York: Prentice Hall Press.

Malkiewicz, K., & Mullen, D. (2005). *Cinematography: A guide for filmmakers and film teachers*. New York: Simon & Schuster.

Mesquita, B. (2003). Emotions as dynamic cultural phenomena. In: R. Davidson, K. Scherer, & J. Goldsmith (Eds.), *Handbook of affective sciences* (pp. 871–890). New York: Oxford University Press.

Millerson, G. (1999). *Lighting for television and film* (3rd ed.). Oxford: Focal Press.

Mitchell, M. (1998). *An introduction to genetic algorithms*. Cambridge, MA: MIT Press.

Moller, T., & Haines, E. (2002). *Real-time rendering* (2nd ed.). Wellesley, MA: AK Peters.

Noh, J., & Neumann, U. (1998). A survey of facial modelling and animation techniques. Technical report, USC Technical Report: 99–705.

Oatley, K. (2003). Creative expression and communication of emotions in the visual and narrative arts. In: R. Davidson, K. Scherer, & J. Goldsmith (Eds.), *Handbook of affective sciences* (pp. 481–502). New York: Oxford University Press.

Ortony, A., Clore, G., & Collins, A. (1988). *The cognitive structure of emotions*. Cambridge, MA: Cambridge University Press.

Perlin, K., & Goldberg, A. (1996). Improv: A system for scripting interactive actors. Virtual worlds. In *Proceedings of SIGGRAPH'96* (pp. 205–216).

Picard, R.W. (1997). *Affective computing*. Cambridge, MA: MIT Press.

Sayre, H. (2007). *A world of art* (5th ed.). Upper Saddle River, NJ: Prentice Hall.

Schroder, M. (2004). Speech and emotion research: An overview of research frameworks and a dimensional approach to emotional speech synthesis. PhD thesis, Institute of Phonetics, Saarland University.

Sims, K. (1991). Artificial evolution for computer graphics. *ACM Computer Graphics, 25*, 319–328.

St-Laurent, S. (2004). *Shaders for game programmers and artists*. Boston, MA: Thomson/Course Technology.

Todd, S., & Latham, W. (1992) *Evolutionary art and computers*. San Diego, CA: Academic Press.

Ventrella, J. (1995). Disney meets Darwin—The evolution of funny animated figures. In *IEEE Proceedings of Computer Animation* (pp. 19–21).

World, L. (1996). Aesthetic selection: The evolutionary art of Steven Rooke. *IEEE Computer Graphics and Applications, 16*(1), 4–5.

Zettl, H. (2008). *Sight, sound, motion: Applied media aesthetics* (5th ed.). Belmont, CA: Thomson/Wadsworth.

Index

A

ACC. *See* Average correlation coefficient
Acoustic features, 217
Acoustic processing model, 134
Action, proposed modes of, 13
Action unit (AU), 159
  based on AdaBoost classification, 164
  based on Gabor feature representation, 164
  inference with a dynamic bayesian network
    learning BN structure, 168–170
    learning DBN parameters, 172
    relationship analysis, 166–167
    relationship modeling, 167–168
  list of, 165
  measurement extraction, 164–165
  recognition through DBN inference, 173
  stages of, 160
AdaBoost classifier, 165
Adams, R. B., Jr., 149, 152
Adult Attachment Interview (AAI), 254
Affect
  and action, 14–15
  and attention, 13–14
  and cognition, relations between, 3
  definition of, 12
  and emotions, 12, 13
    behavioral manifestations, 17–21
    cognitive component, 16–17
  and judgment, 15–16
  manifestation of, 13
  proposed modes of, 13
  sensing from text (*See* Affect sensing from text)
Affective computing, 1, 45
  OCC model for, 270
  sensor system for, 299–300
Affective information processing for HCI, 2

Affective interfaces, design of, 276
Affective physiological sensors, 300
  components
    base unit, 301–302
    sensor unit, 301
  EREC-I, 302–304
  EREC-II, 304–305
Affective reasoner, 31, 77
Affective speech processing, 4
Affective state, 24
Affect sensing from text
  approaches for, 47
    commonsense-based approach, 48–49
    fuzzy logic and machine learning, 49
    valence assignment, 50
  motivation for, 50–51
Affect sensitive human–robot collaboration, 2
Aggressive language, 77
Allwood, J., 234
Altruistic emotions, 26
Amaya, K., 314
Andersen, P. A., 34
Andrasik, F., 294
André, E., 276
Anger emotions, behavioral manifestations of, 19, 20
Anger expressions, 148
ANNs. *See* Artificial Neural Networks
Anticipation, 30
Anvil annotation tool, 235
Appraisal, 25
  dimensions, 270
Arfib, D., 276
Arnold, M. B., 25
Arnott, J. L., 95
Artificial neural networks, 219
Attention, 13

Printed in the United States
130376LV00001B/103-129/P